The Irony of Galatians

The Irony of Galatians

PAUL'S LETTER IN FIRST-CENTURY CONTEXT

Mark D. Nanos

FORTRESS PRESS
MINNEAPOLIS

THE IRONY OF GALATIANS
Paul's Letter in First-Century Context

The author can be contacted directly at nanosmd@home.com.

Scripture quotations are translated by the author unless otherwise noted.

Cover photo: The Marble Court dedicated to the Imperial Cult within the monumental Roman era bath-gymnasium complex of Sardis looms behind the adjacent Synagogue, remodeled from gymnasium halls south of the palaestra in the third through sixth centuries C.E. Photo by Mark D. Nanos. Used by permission.
Cover photo design treatment and book design: Dawn Allman.
Typesetting: Peregrine Graphics Services.
Author photo: Synagogue foundation on the south wall of St. Paul's Church, Pisidian Antioch (Yalvaç, Turkey).

Library of Congress Cataloging-in-Publication Data
Nanos, Mark. D.
The irony of Galatians : Paul's letter in first-century context / Mark D. Nanos.
p. cm.
Includes bibliographical references and index.
ISBN: 0-8006-3214-1 (alk. paper)
1. Bible. N.T. Galatians—Socio-rhetorical criticism. 2. Irony in the Bible. I. Title.
BS2685.6.W5 N36 2001
227'.406—dc21 2001023786

The paper used in this publication meets the minimum requirements of American National Standard for Information Sciences—Permanence of Paper for Printed Library Materials, ANSI Z329.48-1984.

Manufactured in the U.S.A. AF 1-3214

06 05 04 03 02 1 2 3 4 5 6 7 8 9 10

To the victims of the Shoah

C O N T E N T S

ACKNOWLEDGMENTS

This project represents a revised and expanded version of my Ph.D. dissertation, completed and accepted at the University of St. Andrews, Scotland, in 2000. I am especially grateful to my supervisor, Philip F. Esler. He not only helped me to sharpen the arguments and consider details and interpretations that were not always favorable to my thesis, but he helped me to avoid grammatical and technical errors as well. I am also thankful for the feedback of my examiners. The errors that remain are entirely my own.

I have been preoccupied with this project for several years, and I am forever thankful to any and all who indulged me along the way. I am grateful to my family and friends for their encouragement and advice, especially to my wife, Vicky, for her tireless support and good sports(wo)manship. I am also grateful to the many specialists with whom this project interacts, even when in disagreement. And especially with those who have been my conversation partners along the way. Thank you very much. And thank you, Fortress Press.

Finally, I want to acknowledge the victims of certain interpretations of Paul's voice, especially those who have suffered the Shoah. Their suffering cannot be separated from prejudices resulting from those interpretations any more than it can be wholly attributed to them. To them I dedicate the effort represented in this book.

ABBREVIATIONS

ad Aen.	*ad Aeneas*
AGAJU	Arbeiten zur Geschichte des antiken Judentums und des Urchristentums
Ag. Ap.	*Against Apion*
Ann.	*Annales*
Ant.	*Jewish Antiquities*
Athen.	Athenaeus
b.	Babylonian Talmud (Bavli) tractates
B-Greek	Biblical Greek mailing list (http://www.ibiblio.org/bgreek/)
Bib	*Biblica*
BibInt	*Biblical Interpretation*
BibIntSer	Biblical Interpretation Series
BJRL	*Bulletin of the John Rylands University Library of Manchester*
BJS	Brown Judaic Studies
ca.	circa
CBQ	*Catholic Biblical Quarterly*
cf.	compare
Char.	*Characteres*
ConBNT	Coniectanea biblica, New Testament
Contempl. Life	*On the Contemplative Life*
Creation	*On the Creation of the World*
CRINT	Compendia rerum iudaicarum ad Novum Testamentum
CTQ	*Concordia Theological Quarterly*
Demosthenes, *Ep.*	*Epitaphius* or *Funeral Oration*
De or.	*De oratore*
Diog. L.	Diogenes Laertius
Embassy	*On the Embassy to Gaius*
Eng.	English
EPRO	Études préliminaires aux religions orientales dans l'empire romain
Eq.	*Equites*
esp.	especially
ExpT	*Expository Times*
Fam.	*Epistulae ad familiares*
FF	Foundations and Facets
Flac.	*Pro Flacco*
FRLANT	Forschungen zur Religion und Literatur des Alten und Neuen Testaments
GBS	Guides to Biblical Scholarship

Gen. Rabbah	*Genesis Rabbah*
Geogr.	*Geographica* or *Geography*
Hist.	*Historiae* or *Histories*
Hist. Eccl.	*Historia ecclesiastica* or *Ecclesiastical History*
HTKNT	Herders theologischer Kommentar zum Neuen Testament
HTS	Harvard Theological Studies
idem	the same (author)
Inst.	*Institutio oratoria*
Int	*Interpretation*
Inv.	*De inventione rhetorica*
JBL	*Journal of Biblical Literature*
Jos.	*On the Life of Joseph*
JRS	*Journal of Roman Studies*
JSNT	*Journal for the Study of the New Testament*
JSNTSup	Journal for the Study of the New Testament: Supplement Series
JSPSup	Journal for the Study of the Pseudepigrapha: Supplement Series
JTS	*Journal of Theological Studies*
J.W.	*Jewish War*
KEK	Kritish-exegetisher Kommenter über das Neue Testament
LEC	Library of Early Christianity
lit.	literally
Lives	*Lives of the Twelve Caesars*
LXX	Septuagint
m.	Mishnah tractates
Med.	*Medea*
Mor.	*Moralia*
Moses	*On the Life of Moses*
MT	Masoretic text
Names	*On the Change of Names and Answers on Exodus*
Neot	*Neotestamentica*
NICNT	New International Commentary on the New Testament
NIDNTT	Colin Brown, ed., New International Dictionary of New Testament Theology
n(n).	note(s)
NovT	*Novum Testamentum*
NRSV	New Revised Standard Version
NT	New Testament
NTS	*New Testament Studies*
Od.	*Odyssey*
Off.	*De officiis*
OT	Old Testament

P^{46}	Chester Beatty papyrus 46
P.Cornell	Papyrus Cornell
P.Oxy.	Papyrus Oxyrhynchus
QE	*Quaestiones et solutiones in Exodum* or *Questions*
Resp.	*Respublica* or *Republic*
Rhet.	*Rhetoric*
Rhet. Alex.	*Rhetoric to Alexander*
Rhet. Her.	*Rhetorica ad Herennium*
RTR	Reformed Theological Review
SBL	Society of Biblical Literature
SBLDS	Society of Biblical Literature Dissertation Series
SBLMS	Society of Biblical Literature Monograph Series
SBS	Stuttgarter Bibelstudien
SHC	Studies in History and Culture
SJT	*Scottish Journal of Theology*
Spec. Laws	*On the Special Laws*
SNTSMS	Society for New Testament Studies Monograph Series
ST	*Studia theologica*
Symp.	*Symposium*
t.	Tosefta tractates
TDNT	G. Kittel and G. Friedrich, eds., *Theological Dictionary of the New Testament*
Test. Ash.	*Testament of Asher*
THKNT	Theologischer Hardkommentar zum Neuen Testament
TynBul	*Tyndale Bulletin*
Virt.	*De virtutibus* or *On the Virtues*
v(v).	verse(s)
WTJ	*Westminster Theological Journal*
WUNT	Wissenschaftliche Untersuchungen zum Neuen Testament
y.	Jerusalem Talmud (Yerushalmi) tractates
ZNW	*Zeitschrift für die neutestamentliche Wissenschaft und die Kunde der älteren Kirche*

PROLOGUE

Galatians delivers Paul's response with an ironic edge. Like a deeply disappointed parent who has caught his or her adolescent in the act of compromising closely held principles, the consequences far more dangerous than the child seems to realize, Paul immediately attacks his addressees' new interest as betrayal: "I am surprised that you are so quickly defecting." As will be discussed in detail, this rebuke, like others throughout the letter, is shot through with Socratic irony, exposing the victims' naïveté undermining their perception of the situation, rhetorically asking in effect: "Who do *you* think *they* are?" "Who do *they* think *they* are?" "Who do *they* think *you* are?" or perhaps best, "Who do *you* think *you* are?"

The author's anguish is palpable; he cannot get to Galatia to set things straight, but the need is urgent; his children threaten to harm themselves with a change of course imagined to be benign. A letter holds his hopes. The addressees ought to know better, behave appropriately; are they really that ungrateful for the good they have received at his, much less Jesus Christ's, expense? Of this "other message of good" he has already warned them; it is bad news instead, undermining the very meaning of the death of Christ for themselves (1:6-9). "Do they think God's grace shown toward them in the past is now insufficient?"

The time for reasoned argument is past; the addressees stand before Paul's letter without excuse. Ironic rebuke freezes the scene for the victim, clarifying the issues beyond doubt, framing forever the expected, appropriate response. But, ironic as it may be, the interpreter is left instead chasing irony's oscillating shadows, wondering, What did the Galatian addressees know? And whom? Who had persuaded them to depart from the appropriate course set out by Paul? In what way? For what reason? Why would they consider it now, after having begun the course? Did they really think their faith in Christ was now in vain?

Apart from a shared context, irony can easily go unrecognized. When this happens, instead of being uniquely suited to clarify, it can obscure. Thus, it should surprise no one to learn that, if the interpreter wishes to hypothesize and test a proposal for constructing the context of the original author and audience of a letter of ironic rebuke, he or she will need to attend, simultaneously, to Paul's employment of irony at the surface level of the text *and* below it, where irony subverts the ostensible surface meaning. For in the presence of irony, where the two uses of language conflict, there meaning is made.

Because the prevailing interpretations have probed Paul's text without sufficient appreciation of the powerful role of ironic inversion at work, at the formal as well as functional level, the interpretation of the apostle's scathing rhetoric has exaggerated and, regardless of other plans, continues to accentuate the differences that are imagined to separate Christian and Jewish identity, behavior, and even intentions toward God and neighbor. The legacy of this perception of the Jewish other has proven often tragic for Jewish people, at least in a world that has been often dominated by those who look to Paul to shape reality, and for others, as a foil to justify their twisted construal of what is right. But must it be so, or, rather, does the caricature that has resulted represent the heritage that the author would intend or even that the addressees originally understood? And if so, is its perpetuation still morally justified for the historical critic or those whom that critic informs? Moreover, does it properly represent the character of those influencing the addressees in the direction that Paul so opposed, if they were to be taken on their own terms, apart from the ends the author by means of this rhetoric sought to achieve? Should they not have a voice?

To fashion a response, the language that Paul employed must be interpreted in context. What was going on in Galatia; who was involved; and why?

It is the investigation of these and related questions to which this study will attend. For before one constructs a portrait of Paul, his messages must be interpreted. But before his messages can be interpreted, his usage of language in context must be determined or else merely assumed. And this interpretive task, from text to context and back to message, must be undertaken letter by letter.

Where interpretation of Paul's perceptions of Jewish identity and behavior are concerned, Galatians holds pride of place. I have offered, as far as I was able, a reading of Romans with attention to construction of the context there, on its own terms, apart from the influence of Paul's other letters, just as seems to have been required of the original reader/hearer. This resulted in a sketch of the Jewish Torah-observant man who seems to have written it. In this project too, I will seek to read Paul's letter on its own contingent terms. I will only indirectly test the results of the investigation of Romans, because I will not seek to coordinate the two letters, or to offer a comprehensive portrait of Paul and his communities, yet I find him to be the same man. In fact, nothing I have encountered in Galatians has led me to question the working assumption that the Paul who writes this letter is a Torah-observant Jew, known as such by his addressees when he had lived among them. For example, this implication underscores his challenge to the addressees' assumptions about the matter at hand, when ridiculing their naïveté, declaring that if they are to become proselytes they should calculate also that this will oblige them to keep the whole Torah (5:3). However, if they know Paul to be Jewish yet non-Torah observant, such a rhetorical approach holds no promise. They would be expected merely to respond, "We simply want what you have attained, Paul: the advantages of unambiguous identity as circumcised members of the community of the righteous ones, but apart from any concern to observe the Torah as though relevant for ourselves, because we, like you, are Christ-believers too!"

In the case of Galatians, assessing the context in order to get at the message, much less the character of the messenger, has proven to be an extensive task; I have learned much, not least from the many turns that were unforeseen. The study offered here departs in significant ways from some of the working hypotheses with which it was begun. For example, when I turned from Romans to take up the challenge of reading Galatians, I began with the autobiographical narratives; in fact, one of these, the Antioch incident of Gal 2:11-21, was introduced at the conclusion of *The Mystery of Romans* to test the feasibility of the reading offered there, because this incident was considered by many to capture the quintessential core of Paul's beliefs. I found that the traditional and prevailing views as well as my own working hypotheses did not successfully explain the texts I encountered, and that insufficient attention had been paid to the fact that these narratives were constructed to inform the Galatian addressees, but the Galatian addressees' situations must be established first in order to imagine what analogies they might draw from them. So my research shifted along the way to the questions developed in this project: to the Galatian situations and players, and to how Paul's response to them in this letter proceeds. I found that only then could the details of Paul's constructions of the narrative discourses be interpreted in context and not the other way around.

When I turned to examining more specifically the context in Galatia, I again found the prevailing views and my own working hypotheses challenged by the logic of many textual features and discovered the need to reexamine at length, for example, the consensus notion that those influencing the addressees were Christ-believers with a different gospel of Christ (plus circumcision or plus Law), or that they arrived suddenly from outside Galatia, or that they were in some way connected with the interests of the Jerusalem apostles, even if perhaps misrepresenting them. As a result of these and other discoveries made along the way, in order to keep this project manageable for the reader, this study does not attempt to articulate at length the meaning of every verse or to construct a comprehensive portrait of Paul. Rather, the focus is on the context(s) of Galatians: the character of Paul's language and the implied group identities and situations that make sense of what he writes. By attending to these matters, I find that the message of Paul comes through with a new level of force and clarity; I hope you will find the same. I do have plans to address the others in future projects.

No interpretation is independent of context, that realized or assumed for the original author and audience, and that of the interpreter him- or herself. I am a product of many factors, not least the long shadow of the Holocaust, which claimed so many Jewish people, my people, as well as exposure to critical tools now available to the interpreter. It is for the reader to decide whether I have constructed a probable context for interpretation of Paul's voice or the meaning thereof.

The interpretation of this letter matters, and the consequences continue to stare us in the face. It is startling to see how often the portrait of Paul that results from interpretation of this letter finds its way into public discourse, "St. Paul said," cited apart from context, as though self-evident, as well as significant for the matter at hand. It is my deepest prayer that this project will contribute to mutual respect and consideration between those who internalize the message of Paul for their lives and those who do not, as we together seek to understand the context and thus the meaning of the language he employed.

The Consensus View

The prevailing interpretations of the situations Paul addressed in Galatians, especially the identification of those influencing them in a direction to which Paul objects, have not changed that significantly in the history of Christian interpretation. Moreover, the identity of these influential people has not really been developed in spite of the rise of historical and rhetorical criticism. Instead, they have been portrayed in rather stereotypical and dismissive fashion, as straw men against which to measure the superior values attributed to Paul. Although the details of the consensus views will occupy much discussion, a survey of the often overlapping labels and descriptions used to identify these people provides an expedient introduction.

Drawing directly from Paul's polemical language, the consensus view labels these people or groups of people agitators or troublemakers. Other labels such as Judaizers ostensibly stigmatize them in terms of Christian ideals. The tension imagined to have developed sharply between Jewish and Pauline wings of Christianity guides others: they are Paul's opponents. They are usually taken to represent the institution of what is variously called Jewish, Jerusalem, or Palestinian Christianity. They are against Paul and his mission, and he is against them and theirs. Paul's gospel is Law-free, whereas their gospel includes reverence for and the observance of Jewish Law, which is taken thus to involve slavery. And they are understood to be outsiders, usually from Jerusalem or Antioch, or at least motivated by influential people from outside the congregations addressed. They promote another gospel. When regarded as an intra- and inter-Christian affair, Galatians is read as Paul's anathemizing attack on Jewish Christianity for the unacceptable error of imposing the Law of Moses upon the Christian ideal of freedom in Christ, the very heart of so-called Paulinism.

It is important also to note that, methodologically, to the degree that this people's identity is constructed from the rhetoric of Galatians, it is often done with little discrimination among the various discourse units within the letter. For example, the events described in the autobiographical comments of 1:11—2:21 are assumed to govern the setting for the Galatian addressees, as though the players and situations of Jerusalem and Antioch need hardly be distinguished from each other or Galatia. Thus, one frequently finds reference to the influential people in Galatia to be an extension of, if not the very same people as, the "false-brothers" in Jerusalem (2:4), or the "ones from James" or "those for circumcision" in Antioch (2:12), although these terms Paul never applies to the people and groups among the addressees in Galatia.

The Irony of Galatians

It is immediately clear that the consensus views have allowed Paul's polemical interests, not to mention Christian ideological perspectives as well as historical constructions of early Christianity, to shape profoundly the way the influencers' identity, and thus the situations Paul addressed, are construed. They merely provide the backdrop for Paul's message. As a result, interpreters have not generally been concerned with producing a disinterested portrait, that is, with considering their identity, motives, messages, or methods on their own terms. Because the meaning of Paul's message is undeniably colored by the interpreter's understanding of the context of the Pauline letter under consideration, should the interpreter not at least take the polemical nature and interested view of Paul's rhetoric into consideration when seeking to construct the historical context of the setting and players? Indeed, he or she should. And to the degree that the findings of this study are applied, Paul's message in this letter will read very differently.

Reading Paul's letter as ironic rebuke profoundly affects the interpretation, reopening the question of the identity of the addressees and the situations in which those influencing them in Galatia are set, as well as their identification. It also provides cause to reexamine Paul's perspective on the exigence that has provoked this response, as well as the implied perspectives of the addressees and these influencers on the matters at hand. The resulting argument challenges the prevailing consensus in many ways. Consider the following survey of the results.

Those influencing the addressees, the influencers, are not opponents of Paul or of the Christ-gospel per se. Nor are they outsiders who have only arrived in the several Galatian communities addressed after Paul's departure. They are Galatians too. They are members of the larger Jewish communities of Galatia entrusted with the responsibility of conducting Gentiles wishing more than guest status within the communities through the ritual process of proselyte conversion by which this is accomplished. They may be proselytes—former Gentiles—as well. They probably understand themselves to be helping the addressees negotiate the uncertainty and marginalization resulting from their present identity as pagan guests, which is magnified by the present nontraditional expectations of the addressees within their subgroups. This makes sense of the trust the addressees have toward the influencers that Paul herein seeks to undermine. For the addressees perceive them as helpful and their message as good news, even if they might suspect at some level that Paul would not approve if he were present or knew of the addressees' efforts to make this seem to be complementary for themselves.

The addressees are righteous Gentiles within Jewish subgroups, that is, synagogue communities. Paul writes to the Galatian communities ἐκκλησίαις—which language implies several groups meeting in several cities, towns, or villages—who are suffering marginalization for considering themselves already full members of the larger Jewish communities as though they had completed proselyte conversion. This expectation is based upon the good news teaching of the subgroups of Christ-believers. These Gentiles have not completed this course yet appear to consider themselves as having acquired full member status as though they had (based upon the prior teaching of Paul), so they are suffering status dissonance as a result of interaction with the social control agents of the Jewish communities charged with the responsibility of overseeing pagans wishing to make passage into the community. These Gentile addressees have convinced themselves in some way that the influencers' alternative message does not contradict the truth of the good news of Christ as taught by Paul; but, while compromising the rigor of the line Paul had drawn, most likely they want to regard the different message of good now as complementing and augmenting Paul's message of good in Christ in order to escape the marginality they have found themselves experiencing to date. The issue thus becomes one of what action they will take and on whose authority.

This reading challenges the consensus view of the situations as intra- and inter-Christian. The identity problems of these Gentiles are measured not in terms of an intramural dispute among Torah-observant versus supposed Pauline Law-free Christ-believing subgroups. They predate institutional Christian identity, and thus factionalism among rival Christian groups, as well as any division that could be characterized as Christianity versus Judaism, a development that can be clearly traced only in later times. Rather, they are the result of *intra-* and *inter-Jewish* communal disputes regarding the legitimacy of this status claim predicated upon the meaning of Jesus Christ for these Gentiles, a claim that appeals to the dawning of the awaited age to come in the midst of the present age. The good news of Christ claims to challenge the traditional interpretation's limiting of righteous identity to Israelites and thus to inclusion of representatives of the other nations only by way of proselyte conversion. Although it had been appropriate within the limits of the present age, this Jesus Christ–oriented proposition modifies the prevailing interpretation of the fathers by maintaining that this restriction should no longer control the identification of the righteous children of God once God has revealed the fulfillment of the promise made to Abraham of blessing representatives of all the nations in his seed.

Paul's letter implies that the situations of the addressees in Galatia are intra-Jewish. That is, they are taking place within the family, you might say, although Paul will bring into the narrative sections a certain inter-Jewish perspective. In other words, Paul recognizes a difference between the Christ-believing Jewish groups, which together function as a coalition engaged in a specific task for a specific period of time, and other Jewish groups that do not share their convictions about the meaning of Jesus. This is a distinction among Jewish groups that reflects an inter-Jewish tension. His narrative examples reflect similar intra-Jewish situations that have developed elsewhere, as in Jerusalem and Antioch. By stringing together these otherwise independent intracommunal examples, the inter-Jewish nature of the problem is accentuated, that is, that conflict that continues to arise in various settings between this Jewish coalition and its interests, and other Jewish groups. The addressees should now more clearly understand that the larger principles at issue within their current local intra-Jewish situations in Galatia correspond to those experienced by members of the Christ-believing coalition in certain other local intra-Jewish situations.

Moreover, the tensions faced by Paul's addressees suggest an intercommunal dimension to the Galatian situations that brings the pagan context of the Jewish communities into play. The conflicts the addressees are experiencing arise in part because of the constraints faced by the minority Jewish communities with whom they now seek to identify as righteous ones of God. These Jewish communities are embedded within the dominant pagan communities of Galatia; they are not entirely free of concern with the pagan ordering of communal identity and life. The addressees represent pagan guests claiming admission on terms that threaten the prevailing norms of both the pagan and Jewish communities, for until they have begun the ritual process of transformation from pagan to Jewish proselyte identity, the addressees are understood to be pagans. They are still obliged as pagans to observe, for example, the public practices of imperial and local cults. If the addressees remain pagans on the prevailing terms of identity yet fail to participate in pagan activities based on a claim to the rights of Jewish privilege to abstain, apart from proselyte conversion, this represents a threatening proposition for which the leaders of the minority Jewish communities would have to answer to the leaders of the pagan communities.

As for the portrait of Paul implied by this investigation, the author who makes this argument indicates one whom the addressees know to have functioned within the structure and worldview of a Jewish coalition when among themselves, rather than from an outside or sectarian stance. If the addressees' identity was constructed upon sectarian social dynamics, their interest in gaining proselyte identity for themselves is difficult to reconcile with the naïveté of the current consideration of this other message or the authority of its messengers, both of which are confronted in Paul's response. Paul is himself an example of status and observance, and his message in this letter does not abrogate the identity or observance of Torah for Jewish people (i.e., Israelites) in the least but is instead predicated upon their continued validity for himself and other Jewish members of this movement. Any ostensible criticisms of traditional Jewish interpretations, such as they appear, are those of a reformer. They are dissociating arguments limited in scope to modification of what is appropriate because of the meaning Paul attributes to the death of Jesus Christ as it pertains specifically to Christ-believing Gentiles as righteous ones in the midst of Jewish communities, which are also constrained by the interests of the dominant pagan society in which the identity of these Gentiles has been defined, indeed, in the complex of cosmic communal tensions of the present evil age.

Summary of the Book

Part 1
The Methodological Basis for Interpreting This Letter

In part 1, several chapters clarify the argument and the methodological approaches.

It is important to recognize where presuppositions continue to limit the interpretive possibilities. Thus, I will begin in chapter 1 with a general introduction to some interpretive issues for consideration when constructing a hypothesis for the context of those addressed in Galatians.

Any construction of the situations as well as the identity of the addressees and those influencing them is dependent upon the rhetorical information supplied in Paul's letter. Chapter 2 pursues the question of what the interpreter can know about these people and things from the evidence available.

Following the lead of several epistolary specialists, the argument of chapter 3 will concentrate upon the nature of the correspondence as a letter-type, in fact, as a specific example of ironic rebuke. We know something about this genre of letter writing from surviving papyrus examples and from extant handbooks designed to define and illustrate the various approaches that a letter writer might adopt in view of the situations as he or she perceives them. But little has been done to date with many implications that result from consideration of ancient views of irony or of this letter classification where it comes to rethinking the context and message of Galatians. The chapter will offer some modifications of existing interpretations of Paul's feigned expression of surprise and will give particular attention to the way that irony undermines the ostensible meanings implied at the surface level of Paul's rhetorical rebuke. The results of considering Paul's employment of irony will be suggested to exemplify dissociating argumentation in order to modify current expectations within the communities concerning what is appropriate in this age in view of the dawning of the age to come (a reformist approach), rather than dissociating argumentation that seeks to set out a new religious institution over against or in place of the existing communities (a sectarian approach).

In order to examine critically the identity of those influencing the addressees, chapter 4 outlines the epistolary structure of Paul's message and prioritizes the relative weight of the data for constructing the situations in Galatia. The most reliable information in the first instance is from the situational rather than the narrative material. Although all of Paul's argument is concerned with responding to the exigence as he perceives it, it is helpful to rigorously distinguish the material introduced in Paul's argument when creating narratives of past events or metaphors and allegories to illustrate his points, from that rhetoric which is directly engaging the addressees and their situations.

Some rhetoric is directly addressed to the Galatian recipients in their own local situations (thus called hereafter situational discourse), for example, as ironic rebuke, supplication, or instruction. But some discourse units are instead narratives constructed around earlier events that occurred elsewhere. Although situational in the way they are used, and thus directly relevant to the Galatian addressees in their situations as Paul sees things, they are nevertheless not drawn from the events of the Galatian situations directly. These narrative discourses are developed rather from events prior to and outside the Galatian situations in order to illustrate a perspective supportive of his argument to the Galatian addressees about how they should think and behave now in Galatia. This narrative material includes the autobiographical accounts (1:11—2:21), the midrash on Abraham (3:6—4:7), and the allegory of Abraham's two women and their sons (4:22-30). The proposition that is developed from the situational units must, naturally, consider and be tested by the information derived from these units, for its aim is to account for the entire discourse.

Part 2
Identification of the Players and the Exigencies

Part 2 explores the identification of each of the players and the exigence that has arisen in the Galatian situations as it is perceived to require action by each of these players.

Chapter 5 explores the identity of the target recipients of the letter. To whom does Paul write to dissuade them from internalizing as good for themselves "a different message of good [ἕτερον εὐαγγέλιον]" that includes circumcision (1:6-7; 6:12-13)? How are these addressees to be identified?

Paul's letter addresses the exigence, the urgency of moment as he perceives it, that has arisen as a result of the addressees' previous engagement with and consideration as good for themselves "a different message of good" "which is not another [ὃ οὐκ ἔστιν ἄλλο]" (1:6-7). The interests of those offering this other message as good for the addressees presupposes another perspective on what constitutes the exigence. Moreover, the offer of this other message and any accompanying pressure to conform or comply with it creates the exigence from the addressees' perspective: How are they to respond to two ostensible messages of good? Are they as complementary as the addressees would now like to believe? They know that Paul has said otherwise, but they are now confused: What shall they do to reduce the dissonance?

Chapter 6's discussion of each of these perspectives and others will involve consideration of such topics as Jewish communal views regarding Gentiles seeking status among the righteous ones, as well as those views that might be expected to represent the other non-Jewish people with whom these Gentiles and the Jewish communities are in different ways necessarily networked. It will involve consideration of Paul's message of good in Christ as well, for the claims of these Gentile addressees, predicated upon the proclamation of Paul's message, challenge the prevailing Jewish communal norms for the present age. It is thus ironically the addressees' expectations based upon Paul's gospel that have created the initial exigence for the influencers, their response that created an exigence for the addressees, and the addressees' consideration of that response as a welcome way to negotiate the problem that then creates the exigence for which Paul writes this letter.

In other words, I suggest that the situations now confronted by Paul are the result of the innovative nature of the truth of the good news of Christ as Paul had proclaimed it when among the addressees. It has ostensibly offered these Gentiles reidentification as children of Abraham, of God; it has uniquely maintained that they are already honored righteous ones in the present age without completing the ritual process of proselyte conversion, because it claims that the age to come has dawned, thus modifying the terms of identification. This understanding of themselves has shaped their expectations of public standing and the attendant rights of complete membership, but it is in dispute.

The effect of this message among these Gentiles provokes the concerned response of the social control agents and other members of the Jewish communities in which the Christ-believing subgroups operate, perhaps in response to objections raised by civic leaders and others from the addressees' pagan social networks. If so, then it is the unexpected, unprecedented, and unacceptable results of this claim to acquire honor at this level, and likely the concomitant expectation of goods—apart from the traditional means apparently readily available in Galatia—that create the Galatian crisis. Those influencing the Galatian addressees are merely responding according to the communal expectations that have shaped their own lives, whether or not they know of or associate this development with someone named Paul in any way. And their response may have not only their own communal and personal interests in view but those of these addressees and the larger non-Jewish communities in which they must function as well.

Paul's response indicates that the addressees want to reestablish within their new communal identity that which they had thought they already gained by way of faith in Christ. They are concluding that this is done through compliance with the dominant Jewish communal norms. This other message of good news for themselves can appeal for legitimation not only to scriptural precedent but also to traditional interpretation and enforcement, including cooperation with the established norms of the dominant pagan communities within which the Jewish communities dwell.

Chapter 7 takes up the question, How shall we refer to the people influencing Paul's addressees? These people and groups should be both labeled and described in ways that avoid limiting the possibilities for their identity, intentions, or actions. First, the clearly relevant data of the letter will be set out. Then, it will be shown that, by and large, the current labels such as Judaizers, opponents, agitators or troublemakers, and

Teachers (although much less so) are inadequate at the least and overall mistaken or counterproductive for the historical-critical task.

The descriptions of these influential people in the prevailing views may be classified as follows: they are (1) Jewish, (2) Christ-believers, (3) oriented toward the Jerusalem establishment of Christ-believing communities and their leaders, (4) who have arrived as missionaries, (5) and thus they are not Galatians but outsiders. This comprehensive chapter will evaluate these descriptions and explore their weaknesses. This will be done first in terms of the alternate views that have challenged major aspects of the prevailing premises, although usually retaining other premises in their constructions that will be questioned as well.

The chapter will mount a case against all but the Jewish identification of these influential people according to these prevailing or alternate portraits. These people are members of groups involved in persuading the addressees, to be sure, but they are people and groups nonetheless, and involved with the social life of the addressees in various ways and for a variety of possible reasons that our taxonomy and descriptions should make every effort not to further obscure. They have vested interests for both self and group, but so do Paul and those to whom he writes, as well as the interpreter. Thus, as far as the interpreter is able, all of these players should be considered apart from his or her vested interests. Approaching the letter in this way offers the opportunity of rereading Paul in a way that is more sensitive to the original contexts of his readers/hearers, an important aspect of the historical-critical task.

Several additional aspects of the data available in the letter will be considered that do not usually factor into this task. The implications of the circular nature of the letter to more than one group of addressee communities should provoke thought. Also the implied context in view of Paul's evil eye warning in 3:1-5 should be investigated as it may shed light on both the nature of the groups and individuals, as well as the nature of the suffering that the addressees endure. Although they have apparently considered their condition to date an appropriate result of their current status according to the influencers' message, Paul now reveals that it is inappropriate, creating suffering where honor and acceptance should instead be conferred. In addition, Paul's maxim that "a little leaven leavens the whole lump" (4:9) will be considered, for it seems to imply an internal or indigenous rather than an external threat.

Chapter 8 proposes that these influential people or groups are better described by the label *influencers* than by those in current usage. This provides the interpreter a better starting place for imagining them in the situations addressed on their own terms. Some of the social dynamics involved in influencing according to membership and reference group norms will be discussed.

Part 3
The Identity of the Influencers and Situations in Galatia

Part 3 will develop the identity of the influencers, with implications for the identity of the addressees and Paul as well. A construction of the context for the ironic rebuke of Galatians results.

The consensus view is that the influencers are Jewish, yet their Jewishness has not really been explored. Chapter 9 will consider several of the prevailing views and reflect that for the most part their concerns have been trivialized or degraded as merely self-interested, expedient, or worse. Much of this chapter will thus be a new proposal for the identification of the influencers.

The social context of Paul's closing summary of 6:12-13 will occupy much of this discussion, including the concerns for honor and avoidance of persecution of which Paul accuses the influencers. The employment of the substantive participle οἱ περιτεμνόμενοι ("the ones choosing circumcision" [6:13]) will also be examined in this context. These matters raise the issue of the role of these influencers in the rite of passage of proselyte conversion itself. The discussion will note the basic dynamics of this ritual process and the social implications for each of those engaged and will argue that the influencers are involved in welcoming non-Jewish guests into Galatian Jewish communities within which the Christ-believing subgroups assemble. They facilitate the inclusion of any pagans who express interest in becoming full members as proselytes.

The chapter will further explore several aspects of the influencers' identity in Jewish communal terms. These will include the internal communal politics of their role as facilitators of proselyte conversion; the external politics arising from concern to guard communal interests, including their vulnerable position as minority communities that must comply with the dominant pagan communities' civic concerns and norms; and the sincere faithfulness of these influencers to their own core beliefs and concerns as well.

Finally, the discussion will consider the possibility that the influencers are themselves proselytes. If they are former righteous Gentiles, then this identification makes much sense of their role, interests, and policies vis-à-vis the addressees. They can on the one hand empathize with the interests and plight of the addressees but on the other hand not accept any claim to equal standing apart from completion of this rite: "Who do these Gentiles think they are?"

Chapter 10 will examine the influencers in terms of their virtually unquestioned identification as Christ-believers with a different message of Christ than Paul proclaims. The argument here is that they are not Christ-believers and that the message of good that Paul attacks does not concern itself with faith in Christ. Not that the influencers are per se against the Christ-message, this is simply not their own concern.

Paul's references to them and their good news are presented to surprise the addressees by awakening them to the reality of the contrast that they have failed to grasp. Paul's employment of ironic rebuke undermines the addressees' naïve and compromising approach, which has until now allowed them to consider responding to this other message alongside the good news of Christ. But Paul charges that it is actually "not another" (1:6-7)! Although they have not understood themselves to have thus far elevated this other message to the level of the gospel of Christ, Paul says that will be the logical result of the "defection" involved in seeking to resolve the present dissonance of their "unsettled" nonproselyte—and thus marginal—status according to the influencers' point of view.

I propose that Paul is probably the first and only one calling this other message in Galatia a gospel or comparing it in any way with the gospel of Christ. He accuses the addressees, by their inappropriate response to this message, of inherently undermining the gospel of Christ. They themselves have thus given this other message the honor of being compared equal to the gospel of Christ in such a way as to allow the very meaning of the death of Christ—upon which their faith stands—to be twisted so as to turn upside down and empty this of meaning for themselves. All messages of good pale in comparison to the good news of Christ, whether proclaimed by an angel or even Paul himself.

Paul's entire argument in this letter applies specifically to Gentiles who have already believed in Christ and received the Spirit of God as a testimony to their new status as righteous ones among the people of God. Paul's concern is carefully targeted. It is only Gentiles already in Christ (already known by God), who would now thereby subvert the very foundation of their faith if they were to complete the process of proselyte conversion (seeking to be known by God) or alternatively to accept the constraints of pagan identity. Moreover, this action undermines the message and actions of Paul and any other members of this coalition who have sustained this opportunity for the addressees to be in Christ apart from proselyte conversion—as representatives of the nations—at great cost (compare 1:13; 2:5; 5:11).

A brief conclusion, "The Irony of Galatians," will complete this study. By putting flesh on the implied influencers as well as the addressees, making them come alive in an effort to understand their social world and concerns, we might move a step closer to the aspirations of, for example, historical, rhetorical, and social-scientific criticism. Perhaps further consideration of the dynamics of Paul's rhetorical perspective as argued herein will bear some fruit as we make our way forward, Christian and Jew, with differences of opinion, to be sure, but also with respect for the beliefs and actions as well as probable intentions of the other, according to the measure with which we measure our own.

The appendix will offer a brief discussion of the limitations for applying classical rhetorical species to Galatians, in view of which it will be made clear why this topic does not occupy significant space in this investigation. These learned approaches offer organizational and heuristic benefits to be sure, yet this letter does not seem to represent a formal example of any of the three classical species of oration, nor have the situations for which this letter was invented been to date clarified by these approaches. As may be expected, the identification of the situations of the addressees and of these influential people is rather concluded before such rhetorical approaches commence.

PART I

THE METHODOLOGICAL BASIS FOR INTERPRETING THIS LETTER

CHAPTER I

PRELIMINARY QUALIFICATION OF THE SOURCE MATERIAL

It is important to begin an investigation of Galatians by qualifying the source material. This is especially the case when we are primarily concerned with ascertaining the situations among and identities of the several groups of recipients to whom this letter was designed to circulate;[1] and even more specifically, when seeking to identify those influencing the addressees whom Paul resists so vehemently in this response. But we do not know what these situations were,[2] who the players were (or how many), or even that any of this ever existed historically, even as Paul perceived it—apart from this letter, that is.[3]

It is striking to realize that the interpreter of Galatians must approach the task with little to no certain historical information about the *exigence*, the aspect of a situation perceived to require an urgent reaction, that has provoked the response preserved in this letter, except what the letter itself implies. Even the portrait of the author we

1. Paul writes to the ἐκκλησίαις, that is, to more than one "assembly" or "gathering" of those addressed in Galatia (1:2).

2. I will generally refer to situations in the plural rather than *the* or *a* situation, because a plurality of locations suggests a plurality of situations, even if the exigence is addressed by Paul as though undifferentiated. Might this fact not suggest a plurality of influential people or groups?

3. That Galatians represents a letter written by Paul is widely agreed, regardless of whether it was executed by the hand of a secretary (as seems likely on the basis of the subscription beginning at 6:11, in which he puts his own hand to work at writing a summary of the chief concerns expressed throughout the letter; cf. Julius Victor, *Art of Rhetoric 27*, in Malherbe, *Theorists;* Bahr, "Subscriptions"; Richards, *Secretary*, 81–91, 172–75; Weima, *Endings*, 45–56, 118–32, 157–74; H. Betz, *Galatians*, 313). Although much of the argumentation upon which this decision has often been based is actually predicated upon circular reasoning, relying upon a portrait of Paul that itself relies upon the contents of this letter for many of its features, it is assumed herein to be Paul's letter. Even J. C. O'Neill, who takes a relatively more skeptical view of what texts can be attributed to Paul than the consensus, concludes his useful review of the discussion of the authenticity of the letter in modern scholarship by observing that "Paul's original letter has been both glossed and interpolated, though rarely altered" (*Recovery*, 7).

bring to the interpretive task is in important ways predetermined, because we rely upon a prior interpretation of Paul that has itself been shaped by previous interpretations of this and his other correspondence. And so interpreters must question even their working hypotheses about Paul as they approach this task. Did he still regard himself as a Jewish person and behave Jewishly when among them, or does he now when he writes to them?[4] How did the addressees view his practice, or not, of Jewish life? Precisely to what kind of Jewish identity or behavior did he or they subscribe? Or was he, as well as his addressees, already in some way Christian—however anachronistic the term itself may yet be?[5] That is, were they already functioning and thinking of themselves independently of the local Jewish communities, so that their self- and group-identity, such as their interests and behavior, were no longer Jewish, however defined?[6]

4. For example, would he have recognized himself as Torah-observant and synagogue- as well as temple-oriented as portrayed by Luke in Acts (e.g., in 21:26; 24:11-21; 25:8; 26:4-7)?

5. It will sometimes be necessary to retain use of the descriptive label *Christian* or *Christianity,* either to make a point in terms where this institutional identity is appropriate, or in direct quotations of others who use the terminology, or discussions engaging them where its substitution might be distracting. Paul did not use the label *Christian.* I used it only as an adjective in *The Mystery of Romans* but now see that even this is not helpful for communicating the preinstitutional state of the situation as still representing the developments of a Jewish coalition, with Paul as a Jewish reformer. I will refer thus to Christ-believers, those in Christ, and so on. Cf. the example set by Esler, *Galatians.*

6. Although we know a good deal about diaspora Jewish life in general at this time, there is much more that we do not know; and about Jewish life in Galatia in Paul's time, we actually know very little (we know more later; see Feldman, *Jew,* 69–74; Trebilco, *Jewish Communities*). Ironically, this letter is at present our best source for knowing more. By way of Paul's rhetoric, when we consider it alongside other evidence from literary and material remains, we have a good idea that proselyte conversion included circumcision and that identification with Abraham was important; unless, of course, the rhetorical situation only involves people from outside of Galatia who are of this opinion, a position that this study will challenge on the basis of the same rhetorical evidence upon which this view of outsiders is derived.

On the matter of how to translate the reference in Greek to those people to whom the label Ἰουδαῖος applies, I will generally adopt the translation "Jew," and the cognates "Jewishness," "Judaism" or "Judaisms," "judaize," and so on. If the context of a comment brings to the fore the geographic element of their identity, then "Judean" and the cognates will be used instead. Both aspects were present in the usage of this term at this time, and the decision is dependent upon the context as perceived by the interpreter. Shaye Cohen has traced how usage changed dur-

A topic that perhaps best exemplifies the paucity of historical information with which the interpreter begins when approaching this text is the fact that we do not even know where in this large geographic region in west-central Anatolia (= Asia Minor = Turkey) called Galatia that the addressees or those influencing them are located. Are the addressees called Galatians because they are in the Roman province or the ethnic territory?[7] Are they Romans, Greeks, Celts, Phrygians, or from some

---

ing the Maccabean period from generally designating a regional-centered identity (e.g., 1 Maccabees), to often designating a more cultural, religious one (2 Macc 6:6 [cf. vv. 1-11]; 9:1-17 [cf. 6:13; 7:30-38]; see Cohen, "*Ioudaios*"; idem, *Beginnings*, 69–106), even if that identity is yet embedded in politics and kinship (so Malina, *Christian Origins*, 84–85; Garnsey and Saller, *Empire*, 163; Price, *Rituals*). It is in 2 Maccabees that we first meet the term Ἰουδαϊσμός (2:21; 8:1; 14:38), the sense of the Jewishness of being a Jew (Judaism), and its antonym ἀλλοφυλισμός (4:13; 6:25), the adoption of "foreign ways" (heathenism), and more importantly, Ἑλληνισμός (4:13), of "Greek ways" (Hellenism) by Jewish people, against their ancestral ways of life (Cohen, "*Ioudaios*," 219). We encounter here communal boundaries, understood by those outside as well as inside to define the identity of the Jewish people, at least those who behaved as though they were. It is in this context that, although it is safer to speak of Jewish groups, we may speak of Judaism, or Judaisms, if we mean by this a way of life, including religious life, that is embedded in kinship and community (politics), which at this time included not only the laws and customs, variously interpreted by various groups, but also the recognition of the God of the Temple in Jerusalem, regardless of whether someone or some group believed that this God was presently being properly served by those in control of this institution, as well as the level of local patriotism, however that might be expressed in their diaspora location (cf. Kraabel, "Six Questionable"; Goodman, *Ruling Class;* Jones and Pearce, *Local Patriotism;* Richardson and Heuchan, "Egypt." Note Philo's sense of identity with Alexandria as his *patris* [*Flaccus* 115, 123, 158–59, 172; see discussion in Pearce, "Belonging"]). It is now possible to comprehend a person leaving aside their ancestral faith, apostasizing, becoming no longer Jewish, even if still originating ethnically from Jewish parents, or even perhaps from Judea. And it is in this context that we may begin to understand the institutions for conversion for a non-Jewish person into this ethnos, this people.

7. The ethnic territory takes its name from the Celtic tribes that arrived in the third century B.C.E. and settled in west-central and northern areas of Anatolia. When Galatia came under the Roman rule of Pompey in 64 B.C.E., it became a client kingdom; but in 25 B.C.E. it was organized as a Roman province, and in subsequent years its reach expanded. By the time of Paul's letter, the ethnic territory was included within the Roman province, which stretched from the Black Sea to the Mediterranean, and included such cities as Acts describes Paul to be active among (e.g., Pisidian Antioch, Derbe, Lystra, Iconium). Full discussion of the history of these people and lands is available in S. Mitchell, *Anatolia*, vols. 1 and 2.3–51.

other ethnic group? Are they natives of the area addressed? Are their communities proximate to Jewish communities within the villages or towns in which they live, or even in the midst thereof?[8] If so, have they been in the past associated with these Jewish communities, perhaps in some way as righteous Gentiles, or not? Likewise, who are the influencers? Are they from the same background as the addressees? Are they indigenous, that is, are they Galatians too, or have they arrived from somewhere else? Are they natural-born Jews, proselytes, or pagans?

Many more questions could be raised, but posing these few should suffice to make the point that the interpreter of Galatians must be careful to ascertain what he or she really knows apart from the interpretation of the rhetoric of the letter itself.[9] Caught in this circular trap, the interpreter must try to develop a methodological approach that seems most likely to yield plausible results. How does one proceed?

The question of north or south Galatian hypotheses will not concern us here. This issue has not been resolved and contributes to making the point that our historical data is presently limited when it comes to constructions of the situation addressed. The real crux of the issue is felt by those involved in trying to chronicle Paul's life and letters, which involves significant interaction with other letters as well as Acts, topics that are not in view for this investigation. See commentaries and, e.g., Jewett, *Chronology;* Scott, *Paul;* Breytenbach, *Paulus.*

8. What is of interest is the historical situation implied in the rhetoric of this letter, which seems to require the presence of Jewish communal life but as minority groups constrained by the norms of the larger pagan society, as will be discussed. The rhetorical concern with Jewish identity certainly implies a Jewish presence for the context of the addressees (cf., e.g., Davies, *Jewish,* 172–88; Donaldson, "Gospel"). The material as well as literary evidence points clearly to the presence of Jewish communities throughout the southern and central districts of the Roman province. Yet some evidence we have outside this letter indicates the presence of Jewish people in the north as well as south of Galatia, and in regions further north and more distant from Judea than either of these locations; see Acts 2:5-11; Philo, *Leg.* 281–82; Josephus, *Ant.* 12.148–53; 14.114–15; cf. M. Williams, *Jews,* 2–4; discussions in Feldman, *Jew,* 69–74; Trebilco, *Jewish Communities,* 167–85; S. Mitchell, *Anatolia,* vols. 1 and 2.3–51.

9. There is of course much historical and literary information for the various people of the general area and period (cf. sources in above note and S. Elliott, "Anatolian"). Many social and cultural models are also available. For example, the evil eye belief system appealed to in this letter offers important information for constructing a model of that system, providing perhaps our only extant example of an evil eye warning from a gazee detector in antiquity (cf. Nanos, "O Foolish Galatians"; see also J. H. Elliott, "Paul"; B. Longenecker, *Triumph,* 26, 153–57; idem, "Until Christ").

On the one hand, it is useful to consider a variety of hypotheses that the rhetoric might support. The possibilities are many, limited perhaps most by our own imagination. On the other hand, it is prudent to limit them, at least at first, to those that grow out of a close analysis of the rhetoric of the letter itself, rather than imposing some other larger construction, for example, the Pauline versus Petrine hypothesis of Christian origins or the conspiracy theories closely related to this, in which bands of Paul's opponents from Jerusalem or Antioch are thought to dog Paul's trail to undo his work. Or even a less anachronistic construction based on Luke's later portrayal in Acts.[10] It is wise to first listen closely to the rhetoric of the letter written by Paul to these people, whoever they are.

How does an interpreter seeking to know what the original author and addressees might have understood that language to signify proceed? A construction of the situational context of that language is a necessary aspect of such an interpretive task, because the meaning of words is shaped by the context of their usage. But, of course, this move already involves interpretive decisions.

To varying degrees, this circular limitation for the interpreter is now more often realized, and its importance respected, but not always, and certainly not in the long history of interpretation before the development and refinements of, for example, historical, rhetorical, social-scientific, psychological, cultural, literary, and linguistic criticisms. Few interpreters now proceed as though the meaning of the language used is self-evident. They regard as important the difference of time, location, and culture. They are concerned with the semantic domain of usage and other aspects of rhetorical situation that vastly affect the meaning of words,[11] such as when they are used ironically, not to mention the different language of the interpreter of the text from that of the original writer and reader or hearer of this Koiné Greek, which was probably delivered orally and likely performed.[12] Generally respected are the myriad of other aspects of perception that separate the concep-

10. I will refrain from any deep interaction with the accounts in Acts, although some points of possible interest may be noted, and it is sometimes unavoidable when interacting with the views of others who draw upon this material, e.g., Tyson, "Opponents," 244–45. Nevertheless, I believe that the results of this investigation are generally supported by Acts (as I read it).

11. Louw, *Semantics*.

12. Studies indicate literacy was very limited. What did exist, "remained a kind of imitation talking." Moreover, "the concept of the letter was that of written con-

tual location of the interpreter and the original writer and addressees, not least of which is the history of interpretation itself, which clearly reveals the changes in context and worldviews, and how they shape the concerns and perspectives of interpreters. Such distance may always be dismissed as inconsequential by a few who ostensibly express concern only with what the letter holds for today, not what it meant then. But the way that this distance is handled, or not, is nevertheless a fundamental aspect of any interpretation that seeks in any way to represent the voice of Paul, then or now.[13] Thus, immediate attention to the formal rhetorical and epistolary characteristics of the letter, as well as the structure of the argument, comprise an important aspect of our beginning point. First, another introductory matter must be considered: What can we know about a historical situation when we have only a rhetorical document from which to work?

versation. . . . Letters create appearance in the experience of the recipient(s) by evoking the physical presence of the author(s)" (Botha, "Greco-Roman Literacy," 206, 209). It is likely that when delivered orally, the reading was performed (cf. Botha, "Letter Writing"; idem, "Verbal Art"; Loubser, "Orality").

13. See, e.g., Grenholm and Patte, "Overture," 1–56.

CHAPTER 2

ESTABLISHING THE RHETORICAL AND HISTORICAL CONTEXT OF THIS LETTER

If we understand Paul to be the historical figure who wrote this letter to groups of people somewhere in Galatia—among whom, according to this letter, he had proclaimed the good news of Christ at an earlier time (1:9, 13; 3:1; 4:12-20), although now removed from them by some distance—then we take it to be a letter to groups of historical people and not merely a fictional discourse.[1] That is, we are not dealing simply with just any rhetorical discourse but with a specific kind, that of an ancient personal letter.[2]

Letters provided the closest means of face-to-face conversation, albeit one-sided, when the writer was separated from those with whom he or she wished to communicate. The handbooks for letter writing, to be discussed more below, indicate that the writer was to address the recipients as though speaking face-to-face. In the earliest extant handbook for letter writing, Demetrius, appealing to a tradition arguably much older, declares: "Artemon, the editor of Aristotle's *Letters*, says that a letter ought to be written in the same manner as a dia-

1. Mullins, "Formulas," 388, comments on the importance of keeping in mind the fact that this is not a literary project, but these epistolary forms "constitute a social gesture. . . . They show the writer's attitude toward the *audience* to which he is writing, not his attitude toward the *material* he is presenting. The use of epistolary forms, more than any other part of a letter, reflects the fact that it was a letter, not an essay or a theological tract, which was being written" (emphasis his). Although certainly different and not of concern here, even fictional language, like prose fiction, is similar to ordinary speech in some ways, and speech-act theory recognizes that "speech devoid of situation is practically inconceivable" (Iser, *Reading*, 62; cf. 53–68).

Although no unambiguous evidence that Paul wrote any letter to Galatia exists beyond the letter itself, it is clear from Paul's other correspondence (e.g., 1 Cor 16:1; 2 Tim 4:10[?]), as well as the account in Acts (16:6; 18:23; in addition to cities of the Galatian province: 13:13-14; 14:1, 6, 21; 16:6; 18:23), that he traveled through and founded communities in this area.

2. See Stirewalt, *Epistolography*, 1–25, where the various letter settings, including specifically fictitious settings, are helpfully differentiated.

logue, a letter being regarded by him as one of the two sides of a dialogue. There is perhaps some truth in what he says, but not the whole truth. The letter should be a little more studied than the dialogue, since the latter reproduces an extemporary utterance, while the former is committed to writing and is (in a way) sent as a gift."[3] Stowers summarizes the matter well: "The letter fictionalizes personal presence. Thus ancient letters were largely constituted by the literary typification of social situations where two or more people interacted, usually in face-to-face encounters."[4] In other words, a letter was a specific author's or group's effort in time, given the limitation of proximity, to address a specific person or persons, or a group or groups of people with what they wished to communicate if they could be present personally.[5]

Thus the addressees of what we know as Paul's letter to the Galatians existed historically somewhere in Galatia, even if they may have considered themselves and been considered by others—inside or outside of their social context—in ways that are different from those of the author of this letter. For Paul is herein only concerned with certain aspects of their identity and behavior within the scope of his situational rhetorical concerns, his perception of developments that necessitate his action (the exigence), and the response invented in this letter to shape the outcome. Paul thus sets out his understanding of what really matters among the addressees in Galatians.[6] Can we take the other figures, such as those influencing the addressees, to be historical as well? And can we assume that they understood themselves very differently from how they appear when viewed uncritically only through the lens of Paul's polemical stereotyping?

3. Demetrius, *On Style* 223–24 (ca. 100 B.C.E.–100 C.E.; dated to early first century B.C.E. by Kennedy, *New History*, 88–89), see also 225–35; from Malherbe, *Theorists*, 16–19; see also Malherbe's introduction on 1–11; Stowers, "Social Typification"; Deissmann, *Light*, 228–29. Cicero makes the following comments about a letter: it is a surrogate for an actual dialogue; it is speaking to an absent friend as though he were present; it is a speech in a written medium; and it reflects the personality of its writer (cf. Malherbe, *Theorists*, 12).

4. Stowers, "Social Typification," 79.

5. Violi, "Letters," emphasizes that a letter is written because the writer expects something specific to occur as a result, even if only the maintenance of friendly contact.

6. Cf. Perelman and Olbrechts-Tyteca, *New Rhetoric*, 13–51; Berger and Luckmann, *Social Construction*.

The information from which we must work at a historical construction is—even though a letter—after all, rhetorical in nature, and thus limited in that it provides only one side of a conversation, one point of view. In this case, of course, that is the perspective of Paul. As we will discuss, he is not engaged in a level-handed descriptive task, but with the expression of parental-style disappointment and instruction. Thus, his message is delivered by—to name a few aspects of style that communicate his response—irony mixed with ridicule and rebuke; and it is about those influencing the addressees, with criticism of motives and methods through negative stereotyping and excoriating polemic. He goes so far as to wish upon those influencing them a curse (1:8-9), and although sarcastically put, self-castration (5:11). This is no exercise in systematic theology or generalized information to attach to his other more contingent letters.[7] The Galatian discourse is hot: it is written to confront the development of a specific exigence that is entirely unacceptable to Paul and to remove forever the obstacles in the addressees' way.

In what has proven to be a highly influential article for interpreters of the Scriptures, Lloyd Bitzer puts the matter of investigation of rhetorical situation this way:

> The presence of rhetorical discourse obviously indicates the presence of a rhetorical situation. . . . it is the situation which calls the discourse into existence. . . . It seems clear that rhetoric is situational. . . . a work is rhetorical because it is a response to a situation of a certain kind. . . . Let us regard rhetorical situation as a natural context of persons, events, objects, relations, and an exigence which strongly invites utterance; this invited utterance participates naturally in the situation, is in many instances necessary to the completion of situational activity, and by means of its participation with situation obtains its meaning and its rhetorical character.[8]

7. Contra Vouga, "Galaterbrief."

8. Bitzer, "Rhetorical Situation," 1–3, 4–5. In this approach "an exigence is rhetorical when it is capable of positive modification and when positive modification requires discourse or can be assisted by discourse"; it is not rhetorical when it cannot be changed by rhetorical discourse, such as the changing of the seasons (6). Along with the essential constituents of exigence and audience, constraints, i.e., those "persons, events, objects, and relations" that have the "power to constrain decision and action needed to modify the exigence" make up the elements relevant in a rhetorical situation (8). Bitzer's insights have been influentially applied to New Testament criticism by, e.g., Kennedy, *NT Interpretation*, among others.

Beginning with this perspective on the rhetorical situation need not keep an interpreter from recognizing that the context of the situation and the rhetorical action are alive and complex.[9] For example, the understanding of the exigence may be quite different from various and even competing discursive perspectives.[10] Because of different views of what is appropriate in the present age, the addressees or those influencing them may see and interact with the historical moment differently than with each other or Paul, and these views may continue to change as, for example, Paul's letter is delivered and responded to, altering the perspective of the addressees about the situation. Paul's own view of the situation would likely change as well, with the consideration of different aspects of the information he heard and various possible responses, when the letter was being composed, after its sending, and when learning of the response it has received. Likewise, the perspective of those influencing the addressees would probably change as the situation developed and almost certainly after the letter had arrived—whether aware exactly of its existence or not—heightened to whatever degree the addressees internalized and acted upon its message.

This investigation will probe the situation(s) implied in the text of Galatians, provoked by the exigence in the communities in Galatia with which he was concerned, according to Paul's analysis thereof, which is available to us by way of his rhetorical response in this letter.[11] Yet his letter provides only a snapshot of a situation—situations, really—that were likely to continue to develop in various ways even before it arrives, and from an interested view, and about exigencies that will likely change even during its reading, and then again thereafter. Paul's letter itself seeks to anticipate and control the direction of these changes. Naturally, they will change in ways that will be variously interpreted from the perspective of various interpreters, then or now. But it is assumed herein that Paul constructs a discourse that he believes will be salient and hopes will be persuasive for the groups of

9. Bitzer's observations have been variously critiqued by NT interpreters, e.g., Vorster, "Why?" 405–11; Wuellner, "Where?"; Stamps, "Rethinking," as well as by representatives from other fields.

10. Bitzer's later essay in reply to critics ("Functional Communication"), and the further refinements of Smith and Lybarger, "Reconstructed," bring out the roles of multiple perceptions and change, including recognition of multiple exigencies. See also Hester, "Situations."

11. See Louw, *Semantics*, 95.

real historical people to whom he writes.[12] He confesses—perhaps better, hopes—as much (5:10).

Yet at the same time the interpreter should recognize that these groups of people were being influenced in a direction other than the one set out in this letter by another group (or groups) of historical people, although this other group (or groups) almost certainly regarded themselves differently from the way that does Paul in this letter. After all, it is clear from Paul's rhetoric that this group (or these groups) of influential people was (were) even considered differently—positively—by those to whom Paul wrote.

We can thus seek to construct a view of the historical situation or situations that is or are presupposed by an interpretation of the rhetorical situation or situations implied by Paul's argumentative response to the seemingly singular exigence as he is understood to perceive it in this letter addressed to several groups, not just one.[13] The situations he addressed required a shared view on the part of the addressees of some of the particulars of the situations, albeit from apparently different perspectives on what they mean or how they should be resolved.

This consideration of the plurality of addressee groups to which the letter was sent brings to the surface another aspect of the data available that has too often been overlooked. Because most constructions portray these influential ones as a unified group from outside Galatia, it is natural to think of them traveling to the various locations addressed as a unit.[14] That does not adequately consider the possibility that, although the situations that arose in the various communities were similar, these influencers may have consisted of different groups and individuals in each of the locations to which this circular letter was written responding in similar ways, perhaps because they share a similar perspective. The recipients of this letter consist of more than one group; might not those influencing them?

12. Cf. Bitzer, "Functional Communication," 29–30; Perelman and Olbrechts-Tyteca, *New Rhetoric*, 20, note: "In real argumentation, care must be taken to form a concept of the anticipated audience as close as possible to reality."

13. I have chosen construction over reconstruction, respecting the fact that this is an attempt to interpret the historical situation from the rhetorical information available, not reconstruct a prior construction that has been discovered, as would an archaeologist. Such a construction is "only a view of reality, which is not necessarily equal to reality" (Cornelius, "Relevance," 461).

14. E.g., Lightfoot, *Galatians*, 29.

Paul stereotyped the interests and methods of these influential people. Did he purposefully simplify the details of the various situational tensions with a portrait that seems to consist of one undifferentiated recipient group, one group of others, as well as one exigence, or is that simply the result of our own distance, the paucity of information, or perhaps lack of imagination? The letter's circular address implies that the addressees would be in communication and cooperation, or at least could be when they had reason to be; but was this the case with those influencing them?

The way that an interpreter constructs the identity of these influential people is fundamental to the way that he or she constructs the situational context of Paul's letter and the interpretation of its message. Thus, whether the perception that the addressees were being influenced—persuaded and manipulated—precisely in the way that Paul represents the case to be in this letter (from the viewpoint of either the addressees or those accused of such influence), they were being influenced in some ways at some time before Paul wrote this letter by people among themselves whom the addressees considered important enough not to dismiss categorically as harmful to their own interests as believers in the good news of Christ. Instead, the addressees seem to have responded to these influential people as though trusted guides, internalizing—though not yet actualizing—their message of good for themselves.[15] This makes salient Paul's rhetorical subversion of the seeming interest of these influential people in the addressees' best interests, seeking to reveal instead the true character of the influencers' interactions with the addressees. For example, their apparent befriending of the addressees is portrayed rather as jealously driven in order to demonstrate what the addressees cannot have until they comply with their program (4:17; 6:12), and their ostensibly helpful teaching is characterized as obstructing the addressees' progress (5:7-8). Their message of apparent good is actually bad, as it twists so as to turn upside down the message of good in Christ, and thus renders his death meaningless for themselves (1:6-7; 2:21; 3:4; 4:11, 20; 5:1-12; 6:12-14). Their motives are envious (3:1), self-preserving, and self-concerned (4:17; 6:12-13). At least that is how Paul constructed his rhetorical attack in order to undermine the failure of perception he attributes to the addressees, as we will discuss.

15. Internalization is implied by the force and concerns raised in Paul's rhetorical attack; see, e.g., 1:6-7; 3:1-5; 4:16; discussion below.

An additional matter that arises here is the nature of the various discourse units within the letter itself. This will be the subject of thorough discussion, but should be touched upon now, as it relates to the question of what we can know. Within this letter, there is situational discourse, that is, language directed to the addressees about the urgency of their situation in Galatia, and what they should do about it. But there are also units of narrative discourse throughout the letter that Paul constructs to support his situational argumentative points (i.e., 1:11—2:21; 3:6—4:7; 4:22-30). Obviously, stories, such as Paul tells about his own experiences elsewhere, or a midrash or allegory built around historical figures like Abraham, do not provide the same kind of historical data about the situations in Galatia. Information may and probably will be implied by the way that the narratives are constructed and the rhetorical connections with the situational discourse are construed. But extra care must be taken to distinguish what relevance the players in those stories may or may not have for the identification of the players in the situations addressed in Galatia.

These people, that is, Paul, the addressees, and the ones influencing them in Galatia in a way that Paul opposes, existed historically. Yet it is clear that we can only hope to know these historical people and the situations through the lens of rhetoric, and that the information from which we work is limited. These influencers—pronouns may have been sufficient for Paul and the addressees who knew to whom they referred but are problematic for the communicative task of the later interpreter (I will discuss the justification of this label rather than the prevailing choices after evaluating the others)—are ostensibly influencing the addressees with "a different message of good" that Paul does "not" consider "another" (1:6-7). Just who they were and why they maintained the position that the addressees should be circumcised—a view that was feared by Paul to be influential enough for the addressees to provoke this extant response—will be a central element of this monograph. Paul's perception of the danger of their influence creates the exigence that provokes the writing of this letter to the "children" for which he holds himself responsible, and thus this identification is essential to the interpreter's construction of the situation, defining the context for understanding the usage of the language he employed, the task around which the historical-critical interpretive enterprise turns.

CHAPTER 3

THE EPISTOLARY CHARACTER OF GALATIANS AS IRONIC REBUKE

When it comes to unsettling the Galatian addressees, Paul is not to be outdone. An intimidating style of approach is evident immediately in this letter, even in the way it formally opens. Where common decorum called for offering a word of thanksgiving for the recipients of a letter—a move familiar in all his other extant correspondence—Paul does not pause for such pleasant formalities.[1]

Paul does briefly express goodwill toward the addressees (v. 3), but even this common epistolary courtesy is delivered with an edge. It does not stand alone but rather begins an instructive declaration of obligation (vv. 4-5).[2] Moreover, it is framed on the one side by an opening full of implied accusation (v. 1) and on the other with a threatening charge of rapid desertion from "him who called you in [the] grace [of Christ]"[3] (vv. 6-7). Were it not for epistolary convention, the disapproval characterizing the opening is so overwhelming that it makes one wonder whether the addressees questioned if Paul might have preferred to forgo even this courtesy.

More revealing of Paul's disposition is the fact that after the abrupt polemical opening line: "Paul an apostle—not from human agents nor through a human agency . . ." (v. 1), instead of the customary, if formal, note of thanksgiving, they are greeted with an intimidating ironic rebuke (vv. 6-7):

> *I am surprised* [Θαυμάζω] that you are so quickly defecting [μετατίθεσθε] from him who called you in [the] grace [of Christ] for a different [ἕτερον] good news [εὐαγγέλιον], which is not another [ἄλλο], except [in the sense] that [εἰ μή] there are some who unsettle you

1. Cf. Doty, *Letters*, 31–33, 43, takes the reason for this lone exception to be that Paul "was too concerned with the situation in the Galatian church to pause for the customary conventions" (31). The letter closes also in distinctive fashion, without the customary personal greetings (cf. Weima, *Endings*, 159).

2. See Berchman, "Rhetoric."

3. Some manuscripts omit the reference to Christ.

> [ταράσσοντες ὑμάς] and want to undermine [μεταστρέψαι] the good news [εὐαγγέλιον] of Christ.[4]

It will be argued that, just as we might today refer to a certain kind of letter as a Dear John letter, the convention for assessing Paul's choice of epistolary opening—Θαυμάζω in the context of ironic wordplay coupled with rebuke—instantly signaled the writer's intention, adumbrating unmistakably the nature of the social interaction to come. Such an expression of ironic rebuke functioned formally in the epistolary opening to confront a response that the writer considered inappropriate for those addressed. The direction set by this convention did not merely constitute the message of the letter opening but was the start of what the writer wished to say[5] and what the writer would say if able to engage the addressees face-to-face![6] Moreover, any changes that result from the effort of the writer to influence the addressees at any given moment during the discourse become part of the situation for them at subsequent moments of their reading/hearing.[7]

Paul's choice of formal opening expresses the disapproval of developments among the addressees that his message would communicate by way of ironic rebuke throughout, a characteristic of the letter's overall tone that has been recognized even by later interpreters who may no longer have been familiar with the fact that this opening represented a formal epistolary convention.[8] Recognition of the usage of this device in Galatians, as well as a deeper consideration of the nature of the instructive quality of irony, however, offers the interpreter seeking to penetrate the implied historical situation an advantage of significant proportion, to which we now turn.[9]

4. Various aspects of this translation will be discussed below; see esp. chapter 10.

5. Similarly, in terms of classical rhetoric, one purpose for setting out the exordia in deliberative speech is if the hearers are thought to attach too little significance to the issue (Aristotle, *Rhet.* 3.14.12; cf. 3.14.1, 6; Quintilian, *Inst.* 4.1/2.7–49; *Rhet. Her.* 1.4.6–7).

6. Demetrius, *On Style* 223–24 (from Malherbe, *Theorists,* 16–17); Stowers, "Social Typification"; J. White, "NT Epistolary Literature," 1740, notes that Paul "particularizes the qualification, on each occasion, so that the message of the individual letter is anticipated." See also Mullins, "Formulas," 388; Violi, "Letters." For discussion in literary terms, see Rabinowitz, *Before Reading.*

7. Cf. Perelman and Olbrechts-Tyteca, *New Rhetoric,* 490–91.

8. Cf. Roberts, "Transitional Techniques."

9. For a discussion of the present limits of rhetorical classification for Galatians see the appendix.

Defining Irony in Antiquity

In view of the forthcoming discussion of the epistolary character of Galatians as ironic rebuke, it will prove useful to consider what precisely is ironic, how it functioned in Paul's time, and how it is detected. One might even consider it ironic that, in spite of the recognition of the epistolary character as ironic rebuke by some recent interpreters, this has not led to significant new hypotheses for the situation, the identity of the influencers, or even the message of the letter. But it should, because the prevailing constructions have taken their foundational cues from surface readings of the text and not from the ironic level that would have presumably been obvious to those in the situations for whom the letter was addressed.

So what is irony, and how does it work? Irony in Paul's period was a highly developed rhetorical and situational form, even if the use of the term to denote it was rare. The following survey will be augmented by the discussion in chapter 10.

Irony takes many forms. *Situational irony* is a state of affairs that involves a different analysis or outcome than those in view realize at the moment (i.e., the audience awareness of the naïveté of the character's statement or action in view of the more informed view or expectation of the audience; e.g., the cases of David or Oedipus when they fail to realize it is their own fate they foretell, but the reader or audience is aware of the irony unfolding). *Verbal irony* involves an ironist using the technique of saying something but meaning something else in a way that explores the tension between two or more meanings (contrast of appearance and reality) so as to create an unanticipated result, that is, the sudden awareness of what had not been realized before. *Dissimulative irony*, a form of verbal irony, employs exaggeration, that is, over- or understatement, for the purpose of undermining or inverting (twisting) the portrayal. This is accomplished by pretense, by feigning ignorance or lack of capability in order to undermine the confidence or expose the naïveté or incompetence of the victim.

D. C. Muecke has captured the important instructive dimension of ancient irony that involves surprising the confidently unaware victim:

> Simple ironies always function quite openly as correctives. One term of the ironic duality is seen, more or less immediately, as effectively contradicting, invalidating, exposing, or at the very least, modifying the other. In the light of greater awareness, or of prior or subsequent knowledge (sometimes supplied by the ironist himself), an assumed or

> asserted fact is shown not to be true, and an idea or a belief to be untenable, an expectation to be unwarranted, or a confidence to be misplaced. To ironize something (in this class of irony) is to place it, without comment, in whatever context will invalidate or correct it; to see something as ironic is to see it in such a context.[10]

Ancient use of the term *irony* refers to understatement (dissimulation; depreciation) of the *eirōn*'s ability (in contrast to the *alazōn,* who is boastful) for the purpose of undermining the assumed advantage of the other. In this sense, irony creates and exposes a tension between appearance (what is assumed to be the case) and reality, at least from the viewpoint of the *eirōn;* and he or she hopes, following the employment of such irony, that this will be the view shared by the addressees and audience as well.

In early usage, the *eirōn* was sometimes cast in negative terms, as a deceiver or foxlike figure, even a liar who seeks to escape responsibility (Demosthenes; Theophrastus, *Characters;* Aristophanes, *Clouds* 449).[11] But it was also used positively. In the first extant usage of the term, Plato attributed this to Socrates in a positive sense, though he put it in the mouth of an accuser of Socrates who meant it negatively; a perfect ironical beginning for the term's recorded history (*Resp.* 1.337a; cf. *Symp.* 215a–23d). Thus, even in the early usage, we gain a view of the ability of irony to expose the error of appearances, to undermine and thereby correct perceptions through pretense. Indeed, the dialectical method of Socrates was "a novel and fruitful technique for puncturing sham and pursuing truth."[12]

In *Rhetoric to Alexander,* a fourth-century B.C.E. document formerly attributed to Aristotle, but now to Anaximenes of Lampsacus, irony is analyzed as a type of dissimulation that is particularly useful in recapitulation: "Irony is saying something while pretending not to say it, or calling things by the opposite of their real names" (21/1434a18–20). His definitions of irony support the later associations of irony with blame-by-apparent-praise and praise-by-apparent-blame, and opened the door to the more general sense one finds in Quintilian and thereafter that irony is "saying the opposite of what one means" (*Inst.* 8.6.55).

10. Muecke, *Compass,* 23; see also 30 on the element of surprise, 34 on confident unawareness.

11. Muecke, *Irony,* 14; Dane, *Critical Mythology,* 46–47.

12. Knox, *The Word Irony,* 21.

Important for reading Paul here in Galatians (cf. 4:12-20; 6:12-17; not to mention the Corinthian correspondence!) is the example of reality versus appearance that *Rhetoric to Alexander* provides: "On the one hand, those who do evil to our allies seem very worthy, while we, who are the cause of many benefits, seem to be wretches."[13]

The Romans Cicero and Quintilian draw from Greek usage to provide the first extensive definitions of the term and its rhetorical functions. Cicero considers dissimulative irony an "elegant kind of humor" with "an agreeable effect," whether the isolated figure of speech (*De or.* 2.65), or the pervasive habit of discourse exemplified by Socrates (*De or.* 2.67), that is, "in every conversation, pretending to need information and professing admiration for the wisdom of his companion" (*Off.* 1.30). His brief definition is "when you say something different from what you think," which also applies to an entire discourse in which your thoughts are different from your words (*De or.* 2.67).

For Quintilian, irony falls under allegory (*Inst.* 8.6.54), because its "meaning is contrary to that suggested by the words."[14] Quintilian offers a very important insight into how the real meaning of irony is revealed to an audience: "This is made evident to the understanding either by the delivery, the character of the speaker or the nature of the subject. For if any one of these three is out of keeping with the words, it at once becomes clear that the intention of the speaker is other than what he actually says" (*Inst.* 8.6.54).

All in all, Socrates remains the quintessential model of the various forms of irony by his disarming self-depreciation, by which he conceals his real advantage with the appearance of ignorance, for the purpose of instruction. This exaggerated posture or statement unmasks the pretense of the victim, creating a suspicion of appearances that alters the perception of reality. And this is the level on which irony works, even when no direct reference by the label *irony* is present.

This brief survey of ancient irony will not be complete without reference to the biblical material. The critics of irony often fail to account sufficiently for the biblical use of irony, because the term does not occur, and as a result they tend to overlook some important material for defining its usage. Yet this literature is certainly ancient and the use of

13. From Dane, *Critical Mythology*, 47.

14. They were separated finally in Chambers's *Cyclopaedia* (1778–88), so that "allegory imports a similitude between the thing spoken and intended; irony a contrariety between them" (from Knox, "Irony," 628).

irony frequent, wherein irony played overall a positively valued role.[15] Moreover, obviously this literature and its effects on normative behavior and expectations would have been a vital part of Paul's development, and to some degree, of the Galatians' intertextual world as well.

It should be noted that the ironic perspective was attributed to God, the one who sits in heaven and laughs at the foolishly arrogant plans made against him and his people (e.g., Ps 2:1-4; 37:12-13; 59:8 [MT 9]; Wis 4:18). Classic is the case of Job regarding who will question whom, which finally leads to Job's humble reconsideration, ironic interrogation having brilliantly accomplished the task (Job 38–41). God delivers his penetrating view from above ironically, undermining the limited vantage point clouded by self-interest; so too the wisdom and prophetic spokespersons recognize the unmatched ability of irony to penetrate the veil that seeks to mask the (mis)calculated plans of humankind against him and his righteousness and those who are righteous (Ps 2; Wis 1–6). This ironic perspective grants hope to the righteous in the midst of seeming hopelessness (Isa 56–66; Zech 9:9-17), for matters are not really as they appear to be to eyes that do not see and ears that do not hear, to those who "call evil good and good evil, who put darkness for light and light for darkness, who put bitter for sweet and sweet for bitter!" (Isa 5:20), wrongly judging that "tomorrow will be like today, great beyond measure" (Isa 56:12).

Likewise, the positive development of irony pulses throughout the writings of the early movement of believers in Jesus. Note for example the ironic inversion at work in the parables[16] and the Sermon on the Mount (Matt 5:1-12), and the Socratic style employed while engaging both rivals (e.g., Matt 15:3; 16:3) and disciples (e.g., Matt 12:48; 16:8-11; 19:30; 20:16; 23:11-12).[17] Consider, too, the attribution of Zechariah 9 of the king of Zion's ironic arrival upon a donkey, commanding peace in the face of the enemy's mighty horses and chariots, to the entrance of Jesus (Matt 21:2-7; John 12:14-15). Or consider Luke's application of Psalm 2 to the ironic circumstances of Jesus and his followers (Acts 4:23-31). And who could miss the irony of situation in the Roman inscription intended to mock "The King of the Jews"?[18]

15. See Good, *Irony in the OT;* Plank, *Affliction;* Jónsson, *Humour and Irony.*

16. Camery-Hoggatt, *Irony in Mark;* Herzog, *Parables.*

17. Camery-Hoggatt, *Irony in Mark;* Duke, *Irony;* Jónsson, *Humour and Irony.*

18. Muecke, *Irony,* 28–29, 91–92; Juel, *Master of Surprise,* 96–97; Camery-Hoggatt, *Irony in Mark.*

Although we do not know that Paul was ironic in presentation when among the Galatian addressees in the past, or in previous correspondence with them (if there was any), it is safe to assume that he frequently employed an ironic style. Irony is common in his extant correspondence to other communities (e.g., the ironic use of the weakness theme permeates the Corinthian letters),[19] and it is implied by the level and extent of Paul's use in this letter. Interestingly, Luke portrays Paul employing irony even in the most delicate and dangerous of situations (Acts 23:1-10), in addition to indulging in irony throughout his account of the movement.[20] Who could fail to see the irony of situation in Paul, the deadliest enemy of the movement, becoming its spokesperson and object of constant persecution (Acts 26:9-23; 1 Cor 15:8-11; Gal 1:13-16)?

If we simply stay within Galatians in noting that irony and varieties of wordplay were common to Paul, and might be expected by those who already knew him, the evidence is sufficient to suggest that the Galatian addressees could anticipate the use of irony, especially in handling their current compromising state of affairs. When the overwhelming presence of irony throughout Galatians (e.g., 1:13-16, 23-24; 2:2, 6-9, 14-18; 3:1-5, 10-14; 4:8-20, 21-31; 5:1-4, 11-12, 23; 6:3-5, 7-10, 11, 12-13, 14) is combined with the observation that Paul expected them to immediately read/hear this letter on the ironic level—to get the proper meaning from his ironic, even sarcastic tone—we can assume that the addressees know Paul to employ irony in his approach to instruction, especially in correcting inappropriate thinking or behavior, like a mother with a child (cf. 4:11, 19-20). One might even argue that, knowing Paul as the addressees did, they would have expected such an ironic approach from him when expressing displeasure, in which case they would have needed few if any clues in order to per-

19. 1 Cor 4:8-10 is one among many possible examples; see Plank, *Affliction*, on 1 Cor 4:8-13 in particular; Spencer, "Wise Fool"; Reumann, "Irony"; Holland, "Paul's Use of Irony"; Jónsson, *Humour and Irony*, 223–42, 259–75.

20. Outstanding are the reversal of fortunes in Acts 5:17-32 in view of 4:13-21; 5:17-41, and especially Gamaliel's comment in 5:34-39; the irony of Peter's learning God's will for the Gentiles from Cornelius, 10:1—11:18. Reumann, "Irony," 141 n. 5, notes that eleven of the twelve uses of *litotes* (the use of understatement when more is implied than stated; sometimes a term contrary to the meaning desired, with a negative to invert the expression) he observed in Acts in connection with Paul: 14:28; 15:2; 19:11, 23, 24; 20:12; 21:39; 26:19; 27:14, 20; 28:2. See also Jónsson, *Humour and Irony*, 208–22.

ceive it. In other words, it very well may be that they have been prepared for his ironic approach to rebuke in this letter because it was characteristic of the style employed by the Paul they knew in person.[21]

Moreover, once the presence of irony has been realized, it creates a heightened sensitivity on the part of the recipient to detecting other such maneuvers on the part of the author/speaker, which, as already mentioned, is an aspect of the rhetorical situation at work for an audience, regardless of the type of discourse delivered.[22] It is thus important to note that since Paul has begun the letter with a polemic sharply contrasting God's authority with that of human agents or agencies, followed by ironic rebuke, such features will be a part of the addressees' awareness thereafter throughout their reading/hearing of the letter.

Interestingly, it is in precisely those passages of the letter that are specifically connected with the situations in Galatia (1:6-9; 3:1-5; 4:8-11, 16-21; 4:31—6:17), or when Paul was present among them in the past (1:9-16; 4:12-15; 5:21), that we find clear epistolary features characteristic of the ironic and rebuking types, whether derived by comparison with ancient letters or with the handbooks concerned with epistolary style.[23]

Θαυμάζω (1:6) and Ironic Rebuke in Ancient Letters

In antiquity, many letters expressed disappointment for some neglect observed by the sender through employment of the term θαυμάζω (variously translated "I am surprised," "astonished," "perplexed," "amazed," or "wonder about").[24] In recent years, the corre-

21. So too the Corinthians; see Plank, *Affliction*. Notably, in Romans, wherein Paul addresses those whom he has not been among in the past, irony is not as characteristic of his approach. This observation appears to be consistent with recent studies of irony that emphasize that it is a product of community or shared context (cf. Hutcheon, *Irony's Edge;* Booth, *Rhetoric of Irony*). One must share (or at least know of) the values or experiences of the ironist or the context of that which is being twisted in order to get the point. Once employed among those who get it, irony then also creates and reinforces community.

22. Perelman and Olbrechts-Tyteca, *New Rhetoric*, 490–91.

23. Dahl, "Galatians," 35.

24. There are many examples, including both Greek and Latin, extending over a thousand years (400 B.C.E.–600 C.E.). See Hansen, *Abraham*, 34–44; Dahl, "Galatians," 15–35, J. White, *Light;* Roberts, "Examples from Papyri."

sponding characteristics of these ancient papyrus letters with Paul's similar terse opening in Gal 1:6 have led some interpreters to observe that Galatians exemplifies just such a letter of ironic rebuke. The following two papyri are typical of the many from antiquity that could be cited:

> I am very much surprised (πανυ θαυμαζω), my son, that till today I have not received any letter from you, telling me about your welfare. Nevertheless, my master, reply to me promptly, for I am quite distressed (πανυ γαρ θλειβομαι) at having no letter from you.[25]
>
> But I am surprised that no one has brought a letter from you and I am distressed (αθυμω) for this reason.[26]

As these examples indicate, such expressions of θαυμάζω often addressed the lack of response to a prior letter or letters. But they could address many other concerns as well. As in Galatians, this epistolary expression is a formal opening device in the papyrus examples. J. H. Roberts observes that when the usage represents that the writer is "perplexed" "the expression, at the formal epistolary level, fulfils a transitional function, either at the beginning of the letter, leading into the body, or within the body itself, leading to a new topic."[27]

John White observes that the purpose of such complaints "is to shame the addressee into writing"; however, in Galatians, like the common letter, it expresses dissatisfaction and intimates that communication has broken down. He notes: "Expressions of astonishment of this type have two formulaic items: (i) the verb of astonishment, θαυμάζω; (ii) the object of astonishment . . . introduced either by ὅτι or πῶς."[28]

Terence Mullins builds on these observations in a way very relevant to this study, with particular attention to the epistolary characteristics:

> The reproach aspect of the phrase has to be included in any attempt to identify it as a form. The whole point is that the writer is rebuking, even scolding, the addressee. And he is not using θαυμάζω in its common meaning; he is using it ironically, often sarcastically. He is not really astonished; he is irritated. . . . Thus, when a writer says, "I marvel that I have received no answer to my letters," he is not marvelling

25. P.Oxy. 123:5ff. (ca. 300–400 C.E.), from Dahl, "Galatians," 14.
26. P.Cornell 52:5f. (ca. 300 C.E.), from Dahl, "Galatians," 13–14.
27. Roberts, "Paul's Expression," 330–31.
28. J. White, "Introductory Formulae," 96.

> at all. In most cases he knows quite well what the score is. But he is rebuking his lazy correspondent. . . . Since there is no real astonishment in the phrase used this way and since irony and rebuke set the pervading tone, I suggest that if this is accepted as a form, it should be called ironic rebuke.[29]

Nils Dahl brings these epistolary observations directly to bear on Galatians with important results.[30] For example, when θαυμάζω is used ironically or to express disapproval, it does not indicate that the assertion of thanksgiving characteristic of Paul's other letters has been left out but rather "it has been *exchanged* for an expression of astonishment and disapproval."[31] Surprisingly, Dahl also observes that this "occurs more frequently in ancient letters than does ευχαριστω, used to assert thanksgiving rendered to the gods."[32] Although he notes that the evidence provides only for family features of letter styles and not a pure genre, he nevertheless concludes: "The common element is a mood of *disappointment* and a note of *reproach*. A letter characterized by an ironic rebuke and related features differs from a normal letter of friendship much in the same way as Galatians differs from the normal form of a Pauline letter."[33]

He further argues that by taking greater account of letters in literary transmission and of the model letters of the handbooks, the ironic nature of the rebuke in such examples of θαυμάζω usage is confirmed.[34] In addition to wondering about something of which one is uninformed, where θαυμάζω εἰ would of course be appropriate as an expression of surprise, this is not the only sense in which it may be taken. For θαυμάζω is used to express reproach or disappointment, and when followed by ὅτι, as it is here in 1:6, it is a "strong expression of

29. Mullins, "Formulas," 385–86. See also Stowers, *Letter Writing*, 134, 139. Differently, Roberts, "Examples from Papyri," argues that it is not the case that "the verb followed by ὅτι plus object would have to be regarded as a form" (118).

30. Cf. Dahl, "Galatians," 35, 79–81. See also H. Betz, *Galatians*, 47; R. Longenecker, *Galatians*, c–cix; Hansen, *Abraham;* idem, "Paradigm"; idem, *Galatians*.

31. "Galatians," 13 (emphasis his). J. White, "NT Epistolary Literature," 1742, notes the "strained" situation behind this replacement of the epistolary thanksgiving.

32. "Galatians," 13.

33. "Galatians," 35 (emphasis added).

34. Dahl, "Galatians," 13. Although not the topic of discussion here, note that examples of this usage are available outside of letters, e.g., Josephus, *Ag. Ap.*1.6.

disapproval of some action or negligence on the part of the recipient."[35] The sender thereby expresses the expectation that he or she had for some more appropriate kind of action on the part of the recipient.

Moreover, such letters were generally sent to family and friends, not strangers, and they often contain a wish for good health and other positive and intimate statements. Thus, it may be observed that "the ironic rebuke is an indirect expression of affection and concern for the addressees."[36] In business letters, this formal approach is used, for example, to confront the failure to care for the body of a dead brother or the failure to send what the addresser had written about the need of previously. In other words, it is the negligence, inappropriateness, or foolish action of the addressee that is in view in this declaration, not the lack of knowledge on the part of the sender, and it is based on the expectations of friendship or familial relations.[37]

It is interesting to note that perhaps the first extant epistolary use of θαυμάζω occurs, if genuine, in Isocrates' letter to Archidemus (*Ep.* 9:8), which was private in address, yet intended for the public: "I marvel also (θαυμάζω) at those men who have ability in action or in speech that it has never occurred to them to take to heart the conditions that effect all Greeks alike."[38] Demosthenes addressed his third letter to the council and people of Athens with this ironic element, although not in the opening, but nevertheless in a letter to the public along the lines of a persuasive, that is, deliberative speech (*Ep.* 3:11, 23): "I am *surprised* none of you notices that there is something disgraceful here: the Athenian People, which has the reputation of excelling all others in its sense of what is right and in its cultivation, the People which has always offered a refuge to the victims of misfortune, proves to be more callous than Philip! . . . Furthermore, I am *astonished* that any of you fails to perceive yet another thing."[39] Before I turn to the investigation of the evidence of the epistolary handbooks, it may be useful to begin to consider some of the initial similarities of these examples with what Paul expressed in the text of Galatians.

35. Dahl, "Galatians," 14.
36. Dahl, "Galatians," 15.
37. Contra Roberts, "Examples from Papyri" and "Paul's Expression"; see discussion below.
38. Dahl, "Galatians," 15.
39. Dahl, "Galatians," 15–16.

Implications for Galatians

These examples and interpretive observations certainly correspond to the language and tone found in Galatians, and many of the specific features are operating in the immediate context of Paul's declaration of θαυμάζω, whether translated, for example, as "astonished," "filled with wonder," "amazed," "perplexed," or, as I will conclude, "surprised." Once the convention is recognized, Paul's expression of disappointment through this indirect use of language is hard to mistake. Echoing the opening ironic rebuke, Paul's use of interrogatives throughout the letter draws attention to the conflict of Paul's expectations with the unacceptable developments in Galatia.[40] But is Paul actually surprised at these developments, as many interpreters suppose, or have these interpreters perhaps been taken in by Paul's rhetoric?[41] Does Paul not admit to a change of persuasive approach even in his choice of the letter's tone (e.g., 4:19-20)?[42]

The expression θαυμάζω is a stereotypical one that, on the surface, may be taken to suggest that he did not expect this development. That is, it can indicate perplexity, in the sense of confusion resulting from lack of knowledge.[43] But the nature of Paul's usage must be evaluated in the light of Paul's legitimation of his approach as appropriate in view of the situations addressed. Thus he appeals to the fact that he has already made known to the Galatian addressees his opinion of this "other" message of good: "As we have said before, so now again I say" (1:9; cf. 1:13; 3:1; 4:13; 5:3, 21); it is anathema for themselves,[44] even if proclaimed by "an angel from heaven" or Paul himself.[45]

40. Dahl, "Galatians," 26–29.

41. Jewett, "Agitators," 204, expresses the view of many when stating, "that a sudden and unexpected shift of mind came over the Galatians (i.6)." See also, e.g., R. Longenecker, *Galatians*, 14; Hansen, "Paradigm," 33; Dunn, *Galatians*, 39.

42. Thurén, *Derhetorizing*, 30.

43. Roberts, "Examples from Papyri."

44. Hatina, "Perfect Tense-Form," 8–9, noting that the aspect of this having occurred in the past is "indicated by the deictic features in the context such as ὡς and ἄρτι πάλιν, not by the tense form" suggests rather that, "since the perfect conveys the most semantic weight, Paul may have chosen it, instead of the aorist, to draw attention to the previous warning that was given to the Galatians to reject every foreign gospel."

45. It is possible that Paul's first-person plural reference in vv. 8-9 is merely a Hellenistic epistolary plural formula referring to Paul himself (Burton, *Galatians*, 29; R. Longenecker, *Galatians* 16). Yet Paul here appeals perhaps to the group on

Paul delivers this ironic comment in the context of a scathing rebuke for compromising that which is essential by way of that which will upend it, a purpose which is telling for translation and interpretation of the ironic intent. And the style of Paul's argument throughout the situational discourses of the letter is that of rebuke, often by way of irony. Why does he rebuke them? For an inappropriate interest in and trust of the influencers and their message of *apparent* good in view of the *real* good that has become theirs already in Christ.

Paul does not approach the addressees as though they lack prior information or are unable to respond otherwise, for such would excuse them. He accuses the addressees of having allowed themselves to be vulnerable to the effects of the influencers, including:

- an "unsettling" impact that allows the good news of Christ to be "twisted" (1:6-7);
- an "envious gaze" that sends the addressees vainly seeking "completion" (3:1-5);
- policies of "exclusion" that enhance the addressees' desire for acceptance by the influencers (4:17);
- "obstructing," "persuading," "seducing," and "compelling" them (5:7-12; 6:12).

These objectives, strategies, and techniques have now moved the addressees off the "true" course they had been "running so well" (5:7).

For this development, Paul holds the addressees accountable; even if, at the same time, he blames the influencers for their motives and the employment of manipulative methods which are in their own interests rather than those of the addressees. He proceeds to address the recipients as those who "should" have known better than to have considered internalizing as good for themselves that which they learned from Paul, their patron, to be bad for them, as contrary to that message of good in Christ that they have received and from which they have already ben-

whose behalf he writes this letter (v. 2), who are apparently known to the addressees as important witnesses of that which Paul and they hold in common as dear. It also implies that Paul's authority to claim what he herein does is grounded in the community of witnesses with whom he writes, and opposition to Paul represents opposition to them as well as God, from whom his authority has come (cf. Berchman, "Rhetoric," 9).

efited immeasurably with no less than the receipt of the Spirit and even miracles in their midst (3:5).

In other words, Paul indicates that he was not so much surprised as hurt, disappointed, even disgusted. Here, Paul employs the emotional cutting edge expressed by θαυμάζω to undermine their failure to appropriate the knowledge that they have, not their lack thereof,[46] revealing the disloyal character of the action that the writer feels is implied by the inappropriate action of the party being confronted.

In some papyrus examples, instructions given beforehand have been ignored or disobeyed.[47] Paul expected more of them. He had, after all, taught against this error when among them; thus, he had reason to expect, through both general and specific instruction, as well as by the guidance of the Spirit, that they would know and behave otherwise (cf. 1:9; 3:1-5; 5:3, 7-10, 21).[48] He makes it clear that he has been fighting on their behalf to preserve the truth of the good news for a long time and at great personal expense; from his perspective, he has every right to be exasperated by their failure to now remain faithful to it (1:9; 2:2, 5, 11, 14, 20-21; 3:1-5; 4:11-20; 5:1-3, 7-11; 6:9, 14-17).[49]

Such an expression, when directed, for example, at the choice made by a child, is not so much that the parent never imagined the possibility existed. Although the parent (i.e., any authority figure) may appear to declare ignorance at the literal level, seemingly expressing a lack of knowledge or lack of appropriate anticipation in the declaration, for example, "I am surprised that you . . . ," the recipient knows if it is a feigned (Socratic) expression of irony or at least should know. Indeed, the writer may have feared this development, instructed against it, provided personal examples that might help dissuade the recipient from it, all the while praying that the recipient would not succumb. And the recipient knows this only too well. That is how the ironic edge cuts its victim.[50] The writer hoped that such a choice would never be made,

46. Quintilian, *Inst.* 9.2.26, explains that "The *figures* best adapted for intensifying emotion consist chiefly in simulation. For we may feign that we are . . . filled with wonder."

47. Cf. Dahl, "Galatians," 15–24.

48. Note Lightfoot, *Galatians*, 64.

49. Quintilian, *Inst.* 4.2.15, notes that "closely dependent on *ethos* are the skilful exercise of feigned emotion or the employment of irony in making apologies or asking questions."

50. Cf. Hutcheon, *Irony's Edge.*

not by *my child*, if for no other reason than a sense of obligation and respect. But such expressions generally do not indicate so much a lack of anticipation as disapproval.

And that is just how Paul approaches his "little children" in Galatia, with the diminutive twist of Socratic irony employed by a mother who fears her toil has been in vain, indeed, questioning the very labor that has given the addressees life (4:11-21). He reveals that he is "perplexed." Whether Paul is actually perplexed or not, this rhetoric expresses that he is anguished not because of their lack of knowledge but because of their misbehaving in view of what they know and should do instead. They are not without knowledge, but "foolish."[51] Do they think that he is telling them this because it is easy for him to say, because it is for his own good, because he is their enemy? Has he not proven himself a friend—indeed, a messenger of God—when but a stranger, an ostensibly threatening one at that? But they had decided instead to bless him. What do they expect of him now? Oh, that he could be there now and set them straight; indeed, then he could "change" his "tone" (4:20).

Although the incorporation of Paul's ironic rebuke within a formal letter style suggests at least some deliberation on his part, not to mention the role any secretary may have played in the execution of this form, such expressions of disappointment may be entirely spontaneous. Upon discovery of a certain attitude or behavior, it provides an indirect and arguably more effective way to initiate rebuke than statements of fact ("I told you not to do this!" and "Don't do this!") or interrogatives ("Why have you done this?" implying "after I told you not to") that provoke a defensive response. Plutarch noted just this advantage of the Socratic style of irony this response exemplifies: "And a harper delightfully rebuked Philip's late-won knowledge and officiousness: when Philip thought to dispute with him on a question of notes and scales, the harper said, 'May you never fare so ill, Sire, that you have better knowledge of these matters than I.' By seeming

51. Calling someone or their thoughts or actions foolish (ἀνόητος) indicates that one has behaved unwisely, without properly perceiving the situation (cf. Rom 1:14; Aristotle, *Rhet.* 1.10.4/1368b: "mistaken ideas of right and wrong"). This does not mean that they do not "know," but that they do not understand the implications of what they "should" know, indicated by their inappropriate behavior. In honor and shame terms, they are shameless; they do not show proper concern for their honor or the honor of their group.

to ridicule himself he reproved Philip without offence" (*Mor.* 8.634). The advantage of indirect speech in such encounters is summarized nicely by David Worcester: "Rhetorical devices, then, serve to win the reader and to soften the impact of the writer's destructive or vengeful sentiments."[52]

We must remain aware of the profound seriousness of shaming in this culture, more feared than death itself, so that the function of indirect language to soften the effect serves a most important purpose, though even the ridicule of such indirect rebuke would be devastating[53] (we remain in touch with this force in the experience of blushing in embarrassment when the victim of ironic disclosure, an experience that is then seared into our memory).[54] As Paul Radin observed, "The fear of ridicule is . . . a great positive factor in the lives of primitive peoples. It is the preserver of the established order of things and more potent and tyrannous than the most restrictive and coercive of positive injunctions possibly could be."[55] Indeed, ridicule is one of the most effective tools for reinforcing group identity, whether employed to negatively stereotype the out-group as inferior or to evoke shame for the failure to conform to the values that define honor within the in-group, then, and still to this day.[56]

The depth of this insight is magnified by the role of the ancient letter to typify social relations: the "ancient theorists said that authors were to write their letters as if they were speaking face to face with the recipient,"[57] and it is in exactly such facial encounters that honor confrontations took place.

52. Worcester, *Art of Satire*, 14.

53. Cf. R. Elliott, *Power of Satire*.

54. Louw and Nida, *Lexicon*, 25.195–96 and n. 14. See Braithwaite, *Reintegration*, 57–83, for discussion and some examples of the culturally specific modalities of shaming. Pitt-Rivers, "Honor," 504, in a social-scientific analysis with special attention to Mediterranean cultures, notes that the great weapon of dishonor is ridicule, "which seldom employs a moral criterion at all, but destroys reputations on the grounds of a man's pretentiousness, foolishness, or misfortune, not his wickedness." For models of honor and shame in antiquity and in application to the biblical world, see Gouldner, *Enter Plato;* Malina, *Social World*. See Kaufman, *Shame,* for a modern psychological approach to this phenomenon.

55. Quoted in R. Elliott, *Power of Satire*, 76.

56. Cf. Deist, "Boundaries and Humour."

57. Stowers, "Social Typification," 79.

Such letters of surprise, for example, for previous letters that have thus far gone unanswered, solicit a letter and expect to oblige the addressee to comply with that which is requested. The recipient, if for no other reason than obligation in view of the hurt expressed, is likely not to ignore such a request, unless he or she wishes to signal indifference to the concerns of the writer and contribute to a break in the relationship. So too Paul appeals by this comment, and throughout the letter, to the addressees' sense of loyalty in friendship as well as to child-to-parent responsibility, which obliges them to desist from further pursuit of this path.[58]

In view of these points, the translation "surprised" may be preferred over the translation equivalents "wonder," "astonished," "amazed," or "perplexed," although any of these overlapping expressions could effectively perform the ironic task, once recognized as such.[59] Each can resonate with the language of ironic rebuke that is the characteristic of a θαυμάζω opening, capturing the disappointment of a parental figure dealing with a wayward child by an expression of self-deprecation to effect the point. In ironic terms, the use of θαυμάζω here is not an expression of real surprise because of an actual lack of knowledge.[60] It is rather a feigned ignorance, suggesting anticipation, but implying that the nobler expectation that the writer had hoped would materialize has unfortunately not done so; instead, what has developed was that which was feared. In spite of any prior efforts he or she may have made to prevent its occurrence (to which Paul attests; cf. 1:9; implied also in 1:13; 3:1; 4:13; 5:3, 7, 21), these are now revealed as unsuccessful.

But a parent does not give up. There is always hope, and shaming is a powerful albeit often reflexive response to bring the children back into line with the parental values. Here, rebuke set out ironically does some of its sharpest work. The lie the children now seek to hide or justify—according to the values of the parents, and thus by implication, applying to those in their care—is exposed by revealing the *reality* of their compromising behavior, regardless of how they may have previously justified it to themselves, or repressed the fact of it. It is not *the truth*, and will not be tolerated.

58. Similar is Ramsay, *Galatians*, 70.

59. Louw, *Semantics*, 35, 43–45, 62–64.

60. Thus "wonder" and "perplexed" are weaker choices, giving the impression of "thinking about."

Paul's approach to the addressees in ironic rebuke terms continues in the body of the letter. The examples are too many to cite, but consider his accusation of foolishness, that is, the addressees' lack of discernment (ἀνόητοι: 3:1, 3), as well as his expression of "perplexity" (ἀποροῦμαι: 4:20) at the choices being considered or made; likewise, his fear of being regarded now as an enemy for telling them the truth, as though such an act was for his benefit and not rather a sacrifice on behalf of themselves (4:12-16).[61]

As the comments of interpreters have made all too clear, choosing the translation "surprised" tends to be taken literally and can be easily understood by those removed from the context to imply Paul's failure to anticipate that problems would arise. On the other hand, its familiarity at the literal level yet recognition of its employment even until this day when addressing children in Socratic irony may arguably make it the best choice for expressing the oscillating quality of Paul's ironic parental usage here.[62] After all, as Quintilian noted, one of the features of irony is when "we pretend to own to faults which are not ours" (*Inst.* 9.2.49).

Ancient Handbooks on Letters of Irony and Rebuke

The handbooks for letter writing in antiquity sharpen the observations based on the papyri evidence in important ways. Such handbooks were apparently concerned with practical instruction in letter writing for advanced students of rhetoric.[63]

It is important to note that the theory of these letter types "requires that the writer compose according to generic patterns that must fit the circumstances of the author's particular situation in writing."[64] That is, the social relationship of the author with the recipient, including the

61. See also the recognition of rhetorical manipulation in these admissions noted by, e.g., H. Betz, *Galatians*, 129, 233, 236–37; Thurén, *Derhetorizing*, 61–63.

62. It is unclear and surprising that Thurén, who recognizes that Paul's employment of this expression does not reveal that Paul was astonished or irritated, as others suggest, finds the importance of the containment of irony or not in this device "irrelevant" (*Derhetorizing*, 61 and n. 24).

63. Malherbe, *Theorists*, 6–7.

64. Stowers, "Social Typification," 82. The nature of Paul's rhetoric in this letter makes it difficult to understand the proposition that Galatians was not written for Galatia but is a general letter distilling his theology for attachment to the other letters; contra Vouga, "Galaterbrief."

current status and purpose for writing, are to be communicated in the letter as though they were present in person. Stowers observes: "In describing types of letters the handbooks do not specify formal rhetorical-literary features or stylistic traits but picture a typical social interaction that could be transacted through letters."[65]

The classification of letter types is similar to that applied in the classification of rhetoric, each of the three types being chosen for the speech characteristics appropriate for particular social contexts.[66] As the user of these handbooks was a student of rhetoric, he or she would understand how to elaborate the syllogism (enthymeme)[67] of the few terse lines in the model or sample letter given to effect the particular social situation being addressed.[68] These sample letters drew from the ancient institution of Greek friendship (the quintessential type of letter, though of course not the only type) and expressed the occasional concerns of praising and blaming, shaming and honoring, thus naturally sharing many functional parallels with epideictic speech.[69] In other words, the choice of letter type represents rhetorical invention; based upon the exigence, the writer decides upon the letter form that he or she believes will best accomplish the rhetorical task for which the letter is undertaken.

First, the handbook of Pseudo-Demetrius, *Epistolary Types 21*, offers this explanation of the *ironic type* (Εἰρωνικός), one of the twenty-one letter styles for which examples are provided: "when we speak of things in terms that are their opposites, and when we call *bad* men *noble* and *good*."[70]

65. Stowers, "Social Typification," 78.

66. Stowers, "Social Typification," 82. For a discussion of classical rhetorical approaches to the interpretation of Galatians, see the appendix.

67. The literal meaning of Aristotle's technical term is "held in the mind" (Kennedy, *New History,* 59).

68. Stowers, "Social Typification," 83; idem, *Letter Writing,* 52–56.

69. Stowers, "Social Typification," 84–85; idem, *Letter Writing,* 52, includes some corresponding examples between handbooks and epideictic rhetoric, which accounts for many of the letter types (e.g., praising types include commending, consoling, praising, congratulating, thanking, erotic, and diplomatic; blaming types include blaming, reproaching, censure, admonition, threatening, vituperation, reproaching, reproving, ironic or feigned praise), with only two belonging to judicial (accusing, apologetic) and one deliberative (advising).

70. Malherbe, *Theorists,* 40–41 (emphasis added). For a summary of this handbook (dated somewhere between 200 B.C.E.–300 C.E.), falsely attributed to Demetrius of Phalerium, see 4–7; for the full text, see 31–41 (Stowers, "Social

Second and third, in Pseudo-Libanius we learn of two epistolary types from among forty-one defined. The first example, the ironic type (Εἰρωνική), corresponds with many features in Galatians: "I am greatly *astonished* [ἄγαμαι][71] at your sense of equity, that you have so *quickly* rushed from a *well*-ordered life to its *opposite*—for I hesitate to say to wickedness. It seems that you have *contrived* to make, not friends out of your enemies, but *enemies out of your friends*, for *your action* has shown itself to be *unworthy* of friends, but eminently worthy of your *drunken behavior*."[72] The second, the letter of reproach (Ὀνειδιστική), also offers an example that is strikingly similar to Galatians: "You have received many favors from us, and I am exceedingly *amazed* [θαυμάζω] that you *remember none* of them but speak badly of us. That is characteristic of a person with an *ungrateful* disposition. For the ungrateful *forget noble men*, and in addition *ill-treat their benefactors as though* they were *enemies*."[73]

Mixing of such letter types was expected,[74] thus Paul's use of features that exemplify both types simultaneously is not odd. But consider the suggestive similarities! Although no connection with these particular handbooks is implied, it appears that either Paul or the secretary (amanuensis)[75] selected this introductory formula on the basis of its ability to best communicate the sentiments from among the known letter types.[76]

Implications for Classification of Galatians

First, the relevance of Pseudo-Demetrius for our passage obviously recommends itself. Consider Paul's opening. After referring to the

---

Typification," 87 n. 2, says it almost certainly originated before 100 C.E.). Malherbe also discusses other sources.

71. "Atticism accounts for the choice of ἄγαμαι over θαυμάζω" (Dahl, "Galatians," 13).

72. *Epistolary Styles* 56 (fourth to sixth centuries C.E.) from Malherbe, *Theorists*, 74–75 (emphasis added).

73. *Epistolary Styles* 64 from Malherbe, *Theorists*, 76–77 (emphasis added).

74. *Epistolary Styles* 45 from Malherbe, *Theorists*, 73; Stowers, "Social Typification," 86, indicates the need to look for correspondence with mixed types and examples that are simplified in actual practice and not pure ideal types.

75. Richards, *Secretary*, 143.

76. Dahl, "Galatians," 10–11; Malherbe, *Theorists*, 6–7; Stowers, "Social Typification."

"other" message to invert its (mis)appropriation as "good news," Paul makes his real view of this other message as instead "bad" for the addressees with a cutting edge: "it is not another, except" to the degree that you so regard it; and upon its proponents he wishes not good but rather a curse.[77]

The ironic twist on this particular term εὐαγγέλιον is employed in biblical and nonbiblical literature to communicate that what is a good message in the opinion of one of the deliverers or recipients is the opposite, or bad news, for the other (cf. 2 Sam 4:10; 2 Kgdms 4:10 in LXX). This inverted use by Paul parallels Quintilian's observation, which he applies to things as well as people: "It is also irony when . . . we concede to our opponents qualities which we are unwilling that they should seem to possess. This is specially effective when we possess these qualities and they do not" (*Inst.* 9.2.48–50).

Second, in the first example of the ironic type from Pseudo-Libanius, note the issues of speed (quickly), and of the failure to rightly perceive the situation of opposition, although this is not an outright accusation of wrong intentions. These are characteristic of Paul's approach in Gal 1:6-7. Moreover, they continue to function throughout the entire letter (2:6-9, 11-17; 3:1-5; 4:8-21; 5:2-18; 6:1-17).

Paul seeks to set out the stark opposition that he believes has gone somehow, inappropriately, unappreciated to date by addressees who should have known better. Throughout this letter, Paul confronts their foolishness, naïveté, and failure to recognize the magnitude of what is at stake. He does not accuse them of having already apostasized but of acting in a manner that suggests such defection is in the making. Though perhaps not explicitly recognized as such by the Galatian Gentile addressees, their present course demonstrates to Paul that they are in the process of foolishly internalizing the message of the influencers as good for themselves. This involves failing to realize, from Paul's perspective, that allegiance to this other message and its proponents necessarily entails defection from the grace of God toward themselves in Christ while yet Gentiles. It will in effect nullify the purpose of Christ's

77. Quintilian, *Inst.* 7.6.54–58, provides the example of giving "a pleasant or good name for an unpleasant or bad thing." Muecke, *Compass*, 51 (emphasis added), states "Such irony works by asserting a 'falsehood' and *relying upon the reader's or listener's prior knowledge of the truth* to contradict it mentally or vocally by an emphatic counter-assertion, this counter-assertion with all its emphasis being the ironist's real meaning."

death for themselves (2:21; 5:2-4), for it implicitly denies the reality of their decision to believe, as well as their experience of the Spirit, even the miracles performed in their midst (3:2-5).

Paul's comment in 1:9 gives expression to what he "should" be able to expect from the Galatian addressees, but now finds "surprisingly" misplaced. For he has communicated in person at an earlier time—even if presumably not in the same "tone" as he does now—the incongruity of these two messages of good: "As we have said before, so now I say again. . . ." Thus, Paul approaches the addressees as though they ought to know better and behave otherwise. This is not new ground but was covered when he was formerly among them. The writer is justifiably disappointed at their inappropriate behavior, the disregard that reveals their lack of appreciation, by the ingratitude evident in their failure to reciprocate his labor of love and friendship: Paul is "surprised" indeed![78]

The ironic presentation of two contrary messages and messengers undermines the inappropriate equality of place that the addressees have given to the influencers and their message, when from Paul's perspective no such treatment is deserved or permitted. Paul ironically undermines the good that is present in the label "good news," granting this other message a standing "as though" equal to that of "*the* good news *of Christ*," when it is, by his reckoning, instead directly opposed to that news and thus should be regarded oppositely. It is *bad* news, worthy of anathema, that threatens to "undermine" what they have already "received" from Paul, the good news of God's grace toward themselves "in Christ." In fact, I will argue that Paul's comment here indicates that this "other message of good" has nothing to do with a proclamation of Christ, which is what makes the ironic association so unexpected and persuasive.

The friendship theme around which Paul's ironic approach is spun is present throughout the letter. To name but one explicit example: in

78. Muecke, *Compass*, 30: "All that is necessary is the merest avoidable assumption on the part of the victim that he is not mistaken. For one of the odd things about irony is that it regards assumptions as presumption and therefore innocence as guilt." I am not convinced by Roberts ("Paul's Expression") that the choice of translations (e.g., wonder, astonish, surprise, amaze, perplex) can be as rigorously differentiated as he proposes, even in the papyrus examples he cites. If employed ironically, each can function to express the feigned response to what is considered inappropriate on the part of the addressees.

the case of 4:12-20, the parallels are extremely close.[79] The addressees are failing to reciprocate in a way appropriate to their relationship with Paul, instead trusting the influencers as friends and suspicious of Paul as their enemy for telling them the truth.

Interestingly, the accusation of "drunken behavior" in Pseudo-Libanius's example corresponds with Paul's accusations of the "foolishness" that results from having been gazed upon by "the evil eye" (3:1a-b). Paul attributes this "affect" to their having had their own eyes wrongly aimed; instead of looking to the crucified Christ for their identity, they have looked to the influencers instead (3:1c: "before whose eyes").[80] With this and other expressions of disappointment, Paul underlines the foolishness of the addressees allowing themselves to be seduced when they seek the acceptance of "human agents and agencies" after they have already "become known" by the divine (3:2-5; 4:8-10).

Such a charge actually underlies Paul's message throughout. Consider also the accusation that the addressees are being charmed by the manipulative ploys of the lover who "shuts out" in order to fuel the flames of desire (4:17)[81] or of their being engaged by the agonistic, self-seeking methods of attaining honor, instead of living in the service of the other, secure in the status that has already been granted in Christ (4:21; 5:1-4, 13-26; 6:1-10, 12-15). In addition, Paul interprets the addressees' "persuasion" to undertake circumcision as their being victims of an "obstruction," as their being impeded from running on the proper course (5:7: ἐνέκοψεν). Paul accuses the addressees of having been affected not only by the "unsettling [ταράσσων]" of the influencers (v. 10), but by their "seducing [ἀναστατοῦντες]" activity as well. He summarily states that the influencers seek to "compel [ἀναγκάζουσιν]" them (6:12).

To put a point on this important parallel, consider the role irony plays in the opening expression of θαυμάζω in 1:6-7. Whether the "defection" (μετατίθεσθε) that Paul accuses the addressees of being presently engaged in (note the present aspect of verb) is the result of their being affected by the various manipulative means he attributes to the influencers (if passive voice), which charge corresponds with accu-

79. Cf. H. Betz, *Galatians*, 221.
80. See my "O Foolish Galatians" and discussion to come.
81. Cf. C. C. Smith, "Galatians 4:17."

sations made in 3:1; 4:17; 5:7-12; 6:12-13, or is the result of their own doing (implied more clearly if middle [reflexive] voice), Paul's ironic style of rebuke cuts both ways. The expression of disappointment is directed at the addressees, not at the influencers. Yet at the same time, the influence of the influencers by the means of "unsettling" the addressees, motivated by their "wanting to twist the good news of Christ," is present in Paul's accusation as well.

So the addressees' current behavior indicates that they are victims of outside forces; but the ironic dig indicates that these elements are not entirely beyond their control! While Paul attributes the ultimate power affecting them to the influencers, he also indicates that they are themselves at least in part to blame, for these developments are due to their own inappropriate choice, their failure to "stand fast" with their sights on the promise of God that is theirs in Christ, "waiting for the hope of righteousness" (cf. 5:1-12).

Third, Pseudo-Libanius's example of "reproach" suggestively corresponds with Galatians as well. This is especially clear in Paul's accusation of spurned friendship, of the betrayal implied by their current thankless behavior in view of the effort of God and Paul toward themselves, and in his expression of fear that their trust will be further jeopardized by this letter's exposition of "the truth" of their foolishness to date, cast as it is in an ironic style of rebuke. These are the efforts of a loving mother seeking to protect her vulnerable children from the powerful forces of social pressure they find extremely seductive. The children themselves are apparently incapable of calculating the consequences thereof in their present immature state and thus misjudge the results of trying to get away with self-deception; hence, the bite of Paul's unsettling ironic interrogatives in 4:15-16 (and larger context; similarly, 3:1-5): "Will this effort to tell you the truth—for your benefit and at the risk of sacrificing your blessing—lead you instead to regard me now as your 'enemy'?"

Paul confronts the disposition exhibited by their current process of defection implicitly and explicitly throughout the letter as demonstrative of a lack of gratitude, both toward what God has done for them in Christ (1:4-6; 2:21—3:5, 14, 22; 3:25—4:11; 5:1-5), and toward Paul himself (2:5, 11, 14; 4:12-20; 5:10-11; 6:12-14, 17). And he challenges their failure to remember what they ought to already know (1:8-9; 3:1-5; 5:7, 21), that which should have been sufficient among friends and kin to have kept them from allowing, in his absence, such inappropriate developments to surface among themselves: "For it is good always to be jealous of the good, and not only when I am present among you" (4:18).

Dissociating Argumentation in Galatians 1:6-7

Paul's opening approach has significant formal and functional epistolary implications for the recipients of the letter and for the later interpreter too. Additional aspects will be considered as well.

Paul did not waste any time expressing his disappointment with the Galatian addressees for allowing the influencers to affect them or making known his opinion of the influencers' message and methods. These are announced in the letter opening by way of ironic turn of phrase (e.g., "other" for "not another"; "good" for "bad" ["not"]; "complementary" for "contrary"; "help" for "unsettle"; "seeking to be known" when already "known by God") and outright rebuke (e.g., θαυμάζω; "so quickly"; "deserting"; "as we have said before . . . if anyone . . . let him be accursed"; "O foolish Galatians"; the rhetorical interrogatives of 3:2-5; the expressions of fear and ridicule in 4:12-21). This language is intensified by employment of the epistolary convention of ironic rebuke, wherein, by the way θαυμάζω is used in the opening, the addressees are put on alert to the texture of the message to come. In fact, they have already received the story in use, in the "surprising" function of the phrase itself.

This letter opening stole the heart right out of the recipients' consideration of the "other" message as good for themselves and adumbrated the "dissociating" antithesis that the balance of the argument will set out in an unforgettable way.[82] As defined by Perelman and Olbrechts-Tyteca, the *dissociating* approach to argumentation alters the conceptual data upon which notions of reality are predicated. This argumentation proceeds not by breaking the links that connect elements so that they will be regarded as separate and independent, which is how Paul's language has been taken by many interpreters to rather dissociate the two messages of good and the messengers and their religious systems along an axis of freedom in Christ or slavery under Law, and so on. Dissociating is instead based upon an assumption of "the original unity of elements comprised within a single con-

82. Cf. Perelman and Olbrechts-Tyteca, *New Rhetoric*, 411–59; Vorster, "Dissociation."

ception and designated by a single notion."[83] Thus, the argument seeks not to break the links between independent elements but to modify "the very structure of these elements."[84] The dissociation of concepts involves the following dynamics:

> a more profound change that is always prompted by the desire to remove an incompatibility arising out of the confrontation of one proposition with others, whether one is dealing with norms, facts, or truths. There are practical solutions enabling the difficulty to be resolved exclusively on the plane of action; they can prevent the incompatibility from occurring or dilute it in time, or sacrifice one or even both of the conflicting values. At this practical level, the dissociation of notions amounts to a compromise, but, on the theoretical level, it leads to a solution that will also be valid for the future, because, by remodeling our conception of reality, it prevents the reappearance of the same incompatibility. It preserves, at least partially, the compatible elements. The operation, though bringing about the disappearance of the object, is nonetheless carried out at a minimum cost, because the thing that is valued is given its rightful place in the thought, and the latter is given a coherence that is beyond the range of difficulties of the same order.[85]

As they discuss by way of example, this is precisely the process employed when dealing with such seeming incompatibilities as the existence of evil or death in a world created by a God of good and life. Thus, the notion of original sin dissociates the concept of humankind into categories of "created good" but "fallen," where the second term, *fallen*, modifies the first term, *created good*, rather than replacing it. This solution seems to some interpreters to resolve these perceived incompatibilities.

Consideration of dissociation leads to recognition of a dynamic that is important for consideration of Paul's emphasis on incompatibility, for if new concepts are sufficiently consistent, they may "appear so indissolubly linked to the incompatibility whose removal they make possible, that the forceful presentation of the incompatibility may seem to be another way of stating the dissociation."[86] Thus many interpreters

83. Perelman and Olbrechts-Tyteca, *New Rhetoric*, 411–12.
84. Perelman and Olbrechts-Tyteca, *New Rhetoric*, 412.
85. Perelman and Olbrechts-Tyteca, *New Rhetoric*, 413.
86. Perelman and Olbrechts-Tyteca, *New Rhetoric*, 413.

of Galatians emphasize the ostensible antithesis between pairs, when it is the modification of the first term by way of the second that is in view if Paul's argument is approached as exemplifying dissociation instead.

Paul emphasizes dramatically the incompatibility of these two messages of good for his addressees ("a different good news, which is not another, except"); turning toward it represents "defection" and will have perilous results, upending the very meaning of Christ's death, of the very grace of God toward themselves in the midst of the present ("evil") age. The perceived incompatibility has proven decisive for the interpreter who has internalized as good ("consistent") Paul's notion as though seeking to create something separate and independent, something now understood to replace rather than modify what was good before. This is natural enough, for there are several adjustments Paul must make to resolve the relatively singular incompatibility of these two "messages of good," for there are two theoretical and social systems that are represented therein. But Paul's approach is predicated upon the elements it shares with the traditional good news, the message of good proclaimed beforehand to Abraham (3:8). Paul thus modifies rather than replaces the traditional meaning in view of his understanding of what has changed in the present time because of Christ's death. Now, the historical righteous ones of God interface with those from the nations who join with them in the worship of the One God, demonstrating the arrival of that which is expected when the age to come has dawned.

Rather than pushing for replacement, Paul takes the difficult road of compromise, which calls for "the greatest effort and is most difficult to justify because it requires a new structuration of reality."[87] Once established, this involves the dissociation and restructuring of concepts, for "compromise tends to appear as the inescapable solution and to react on the aggregate of concepts into which it is inserted."[88]

Thus, we can understand the effectiveness of Paul's reliance upon irony, for it dissociates appearance from reality, revealing the incompatibilities of the two appearances—the good message of inclusion by circumcision versus the good message of inclusion apart from circumcision—that are on offer in the addressees' situations.[89] That is, Paul

87. Perelman and Olbrechts-Tyteca, *New Rhetoric,* 415.
88. Perelman and Olbrechts-Tyteca, *New Rhetoric,* 415.
89. Cf. Perelman and Olbrechts-Tyteca, *New Rhetoric,* 415–59, esp. 415–19.

argues from a revealed perspective for how Israel is to deal with non-Jewish people who seek incorporation among the historical righteous ones as full members, which is how things now are proclaimed to be in view of the meaning of God's actions in Christ, regardless of how they might to others merely appear to be apart from the meaning of Christ's death. It is that meaning that provides the "agreed value" of perspective for Paul and the addressees, providing the dissociation by which the rival appearances of the two paired "messages of good" for the addressees must be evaluated. For "while appearances can be opposed to each other, reality is coherent: the effect of determining reality is to dissociate those appearances that are deceptive from those that correspond to reality."[90] In other words, Paul dissociates the meaning of "good news": what is truly "good" for these non-Jewish addressees now in view of the good news "of Christ" has been modified with the changing of the aeons. Paul does not call for a new message but for a modification of the understanding of the traditional one.

The addressees will never again be able to imagine that this "other" message, which is really "contrary" to the meaning of the death of Christ for themselves, could appear complementary. They will now know not only at the intellectual level but at the deep emotional level where irony shames its victim that this "other message of good" now rather subverts the good news of Christ for themselves as Gentiles in the present age, turning its meaning upside down, because adherence to the one message necessarily represents defection from the claims of the other one.

The message that follows indicates that Paul approaches the addressees in this way not because they ought not to already have known better—they should have—but rather in view of the fact that he is certain they would not entertain such a course if they really understood that it had such an implication for themselves in terms of Christ and will judge the situation properly now in view of this message. He attacks throughout their naïveté, their inappropriate thinking and behavior, in view of who they already are as Gentiles in Christ who have thereby experienced the grace of God of the age to come, having had this identity confirmed by the receipt of the Spirit as well as miracles.

90. Perelman and Olbrechts-Tyteca, *New Rhetoric*, 416.

Conclusion: Interpreting Galatians as a Letter of Ironic Rebuke

Many interpretive possibilities emerge from consideration of the epistolary aspects of ironic rebuke. It has been demonstrated that additional attention to the dynamics of irony provides significant insights into this profound letter, which have been coupled with the examination of the formal epistolary features of ironic rebuke at work in the opening frame, their detection, and their implications. These insights grant the interpreter entrée not only into the epistolary frame and structure of the letter but, as we have already seen, into the body of the letter itself. In fact, once the ironic texture of this discourse is recognized, many other seemingly inscrutable aspects of the letter's implied situation and meaning come to light. To some of these we will eventually turn, especially as they reflect upon the identity of the influencers.

As most any parent knows, when one addresses his or her teenage children in the struggle against the powerful seduction of their peers, when principles considered sacred threaten to burst at the very seams, when ironic rebuke and vituperation are sharpened to pierce the armor of indifference, such rhetoric is not meant to portray the peers accurately, nor their parents, whose ability to parent adequately may be summarily dismissed as inadequate or immaterial to the point at hand, if not outright incompetent, mistaken, even wrong. What parent has not blasted the "other" (including the failure of the other children's parents) in exasperated response to a teenager's appeal to the behavior of the other's values and behavior as superior, as normal, as that which everyone thinks and does? Who has not said, "I do not care what other parents think or let their children do; we do not think this way, and you will not do this!"? Or sometimes more cleverly, "If so-and-so jumped off a cliff, does that mean that you should too?"

When such ironic rebuke is employed to address one's own children, one assumes that no one else will hear the bitter denunciation of the other children's or their parents' character or upbringing; that one will not have to answer for their accusations as though public statements of fact. On the contrary, one assumes that the other children and their parents will never hear of this charge; in fact, sometimes this discretion is explicitly commanded to avoid just such misunderstanding.

For that matter, one may not even suspect the other children or their parents of that which one's own child attributes to them. But that is not the topic of a parent's concern in this engagement with the wrongheaded views or behavior being expressed by his or her child. The rhetoric is intended only to shock and forever render unimaginable the powerful charm of acceptance by another court of reputation, one might say, a suddenly more immediate and important part of the child's identity and ambitions, when this involves compromising the principles most essential to a family's survival or honor, and to a child's health and opportunity to rise above the tempest of puberty. This is the time not for another rational argument, although such an appeal will likely be made as well, but for the emotions to be engaged. Just as Paul proceeds in this letter, the appeal will likely include disclosure of one's own sacrifices for the principles in question, in spite of the opinion of others, with an appeal to nobility and integrity, and a call to wait patiently for the acceptance and satisfaction one so desperately seeks, perhaps appealing to well-worn maxims such as, "As you sow, so shall you reap"; or "The just will triumph in the end."

It is in just this kind of spirit that Galatians was written, I believe: by a parental figure anxious that his children would take the road to compromise that would delegitimate the very honor of the death of Christ upon which their faith, and Paul's, stood, and destroy themselves before they have had a chance to "grow up," to stand on their own as adults; by a parent determined to prevent this result. When Paul's smoldering rebuke is given its rhetorical place, the possibilities for evaluating the situations and players from a historical perspective are immeasurably increased.

CHAPTER 4

THE STRUCTURE OF PAUL'S ARGUMENT

In order to isolate the data most precisely bearing upon the implied identity of those influencing the Galatian addressees, that is, those who are involved now in Galatia, the structure of the letter providing the information must be considered. Some of the argument Paul makes is *situational*, directly written to the addressees, for example, by way of ironic rebuke, to persuade them to take or not take a specific course of action. It is epistolary rhetoric having to do with the exigence in Galatia, namely, that the addressees are to remain faithful to the good news of Christ and not take the other course of proselyte conversion to which they are ostensibly being persuaded by the influencers. Other aspects of his argument are *narrative* in character, drawing from other experiences or stories to support the lines of argument taken up in the situational discourse, that epistolary rhetoric Paul constructed specifically to persuade the Galatian addressees in their own context.[1] The details of this narrative material are not necessarily relevant for construction of the situations or players in Galatia; rather, it is the rhetorical points of this material as they support the situational discourse that matter. As John Muddiman so cleverly put the case in anatomical terms: "In dissecting Galatians, then, it is vital to avoid the mistake of identifying the organs that belong to one system as though they belonged to another."[2]

The texts of the letter will be separated for the sake of clarity into situational and narrative discourses. These are joined by *transitional* material that creates seams when the writer moves from the one discursive element to the other.

The situation-related discourse units should be expected to contain the primary rhetorical information from which we may derive details of the exigence in Galatia that has provoked the letter, as Paul sees it anyway, and thus is that from which a hypothesis of the situations and

1. Cf. Cicero, *Inv.* 1.19.27–21.30; see Perelman and Olbrechts-Tyteca, *New Rhetoric*, 350–410.

2. Muddiman, "Anatomy," 258.

players will be constructed as well as tested.[3] Paul's rhetoric implies that he is addressing a particular audience with a particular exigence arising from a particular situation, as he understands it. This information might be expected to be most clearly evident in the epistolary opening and closing, especially the summary of the letter of 6:11-18. And indeed it is, but the body of the letter also involves the communication of Paul's reaction to the social situation, in keeping with the character of ancient letters.[4] The interpretive task includes attention to what is implied for the situations of the Galatian addressees in Paul's rhetoric and not necessarily something else that has occurred at another time or location, for example, in the life of Abraham or in Jerusalem or Antioch. Thus, the body of the letter must be carefully analyzed for its relative value as it pertains precisely to the situations in Galatia.

The narrative discourses that Paul constructs to illustrate or further particular lines of argumentation begun in the situational discourses must be analyzed for the salient rhetorical connections with that material that should be expected to arise for the addressees. However, with respect to details of the exigence in Galatia, they provide secondary data. Thus, this material is better suited to testing the hypothesis formulated from the situational discourses and less so that from which it can be reliably constructed. There are, after all, only two explicit digressions in the autobiographical narratives beyond the strict limits of the telling of the stories themselves (Gal 1:20; 2:5).[5] The narrative units thus play a smaller role in this discussion. But their importance in the history of the interpretation of Galatians is not meant to be slighted, just qualified, and for the most part in a way that puts them outside the scope of this investigation. The point is made succinctly by Nils Dahl, when he observes that the historical and theological arguments of 1:11—2:21 and 3:6—4:7 "have given the letter a permanent importance. *But* within the epistolary structure

3. I do not mean by this the rhetorical device common to forensic rhetoric labeled *narratio,* referring to that part of an oration that sets out the events that have brought the case to court (see Kern, *Rhetoric,* 104–5).

4. Stowers, "Social Typification," 85, takes exception to the idea that "the body is merely the message to be communicated." Rather, according to ancient epistolary theorists and the handbooks, "the body is not mere information to be communicated but rather a medium through which a person performs an action or a social transaction with someone from whom he or she is physically separated."

5. Cf. Cicero, *Inv.* 1.19.27.

they are *subordinate* to the framework provided by the statements of Paul's dissatisfaction and fear."[6]

The examples brought forth in the narrative units, whether from Paul's own prior experiences in Jerusalem, Antioch, or elsewhere (1:11—2:21), or Abraham's as found in the Scriptures (3:6—4:7), or in an allegory (4:21-30), are constructed to support the points he seeks to make to the Galatian addressees about their own current situations; however, their situations may or may not conform to the particulars that are used in constructing the examples. Failure to recognize this limitation accounts for much confusion and lack of precision in identifying the implied rhetorical and historical situations of the addressees themselves—not an earlier case such as in the examples from Jerusalem or Antioch—and Paul's specific response to the developments in Galatia for which this letter was written.

In articulating the limitations of the narrative discourses for providing the starting place for the identity of the influencers and situations addressed, it is useful to consider their methodological purpose within the framework of the letter. It is clear and generally agreed upon that in 1:12—2:14 (-21)[7] Paul tells a story of aspects of his life since the revelation of Christ that do not take place in Galatia, and thus the details of this autobiographical discourse have no situational connection with the experiences of the addressees, apart from Paul's direct connection in 2:5, and as they are connected to the rhetorical situations by the reader/hearer in Galatia (or the later interpreter).[8] However 2:15-21 is viewed, it is only at 3:1 that Paul returns to the ironic rebuke of the Galatians begun in 1:6-9.[9]

It is not self-evident how this autobiographical discourse is to function in the letter unless we first determine the situations in Galatia that

6. Dahl, "Galatians," 81–82 (emphasis added). In another vein, it has been noted that Galatians is a singular argument (e.g., H. Betz, *Galatians*, 14–25; T. D. Gordon, "Problem," 33–34); such observations are not in dispute.

7. The transitional verses 1:10-11 may be argued to apply to Galatia. And the presentation of 2:15-21 has been argued by some as what Paul's view of the Antioch incident was upon reflection, or perhaps what he wished he had said to Peter (so Dunn, *Theology of Galatians*, 13–17, 72–75). Although it is unlikely that Paul is recounting word for word what he had said to Peter some years earlier, it is likely what he thought at the time and in some way communicated to Peter and those who witnessed the incident in Antioch. Regardless, these verses do not mention the influencers and are not those around which identity decisions are constructed.

8. Cf. Bitzer, "Rhetorical Situation."

9. Cosgrove, *Cross*, 5, 26–38, notes similarly.

have provoked this response.[10] Likewise, the midrash on Abraham and appeal to scriptural precedent and chronological logic in 3:6—4:7 provide material to amplify the point Paul has made directly in the ironic rebuke of 3:1-5, explaining how these Galatian Gentiles' new identity is the result of faith in and of Christ, and witnessed already in their own experience of the Spirit.[11] Similarly, the allegory of Abraham having children through both Sarah and Hagar (4:22-30) does not reflect events in Galatia at the literal level and, as such, represents an example explicitly labeled as allegory by Paul; in the same way, neither do his examples of the mountains of Sinai and Jerusalem, nor the heavenly versus earthly Jerusalem.[12] Any association with groups from Jerusalem, Antioch, or elsewhere (has anyone suggested Sinai, which is also mentioned?) should not be presupposed but must be derived from interpretation of Paul's rhetorical application of these examples to the Galatian situation, which is precisely what is under investigation. He presents this analogy as an allegory, but the basis for interpretation is predicated upon what the addressees know about the situations that the later interpreter does not and, in the case of this investigation, now seeks to understand apart from turning to such interpretive matters as the meaning of this allegory.

It should be clear that someone making a point may construct examples for any number of reasons in support of it and thus that an interpreter of Paul's letter must attend to the methodological separation of the narrative examples from the situational discourses directed to the Galatian addressees for analysis of the exigence in Galatia[13] and, in this

10. So too Cosgrove, *Cross*, 13, 31.

11. Note Schmithals, *Gnostics*, 41; Cosgrove, *Cross*, 28, 32.

12. Even if, as argued by S. Elliott, "Choose," they may have some contextual connection for the addressees with mountains in the area of the Galatians.

13. This separation of units of discourse may also be supported by appeal to the elements of rhetoric, classical or new. Although I question whether Galatians exemplifies handbook rhetoric (see appendix), each of the species of such rhetoric accounts for the use of examples within argumentation. Each of the classical genres of classification accounts easily for Paul's use of examples in order to persuade the addressees to make the appropriate choice for themselves in view of what may be learned from the experiences of the past (cf. Aristotle, *Rhet.* 1.9.40; 3.16.11; 3.17.5; *Rhet. Her.* 3.2.4; *Rhet. Alex.* 32 [see also 8]; Quintilian, *Inst.* 3.8.36; Cicero, *De or.* 2.335). Some commentators adopting the deliberative species for their interpretation have made much of this point (cf. Witherington, *Grace in Galatia*). For application of examples in forensic oration see, e.g., Aristotle, *Rhet.* 1.9.40; 3.17.5; Cicero, *Inv.* 1.19.27–33; for epideictic, see, e.g., Aristotle, *Rhet.* 3.17.11. And the new

case, for the special emphasis upon the identity of the influencers. The failure to keep this distinction within the discourses of the letter in view may be noted in the methodology and conclusions of many if not all commentaries that take up the issue of the influencers' identity.

More attentive to this problem, although not always following his own advice, Ben Witherington notes that this language is properly considered exemplary in nature and not situational.[14] The point of these examples is that as Paul has acted in the past "so also they [the Galatian addressees] must oppose the agitators with similar agendas in their own churches."[15] And although not precisely correct or helpful to call the autobiographical discourse "analogies" rather than examples,[16] Witherington offers a corroborating point with regard to how this discourse should or should not be applied to the task of identifying the influencers now in Galatia, observing that "analogies are not identity statements."[17] That is the point or at least very close to it. The issue is all the more clear when it is recognized that in the case of constructing the autobiographical examples Paul does not present them even as analogous to the Galatian situation or in any way draw an analogy with the players involved. The only point of comparison is made explicit in the Jerusalem example, with the united resistance to the circumcision of Titus in 2:5 being cited in order to make the point that this unflinching response to advocates of circumcision of Christ-believing Gentiles was "that the truth of the good news might be preserved for you," that is, the Galatian addressees. Even this case is thus not presented as an analogy but a historical event the consequences of which are made explicit for the addressees and in this sense representing a situational comment.

---

rhetoric maintains that examples imply disagreement over a particular rule but assume earlier agreement that provides the possibility for arriving at a generalization that the example is invoked to establish (cf. Perelman and Olbrechts-Tyteca, *New Rhetoric*, 350–68).

14. The inconsistency of identification surfaces in his comments, and in his construction of the situational dynamics; see, e.g., *Grace in Galatia*, 25, 203, where he draws a direct association with the Jerusalem Christ-believing apostles, which he can only do by making more of these narrative examples then his comments would otherwise suggest appropriate (care is apparent, however, often; e.g., 136, 160–62, 448).

15. Witherington, *Grace in Galatia*, 23.

16. Discussion in Perelman and Olbrechts-Tyteca, *New Rhetoric*, 371–98; however, the allegory may be thus described (398–405).

17. Witherington, *Grace in Galatia*, 23. Also Cosgrove, *Cross*, 31; Lyons, *Pauline Autobiography*, 163.

Examples are developed for the purpose of supporting one's case. As such, they must be examined for their rhetorical connections with the argument in the situational and, in this case, epistolary discourse. Any details must remain within their respective spheres, whether in the examples themselves or in the situation now being addressed. This information is to guide the future course of the Galatian addressees, and any details brought to bear from other examples need not compare to the details of the situations in Galatia now, except as they exemplify the rule Paul seeks to clarify, that is, the truth of the gospel where it concerns the identity of these Gentiles and concomitant indiscriminate fellowship with them by all Jewish people who share this conviction.

The letter's structure breaks down as follows.

Situational discourse is that most pertinent for seeking to construct the situations in Galatia and is to be found in the following passages:

- the opening language of 1:1-9, and the transitional language of vv. 10-12,[18] in which Paul sets up the fundamental political antithesis between human agents and divine, and strikes out in ironic rebuke;
- a tone that he picks up again in 3:1-5, after the autobiographical information;
- and again in 4:8-21, following several direct applications of the Abraham material;
- finally providing extensive instructions in the concluding arguments of 4:31—6:10, with the overall argument summarized tersely in the accusations and challenges of 6:11-18.[19]

18. For division of these verses see the commentaries and Holmstrand, *Markers*, 147 n. 8, 148–55; J. White, *Form and Function*, 32–51, 79–84; idem, "Introductory Formulae"; idem, "Epistolary Literature"; Mullins, "Formulas," 387–88; Dahl, "Galations"; Silva, "Text," 278; Parunak, "Dimensions," 224–26. In this case it seems that v. 11 functions as a signal opening the transition to the autobiographical section, since the θαυμάζω of v. 6 had already opened the letter's body. And the tense changes in v. 11 to describing the past, and this is then built upon clearly in vv. 13 through the autobiographical narrative ("former [ποτέ]"). It thus seems likely that v. 10 wraps up the first section of vv. 1-10 and signals the transition restating this theme of antithesis in vv. 11-12 for amplification in the autobiographical section of 1:13—2:21.

19. This basic structure is confirmed by various methodologies, including the multidimensional discourse analysis of Parunak, "Dimensions"; and the literary analysis of Cronjé, "Defamiliarization," 217–19.

This assessment conforms closely with Dahl's conclusion: "These sections are clearly written in epistolary style. Conventional epistolary formulas cluster within and around them. They, along with the opening and conclusion, provide the framework into which more general, somewhat self-contained units have been inserted."[20]

In other words, although material directly relevant to the Galatian situations is also identifiable within the rhetorical asides contained in the narrative discourses at 1:20; 2:5; 3:7, 13-14, 22, 25-29; 4:3-7, 28-29, 31, most direct information is contained in the situational discourse units. These are the places where Paul first sets the tone of ironic rebuke and later summarizes his perspective of the influencers, their motives, and the appropriate Galatian response. In fact, the most important details from which the interpreter can seek to construct the situations and the identity of the players are contained specifically within the sections of the letter wherein Paul expresses ironic rebuke. These discourse units share the theme and mood of the epistolary opening. They include 1:1-9 (10-12); 3:1-5; 4:31—6:10; 6:11-18. Special attention should be given within this situational material to the epistolary opening (1:1-9 [10-12]) and closing (6:11-18) sections.

As a result of these epistolary observations, the situational discourse units will be the focus of this study into the identity of the situations and players in Galatia. With regard to the influencers in particular, Dahl observes: "These situational passages have the 'I-you' or the 'I-you-they' style and contain all the explicit references to the troublemakers."[21]

Narrative discourse units include

- the autobiographical section of 1:13—2:21;
- the discussion of Abraham and his rightful heirs in 3:6-24, which continues in principle until 4:7, with 4:8-11 serving a transitional role back to situational discourse;[22]
- and the allegory of Abraham's sons in 4:22-30.[23]

20. Dahl, "Galatians," 35, breaks this down slightly differently, after the opening, he includes 3:1-5; 4:8-11, 12-20; 5:2-12; 6:11ff.; and on 79, he groups under this heading 1:1-5, 6-10; 3:1-5; 4:8-11, 12, 13-20; 5:2-12; 6:11-16, 17, 18.

21. Dahl, "Galatians," 79.

22. Note that Chrysostom's outline as constructed by Fairweather is very similar to mine, and he regards 3:6—4:11 as persuasion based upon "ancient narratives" (Fairweather, "Rhetoric: Parts 1 & 2," 16–18).

23. Dahl, "Galatians," 79.

Some of the parenetic material in chapters 5–6 may also reflect formal discourse rather than actually articulating particulars directly evident in Galatia, such as the catalogs of virtues and vices (5:19-23), even if many of the particulars, like the overall section in which they are placed, may be directly contingent to the agonistic context addressed.[24] Each of these unit breaks is identifiable on both thematic and semantic grounds, though with some overlap in transition and application at the seams, reflecting an all-out argument to dissuade the addressees from a course that he fears they may have already had their deepest desires awakened to pursue.

The transitional statements often found between the narrative and situational discourses (cf. 1:10-12; 3:23—4:7; 4:8-10, 11, 21; 4:30—5:1) will also be considered in constructing the hypothesis, as well as testing it, because it may be expected to contain relevant situational information as the writer turns either from or to situational discourse. For example, Gal 3:1-5 begins an ironic rebuke that is sharpened by lack of transition, picking up where Paul had left off in 1:6-9, so that these two sections function as an *inclusio* for the autobiographical sketch (1:12—2:21), introduced by the transitional material of 1:10-12, and perhaps concluded by a kind of transitional statement offering rhetorical explanation of the force of Paul's confrontation of Peter (2:15-21), yet one that is not of itself actually taking place in Galatia.[25] When the general

24. See Fletcher, "Singular Argument," 99–271, for good discussion of the limitations of taking this material as parenetic as defined by Dibelius, or Vetschera, from whom he drew. He notes among other matters the structural problem of a lack of a clear beginning point for such a transition of function (119–42). Instead, he argues that it is better to recognize that this material is bound together fluidly with the argument of the rest of the letter. See also Fitzgerald, "Catalogue," noting numerous functions for this device, especially amplification, and how "while the catalogue itself generates the feeling of greatness and size, concluding formulae indicate the ultimate inexhaustibility of the catalogue's subject" (288), which is explicitly the case at the end of both lists, in Gal 5:21 ("and the like") and 5:23 ("against such").

25. Arguments for the identity of the influencers have drawn often from the autobiographical material, but not generally from 2:15-21, so it is not that important of an issue for this study. Some argue that vv. 15-21 are transitional or even situational. The majority of commentators take this to be part of the autobiographical narrative, which I find convincing on both epistolary and functional rhetorical grounds. The logic for the narratives is the same throughout; it is an argument constructed to support the situational arguments. Apart from this, one would have to argue that Paul was engaged in the balance of the narratives in some other enterprise that was not deemed directly relevant to the case he seeks to make for the

nature of much of the material in 3:23—4:7 is recognized, the intensity of the epistolary emphasis of 1:6-9 and 3:1-5 is continued across this seam into 4:8-11, 12-20, and by way of v. 21 into the allegorical discourse as well. This transitional material may contain information that is directly useful for identifying the situations or influencers, and it will be carefully considered in this light.[26]

Outline of the Flow of the Letter

Below is a schematic treatment allowing one to see how the situational discourses (left column) would read without the narrative discourses (right column). Note how the information for assessing the rhetorical situations in Galatia remains. Now, the rhetorical connections in the narratives as they are brought to bear upon the situations addressed can be analyzed. This should help us minimize the bleeding across of the material within narrative examples that Paul constructs around other occasions, into the discourses specific to the exigence now addressed in the situations in Galatia. Transitions between situational and narrative discourses are very important for making rhetorical connections that explain the implied usage of the examples for the situational point, but they are difficult to include in a linear treatment like this, because, without the narratives, they would not be present. This is perhaps more so for the transitions from situational to narrative discourses than when coming the other direction. Galatians 4:31 is a good example of transition from an example to the situations addressed in Galatia. Where clear situational material may be derived from the transitions, these are included and marked.

Galatian addressees. In addition to Dahl's argument ("Galatians," 42) and the above discussion of the epistolary frame, consider, e.g., the rhetorical arguments against Betz's analysis by Fairweather, "Rhetoric: Parts 1 & 2," 14–15; Classen, "St. Paul's Epistles," 287–88; Anderson, *Ancient Rhetorical Theory*, 134–35. The extensive treatment of Holmstrand (*Markers*, 147, 157–65) provides a linguistic analysis with eight specific reasons why Paul does not abandon the narrative level of the text to turn to the Galatians and embark upon a theological discussion; see also Parunak, "Dimensions," 216–18, 231–37. For the opposite view, see H. Betz, *Galatians*, 113–14; Esler, "Making," 309–10.

26. Dahl, "Galatians," 80. See also Cronjé ("Defamiliarization," 223), who notes that, like a good stylist, Paul shows a concern for arrangement of his material (a valued Hellenistic trait) in the employment of *defamiliarization* (a technique with a high level of estranging effect), by alternating the "passionate sections" (he cites 1:6-10; 3:1-6; 4:8-20) with the less emotional ones (the principle of μεταβολή).

The reader may thus see the flow of Paul's argument, sometimes speaking directly to the addressees, and at other times amplifying his point by the construction of example, midrash, analogy, and allegory. This allows attention to the implied rhetorical situations to be carefully differentiated from the narrative material constructed to support his response.

This is a linear treatment of the *flow* of the letter based upon the structure traced above (transitions in []; narrative in {}; -> for flow).[27]

SITUATIONAL	TRANSITIONAL	NARRATIVE
1:1-5 Opening greeting and theme introduced ->		
->1:6-9 Letter body: ironic rebuke and theme applied to exigence ->		
	->[1:10-12] [28] Restates theme ->	
		->{1:13—2:21} Autobiography illustrates theme in Paul's life[29] ->
3:1-5 Ironic rebuke restates theme of exigence ->		
		->{3:6-14; 15-22} Midrash illustrates theme historically ->
		->{3:23—4:7, 8-10, 11}[30] Applying midrash->

27. The results of discourse analysis confirm many of the features of this outline (cf. Pelser, et al., "Galatians"). For a survey of prevailing outlines see Kern, *Rhetoric*, 91–92; Fairweather, "Rhetoric: Parts 1 & 2," 16–18. For those more epistolary in character see Dahl, "Galatians"; Hansen, *Galatians;* idem, *Abraham;* Cosgrove, *Cross;* Boers, *Justification*, 49–75.

28. Parunak, "Dimensions," argues that 1:11-12 provide an "introductory chiastic summary" (237). Note also discussion of Roberts, "Paul's Expression," 332–33.

29. Galatians 2:5 draws explicit historical inference that has resulted from this prior engagement in Jerusalem on behalf of the addressees in Galatia.

30. This unit has a situational quality about it, as Paul here applies the insights, although it is still structurally a part of the larger narrative unit.

SITUATIONAL	TRANSITIONAL	NARRATIVE
->4:12-20[31] Ironic appeal to previous experience of theme ->		
	->[4:21] Ironic rebuke ->	
		->{4:22-30} Illustrates theme allegorically ->
	->[4:31—5:1] Application of allegory->	
->5:2-18 Parenesis: application of theme for communal lifestyle ->		
		->{5:19-23}[32] Vice and virtue catalogs ->
->5:24—6:10 Parenesis (cont.) ->		
6:11-17 Restatement of letter/theme ->		
->6:18 Closing greeting		

31. Note that this is Paul's first direct request in the letter. Dahl has suggested ("Galatians"), and Hansen (*Abraham; Galatians*) then developed, a division here of the letter along a line of rebuke until this point and thereafter a request, which can be seen in some papyrus letters. But Paul's rebukes have not ended nor has his delivery of them in ironic style (e.g., 4:21; 5:2-9).

32. The lists of the fruit of the Spirit or flesh appear to be developed into a general kind of list. The occasional application is implied overall; the relative weight of each element is not distinguishable on its own but only when compared to the rhetorical weight of emphasis throughout the letter. For example, envy is mentioned, and the evil eye context of Paul's language combined with the agonistic material suggests that this is a particularly pertinent element among those on the list, but its location in the list itself would not suggest this importance. Many have argued on the basis of comparison with other vice and virtue lists of the period that this is a general list and not developed especially for the Galatians (see commentaries).

PART 2

IDENTIFYING THE PLAYERS AND EXIGENCIES

CHAPTER 5

THE IDENTITY OF THE ADDRESSEES

Paul addressed "the assemblies [ἐκκλησίαις] of Galatia" (1:2), marking his correspondence thus as a circular letter to at least one or more locations consisting of one or more groups of people (the addressees), who may be among one or more groups of people influencing them (the influencers), somewhere in the region of Galatia. Paul indicates from the formal greeting straight through to the closing blessing that these groups of addressees collect together because of a shared faith in Jesus Christ.[1] Their group formation around this belief was the result of their

1. It is not clear how the term ἐκκλησία functioned at this time for Paul or those to whom he wrote. He clearly has in view more than one target audience of Christ-believers assembling in more than one place for the hearing of this letter. On the one hand, it was widely used interchangeably with συναγωγή in the Septuagint to render the Hebrew *qahal* (קהל), an assembly or act of assembling, for any number of reasons and consisting variously of different persons, and not always for the gatherings of Israelites (e.g., compare Deut 5:22 συναγωγή for קהל, but ἐκκλησία for קהל in Deut 4:10; 9:10; 10:4). On the other hand, ἐκκλησία was used to refer to the assembling of free citizens to vote and for other political purposes throughout the Greco-Roman world or for any kind of civic assembling for all kinds of reasons (e.g., Acts 19:32, 39, 40; Josephus, *J.W.* 4.159). Both usages are found in Josephus (e.g., *J.W.* 1.550, 654, 666; 7.412; *Ant.* 3.292; 6.86; 12.164) and Philo (e.g., *Good Person* 138; *Virtues* 108). It is not clear at this time to what degree the assemblies Paul addressed were constituted along synagogue or voluntary association lines, or both (ἐκκλησία is used by both), especially to the degree that the Jewish community is considered to be constituted along the lines of a polis itself (see Levine, *Ancient Synagogue,* 74–159). However, the intra-Jewish character of the setting implied in the rhetoric of this letter suggests Paul is addressing synagogue subgroups, as will be discussed. Paul's usage of this term has often been taken to indicate a sectarian identification of his groups, but it implies no such thing on the available evidence. It may be noted that A. Saldarini argues that as late as Matthew's Gospel (some twenty to forty years after Galatians) the usage of this term did not yet denote sectarianism ("Boundaries"). It could be argued, to the degree that the stress is on the assembly or meeting for a purpose rather than the body of people or congregation itself, that Paul refers by his use of ἐκκλησία to an assembly that recognizes itself as a particular subgroup gathering for a particular purpose (i.e., a coalition) within a larger synagogue community (cf. Levine, *Ancient Synagogue,* 128–34). Certainly, this phrase became associated with particularly

relationship with Paul, who had apparently stopped in their region because of "a weakness of the flesh [ἀσθένειαν τῆς σαρκός]," and thus proclaimed the good news among them (1:6-9, 13; 4:8-20; 5:7-12; 6:11).[2]

In what ways, if at all, these people had functioned together as groups before their common bond through Paul and the shared faith that resulted through his work among them—besides their apparent affiliation by way of shared location, such as the politics of patronage, and perhaps other cultural dynamics of kinship that might have applied—is not clear. It is common for interpreters to suggest that they were formerly "righteous Gentiles" ("God-fearers") and thus would have had a Jewish group affiliation prior to Paul's interaction with them.[3] For example, V. Jegher-Bucher's epistolary and rhetorical investigation of this letter led to the conclusion that the occasion and theme indicate it was essentially written to the righteous Gentiles—so-called God-fearers (σεβόμενοι)—that is, their identity was defined in Jewish terms.[4]

The competence of reader/hearer presumed by the author of this letter implies familiarity with Jewish communal life and Scriptures among the addressees. What is not clear is whether the addressees' implied competence or claim to identity as righteous ones, hence righteous or God-fearing Gentiles, was acquired prior to their interaction with Paul. Instead, might not the indications of this kind of identity among them at the time of Paul's writing be accounted for precisely as

---

Christian assemblies and buildings, churches, but that is a later development. It is not clear that at this time, and especially in these various groups addressed in Galatia, that permanent structures dedicated to assembling were yet in use; the evidence suggests rather that assemblies met in existing homes (L. White, *Social Origins*). For discussion of this term with different conclusions, see, e.g., Schmidt, *TDNT* 3.501–36; J. Campbell, "Origin"; Winter, "Problem"; Meeks, *First Urban Christians;* McCready, "*Ekklēsia* and Voluntary Associations"; Kloppenborg, "Churches." The interesting point to consider is the plurality of audiences addressed, as this may have some significance for constructing a probable social context for the addressees and those who are influencing them.

2. Why or when he was present or the nature of the "weakness" are not clear (4:12-14); see discussion below in context of the semantics of the evil eye belief system.

3. E.g., Davies, in *Jewish*, 172–88. See also Harvey, "Opposition," 326; Munck, *Salvation*, 131–33.

4. Jegher-Bucher, *Galaterbrief*, 114.

a result of his influence upon themselves, so that now when he writes it is implied as a present aspect of their personal and group identity?

It is not clear how long Paul had remained among these groups or how long it has been since his departure, so we do not know how long the addressees would have had since their response to Paul's message to have become familiar with Jewish thought and Scripture and life, to become righteous in lifestyle themselves. This possibility appears not to have been often considered, perhaps because most interpreters assume—on the basis of their prior view of Paul—that Paul's Gentile converts were not encouraged to such behavior or identity, that is, in terms of Jewish communal life. Because Paul is taken to be involved in establishing communities and ideologies independent of and even contrary to Jewish communal identity and behavior, wherein such righteous Gentiles would emerge from former pagan identities, it is concluded that any such evidence of this identity and behavior is the result of choices made in their former lives, that is, prior to affiliation to Paul. But if it is assumed that Paul was still affiliated with and actively promoting a life of righteousness as defined within Jewish communal norms, as I do, then such a conclusion is not warranted. This is not the argument to be taken up herein; the present point is simply that the evidence for their status as pagans or righteous Gentiles prior to involvement with Paul, apart from arguable interpretive moves, is not clear.

In addition to their meeting together in several locations somewhere in the immense region of central Anatolia—whether in close proximity is uncertain—it is clear from the rhetoric of this letter that the implied, intended, or target recipients of this message are not circumcised (e.g., 2:2-5, 12; 3:1-5; 5:1-12; 6:12-13). This state indicates that it is not Jewish people in these groups to whom Paul is writing, although it appears from the context of his concerns that there are influential Jewish people either in these groups or at least in other groups with whom the addressees' groups are intimately associated (e.g., 5:7-12; 6:12-13).

It is theoretically possible that the addressees are Jewish people who were not circumcised as children, although such a case for communities of people of this time is highly improbable historically, because it is unparalleled according to our sources of information.[5] Moreover, and

5. Even Philo's rhetorical comments ostensibly against such a presumably rare case are perhaps only theoretically constructed to make his point (cf. *Migration* 89–90; *QE* 2.2).

more importantly, the rhetoric implies throughout (e.g., 2:2-5, 7, 9, 12-15; 3:8, 14; 3:15—4:11, 21; 5:2-12; 6:12-15), and in at least one explicit comment indicates, a pagan background of identity for the recipients. Here, Paul ridicules the addressees as former pagans (4:8-9). And elsewhere he continually undermines any confidence they might have in their own desires to be "under the Law," because they are presently still naïvely unaware of what such interest implies (4:21 to set up the allegory and lead to the points made in 5:1-12, especially vv. 2-5).

Yet even this need not imply that they were not affiliated with the Jewish communities of Galatia prior to Paul's influence, or thereafter, but it at least indicates that their identity is vulnerable to characterization by birth into the world as non-Jewish people.[6] Such characterization marked freedpersons in a similar way, inscribing forever the place in the world from which they had come, that is, as the world was seen through the eyes of those who were not and had not been slaves. This past identity could be exploited by others—or even inadvertently raised—after they had been freed, for example, to describe their social classification, which naturally put them in their place, after the transition to freedom had been completed, even if it had been completed in the life of their parents before their own birth.[7] Former slavery is always implied in the mention of "freed"! Attesting to the importance of negotiating this problem are the many strategies that were employed to escape its grasp.[8]

On the basis of Paul's ridiculing comments, some interpreters have suggested that the addressees are backward. For example, Jerome took this accusation to mean literally that the addressees were stupid, and thus Gauls. This was on the basis of the comment of Hilary, the Rhone of Latin eloquence, himself a Gaul, that the Gauls were *indociles.* Yet Lightfoot observes that this misses the point, as the Galatian addressees were known to be "intellectually quick enough," referring to a comment of their inquisitive nature for news in Caesar, *Bello Gallico* 4.5, so

6. Cf. Porton, *Stranger,* for rabbinic evidence.

7. See M. Gordon, "Freedman's Son"; Duff, *Freedmen,* 36–71; Garnsey, "Descendants"; Garnsey and Saller, *Empire,* 118–23; de Ste. Croix, *Class Struggle,* 174–79; Lanci, "Behind the Boasting"; Weaver, "Social Mobility," 121–40; Meeks, *First Urban Christians,* 20–23.

8. Strategies for identity transformation included acts of public benefaction, so that one might refer to one's self as "the son of so-and-so who gave our town this fountain," moving to new locations; in the same way affiliation with Jewish communities may have been a means employed by some.

that Lightfoot takes the reference to be not to their obtuseness, but to their "fickleness and levity: the very versatility of their intellect was their snare."[9] Lightfoot's first point is often noted: the letter does imply a certain level of learning, or at least, unlike Hilary, the capacity to learn, although interpreters are not always clear just how their education is to be accounted for, especially by those who regard them as rural or Celts, to whom they do not attribute much education or opportunity for learning.[10] Against Jerome's view, it is cruel and sarcastic to call someone who is actually a fool a fool, and it is not the rhetorical nature of Paul's ironic rebuke here, which is to surprise. As the discussion of this kind of parental ridicule employed by Paul has shown and will further show, in addition to the discussion of the exigence, Lightfoot's solution does not work. It is not fickleness or levity that is attacked in Paul's rhetoric but rather foolishness, the failure to appropriately judge their present situations and the danger inherent in their consideration of adopting for themselves the other influential message of good.

More important to consider is the fact that a few interpreters have argued that at least some of the addressees have already been circumcised.[11] But this is not the case for those to whom Paul writes, at least at the time that the news to which he now responds was generated. It could be the case that some others among them have indeed already completed circumcision or that others to whom he intended to speak by way of this letter have done so in the interim. But they are then no longer his rhetorical addressees, or differently put, the implied, intended, or target audience.[12] For the Gentiles now addressed by Paul

9. Lightfoot, *Galatians*, 242, and n. 3. See Dahl, "Galatians," 48.

10. Cf. H. Betz, *Galatians*, 1–3, although on 27 he rather implies that they may not be all that sophisticated in these terms: "these Galatians were no longer the 'hicks' of that rough and ungovernable area in central Anatolia. They were avant-garde, a 'new creation.'" One wonders what might account for the change in the level of intellectual sophistication Betz later assumes for them.

11. They cite, e.g., 1:6; 3:1-3; 5:7; 6:13; cf. e.g., Tarazi, *Galatians*, 322–23. Davies, *Jewish*, 181, suggests that some were likely proselytes who may have "backslid either to paganism or to a more observant form of Judaism than Paul demanded." Munck's view is based upon the circumcision of some of the addressees, although he sees those now as "circumcised gentiles" (*Salvation* 89, 129–34) rather than as (Jewish) proselytes. See also Brinsmead, *Dialogical Response*, 67–69, 168, 187–92, who argues for a seamless identity of the influential ones and the addressees, and a level of embracing of apostasy that would seem to imply some have completed this course.

12. Perelman and Olbrechts-Tyteca, *New Rhetoric*, 19, note that "it is preferable to define an audience, for the purposes of rhetoric, as *the ensemble of those whom the*

had not already become Jewish proselytes; note, for example, among other indicators that we will discuss, the present aspect of 6:12-13 and the cognitive present of 4:9.[13]

Paul's argument is directed throughout to Gentiles who have become "known by God" in view of the faith of/in Christ (4:8-9), but who remain, somehow, unsure of their place apart from conformity with the traditional communal norms for attaining the identity of righteousness by becoming proselytes (3:1—4:9; 4:21; 5:1-12; 6:12-13). He seeks in this letter to persuade them not to follow through on what they have begun to internalize as "good" for themselves (1:6-9; 3:1-5; 5:7-12). To do so would consist of allowing obstruction of the course set by the gospel of Christ that they had successfully begun to run (5:7).

His rhetorical expression of certainty that they will return to that course as a result of this letter (5:10), regardless of how certain he may actually be, indicates that Paul believes he is dealing with those who have not yet taken the step in view (1:6-9; 3:1-5; 5:2-6). In the narrative discourses, even Paul's usage of first-person plural pronouns often seems to maintain the distinction between the Gentile addressees and Jewish people,[14] which is what Gentile proselytes become. For there is to our knowledge no such thing, at least in the context of Jewish communal life, as circumcised Gentiles; when circumcised at the completion of the ritual process of conversion they are no longer Gentiles. So we should speak not of circumcised or proselyte Gentiles but only circumcised or proselyte Jews,[15] and to proselytes Paul's letter is not addressed.

Paul's rhetoric implies, however, that the addressees now *want* to acquire Jewish status (by circumcision) to ensure their social position among the people of God as righteous ones (as children of Abraham

---

speaker wishes to influence by his argumentation. Every speaker thinks, more or less consciously, of those he is seeking to persuade; these people form the audience to whom his speech is addressed" (emphasis theirs).

13. Also 5:1-2, 7, 10, 13; see Dunn, *Galatians*, 225–26; Burton, *Galatians*, 18–19; Jewett, "Agitators," 209; H. Betz, *Galatians*, 45–47; Lyons, *Pauline Autobiography*, 126–27.

14. Cf. 2:4, 15; 3:13-14, 23, 26; Robinson, "Distinction." It should be noted that the passages discussed are all in narrative rather than situational discourses; they thus can imply a level of identification by rhetorical association, if the addressees understand themselves in similar terms.

15. Nolland, "Uncircumcised Proselytes?"

and Sarah).[16] Moreover, this is explicitly indicated in the Socratic interrogation of 4:21: "Tell me, you who *desire* [θέλοντες] to be under law. . . ."[17] Paul is turning what they actually desire on its head by way of irony, for it is rather gaining undisputed acceptance that they want, and thus their interest he undermines as "desire" to become what they feel "constrained" to become in order to escape the present results of nonconformity. However, this comment is seemingly mitigated by the prior statement made in the ironic rebuke of 4:9, where Paul addresses their "desire [θέλετε]" to become slaves of the elements (στοιχεῖα) once again by returning to idolatry (4:8-10). That comment seems to be more directly ridiculing their desire to return to some pagan practices rather than to beginning the process of proselyte conversion. It is likely that the addressees do not wish either to behave like pagans or to become proselytes per se, but rather they "desire" to escape the constraints concomitant with their ambiguous nonproselyte status, which they believe can be gained by way of seeking proselyte identity, and thus, in the meantime, they have accepted such constraints as appropriate to their as yet pagan identity in returning to social expressions of idolatry deemed by others appropriate to those who are merely guests. The point to be made here is that Paul works with the reality of their own interest in gaining proselyte standing, in completing in the flesh what they had begun in the Spirit (3:3). This is throughout implied by the way Paul's concerns are rhetorically put, expressing genuine fear that the addressees have been effectively engaged, as mentioned—"defecting from" or "obstructed on the course" he had set for them as Gentiles, instead of "running" it still, that is, "obeying the truth [of the gospel of Christ]"—because of the influencers' persuasive speech and manipulative tactics (5:7-12; cf. 1:6-7; 4:17; 6:12-13).

16. E.g., Davies, *Jewish*, 172–88; Donaldson, "Gospel"; Lull, *Spirit*, 32–33, 42. It is implied even in such comments as occupy Paul's closing instructions to be satisfied with the honor they have as spiritual ones instead of seeking the acceptance of others and the mistake that is made by those who seek such honor from others, instead of in their own standing as is established by God alone (6:3-5, 14). I would suggest translating v. 4 as, "But let each one certify [guarantee as the real thing] his or her own work [status], and then he or she will have the claim to honor in him- or herself only, and not in the other." This seems to imply that the opposite concern is present among the addressees, the claim to honor on the terms of "the other," that is, acceptance of this claim by the influencers.

17. Also Jewett, "Agitators," 209.

Paul's argument is constructed to secure the identity of uncircumcised people in Christ as equal to that of circumcised people, which naturally implies that it is Gentiles and not Jewish people whom he regards as in need of being assured of the equality of their status (2:2-5, 8, 14; 3:8-9, 14; 3:26—4:7; 4:8-9; 5:2, 5; 6:12-15). For the desired status Paul proclaimed as already guaranteed, witnessed by their receipt of the Spirit through faith (3:1—4:7)—apparently accompanied by miracles (3:5)—and their shared experiences with Paul (4:12-16), has occurred for them apart from completing the ritual process of proselyte conversion. They are in this sense those whom Paul calls "the spiritual ones [οἱ πνευματικοί]," born of the Spirit but not of the flesh, as would be proselytes by way of circumcision, and must pull together to resist the temptation each one faces to gain indisputable status as the children of God on the traditional terms by seeking proselyte conversion, however attractive this might seem (6:1). Do they not realize that this "other" course—"seemingly" complementary—is "really" contrary to the one on which they have begun, that it in fact will "twist" so as to "turn upside down [i.e., subvert or undermine] the good news of Christ" (1:7) and is thus anathema (1:8-9)? If not, this letter will set them straight, or so Paul intends (5:10; cf. 1:6-9; 3:1-5; 5:7-12; 6:12-14; passim).

Further confirmation of this implied identity is derived from the polemical rhetoric of 5:2-4 and 6:12-13: they are not now circumcised and thus not currently expected to observe the whole Law; yet they are interested in obtaining the identity that the influencers offer, which would thereafter oblige them to live as Jewish people. It is important to note that this is not the same thing as wanting to observe the Law, and it is just this potential oversight that Paul undermines in 5:3! Identity as proselytes is in view, not Torah observance.

There is a vast difference in Jewish expectations toward Jewish versus non-Jewish people, proselytes versus so-called righteous Gentiles. I suggest that failure to recognize that Paul's rhetoric does not concern itself with opposing Jewish practices but only with proselyte conversion for Christ-believing Gentiles has led to uncertainty about the Gentile makeup of the targeted addressees, regardless of whether Jewish people were also present in these subgroups of Christ-believers. Many interpreters do not make sufficient distinction between the concern with identity that proselyte conversion entails, some even imagining that this is an act of Torah observance for the Gentile candidates.[18] Such a con-

18. Contra, e.g., Dunn, "Theology of Galatians," 130–31.

cern is very different from that of Jewish persons to observe Torah as a part of their already ascribed or, in the case of proselytes, acquired status under the Law, which is a privilege, as well as a responsibility based upon a consciousness of the divine will for themselves as righteous ones and in conformity with the social concerns of identity and behavior that would be expected of Jewish communal life. Circumcision is an action of the Torah-observant parent, obviously not of the eight-day-old baby; the child does not formally decide to observe for himself until the rite of adult passage is performed.

The logical result of interpreters supposing that Paul is opposing Jewish observance is to postulate that Jewish people are in view, because the implications of Paul's own position (expressed in 5:3), in keeping with that of other Jewish people and groups of which we know, is that Jewish people alone would be required to observe the whole of Torah.[19] Gentiles would not, although righteous Gentiles would observe some elements of righteousness. And proselyte candidates would be likely observing most, if not all, of the commandments by the time that they were ready to complete the process of conversion, for in effect completion of this process really confirms the new identity as Jewish people that they have already long embraced by the time proselyte rather than candidate status is conferred. They would now, as Paul says, be obliged to observe the whole Law.

This point brings to the surface an important issue of interpretation. Paul approaches the addressees as Gentiles seeking entrance to identity as righteous ones, not as ones trying to observe Torah per se, and thus does not indicate a denunciation of Jewish identity or behavior, for Jewish people, or even for Gentiles seeking proselyte status who are not connected with Christ-faith.[20] If Paul responds from within a Jewish coalition, and if the ostensible antithesis is recognized as dissociation instead (see discussion in chapter 3), then the implications are quite the opposite. If Paul is employing dissociating rhetoric, it indicates the pragmatic response of a reformer from within a minority

19. We have such discouraging of converts laid out clearly in the Babylonian Talmud (*b. Yeb.* 47a–b; cf. *Sifra Qedoshim* 8.3; *t. Demai* 2.3–5), though it is not clear that this was the case in our period (cf. Porton, *Stranger,* 13, 30, 47–50, 87, 98–101, 122, 196), but it is a reasonable assumption with the dangers proselytes present to such a minority culture that this was the case (Josephus, *Ant.* 20.34–41, 75–77, 81; Juvenal, *Satires* 14.96–99; cf. Segal, *Paul,* 96–105; Sanders, *Paul, the Law,* 29 and notes, 206), and thus for Paul.

20. The clear implications of Sanders, *Paul and Palestinian.*

group calling for a modification of the existing majority position based upon the incompatibility of the two messages of good in view of this coalition's understanding of the meaning of the death of Christ for themselves.

The issue is then the confirmation of the non-Jewish addressees according to Jewish expectations and norms, including those maintained by Jewish communal leaders in order to conform with the constraints of the prevailing Greco-Roman pagan world in which they exist, as these expectations and norms come into conflict with a new hierarchical structure for perceiving reality claimed by this Jewish subgroup.[21] Note that it is only the addressees whom Paul indicates would be implicitly stepping down from that which they now have in Christ if they were to seek status on the influencers' terms (4:8-9: having been already known by God, do they now seek to be known by God?). Paul does not absolutize Jewish identity to an inferior status for anyone but the non-Jewish addressees, if they were to seek it in order to elevate their status; so that even the issue is put rhetorically for them in terms of motives or means (why) and not the actions themselves (what). The implied Jewish status of the influencers as already righteous ones by way of their identification as the historic people of God (i.e., as high status) remains intact, for it is implied in terms of the elements upon which Paul predicates his dissociating solution (e.g., God, Abraham, Israel, Scripture, revelation, evidence of God's Spirit at work or being known by God, unification of humankind in the awaited age according to promise, suffering in the present evil age for those who wait for righteousness until God comes to bring to pass the reaping of what has been sown, even the belief in the figure of a Christ-Messiah). This dynamic also explains—although it may not excuse—Paul's vehement curses and other expressions of disgust, for he holds the influencers accountable to recognize the addressees' claims on the basis of their own Israelite expectations according to Scripture for what would be evident when the awaited day dawned, such as the expression of the Spirit of God at work among them (3:5). To this matter we will return.

21. Vorster, "Dissociation," 303, makes some similar points, although he concludes quite differently that Paul's argument involves status inferiority for the influencers (305) and regression to "an inferior status" for "adhering to the Law after the advent of the time of faith," because the Law "has been relegated to a past era" (306).

In Galatians then, Paul does not express an opinion about the value of Jewish practices for Jewish people, not even proselytes—they are not the addressees (in my view, his rhetoric implies a positive view of Torah observance for Jewish people, including himself, because his argument is predicated upon this foundation in order to make the dissociating case for the incompatibility of the two ways of including Gentiles among the righteous ones of God). Rather, he confronts Christ-believing Gentiles who are considering conversion to proselyte status. This is the case even though they may not have considered sufficiently the Jewish practices that they will be obliged to observe once they acquire this status.[22] And the dissociating message, in short, is that they must not complete this course, for to do so is to compromise the good news of Christ for themselves by trying to live according to two incompatible realities in view of the claim that the age to come has dawned in Christ; indeed, it would subvert the very meaning of the death of Christ, rendering it, for themselves as Gentiles, gratuitous.

The target audiences are thus not Jewish people, or (Jewish) proselytes, Christ-believing or not, although their circumstances as Paul addresses them implies the presence of Jewish people and groups, and probably Jewish proselytes as well, who have created the social constraints Paul seeks in this letter to undermine on behalf of the addressees.[23] This does not mean that none of Paul's former Gentile converts to the gospel of Christ has become a proselyte before he writes this letter or before its arrival, but those are no longer the addressees and may be now part of those influencing the recipients in the direction that Paul opposes; if so, they are now not the "us" with whom Paul is concerned but "them." These people should no longer be classified as the rhetorical addressees or implied, intended, or target audiences: those to whom Paul addresses his letter are Christ-believing Gentiles.

Before proceeding to the matter of identifying those influencing the addressees, one more area needs to be assessed: What was the exigence in Galatia as considered from the perspective of each of the players; or to put this another way: For whom is circumcision of the addressees considered good news, and why?

22. Although perhaps not actually the case, this is suggested by Paul's rhetorical aside calling into question whether they understand the end result of this other message, namely, the proselyte's obligation to observe the whole Law (5:3).

23. This point is too often obscured by reading Galatians as one seamless discourse; contra Lategan, "Argumentative Situation," 259.

CHAPTER 6

VIEWING THE EXIGENCIES FROM MULTIPLE PERSPECTIVES

The Gentile addressees to whom Paul writes in Galatia are being persuaded to consider the value of circumcision for themselves. Such is the exigence—the urgency of moment demanding reaction—to which Paul responds with the letter to the Galatians. This statement seems as close to a historical fact as any interpreter of this extant letter may claim, at least according to the rules of interpretation of rhetorical and historical situation as set out above.

What this exigence or the exigencies meant or mean from the various perspectives of the addressees, the influencers, or Paul may appear different; in fact, did appear different. This dynamic of interpretive perspective is still witnessed in the differences of opinion that arise among later readers of this letter. The reasons are too many to name but emerge from the simple fact that the urgency of moment is considered differently from each person and group's point of view. It was Paul's purpose, with their reading of this letter, to change the meaning of the urgency of moment for the addressees and thus by implication to alter forever the nature of the exigence from the perspective of those influencing them, who have themselves created, from Paul's point of view, the present unwelcome situations.

Paul's is not the only perspective the interpreter must consider to construct the historical or rhetorical situations, and I suggest that it is actually Paul's past work among the addressees that has instead created the initial exigence for those influencing them in Galatia. The exigence begins for the influencers when they become aware of the addressees' claims to identity, and probably to concomitant resources, predicated upon an appeal to norms that the influencers find surprising and unacceptable based upon traditional prevailing norms to which they themselves subscribe, and in addition, in the interest of compliance with those norms and expectations of the dominant Greco-Roman pagan communities by which their own communal policies are constrained. The reflexive response of the influencers to this exigence then creates the exigence of identity dissonance for the addressees, and it is the concern for reduction of this that creates the exigence to which Paul responds. His letter will thereby find Paul, ironically, also initiating, this time from afar, the next round of exigencies, for both the addressees as they seek to come to terms with his uncompromising call for resistance to the influencers and their message of seeming good and for the influencers, to the degree that the addressees comply, much less conform, with the letter's appeal. And then, depending upon these results, the spiral of action and reaction will continue for each of these parties, including Paul.

As already shown, Paul's threatened reaction as measured by his response implies that he assesses the exigence in these terms: the Gentile addressees as a whole are now *considering* to some degree the pursuit of circumcision for themselves (1:6; 3:1-5; 4:21; 5:2-7; 6:12-13), but movement in that direction would represent a departure from the course of "walking straight toward the gospel of Christ" that they had begun under his influence (1:6-9; 3:1-5; 4:8-11, 12-20; 5:1-6, 7-12; 6:12-14; passim); moreover, he perhaps fears at least some of them have already departed from the now "obstructed" way they had begun to "run" in order to go down the alternate, albeit *traditional* path, although his target audience consists of those who have not yet "completed" any such course (1:6; 3:1-5; 4:8-10; 21; 5:3-4). At the same time, there seems to be a threat of them turning in an entirely different direction, returning to pagan practices associated with the public expression of idolatry (4:8-10), a dynamic that we will discuss in the next section.

Thus Paul is reacting to a combination of perceived threats. On the one hand, the addressees seem to be interested in beginning the course of proselyte conversion, but on the other they seem interested in returning to public expressions of idolatry. He writes urgently to ensure that those who hear his words will not regard themselves as in need of initiating the process for becoming proselyte candidates, or of completing this rite of passage, but at the same time as not thereby considering themselves as in some way still pagans in need of continuing or returning to the displays by which they would thus be constrained by pagan social norms. Yet these are norms to which a minority Jewish community would consider them confined as well, unless they declared themselves turning toward incorporation by way of proselyte conversion and thus no longer pagans.

Paul writes to ensure that the Gentile addressees see themselves as already incorporated members of the household of God, although not proselytes, and thus not conforming to the prevailing norms of either

Jewish or pagan society in the present evil age, so that they will dismiss this other message of ostensible good as bad for themselves, because they are among those for whom the age to come has dawned by way of Christ Jesus.

But that is not the only exigence with which he must be concerned! He also anticipates the process of deliberating upon the consequences of accepting this message when received, and, if observed, the undesirable consequences that resistance to the influencers' norms will likely bring for the addressees. Thus, the letter anticipates an unfavorable response on the influencers' part to the addressees, if the addressees obey him, as Paul expresses confidence they will do (5:10). For the addressees, the message of the letter anticipates the call that finally becomes explicit only at 4:12 and then is clarified for their own intracommunal situations thereafter. That is the call to identify with himself as marginalized within the historic people of God for the good news of Christ (which in this sense seems bad perhaps)[1] and thus serve one another, instead of striving with one another for honored identity, within this coalition, as they together "wait" for the ultimate good that God has promised them in Christ, "the hope of righteousness" (5:5).

It cannot be proven, but is generally agreed among interpreters who may disagree about virtually everything else regarding what this letter meant or means, that the context of this language regarding circumcision is that which arises in terms of Jewish proselyte conversion.[2] Yet this symbolic meaning is considered by most interpreters apart from a salient communal context in which this interest for or pressure upon Paul's Gentile converts makes psychological or sociological sense. Proselyte conversion involves a ritual process. It is a rite of passage, the completion of which, for males, is signaled by circumcision. Circumcision symbolizes, albeit oversimplified and overindividualistically set out, the completion of this rite of passage—along with, for example, ritual washing and declaration of completion by the initiate and initiator(s), and prayer and thanksgiving. Together, these actions signal the

1. I suggest that the call to become like Paul in 4:12 is to his marginality for upholding the nonconformist "truth of the gospel" for the inclusion of Gentiles as Gentiles rather than proselytes, not, as many interpreters suppose, to a Gentile or Law-free lifestyle for Jew and Gentile alike.

2. E.g., even those who explore other facts of the implied situation, such as S. Elliott, agree, attributing this to the urging of those whose reasons are "probably based on motivations stemming from the Jewish context" ("Choose," 679).

final actions of the transition process that takes place when a non-Jewish person passes from being regarded as a pagan to a liminal proselyte candidate to a proselyte (Jew).[3]

Since the circumcision of Abraham and his sons (the governing statement is of course Gen 17:9-14), it was recognized among Israelites as an important mark of ethnic and national identity beyond dispute. Jonathaan Smith observes that earlier, before the Priestly tradition, the biblical legal codes and Deuteronomy contain no injunction of circumcision for the Israelite; rather, in the Hebrew Scriptures, circumcision "is assumed to be characteristic of the Israelite rather than enjoined."[4] Whether Smith's interpretation of the early Israelite evidence is correct (cf. Exod 12:44, 48; Lev 12:3; Deut 10:16; Josh 5:2-7), this symbol of identity took on additional purpose in the context of Hellenistic cultural encroachment as well as policies (cf. 1 Macc 1:15, 44-48, 60-61; 2:45-46; 2 Macc 6:10), identifying the people Israel as the people of God, "righteous ones" among the other nations of the world.[5]

One might say, during Paul's period, for Paul as well as other Jewish voices of which we know, that it had become the symbol of Jewish identity sine qua non, even employed as a technical term: to be circumcised was to be a Jew, whereas to be uncircumcised was to be a non-Jew.[6] Although a variety of views must be always recognized, circumcision among Jewish people of this time generally describes as well as labels the boundary of Jewish identity in the midst of a non-Jewish world (Gal 2:7, 9; 5:3; Phil 3:4-5; Acts; 1 Macc 1:15, 44-48, 60-61; 2:45-

3. We do not know the details of this ritual process during Paul's time, but we have evidence from the rabbinic period; see *b. Yebamot* 47a-b; *Gerim* 1.1; discussions in S. Cohen, *Beginnings*, 198–238; Porton, *Stranger;* Hoffman, *Covenant of Blood.*

4. J. Smith, "Fences," 10.

5. S. Cohen, *Beginnings*, esp. 109–39; Hengel, *Judaism;* Schultz and Spatz, *Sinai and Olympus;* Tcherikover, *Hellenistic;* note the cautions of Goldstein, "Jewish Acceptance."

For how such symbolism works in terms of defining group identity at the boundaries, see F. Barth, "Introduction"; A. Cohen, *Symbolic Construction;* Jenkins, *Social Identity;* Banks, *Ethnicity.* A group's identity (ethnicity) is socially constructed, and this identity is salient in terms of category comparison with other groups. Ethnicity is then defined at the boundaries both by themselves and others. These boundaries continue in spite of the flow of people and things, like communication, across them.

6. J. Smith, "Fences," 9–15; S. Cohen, *Beginnings*, 156–74, 219–21, passim; Segal, *Paul*, 72–109; Feldman, *Jew;* 153–58; Nolland, "Uncircumcised Proselytes?" 173–94; Marcus, "Circumcision"; Schäfer, *Judeophobia*, 93–105.

46; 2 Macc 6:10; *Jub.* 15.25-34; Josephus, *Ant.* 1.192; 13.318-19; 18.34-48; 20.38; *Ag. Ap.* 2.137, 140-42; Philo, *Spec. Laws* 1.1.1-1.2.11; *Migration* 92. This function is attested also in the later rabbinic material: *y. Megillah* 3.2.74d; *b. Yebamot* 47b [after completion of ritual process a proselyte is "like an Israelite in all respects"]; Midrash *Ex. Rabbah* 30.12; Hillel and Shammai in *m. Eduyyot* 5:2; *b. Pesaḥim* 8:8).[7]

Moreover, the recognition of this identity marker and even reference to circumcision as a sufficient label for descriptive purposes can be observed sometimes in stereotypical and less than generous terms by non-Israelites as well. Surviving examples from various elites of the period include Strabo, *Geographica* 16.2.37 (64 B.C.E.–20 C.E.); Diodorus Siculus, *World History* 1.55 (late first century B.C.E.); Horace, *Satires* 1.9.60–72 (65–6 B.C.E.); Petronius, *Satyricon* 68.8; 102.13–14 (died ca. 65 C.E.); Persius, *Satires* 5.179–84 (34–62 C.E.); Martial, *Epigrams* 7.35.3–4, 82; 11.94 (40–104 C.E.); Tacitus, *Histories* 5.5.2, 8–9 (56–120 C.E.); Juvenal, *Satires* 14.96–106 (50–150 C.E.); Suetonius, *Domitian* 12 (69–120s C.E.); Paulus, *Sententiae* 5.22.3–4 (late third century C.E.?).[8]

That is not to say that this custom of identification is not attested among other ethnic or national groups of people. It appears that it was practiced by Israel's neighbors in ancient times, for example, according to Herodotus, by the Egyptians, Ethiopians, and Phoenicians.[9] Philo too considers it a custom "practiced to no slight degree among other nations also, and most especially by the Egyptians" (*Spec. Laws* 1.1.2). And Josephus attributes this custom more specifically to the Egyptian priests (*Ag. Ap.* 2.141). Yet whatever the case may have been at this time, these people and their customs do not constitute the rhetorical context of Abrahamic descent of this letter sent to Anatolia.

Paul himself is a person identified by way of Jewish circumcision. It is because of the honored status of this standing that Paul is able to argue from a position of strength; on the one hand, with Jewish people such as Peter on behalf of the Gentiles' equality of status by way of

7. See S. Cohen, *Beginnings*, 198–238; Feldman, *Jew*, 153–58, 292; Hoffman, *Blood;* Porton, *Stranger*, 132–154; Segal, *Paul*, 79–104.

8. Note Josephus, *Ant.* 8.319, attributes to Strabo on the authority of Timagenes, a first-century B.C.E. Alexandrian historian, the recognition of circumcision as a Jewish custom, and no negative tone is implied. Josephus, *Ag. Ap.* 2.137, 140–42, attributes to Apion a negative attitude toward this distinguishing practice.

9. Herodotus, *Hist.* 2.36, 37, 104; also Strabo, *Geogr.* 17.2.5. Josephus, *Ant.* 8.262; *Ag. Ap.* 1.168–71, says the "Syrians of Palestine" in this reference are the Jews (note also 2.142). Schäfer, *Judeophobia*, 93–95.

Christ (1:13—2:21), and on the other, with the Gentiles themselves to remain in their state as a testimony to the meaning of the death of Christ on their behalf (5:1-6; 6:12-15). Sometimes this appeal is not merely implied but quite overt instead (e.g., 2:15; cf. Rom 9–11; 2 Cor 11:21-24; Phil 3:4-5).[10]

That is not to say no disputes arose over questions of Jewish identity; they did to be sure, and perhaps in a few cases even over whether circumcision is a required marker, although the evidence of this on the part of a community is virtually nonexistent.[11] But Paul's rhetoric is not addressing questions of Jewish people about their own identity, for these people would already be circumcised as infants, before they could have experienced any "hearing of faith" (3:2). Whatever the prevailing prejudices or concerns that might be expressed by their pagan contemporaries toward circumcision or Jewish identity, communal or personal, it appears that the addressees of Paul's Galatian letter are interested in reidentification within Jewish terms. In fact, it appears that they desire it. The issue that arises from the rhetoric of Galatians is not the circumcision of Jewish children but rather of Gentile adults: What would such interest involve for a non-Jewish person in Galatia?

The conclusion that circumcision in Galatians symbolizes the completion of the ritual process of proselyte conversion means that the rhetorical situation must be considered from a perspective on Gentiles that is much more immediate and variegated than might at first appear to be the case.[12] It is immediate in that it assumes social involvement with Gentiles in Jewish communal terms of identification and variegated in that it indicates that these Gentiles are regarded in some way differently from the rest of the non-Jewish world by the Jewish community members involved in influencing the addressees to complete this passage as appropriate for themselves. Both of these implications have significance for this investigation.

On a purely theoretical level, that is, if no social engagement is actually involved, the category of righteous Gentiles need not be very carefully considered or nuanced. For example, they may be described in

10. This is the case throughout Acts as well.

11. See Goodman, *Who Was a Jew?;* idem, *Mission;* Feldman, *Jew* ; S. Cohen, *Beginnings*, 150–62, 219–21.

12. Cf. A. Cohen, *Symbolic Construction*, 74–96.

largely theological and ethical ways, as those who do not believe in idols but in the Creator, and do not commit murder and other heinous crimes against fellow humans. The concerns for definition may stop at the level of the theoretical question, like what about the "heathen" in a distant land?[13] But the issue changes profoundly when it is forged in the crucible of social contact and even more when interest is expressed in acquiring communal incorporation.

From a Jewish communal perspective, a general category of righteous Gentiles exists in distinction from the rest of the pagan or non-Jewish population, especially those who are regarded as idolaters or in some way engaged in activities that may be harmful to the Jewish people or their interests. The various responses and evaluations are as many as the persons and communities involved. But a simple model of the major categories may be set out, as long as it is recognized that this is a gross oversimplification of what takes place in the minds and actions of the various people and groups involved on either side of the developments at any time or place. Due to the limitations of space, prior description of my own views and those of others, I will not review this matter.[14] The important point for this work is to remind the reader of the necessary sensitivity to the fact that there are many reactions, many different and changing perspectives upon the situations, depending upon the people and their interests at any given time and place. What is pertinent to the present task is to set out some of those that will help us interpret what is implied in the rhetoric of Galatians.

In general, regardless of how they were labeled, the non-Jewish people who were considered righteous Gentiles, for a variety of reasons, were themselves in contact with Jewish people and communities. Those who were respectful or helpful were naturally considered friendly to the interests of the Jewish people and life. Those who sought to associate at some level were generally welcome as guests and respected as differentiating themselves to some degree from the broader population. Naturally, when associating within the community, proper decorum would be respected, regardless of what they might do when away. No doubt some would embrace these as norms they practiced apart from association, when they went home, one might say, and

13. Novak, *Image.*

14. Novak, *Image;* Segal, *Paul,* 194–201; S. Cohen, *Beginnings,* 140–74; Fredriksen, "Judaism"; Donaldson, *Paul,* 51–78; Nanos, *Mystery,* 50–56, and the sources listed there.

to degrees that would vary for different people according to time and place. They might or might not continue this association after it began, and the reasons for starting or stopping it are too many to consider but certainly would include changes in proximity itself. And these righteous Gentiles might or might not express an interest in making passage from this standing as righteous Gentile guests into full membership within the Jewish community, for example, from personal conviction or to facilitate marriage or some other social bond that might require consideration of such a transition.

When Gentiles or their family members declared this interest, many things changed for themselves and everyone else associated with them. Such moves not only directly impacted upon the rest of their family, but they had direct repercussions for extended kinship and the local political networks in which their social life took place, and if deemed by them to be threatening, they became the concern of the guardians of the Jewish community that had to respond. Apart from expression of an interest in proselyte conversion, it is likely that, as pagans, these guests or friends continued to participate in public expressions of idolatry according to the norms of non-Jewish Greco-Roman and indigenous societies in which they lived, not least the public observances associated with the imperial cult. It is also likely that until the Gentiles' expressed the intention to become proselytes, the Jewish community would also expect and accept these expressions of solidarity with their pagan family and neighbors to continue, for as guests they were not entitled to the exemption that was extended to the Jewish populations of the diaspora to refrain from such idolatrous activities, with daily burnt offerings in Jerusalem offered instead once the decrees of Julius Caesar established this special privilege (see chapter 9).

For these people and their families, the rite of proselyte conversion facilitated the negotiation of this boundary crossing. The initiating of this ritual process created expectations for those on both sides. For the Jewish community members, especially those responsible for social control, it marked a radical break from the pagan past of these initiates as they turned to the One God and the community of Israel, the historic people of God, those responsible for living in righteousness on behalf of God and all humankind until the arrival of the promised day. Such initiates had liminal status as they prepared to pass through the threshold (i.e., limen) and into proselyte identity and life. More was expected of them than other Gentile guests along the way and certainly upon completion of this passage, and more was required. By the time that the ritual passage was completed and the person became a proselyte, which for males was marked by circumcision, the former Gentile had presumably internalized Jewish values and norms, and to a large degree his lifestyle was probably difficult to distinguish from that of any other Jewish person. This became obligatory upon completion, although a process of growth and change continued; life is seldom as neatly configured as the rituals may be taken to suggest.[15]

From the initiates' perspective, they had made an important decision to turn from their former life and networks in which that life was carried out, in most cases with enormous consequences for their identity and interests. They had broken with family and the politics of their Gentile networks of social life and turned to a new community to replace those, of course, to different degrees depending on many factors, not least the level of integration of this particular Jewish community within the network of the Gentile society from which they had begun to move. They understood themselves to be liminals and as such obliged to learn new ways to perceive life as well as to live it, investing a new level of trust in the authority of the leaders and members of the community to which they turned. And they expected to be respected in new ways by them, especially upon completion of the rite.

But during this passage, these Gentiles experienced status ambiguity, for they had chosen a road that inscribed their marginality in both communities. They were yet Gentiles but then again not the same as other Gentiles, even righteous ones. They likely shared a special bond with the other liminals during this dangerous and ambiguous time of crossing, or, if they had not begun this rite, as jointly sharing the unexpected status of mere guests.[16] But their primary need for identification and guidance came from the response of those to whom they now turned to direct their passage. These influencers would make possible successful negotiation of that which had been begun. They would profoundly affect their self-concept, their self-esteem at every stage along the way. Those who guided them were primary influencers indeed.

Because of space constraints, this brief and oversimplified discussion of some of the dynamics of the ritual process of proselyte conversion with special attention to the issues of identity for these Gentiles will have to do here, although additional dynamics we will discuss in chap-

15. A. Cohen, *Self-Consciousness*, 128–31.

16. Turner, *Ritual Process*.

ter 9. It should prepare us to recognize that the rhetoric of Paul's letter implies very complicated situations for those being addressed and those influencers with whom they are intimately engaged, much to Paul's chagrin. The issues of identity for each of the players are many and complex, but the interpreter who considers the social aspects of communal life and identification has a chance to begin to understand them, to some degree at least. Thus, even if circumcision is hardly the most important aspect of identity among the communal members, or the proselyte for that matter, being a private mark not generally open to public witness or verification, and limited to male participants, it symbolizes a public social act of transfer for a non-Jewish person into the Jewish community and thus places him in subordination to its norms, which will be especially prominent when these norms conflict with those of the community outside of this bounded identity from which he has come.

In other words, whatever the precise actions accompanying the culmination of this ritual, it seems that circumcision symbolized that public action that defined the moment in terms of communal identification, that is, boundary maintenance, such as is at issue in our text, regardless of nuanced distinctions that may have pertained for the participants, especially those involved in the administration of the community's norms, particularly overseeing the ritual process itself. Circumcision functioned to distinguish the identification of the community of the righteous ones of God, thus guarding the communal boundary, and would need to be negotiated by any male wishing to make a complete crossing.[17] As Anthony Cohen expresses the social dynamic, "the symbolic expression and affirmation of boundary heightens people's awareness of and sensitivity to their community." To this end ritual is well suited, for whatever the participants' "motivations or ostensible purposes, it would seem that much ritual also has this capacity to heighten consciousness. It should not be surprising, therefore, to find ritual occupying a prominent place in the repertoire of symbolic devices through which community boundaries are affirmed and reinforced."[18] It is thus a social or communal definition of identity that

17. See Esler, *Galatians*, 141–69, on the identity issue of righteousness; although he takes the communal implications for the identification of the influencers as well as the addressees to be different than suggested herein, his argument for the social aspects of the claim to be righteous ones is similar and helpful.

18. A. Cohen, *Symbolic Construction*, 50.

gives this symbolic action meaning, and at the same time this symbol gives the community meaning too.[19]

Circumcision is a symbolic action, a means of expression, but what it means may vary with the perspective of the parties concerned with its interpretation, for themselves, for others within their community, and for those without. Perhaps most elaboration will occur because of those who are at the boundaries seeking either to challenge their value or negotiate passage by this media.[20] It is along precisely such a line that we find Paul arguing for a new way to understand what is taking place at the boundaries of Jewish communal identity, because of these Gentiles' relationship with God in Christ. For in order to settle the matter of the certainty of the addressees' identity already—now, in the present age, as though the age to come had already dawned, although the addressees have remained to date uncircumcised—Paul confronts as now incorrect the traditional Jewish communal reflex. That response to the expressed interest of Gentiles for acquiring full standing as righteous ones is to direct them to complete the rite of passage into Jewish or Israelite identity. But for these Gentiles, according to Paul's response in this letter, that will no longer do: Gentiles in Christ are not to regard themselves as liminals on the way to becoming proselytes and certainly not as mere guests needing to now commence this process!

It may be useful here to make the point more concrete by brief interaction with an ostensibly sympathetic aspect of Terence Donaldson's argument.[21] This particular example is a tribute to the logical social implications of what he claims to find in the rhetoric of Galatians, where it seems that many interpreters are content to ponder this language in merely theological terms. He proposes that the Israel-centered framework of Paul's gospel is evident in the rhetoric of Galatians, although the letter is notably dealing with the identification concerns (salvation) of non-Israelites, observing that, for example: "The question, then, has to do with the conviction—held by all three parties at least by the time of the writing of Galatians—that membership in Abraham's family is not only desirable but essential for salvation."[22] In this light Donaldson observes that to which the addressees'

19. Cf. A. Cohen, *Symbolic Construction*, e.g., 11–19, passim.

20. Cf. A. Cohen, *Symbolic Construction*, 11–19, 50–63; F. Barth, "Introduction"; Berger and Luckmann, *Social Construction;* Goodman, *Who Was a Jew?*

21. "Gospel." See also his *Paul*, where he works out this position more fully.

22. Donaldson, "Gospel," 181.

beliefs would lead for themselves: "A status ambiguity that would become immediately apparent should they walk through the door of a synagogue, or even encounter Jewish Christians of the more conservative variety!"[23]

This perceptive observation is predicated upon theoretical contemplation of the social world implied in Paul's rhetorical approach. It seeks to make Paul's rhetoric relevant. Yet the way Donaldson frames this point, in a footnote and as an aside, brings to the surface an instructive difference between the approaches of Donaldson—and with him most interpreters of Galatians—and the interpretation proposed herein.

Throughout this article and later in his book, the Israel-centered framework he applies to Paul's concerns for the identification of the Christ-believing Gentiles to whom he writes frames the issue within the theoretical spheres of Jewish theology, to which Paul is understood to appeal. This approach is revealed by the pause taken in a footnote, when Donaldson observes what would happen if this was considered in concrete social terms: "*should* they walk through . . . or encounter." Highlighting a comment like this one brings to the fore the difference of emphasis.

I take Paul's Israel-centered rhetoric to indicate that a salient Jewish social setting is the framework already active in the life and interests of the addressees as well as Paul, and thus that which really makes his rhetoric a word on target. Thus, by way of comparison, I would not emphasize that it is the theoretical entering of a synagogue per se, as though this was a random or unexpected event to be contemplated in a footnote, the implications of which they or Paul would now have to unexpectedly confront. For this implies that their lives had not been and still were not lived in this kind of social reality! This would suggest that Paul's work with them and their social identity have taken place outside of a Jewish social context, apart from a social concern shaped by one for that matter. It presumes that the differences upon which the premises of social identification for Gentiles within this coalition are predicated would only become apparent in terms of an Israel-centered framework operating in significant social ways *if* their social life was altered, by choice or not, by the entering of Jewish communal space, or engagement with a Jewish person outside such space.

23. Donaldson, "Gospel," 191 n. 72.

Rather, I take the Israel-centered framework of Paul's rhetoric, and the specific approach of this letter, to imply that the addressees have entered into a different ("another") synagogue, that is, most likely into the sphere of influence of the larger Jewish environment and the traditional message of good for Gentiles seeking identity as righteous ones. Such a movement for the addressees—even if only a change in the degree of association after some time has passed, because their participation within the boundary of the larger community has been lived primarily within the parameters of the subgroup of believers in Christ—brings into clear view the status ambiguity.[24] The social framework is intra-Jewish, among rival Jewish groups. Moreover, this approach makes immediately relevant and imaginable the powerful force of the argument for already completed or merely liminal or even preliminal status for these Gentiles that is at dispute in this letter. They must now reconsider and renegotiate their concept of who they are and how they fit in: What norms will they embrace to accomplish this task?

The addressees as Gentiles need to reduce the dissonance that arises from the new or intensified awareness of marginality that results for themselves when making and living on the basis of a claim to status constructed around Paul's gospel. Where it runs up against the traditional and normative opinion of reality—the "other message of good" for themselves—especially to the degree that these control the access to honor and goods, decisions with life-threatening implications must be made. It is to be expected that those on the margins are seeking predictability by way of conforming to membership criteria and behavior thought appropriate in order to overcome the ambiguity and uncertainty of their identity: "Strong pressures encouraging conformity—with penalties attaching to deviance—may oppress most those whose membership or social identity is insecure."[25]

The Gentile addressees appear to be outgrouped quasi-insiders, seeking the dominant in-group's full acceptance. They are considered by the influencers to be righteous Gentile guests or perhaps liminals who appear to want to be adopted into the family. For the addressees in these social situations, completion of the ritual process of circumcision may seem but a small price to pay. For the rights they have con-

24. Cf. A. Cohen, *Symbolic Construction*, 69–70.
25. Jenkins, *Social Identity*, 124.

sidered theirs as a result of their incorporation into this Jewish community only exist to the degree that these rights are recognized by the guardians of the communal norms.[26]

But from Paul's perspective, there are other Jewish communal symbols active in the experiences of these Gentiles that demonstrate that the change of aeons has occurred with the meaning of the death and resurrection of Jesus Christ, where these Gentile addressees, and those Jews who meet with them now within the *ekklēsias* as indiscriminate equals, are concerned. The receipt of the Holy Spirit of God and miracles wrought among themselves bear witness that they are righteous ones—while yet remaining non-Jews—for they are children of Abraham, indeed children of God, and thus full heirs.[27]

These Gentiles, in Paul's view, as demonstrated by these manifestations, are now equal in status with the historical righteous ones of God, even with those who would have them complete circumcision to gain such status (e.g., 3:1—4:9; 5:1-6; 6:12-14). Thus, Paul maintains, even for those communal agents who may not share this conviction, a different response to their claim to identity among the righteous ones of God is required. The righteous life they now manifest, while still Gentiles, and the miracles of God wrought in their midst, demand reevaluation of the basis upon which the traditional reflex legitimates its right to deny this reality.

Paul is not arguing, on my reading, that the boundary has collapsed so that there is no longer Jew or Gentile, circumcised or uncircumcised, any more than he is arguing that the social boundary of difference between male and female or slave and free has been eliminated; both kinds still exist, and they are different with respect to one another. These Gentiles have not become Jewish proselytes but fellow heirs of Abraham while remaining members of the nations.[28] For Paul, the dif-

26. Cf. Jenkins, *Social Identity*, 135.

27. Scott, *Adoption;* Lull, *Spirit;* Hansen, *Abraham*.

28. Contra Donaldson, "Gospel"; idem., *Paul*, who draws a different conclusion regarding Paul's view of the Gentiles, in that he attributes to Paul the view that Gentiles in Christ are now proselyte Jews and thus Israelites without circumcision, where I believe that they are rather equal with them, though actually remaining righteous Gentiles, so that both Israel and the nations are represented as one in the new community of Christ-believers, though different relative to membership in Israel. I think this difference of view is symptomatic of the above difference in terms of approach as theologically rather than socially framed. How else but in theological orientation could Paul be thought to regard as proselytes those who are

ferences of identity remain, but the discrimination that accompanies such roles in the present "evil" age does and must not remain, for those in Christ, those of the age to come (cf. 3:26—4:7).[29] They have become the equivalents of proselytes—righteous ones of God though not of Israel, of a new community creation consisting of Israel and the nations worshipping together—by the act of God in Christ. This is how he now calls them to live.

This position would be in keeping with a Jewish understanding, albeit not the only one available, for what would be appropriate to expect when the age to come has dawned, that is, if it had dawned. For in that age, the dawning of which he believes has now begun—a position that Paul himself seems to have arrived at by way of a miraculous revelation and then reexamination of the Scriptures and not merely by the articulation of this view beforehand or by examination of the empirical evidence itself—Israel and the nations would together worship the One God, the Creator of all, together as one, although remaining Israel and the nations.[30] The difference of identity would remain on the level of national historical identity, but the discrimination that had characterized interaction at the boundaries of that distinction in the present "evil" age, such as is now the case for the addressees in their interaction with the influencers, would no longer obtain.

Paul does not denigrate the role of circumcision or Jewish identity for Jewish people. This may be assumed, however, to be the implied result of Paul's position in the view of the influencers, who do not consider Paul's modification appropriate in the present age, because it may seem to them to collapse a necessary boundary of righteous Israel in service of the nations until the age to come arrives, which they do not believe to have happened. Paul is arguing for the recognition of the identity of these Gentile addressees in Jewish communal terms, although his letter is not directed to the other Jewish people who are involved in determining their identity. Instead, it is written to the addressees, so they will thereby understand themselves regardless of how other influential people react who may not confirm this identification of them.

---

socially yet Gentiles, even by Paul's own terms of personal identity as a circumcised Jew?

29. Contra Boyarin, *Radical Jew*, among many others; see my *Mystery*, esp. 179–92, 286–87, 353–59.

30. Cf. Donaldson, "Proselytes"; idem, *Paul*, 51–78; Nanos, *Mystery*, 50–56.

Thus, although the addressees are not Jewish, Paul seeks to clarify their identity in Jewish communal terms. The situations in which the exigence that Paul addresses would arise are intra-Jewish communal ones, although his response brings to bear an inter-Jewish template on the principles of this coalition.[31] At the same time, an intra- or inter-communal dimension is at work between these Jewish communities and the dominant pagan society in which they coexist, accounting for the severity of the concern to conform with the constraints placed upon these pagan addressees by the norms and expectations of their family and neighbors as long as they are not proselytes, that is, that they will not threaten the interests of their village, town, or city by failure to participate in applicable public expressions of pagan life.

Moreover, although Paul's address is not directed to the influencers, it is predicated upon values that they will recognize as their own, anticipating the response that will arise when the addressees appeal to this correspondence to legitimate their (renewed?) resistance to the traditional communal norms. Paul thus anticipates the influencers' (most likely continued, because traditional) appeal. He anticipates the need to legitimate his position according to several Jewish elements. These include Scripture, which is the basis for the interpretation of the promise made to Abraham, and thus the basis for any interpretation to alter expectations in view of current implications, and revelation, to which the traditions also appeal for their legitimacy. Paul also supports his contention on the basis of the witness of God's Holy Spirit at work in the lives of the righteous ones of God, inclusive of the experience of miracles.

The question then between these two reference groups is, What is appropriate for these Gentiles to gain full membership "presently"? This includes the appropriate response to them now for the communal agents who protect the interests of the Jewish people in the midst of the present "evil" age, not to mention the interests of any Gentiles seeking to pass legally into the status granted to proselytes among them, such as the right to abstain from continued participation in the celebrations of the imperial cult. The various responses to this question revolve around the issue of time: Has the age to come dawned with the meaning of Jesus Christ's death and resurrection, or not? What is the time? And therefore, what is appropriate?

31. See arguments herein and my "Inter- and Intra-Jewish."

This discussion sets the stage to investigate the question of exigence: What does the perceived interest of the addressees in proselyte conversion mean for evaluating the perspective of each party regarding the exigence? The answers, for each of these players, appear to be different.

The Exigence for Paul

The exigence from Paul's perspective arises from the failure or at least temptation of these Gentiles to depart from the course they had been running since their positive response, as Gentiles, to the good news of Christ. This development has been precipitated by interaction with those who have put the obstacle in their way by prohibiting them to understand themselves and gain what they seek among the righteous ones of God on the basis of that claim. These others have instead insisted upon the traditional methods for gaining that identity, inviting the addressees to regard themselves as liminal, and are in a position to make a compelling, if not yet fully convincing case.

This is evident to Paul, for the addressees have to some degree begun to consider seriously and perhaps already to internalize as good for themselves this "other message of good," which proposes, by way of completion of proselyte conversion, that the addressees can indisputably acquire the (Jewish) status that they desire on Jewish communal terms. This is apparent in his ironic approach and in such direct comments about their current state of "defection" (1:6), of being "affected by the evil eye" (3:1), engaging in practices to become known by God (4:8-10), "desiring to be under Law" (4:21), or having paused in the running that they had begun toward obeying the truth of the gospel of Christ (5:7). In this way, the addressees have made this other message such an active force among themselves to date, instead of resisting this influence, as he had warned them to do when among them in the past. The threat has grown with time that the addressees will not resist the powerful drive for unequivocal acceptance on the terms that the influencers serve as guardians thereof, and thus seemingly, in superordinate position to the addressees in terms of controlling the access to indisputable honor, and with this concomitant access to goods. Paul must dissuade the addressees in no uncertain terms from contemplating or continuing on this alternate course. In this letter, he sets out to make it compellingly clear that it is "not another" good news, because it is incompatible with the good news of Christ and thus not complementary, as they seem to wish to suppose.

Although Paul blames the influencers' influence and attacks the addressees' naïveté for precipitating the exigence, he does not absolve the addressees of the responsibility to know better and to behave properly, to continue to run straight toward the truth of the gospel of Christ, regardless of the obstacles, such as this status ambiguity they now suffer.

These moves allow the addressees to save face to a certain degree, but they are confronted face-first as well, by way of ironic rebuke and ridicule, for repressing what they know to be truth in the developments they have permitted at least in part to shape themselves to date. He calls them to bear witness to the truth: the truth about how God has acted graciously to them by way of Christ, the truth about having received God's Spirit and experiencing God's miracles wrought in their midst, the truth about conforming to the kind of expectations that should govern the lives of those who look to Christ crucified. However, ironically, this behavior will lead to being shamed by the powers that rule this present age—as Paul is persecuted, ironically, stigmatized for upholding this disputable position on their own behalf—while they "wait for the hope of righteousness" (5:5).

For although Paul ridicules the naïveté of the addressees by way of an evil eye warning for having failed to realize that their current "suffering" of marginalization was the result of the influencers' envious rather than generous designs, he accuses the addressees of having had their own eyes where they should not be, that is, on what the influencers' message ostensibly offered as good. This has had a deleterious effect upon them, but it is one that would and could be prevented by fixing their eyes upon the one publicly portrayed as crucified, shamed beyond comparison as a threatening social deviant according to the ruling powers of this age, the Roman regime itself. Indeed, the addressees were themselves to blame for treating this other message as though complementary, when they had been prepared beforehand to resist it as contrary instead.

Yet Paul proceeds in his argument on the assumption that the addressees would not pursue this course if they actually understood that it would result in so twisting the good news of Christ that it rendered meaningless the death of Christ for themselves. They have not properly considered this to be the ineluctable result. This is where their naïveté is addressed, and this is the issue (or stasis) anticipated in Paul's rhetorical approach. It represents that point where Paul may pause in his argument, with no need to explain or go further to support his point, because it is bedrock upon which the addressees are certain to agree (anticipating the need for a stasis of definition, followed by anticipation of an appeal to stasis of quality). This is a point worth some consideration for getting at the exigence and situations in Galatia implied by Paul's rhetorical approach.[32] For this indicates an aspect of the exigence from Paul's perspective as it is anticipated in his rhetoric: he does not approach the recipients of Galatians as though they have any explicit intention of abandoning their faith in the proclamation of the good news of Christ for themselves. That is not the urgency of the moment; rather, Paul must dramatize that this will necessarily be the implicit effect of taking the action that they are contemplating as though this other message was simply "another," requiring an additional action to a complementary message of good.[33]

It is perhaps possible that the addressees were not even admitting to themselves what may seem to be an obvious overlap of conflicting meanings for Paul, or even the later reader, who only begins to consider the issue after engagement of this text—not before it, in this sense—with the addressees![34] In other words, it may have been that the addressees, like teenagers caught between two rival courts of reputation composed of peers and parents, may want to convince themselves that they could regard the two messages as good for them in different spheres, so to speak: one pertaining to their membership in the subgroup of Christ-believers, wherein they are in-group members, and the other with respect to their membership in the group of which the influencers represent the in-group and its norms and values. The addressees seem to be asking themselves, and this may be the influencers' question to them on the matter as well: Have the addressees found or rendered themselves, because of resisting to date the influencers' way to negotiate acceptance, as out-grouped in terms of the influencers' reference and membership group norms, perhaps needlessly so?

32. Cf. Nadeau, "Hermogenes' *On Stases*," 361–424; Aristotle, *Rhet.* 1.13/9–19; *Rhet. Her.* 1.11–17/18–27; Quintilian, *Inst.* 3.6; Cicero, *Inv.* 1.8/10.

33. This tells against Martin's application of stasis theory to conclude that the addressees are turning back to paganism, rejecting faith in Christ because they now find that it includes proselyte conversion, which they reject for themselves ("Apostasy," 440–41).

34. See too Mitternacht, *Sprachlose*, who also seeks to give voice to the "speechless" addressees, with many observations sympathetic to those argued herein, as well as significant differences, especially for what is implied about Paul.

Although his strained approach undermines his declaration, Paul makes known to the addressees his anticipation, once this letter is read (5:10): he is certain they will comply with his wishes, because they represent their own core beliefs and interests as ones defined in and by Christ. The message of the letter is predicated upon Paul's conviction that the age to come has dawned in Christ,[35] and he writes based upon the assumption that the Gentile addressees share the same conviction. But the anticipation of his rhetoric reveals that he believes they would like to fool themselves by repressing what they should know better than to think or do, so as to avoid the unwelcome consequences of social marginalization.

Paul appears to realize that the addressees are struggling to find a way to reduce the so far unavoidable dissonance created by interaction with the influencers, to the degree at least that the addressees have resisted enlisting or completing proselyte conversion on the basis of appeal to Paul's gospel of Christ. Running straight forward on such a course as Paul would have them navigate without accommodating the demands of this other communal norm will precipitate rather than reduce the dissonance. Where they had sought to explore a nuance and negotiate a compromise, Paul, by way of dissociating rhetoric, now closes the possibility of escape.

The bedrock conviction that Paul believes the audience to share, and thus that he can anticipate appealing to without explanation or justification to win the dispute, is the good news of Christ: his death by crucifixion, as well as God's raising him from the dead, and the great benefit of these events for themselves. Although perhaps these are in dispute among the influencers, Paul is not writing to the influencers, and these are not controversial for the addressees. Paul relies upon this issue of agreement throughout his argument by way of appeal, without explanation.

The Exigence for the Addressees

The exigence from the addressees' perspective arises in Galatia when the message of the influencers seems good to themselves to resolve the conflicting ways of ensuring their identity as righteous ones of God according to two sets of communal norms; the differences are not in

35. Sympathetic is the point made by Silva, "Eschatological Structures."

kind but in time. Because the addressees have internalized as good for themselves the message of Christ as proclaimed by Paul, they have believed themselves to have already gained the status of the age to come in the present age; moreover, because of this, they have expected to be honored by others who share this claim to status and to become part of their communal life, anticipating full access to honor and the goods associated with full membership. It has shaped their identity, albeit in ways that are new and thus fragile, so that they understand themselves to be already equally righteous ones of the historic community of God, because of the good news of Christ by which they have been graciously called by God and become known.

The addressees had thus not considered themselves in need of becoming proselyte candidates according to the traditional Jewish communal norms—whether they were aware that this was a choice they were making initially is not clear—instead claiming the status of righteous ones of God on the basis of their relationship with God in Christ. But this is a status, with regard to non-Jewish people, according to traditional Jewish interpretation, that was considered to be impossible to acquire apart from completion of the ritual process of proselyte conversion, in the present age anyway; in the age to come perhaps equal or even greater status may be granted![36] Thus, they are confronted with a crisis of identity that is at the same time religious, political, and familial: Who are they and how do they belong or not?[37] The addressees believe the age to come has dawned in Christ, but they have failed to consider turning to this other message a denial of that reality, for it is still clearly the present age, where communal acceptance by the influencers is desirable.

The Exigence for the Influencers

The exigence from the influencers' perspective is different still. In response to this unanticipated and unacceptable claim on the part of these Gentiles, the influencers wish to encourage and ensure the compliance of these Gentiles with the traditional way to acquire the status desired, but which inappropriately already claim, by completion of proselyte conversion in the present age.[38] Regardless of the

36. Cf. *m. Sanhedrin* 10.1; Segal, "Conversion and Universalism."
37. Similar is Barclay, *Obeying,* 73.
38. Similar is Esler, *Galatians,* 73.

influencers' nobility of intent (denied by Paul and not considered by most interpreters of his polemic either!), they have engaged in persuasive tactics that appear to be normally associated with the accomplishment of this kind of goal, namely, communal boundary maintenance—social control.[39]

As we will discuss more fully, Paul's rhetoric implies that the influencers' methods of social control include—apparently, based upon application of historical suspicion in analyzing Paul's accusations—didactic endeavors such as teaching, exegesis of Scripture, and appeal to tradition, as well as social control techniques such as shaming,[40] for example, exclusion from the level of association that the addressees seek when it is presently considered inappropriate according to the communal norms (cf. 4:17). Combined, these techniques are employed strategically, or perhaps reflexively, to put the addressees in their proper place until compliance is gained.

Thus, Paul's rhetoric does not imply that the influencers have created the exigence per se, that is, from their own perspective on this need for urgent action, although Paul does not express this view. Rather, the urgency of the moment for themselves has been created by the addressees' "inappropriate" expectations of communal identity. These claims have resulted from the addressees' internalization of a status not yet conferred on the influencers' communal terms—which expectations have been revealed to the influencers to whatever degree the addressees have appealed to date to their understanding of Paul's good news of Christ to legitimate those claims or to the degree that the influencers have interacted with Paul when he was present in Galatia or somewhere else—until the completion of proselyte conversion has occurred. The integrity of the communal norms and values, founded on Scripture and tradition, which are themselves based upon revelation, as well as those of the dominant Greco-Roman society by which they are constrained, have been threatened, and the influencers must act to ensure that they are not compromised.[41]

39. Pitts, "Social Control," 381–96.

40. See Braithwaite, *Reintegration*, 57–83, for discussion and some examples of the culturally specific modalities of shaming. See also Pitts, "Social Control," 390.

41. A. Cohen, *Symbolic Construction*, investigates the way symbols are resourcefully employed to "re-assert community and its boundaries when the processes and consequences of change threaten its integrity" (28). Here, the rabbinic story of Rabbi Eliezer and the debate on the susceptibility of a specific oven to ritual purity seems a later parallel; cf. *b. Baba Meṣia* 59b; Nanos, "Inter- and Intra-Jewish."

Thus, it is the place of these influential agents to respond by informing the addressees that they have taken a seat at the table that is reserved for someone else and of their need to step down to the other end thereof, until, that is, they have acquired the appropriate status. They seek to shame them. The dynamics are articulated by many interpreters of Mediterranean cultures and of Paul's time.[42]

In the context implied in Galatia, how may the influencers accomplish this task? Articulation of the symbolizing act of proselyte conversion, completed by circumcision, naturally rises to meet the occasion.

It remains important to note that such an approach to the acquisition of equal standing by way of a rite of conversion, while ethnocentric, is not exclusive, contrary to many recent approaches to the topic; the fact is that it is quite the opposite.[43] It is inclusive, as it ritualizes the process for negotiating the boundary, rendering it permeable so that Jewish identity can be acquired and not only ascribed. And it is righteous, because it is a boundary not of their own creation but revealed by God to mark a holy community of righteous ones who will enlighten all of the other nations until the awaited age has come.

From the perspective of the influencers, the exigence has arisen because of the need to confront the results of these Gentiles' internalization of expectations, because they are considered wrong, and lead to claims and actions that are inappropriate for the present time.

To return to the subject of the addressees' own exigence, it is now easier to see that they wish to reduce the cognitive dissonance that has arisen as a result of becoming aware of, and to varying degrees internalizing as desirable for themselves, both Paul's message of good in Christ, by which they become righteous ones of God but must remain Gentiles, and the influencers' "other" message of good, by which they

42. Aristotle, *Rhet.* 2.6.2, 12, defines shame (αἰσχύνη) under emotions as that which motivates one to obtain a good one ought to have gained but failed for some reason to secure, whereas shamelessness is "contempt and indifference in regard to these same things." The positive counterpart of shame is emulative jealousy (ζῆλος), which includes the ambition to maintain status among peers (cf. *Rhet.* 2.11.1). See discussions in Pitt-Rivers, "Honor," 504. Cf., e.g., idem, "Honour and Social Status"; Gouldner, *Enter Plato;* Malina, *Social World;* Nanos, "O Foolish Galatians."

43. Ethnocentrism is appropriate for describing the requirement of proselyte conversion for inclusion, when defined in the general social-scientific sense as "evaluative preference for all aspects of one's own group relative to other groups"

must instead become proselytes (be circumcised if male). The urgency for action arises for the addressees because these two approaches to their identity have become more pressing in view of the continued and increasing presence of the influencers, and the immediacy of their authority to determine what is good for the addressees, coupled with the distance that accompanies the growing absence of Paul, and with this a suspicion that the differentiations he seemed to make were too rigorous. In the meantime, the threat of suffering continued identity marginalization and concomitant deprivation of opportunities and goods within the community—under the influence of the norms as understood by the influencers—have dimmed their own perception of the problem, or at least led to the repression of what they ought to know. They have lost touch with the honor at stake: Paul calls them foolish, because they have contemplated a shameless route for themselves in view of faith in/of Christ. They have, in effect, like Peter at Antioch, chosen to mask their conviction by indulging in a lie in order to avoid social consequences in the presence of advocates who oppose the legitimacy of this truth for Gentiles.

Status uncertainty has resulted from their resistance to date, and to the degree that they interface with the influencers, the marginalization has increased, which is even inscribed in the ritual distinction that obtains.[44] For the addressees are—according to the values embraced and presumably internalized by the influencers, in conformity with those norms represented by their communal leaders (cf. 6:12-13)—not yet incorporated members, as they would be if they had already become proselytes according to the influencers' terms of identity, but merely, on Paul's terms, liminals. Or worse yet, they are even preliminals; to the degree that they have not even begun down the path toward proselyte initiation, they are but pagans! Albeit the influencers' level of interest, rather than rejection, implies that the addressees are welcome, of course—not as they want to claim but instead as guests.

(Hogg and Vaughan, *Social Psychology*, 365). The charge of ethnocentric exclusivism has been an aspect of the so-called New Perspective approach. There is not space to discuss this fully, but it is a judgment that fails to recognize the point being made. I formerly failed to recognize how "ethnocentric *exclusivism*" is an incorrect description for an inclusive policy and also how it might continue negative stereotyping, in *Mystery*, which was properly criticized by Neil Elliott in his review in *CBQ* 59 (1997): 587–89.

44. Cf. Kertzer, *Ritual;* Leach, "Ritual," 524.

CHAPTER 7

ENGAGING THE PREVAILING INTERPRETATIONS

Paul makes many explicit comments about those who are influencing his addressees in Galatia in a direction that he opposes. His rhetoric offers many implicit indications about them as well. It will be useful first to set out the data and try to organize what is available for evaluating their identity. The construction that results must seek to account for all of the data in the letter, yet for the sake of space and clarity this section will focus on those passages that appear to provide the most essential data, recognizing that while this move is efficient, it is flawed. For categorization of the data already interprets or allows other prior interpretations to govern the scope of the data of the text, organizing in a way that may limit what is relevant before that data has supposedly been interpreted. Might not a different set of presuppositions or conclusions lead to a different organization and even recognition of the potentially relevant data? Every word written and every syntactic connection contributes information that is essential to the interpretive task; conversely, every word left out and every break in syntax—at least to the degree noticed or notable, so that it gives the interpreter pause to inquire if this move represents a conscious choice that is itself meaningful—can also be considered essential. In fact, on the basis of the work that has been carried out in this and other investigations of my own, after the analysis of other constructions, I will suggest some additional data that should be examined that is not usually taken to pertain but that may alter the conclusions if it is.

Paul accuses someone or ones of influencing the addressees, and these passages often express Paul's opposition to this influence. Paul warns the addressees that they have been the objects of "persuasion" (5:8) in various ways.[1] In some cases, it is their motives that are in view, in others their objectives, strategies, or techniques. Leaving aside for the moment the verbal tenses in which these ways are set within Paul's

1. Πεισμονή: contrived persuasiveness; see R. Longenecker, *Galatians*, 230–31; Morland, *Rhetoric of Curse*, 147.

statements, or any assessment of the perspectives Paul expresses, this data may be grouped together as follows:

- These people are accused of trying to "compel [ἀναγκάζουσιν]" the addressees to become circumcised (6:12-13):
  - in order to "make a good showing in the flesh,"
  - and "in order that they might not be persecuted for the cross of Christ" (cf. 2:14),
  - a result that they "desire,"
  - in order to "glory in the [addressees'] flesh."
- They ("some" or "certain ones"; τινές) are "unsettling" the addressees (ταράσσοντες; 1:7; 5:10: this can also be translated as "troubling," "agitating," "disturbing," "stirring up," "frightening," "intimidating," among others),[2]
- and want (θέλοντες) to "twist [μεταστρέψαι] the good news of Christ"; which, along with "unsettling" them, has had the result of causing the addressees to "defect [μετατίθεσθε] from the one who has called" them "in grace" (1:6).
- They are "bewitching" or "evil eyeing" the addressees (ἐβάσκανεν; 3:1), "before whose eyes Jesus Christ was publicly portrayed as crucified."
- They are "jealous" for them (ζηλοῦσιν or "courting," "zealous"), yet "not for good" but rather in order to "exclude" them (ἐκκλεῖσαι; or "shut out"),[3] and they do so in order that the addressees will be "jealous" of themselves (ζηλοῦτε) (4:17).
- They are "hindering [ἐνέκοψεν]" their progress, in the sense of "obstructing" the course set by Paul on which the addressees had been "running," that is, getting in the way of the addressees' "obeying [following] the truth" (5:7),[4]
  - this may also be considered "subverting," "seducing," or "troubling" the addressees (ἀναστατοῦντες; 5:12);[5]
  - as well as "unsettling" them (ταράσσων; 5:10; cf. above on 1:7).

In addition to the data of 6:12-13, several of the accusations include reference to the specific goal of these influential people as wanting to

2. In some cases the referent is plural (e.g., 1:7; 4:17; 5:12; 6:12-13), in some singular (e.g., 1:9; 3:1; 5:7-10; 6:17); see discussion below.

3. Cf. Bligh, *Galatians*, 172; C. Smith, "Galatians 4:17."

4. See Stählin, *TDNT* 3.855; Lightfoot, *Galatians*, 205.

5. See discussion below.

have the addressees circumcised (e.g., 4:21; 5:1-12). And this is implied as well in the digression from the narrative at 2:3-5, where the reader is told that the apostles in Jerusalem "did not yield" to those wishing to have Titus circumcised in order to ensure that "the truth of the gospel might be preserved for you," that is, for the Galatian addressees, who were not present in Jerusalem; and also in 3:3, where Paul ridicules the addressees' naïveté to think that they should follow the lead of these influential people and "complete [ἐπιτελεῖσθε]" that course which the addressees had instead begun by "hearing faith," "in the Spirit."

Paul's opposition to these people is clear in the following passages:

- He wishes a curse upon them twice (1:8-9);
- assures the addressees that "he" who is "unsettling" them will "bear his judgment, whoever he is" (5:10);
- and sarcastically wishes that "those who unsettle you would mutilate [castrate] themselves" (5:12).

Many interpreters have taken Paul's assertions of his authority as an apostle of God and not of humans, coupled with his autobiographical sketch to support that contention, as indications that those influencing the Galatian addressees have challenged Paul on this matter. More specific direction is often taken to be implied, so that the issue of authority is about Paul's right to consider or call himself an apostle vis-à-vis the Jerusalem apostles, who can appeal to personally knowing and being appointed by Jesus. Much is also made of his supposed concern to assert independence from these other apostles, or, some rather argue, his dependence, and a few propose that both dependence and independence are at issue. Thus, it is necessary to include as possible data, in addition to those comments in 1:13—2:21 taken variously to denote dependence or independence from the Jerusalem Christ-believing coalition's apostles, the following:

- Paul's startling opening: "Paul an apostle—not from human agents nor through human agency, but through Jesus Christ and God the Father" (1:1).
- Further comments are along this line, such as the rhetorical questions and claims of vv. 10-12, that Paul does not seek "approval [πείθω]" or "the winning of favor [ἀρέσκειν]" from "humans" but from "God," otherwise he would "not be a servant of Christ"; moreover, his good news proclamation was not "received [παρέλαβον]" from nor "taught [ἐδιδάχθην]" to him by "humans"

but by "a revelation [ἀποκαλύψεως] of Jesus Christ," it is therefore not "according to humans."[6]
- Paul's argument is that if he "still" proclaimed circumcision this would remove "the stumbling block of the cross," so he asks: "why am I still persecuted?" (5:11).

Additional aspects of their identity may be implied in Paul's instructions to the addressees. They are to resist their influence, as the data above shows, but they are also to think and do certain things that presumably might run counter to those things important to these influential people. This is a tricky area, but the data that may apply, and that is often considered to apply, should be set out. For example, Paul's first admonition in this letter is in 4:12, notably well into the letter, where he calls the addressees to "become as I am, for I also have become as you are." This instruction puts the entire autobiographical character of his argument in perspective, making commands out of many statements Paul makes about his own ethos[7] and contextualizing the generalizations that occur throughout the letter. Many additional instructions quickly follow in the parenesis of chapters 5 and 6. It is thus possible that Paul has them in mind, by way of contrast with the thinking and behavior to which he calls the addressees in their posture of resistance in 5:1—6:10, when he instructs the addressees instead

- "to freedom," but warns them not to use this "as an opportunity for the flesh," instead, rather to "through love be servants to one another" (5:13);
- not to engage in an agonistic struggle with one another, which Paul puts thus: "But if you bite and devour one another take heed that you are not consumed by one another" (5:15);
- to "walk by the Spirit, and do not gratify the desires of the flesh" (5:16);
- by again "warning" them "that those who do such things shall not inherit the kingdom of God" (5:21);

6. See Schütz, *Paul,* 114-58; esp. 124-35. The matter of dependence, independence, or both, is discussed also by commentators and, e.g., Holmberg, Paul; Lyons, *Pauline Autobiography;* Howard, *Crisis;* Taylor, *Paul,* but it is clearly a circular road, and thus such contradictory claims can appeal to this language for substantiation, but without convincing those who have contrary proposals.

7. Cf. Lyons, *Pauline Autobiography,* 132–76; Kraftchick, "Ethos and Pathos," 209–80; Dodd, *Paradigmatic,* 13–32, 133–70.

- not to engage in agonistic struggles for honor: "If we live by the Spirit, let us also walk by the Spirit. Let us have no self-conceit, no challenging of one another, no envying of one another" (5:25-26);
- to be circumspect: "For if anyone thinks he is something, when he is nothing, he deceives himself" (6:3);
- not to be "deceived; God is not mocked, for whatever a man sows, that he will also reap. For he who sows to his own flesh will from the flesh reap corruption" (6:7-8).

In addition to the material set out above from the situational discourses with respect to the situations of the Galatian addressees, additional data about influential people in other situations elsewhere is included in the narrative discourse units of the letter. Paul provides polemical descriptions within each context suitable for my present purpose:

- In Jerusalem there are "pseudo-brethren" who are "informants [κατασκοπῆσαι; or "spies" or "inspectors"]" (2:4).[8]
- In Antioch (2:12) there are:
  - "certain ones from James";
  - and "ones for circumcision."
- The allegory of Abraham includes mention of:
  - "the present Jerusalem" "in slavery with her children"; in contrast, "the Jerusalem above is free, who is our mother" (4:25-26);
  - and a figurative "persecutor" (4:29).

To be sure, these are influencers too, but they are not the influencers in Galatia. They rather populate narratives constructed from examples of tensions elsewhere. Determining how these situations arose, who was involved, and how they were resolved by Paul and the other apostles for the benefit of the Galatian addressees involves several interpretive moves.

Finally, there is other data that interpreters have appealed to, or which I will bring up in the following arguments, that cannot be so easily set out. For example, less clear in terms of direct data are such matters as whether they are appropriately referred to as Judaizers; whether they are opponents or opposing Paul or his gospel of Christ in any way;

8. See below and Nanos, "Intruding 'Spies.'"

if or to what degree Paul knows who they are, in general or specific ways; if they have arrived from somewhere else after Paul's departure, and if so, how recent or sudden it was, from where, and why; if they are in any way associated with the leaders of the Christ-believing coalition in Jerusalem, Antioch, or somewhere else, or even if they simply claim to be but misrepresent themselves; even whether they are Christ-believers themselves or their message a gospel of Christ, however else it may be characterized. The data for consideration of these and many other matters is not unambiguous; being the result of interpretive moves, its close inspection will be the subject of this investigation. We will take up these examples in the arguments below.

Previous Labels and Their Shortcomings

Many labels have been proposed for those influencing the addressees. Paul does not actually call them by any name, although he does describe them in various ways (the description closest to a label is the substantive participle in 6:13, οἱ περιτεμνόμενοι; see chapter 9). For example, Paul writes of "certain ones [τινές]" in the plural, or "he" or "it" in the singular "who" "unsettle" or "agitate" the addressees, but he does not actually label any of these persons "unsettlers" or "agitators" (cf. 1:6-7; 5:7-10).

Thus before turning to the issue of how the influencers are described, let us consider how they are labeled. The popular taxonomies include (1) Judaizers, (2) opponents or rivals, (3) agitators or troublemakers, (4) teachers.

Judaizers

Through the history of Christian interpretation, these influential people have been thought to be Jewish and labeled *Judaizers*.[9] This identification underwent significant changes when F. C. Baur painted a monochromatic portrait of supposed "Jewish Christian" opponents of Paul from the Jerusalem churches who dogged his trail. Baur found them in all of Paul's letters but derived the main thesis from Galatians, especially the narratives of chapter 2, which were approached by way of his conclusions from the controversy he perceived in Corinth. The singular

9. This can be traced back to Marcion's prologue to the letter in the mid-second century; see Schmithals, *Gnostics*, 13–29. When not so labeled, still so described; e.g., Barclay, "Mirror-Reading"; Martyn, *Galatians*, discussed below.

brushstroke for painting this portrait Baur found supplied by way of supposed parallels with particular passages in the later (second to third century) *Pseudo-Clementine Homilies* (combined with other later literature). On his reading of "Homilies II.17.2-3; XVII.16.1—19.7," Peter avenges the challenge of Paul at Antioch as told in Galatians 2. Peter undermines the right of Paul, veiled as Simon Magus in this later account, to consider himself an apostle. This literature thus provides in a single broad stroke the witness for a trajectory from the Jerusalem churches to Petrine Christianity—whether or not direct developments of Peter's intentions—thus providing an explanation of the supposed opposition to Paul and his groups from the beginning, and for centuries thereafter. These opponents Baur and those who follow him call "Judaizers."[10]

The hypothesis has proven extremely influential to this day, not only by explicit champions of this or similar views, but the lasting impression it has made continues to be evident in the shaping of the issues and constructions of subsequent interpretations that have taken exception to the conclusions, or various aspects thereof. However, at the linguistic level, this particular taxonomy, regardless of one's position on the theory itself, is suspect.

While judaizing is something that Gentiles seeking Jewish status may engage in, it is not appropriate for describing Jews who may be involved with initiating the interest in or facilitating this process among Gentiles.[11] The verb is intransitive, so that the terms *judaizing* and *Judaizers* refer to Gentiles who choose, at various levels and in various ways, to become or to live like Jews.[12]

10. Baur, *Paul*, passim, esp. 1.253, 256.

11. Moreover, it is not as clear as most interpreters think it to be that a pro-circumcision position toward Christ-believing Gentiles characterized Jewish believers in Christ, at least not on the NT evidence (contra, e.g., the a priori position of Hawkins, *Opponents*, 79–80; better is his comment on 81 that any characteristics should arise from the text of Galatians). In Acts 15, a minority of advocates of this view begin to bring sufficient pressure to bear to make it necessary to resolve the issue, and their view is reportedly vetoed (cf. Jervell, "Mighty Minority"). On my reading of Paul, in this project or others on Galatians (e.g., "Intruding 'Spies'") and in my work to date on Romans (cf. *Mystery*), there do not appear to be any Christ-believing Jewish advocates for circumcision of Gentile believers in Christ (so too, e.g., Munck, *Salvation*).

12. See Gaston, "Judaism of the Uncircumcised," 35–36; Dunn, *Theology of Galatians*, 10. For a full treatment see S. Cohen, *Beginnings*, 175–97, who includes a useful critique of the way this has been used for negative characterization in Christian interpretive tradition (cf. 185–97).

The same point may be made with respect to those who are hellenized; this takes place when a non-Greek chooses to live as a Greek, or "Greekly," one might say.[13] To speak of judaized Jews, like hellenized Greeks, makes no sense, although it is conceivable to speak of the rehellenization of a Greek person or people, say, expatriates, just as we could refer to the rejudaizing of some Jews, for example, by the Maccabees, when these people had left behind Jewish identity and ways of life, upon their return to them.[14]

Judaizers is a label not therefore best applied to the Jewish people who might promote the circumcision of Gentiles but to the ritual process (judaizing) or to the ones who are being circumcised. "Judaizers" is in most cases applied correctly only to former Gentiles who are now proselyte (Jews): judaized former Gentiles who are now proselytes.[15] If such proselytes are the ones involved in facilitating the ritual processes concerned with the proselyte conversion of Gentiles, then they might technically be considered Judaizers, not for their actions toward others but rather for their own prior action of becoming proselytes themselves.

On different grounds, J. Louis Martyn objects to the choice of *Judaizer*, because it has become in modern parlance usually a reference "to someone who wishes to hem in Gentile Christians by requiring them to live according to 'narrow' Jewish practices," when, by his reckoning, "the Teachers are embarked on an ecumenical mission" instead.[16]

This brings up a topic I will only touch upon here, but it flows naturally from the negative cultural valence, "a nasty or a comic edge,"

13. Ward, "Opponents," 186 n. 11; while noting the point, he does not adopt the conclusion.

14. That situation among "Judeans" tells against those who might maintain that there is no identifiable religious or cultural component that is sometimes most salient for translating the word Ἰουδαῖος and its cognates as "Jews," "Judaism," "judaize," etc. The "apostates" were still Judeans, but "bad" Jews until they rejudaized, for the term *rejudeanized* fails to capture the cultural (religious) nature of what was at dispute.

15. Cf. Esth 8:17 (LXX); Josephus, *J.W.* 2.454; similarly taken by H. Betz, *Galatians*, 112; Esler, *Galatians*, 137–38; differently translated ("to live like a Jew") but to the same conclusion ("to become Jewish proselytes") is Tomson, *Paul*, 229–30. Space does not permit argument here, and this interpretation is not necessary for this discussion. See my *Mystery*, 342–58.

16. Martyn, *Galatians*, 122.

that verbs with *-izein* (Eng.: *-izer*) endings typically connote.[17] What Martyn's comment seems to turn around is an implicit differentiation of the Christ-believing Jewish people in view and other Jewish people of the time—non-Christ-believing Jews or nonecumenical Christ-believing Jews—who are presumably "narrow" in their Jewish practices, namely, in terms of not viewing or relating to others, such as these Gentiles, in a way that Martyn would characterize (on what seems to be an anachronistic platform for measuring values of Paul's time) as "ecumenical mission." These people Martyn would presumably not object to identifying as Judaizers, because he accepts the "modern parlance"—however anachronistic that may be for the historical-critical task—applying it to a historical evaluation, and on the basis of the criterion that narrow Jewish practices are nonecumenical and thus judaizing. Thus, this ostensibly sensitive comment seems to carry within it a hidden critique that involves a disputable value judgment about the character of "ecumenical" (might not Martyn's criterion for defining ecumenical intentions for the influencers be judged by someone else as itself narrow, or even worse; if so, would that mean it was appropriate to call his view judaizing; moreover, in a supposed historical-critical application of the term?).[18] Martyn's inference is in keeping with the ineluctable value-laden nature of *-izein* verbal forms.

Ironically, this example, by way of defining the values buried in its ostensibly positive ecumenical point against applying the description to these people—both implicit and explicit—provides continued evidence for the negative ideological evaluation that has characterized usage of the terms *Judaizers* and *judaizing* in the history of Christian interpretation: a negative assessment of things Jewish where they are thought to differ from what is valued positively by the Christian interpreter as Christian.[19] Is this not sufficient cause to desist from its usage? Even if, for example, it was restricted to its proper theoretical usage as a synonymous reference to proselytes, these words have become inex-

17. S. Cohen, *Beginnings*, 175–79; *hellenize*, as used by Greeks, represents a positive turn of phrase, although it may not for even a so-called hellenized Jew like Philo (*Embassy* 147).

18. See N. Elliott, *Liberating*, 66–72, on the dejudaization of Paul characteristic of most traditional as well as New Perspective approaches.

19. In the context of this discussion, consider too the subtle value judgments and the implications that emerge from the extension of Martyn's justification for the adjectival or nominal use of "Jewish Christian" and "Christian Jew" in his commentary (*Galatians*, 118 n. 96, 588).

tricably tied up with communicating Christian distaste for things Jewish, at least that is what is implied when the phrase can be cited so often without adequate explanation as to why this identity or such activity would be necessarily valued negatively. In other words, would most Jewish people—or the historical Jewish Christ-believers in view in this text, to sharpen the point—agree with this negative value assessment per se? Is that how they used the term ἰουδαΐζειν?[20]

Where a term like *evangelist* or *missionary* is often imbued with a positive value, *Judaizer* or *proselytizer* is negatively valued, among past interpreters of Galatians anyway. It seems often simply ideological in appeal, because its usage has been provocative, appealing to a fear of compromising the freedom of Christ for slavery to Law among Jewish and Gentile people as though undifferentiated with respect to what the Law means for themselves, although this is arguably not the conflict of which Paul wrote when employing such contrasts. It is at least arguable that the freedom Paul has in view implies that Law observance enslaves; it does not in any of the documents of which I am aware, and on my reading this conclusion is not shared by Jewish believers in Christ who remained Torah-observant for themselves.[21]

Is it not clear that the descriptions and the label *Judaizers* have taken the wrong referent for the verbal phrase, are not appropriate for value-free efforts at historical inquiry (the inference being contained in the verb stem itself), and are not helpful for the advancement of interreligious dialogue or communal respect?

Opponents or Rivals

The concept of the influential ones as opponents or rivals of Paul, and his particular proclamation of the good news to the Galatian Gentile addressees, is well established (hereafter just *opponents*). This conclusion has shaped the view of their identity and disposition to Paul and his brand of belief and message as much as any.[22]

20. Martyn's view of *ioudaizein* is qualified further (*Galatians*, 236), where he observes that it "seems to have about it a ring that is artificial—perhaps even somewhat false—referring to Gentiles who take up wholly or in part the Jewish way of life, without thoroughgoing conviction from the heart"; yet on 154 it is defined as having the historical meaning "to live in a Jewish manner."

21. So too, e.g., Fredriksen, *From Jesus*, 146.

22. Instructive is the title of Hawkins's 1971 dissertation: "The Opponents of Paul in Galatia," although this language is found in the titles and arguments of the majority of works dealing specifically with this matter.

The dynamics of this identification have played an important and in some ways new role in recent debates on Galatians, its rhetorical and historical situations, and its message.[23] As discussed in the appendix, this development is readily apparent to the reader who engages the past twenty-five years of Galatians research, since the move to classical rhetorical genres was initiated by H. D. Betz's work.[24] His thesis maintains that Paul was engaged in forensic speech in order to "defend" his apostleship and message, an approach that highlights mirror-reading to pose explicit opposition to Paul, thus interpreting Paul's response to those labeled as his opponents.

Although other rhetorical approaches have often challenged the characterization of the letter's rhetoric as judicial, they have less often dismissed the prior understanding of the situation upon which classification of the letter under this genre is determined. But this classification cannot arise from the invention and arrangement aspects of the rhetorical process, as it would have for the author facing a situation. We are approaching the task precisely backward, from the expressions that seem to us to appear within the rhetoric to trying to construct the situation; we must hypothesize the historical situation that would make sense of those elements. Thus, Betz's approach, in which he first describes the situation as though certain, and then applies the rhetorical category he deems as most fitting, is open to criticism. (This criticism characterizes the other classical rhetorical evaluations of the letter too.) For his thesis, a prior situational sketch that involves opponents of Paul is essential.[25] But this hypothesis must be proven from the rhetoric, because it cannot, with our present information, be otherwise known.

Indeed, although it is clear from Paul's rhetorical response that he opposes the influence of these people, several interpreters have chal-

23. In a different direction than the rhetorical approaches, e.g., Tarazi, *Galatians*, 1–5, argues that Paul has made multiple trips to Galatia, expressly because each time after his departure these opponents supposedly return in an effort to undo his work.

24. "Literary Composition," 353–79; *Galatians*. Evidence of usage throughout interpretive history is traced by Classen, "St. Paul's Epistles"; Fairweather, "Rhetoric."

25. See H. Betz, *Galatians*, 1–9, where the introduction sets out the situation of the addressees, including the "anti-Pauline opposition." In his "Literary Composition," a sketch is not given, the "opponents" are just assumed, not even announced (357), on the basis of prior genre selection and evaluation of the rhetorical structure.

lenged the assumption that the ones influencing the addressees are or intend to be opponents of Paul. For example, Dahl argues that they did spread some "false reports about Paul"; nevertheless, "the results of my literary investigation challenges the traditional picture of Paul's 'opponents': they may not have considered themselves as opponents of the apostle but rather understood their own advocacy of circumcision and other observances as a continuation and completion of his work."[26] Dahl's conclusion that they know Paul's work is related to his understanding that these people are proclaiming a message of Christ and have knowledge of Paul as insiders to this coalition, a position that will be questioned below. But these advocates for circumcision of the addressees may well think—apart from much if any knowledge of Paul, or others of this coalition, and without sharing any faith in Jesus Christ's death as meaningful for themselves—that the interests of the addressees would be well served by what their message of good promises them. Moreover, Dahl wondered if those in Galatia who are turning toward the influencers' message have done so "quite possibly on the assumption that Paul would approve what they were doing."[27] Dahl advances a suggestion of M. Luther Stirewalt, "who assumes that representatives of the Galatian churches have asked Paul whether they ought to undergo circumcision," and concludes: "I find this convincing. The recipients may well have wondered why Paul delayed his reply and wrote an ironic and rebuking type of letter."[28]

An elaborate challenge to Betz's view on this point is sustained by George Lyons. He shows the logical and methodological problems with assuming Paul's response is apologetical or framed by formulations of his opposition. Instead, Paul's rhetorical approach reflects his own argumentative style, and his autobiographical remarks support the larger rhetorical aims of the letter, demonstrated also in the differences Lyons finds between Galatians and 1 Thessalonians.[29]

The "function of Paul's autobiographical remarks," he observes, "depend on the answers to two prior questions: Who are Paul's opponents? and, What are their charges against him?" which lead to historical reconstructions largely dependent upon "mirror-reading" to guide

26. Dahl, "Galatians," 50.
27. Dahl, "Galatians," 49.
28. Dahl, "Galatians," 90–91.
29. Lyons, *Pauline Autobiography*, 78–79, 104, 224–27.

interpretation."[30] This move, he argues, is a "fundamentally mistaken" approach that necessarily skews exegesis.[31] Although the weakness of various aspects of the construction are often noted, this method is indebted to the legacy of F. C. Baur, which is predicated on the notion that "Paul's autobiographical remarks respond apologetically to specific accusations made by invading Judaizing opponents, against which he defends the independence and/or consistency of his gospel and apostleship."[32]

Thus, regarding opponents, in a way that sets up nicely several other aspects for critical evaluation of their identity we have considered already or will now, Lyons concludes that the designation is simply inappropriate:

> Certainly Paul opposed some he identified as troublemakers and perverters of the gospel, but this need not imply that they had previously opposed him. It is not certain whether the opposition was mutual or only from Paul's side, whether the intentions of the "opponents" were malicious or well-meaning, whether they understood Paul's position correctly or not and vice versa.[33]

A growing number of interpreters observe that the notion these influential people are opposing, for one, Paul's apostleship, the case as it has been historically understood, is highly questionable.[34] Second, there has been an emerging realization that it is possible those influencing these Gentiles were so unaware of the conflict, clever, or just misinformed as to present their message of circumcision not in intentional opposition to Paul's gospel, but as even complementing or completing what the addressees have already "begun," a proposal Paul denied vehemently (3:3; 5:11). Along this kind of line, for example,

30. Lyons, *Pauline Autobiography*, 80–81: "The designation 'mirror reading' arises from the presumption that what Paul denies, his opponents have asserted and/or that what he asserts, they have denied."

31. Lyons, *Pauline Autobiography*, 75–121; also Barclay, *Obeying;* idem, "Mirror-Reading."

32. Lyons, *Pauline Autobiography*, 76–77.

33. Lyons, *Pauline Autobiography*, 79.

34. In addition to Dahl and Lyons, see, e.g., Vos, "Argumentation"; Lategan, "Situation"; Muddiman, "Anatomy"; Vorster, "Dissociation," 302; Koptak; "Rhetorical Identification"; Verseput, "Mission"; Sumney, "*Servants*," 149–50, 156, perceptively notes that the issue in Jerusalem and Antioch was Paul's gospel, not his apostleship.

Robert Jewett argued that Paul's use of ἐπιτελεῖσθε in 3:3 indicates that they represented themselves as "completing" Paul's work,[35] although the reason he gives for their maintenance of this view, the promise of perfection, is arguable.[36] Second, Terence Donaldson argues that it is implied in Paul's use of "still [ἔτι]" in 5:11, as an answer to a claim that he continued to preach circumcision.[37] My work below will add some different angles to develop along this line, but some current suggestions are well summarized by George Howard: "it is possible even to go further and argue that the opponents did not charge Paul at all, directly or indirectly, but actually considered him to teach circumcision as they themselves did and in fact treated him as an ally. . . . One can argue that the agitators not only preached a Jewish gospel but actually used the example of Paul to support their views."[38]

It is thus fair to note at the outset that, whereas Paul opposed these people and their influence in no uncertain terms, their opposition to Paul is not certain.[39]

At the same time, however, Paul does oppose the influencers without compromise, cursing them doubly (1:8-9), which is severe indeed;[40] sarcastically wishing the knife they wish to wield on the addressees' member will slip and castrate their own honor-seeking flesh instead (5:11); accusing them of envious and self-seeking motives (3:1; 5:7-12),

35. Jewett, "Agitators," 206–8; cf. Schlier, *Galater*, 123–24.

36. See the critique by Donaldson, "Gospel," 179–80; and my discussion below.

37. Cf. Donaldson, "Preaching Circumcision"; Borgen, "Paul"; R. Longenecker, *Galatians*, xcvii–xcviii, 12–20; Lyons, *Pauline Autobiography*.

38. Howard, *Crisis*, 8–9 (cf. 11); Hansen, *Abraham*, 98, suggests that this appeal was convincingly made by way of the Abraham story. This approach to Paul as having left matters unfinished is turned in a negative direction by Tarazi, who argues that this was an effort to deceptively outmaneuver Paul, and where this failed, they attacked his inconsistency as well (*Galatians*, 12–13).

39. Sumney, "*Servants*," 145–46, observes that it is likely that "the opponents claim that Paul does preach circumcision," that they "are not attacking Paul or his teaching," and that "it is unlikely that they also attacked his apostleship"; moreover, he concludes that "these Galatian teachers do not view themselves as opponents of Paul" (158) and "do not know they are Paul's opponents until his letter arrives" (159); nevertheless, Sumney surprisingly continues to label the influencers "opponents."

40. The issuing of the curse wish shows the level of Paul's concern that other approaches may fail to persuade. Brichto, *Problem of "Curse,"* 215–16; Morland, *Rhetoric of Curse* (on double curse, see 156–71).

manipulating methods (1:7; 4:17; 5:7-12; 6:12-13), and even veiled, spineless, self-protective interests that they represent as good news for the addressees instead (6:12).[41] But is it not perhaps Paul's own anticipation of this response that drives his defensive moves?

To put this another way, does not Paul anticipate the results to come after the influencers learn of his letter—assuming they will—thus preparing in advance a response to the most natural line of attack for this opposition to take: questioning, for example, his authority, his credentials, and the accuracy of his representation of this opinion as one widely shared by other Jewish authorities, perhaps doubting even the existence or reach of the influence of such supposed pillars of this coalition? Does Paul not expect that they will naturally then oppose his influence as harmful, indeed perhaps with the same kind of descriptions of motives and methods of which Paul has accused them—accusing him, for example, of unsettling, hindering, subverting, compelling—while appealing to the Scriptures and the long-standing traditional understandings and norms that follow therefrom? These, after all, have been arrived at by consensus, not as the result of the musings of some maverick who had traveled through their town now calling for the addressees' resistance based upon unacceptable membership norms.

It is highly probable that the subversive moves Paul makes, which have been interpreted to be defensive in response to direct opposition, rather anticipate the reactions he expects might follow from the profound impact that he hopes this letter will have upon the addressees.[42]

41. Lightfoot, *Galatians*, 222, although for reasons to be challenged below.

42. Similar is the position of Schütz, *Paul*, 128. This general dynamic for letter writers is noted by Stirewalt, *Epistolography*, 3, 6. Esler, *Galatians*, 66–68, discusses the theory of anticipatory rhetoric, especially in *Rhetorica ad Alexandrum* 1432b, 1436b–1437a (*prokatalepsis* or *prolepsis; praesumptio*); however, Esler limits the application in a way that is not dissimilar from mirror-reading and makes this point in fact directly against Lyons. Yet the rhetoric of anticipation need not have any sense of responding to an accusation already made or even thought to have been made. It can refer, as I am suggesting here, simply to the anticipation of the kinds of objection that will arise upon the hearing or reading of the rhetoric itself: the letter creates a situation that the author seeks to anticipate so as to succeed at the rhetorical task.

Although dealing with oration in a formal setting such as a court of law, which is different than the case we are considering in this letter (see appendix), and thus with opponents, which is a matter for Galatians at dispute in this project, the author of *Rhetorica ad Alexandrum* begins his treatment thus: "Anticipation is the device by

At least he expresses such conviction (5:10). Surely Paul could anticipate that these influential people would engage the addressees in new ways when, for example, their authority to proclaim this message as good for the addressees, or their motives or techniques of social control to achieve compliance, are jeopardized by this message of resistance. I suggest that it is such anticipation, perhaps purchased with the high price of prior experience, not only as a result of the views he defends (5:11) but having formerly opposed the Christ-believing coalition's appeal to such norms so vehemently himself (1:13), that lies behind the authority issue of dissociation that marks Paul's letter so strongly throughout.

Paul naturally considers the developments in Galatia to imply an opposition to the fundamental truth of the good news of Christ that he has proclaimed. Although not necessarily directed toward Paul by the influencers, their reaction—to the degree that it is a reaction to the claims of the addressees considered inappropriate to their present standing as Gentiles, and to the degree that Paul is aware of this reaction and any accompanying response—is a veiled opposition, from Paul's perspective, to the legitimacy of the addressees' claim predicated upon the work that God has done in Christ and through Paul's ministry. The influencers' response, because disputing that claim, or at least modifying the means whereby it can be achieved on the normative terms that they uphold, is itself taken by Paul to be oppositional. And surely some justification for the influencers' reaction will have been offered to the addressees, of which Paul may have learned. But this is quite different from intention to oppose Paul per se. It is quite possible that the influencers have presented their response as helpful and compatible, able to complete that which their association with the message of good in this Christ had begun.

Paul's defensive posture has so defined the interpretation of this letter, not least by proponents of forensic rhetoric, that it has led most

---

which we shall remove ill-feeling that we encounter by anticipating the criticisms of our audience and the arguments of those *who are going to speak* on the other side" (1432b; emphasis added); and again: "This is how when speaking *first* we must *anticipate* the things that *are probably going to be said* by our opponents, in order to discredit them and weaken their force" (1433a; emphasis added); and finally: "Anticipation is the method by which you anticipate the objections that *can be advanced* against your argument and sweep them aside" (1439b; emphasis added; see also 1442b).

interpreters over the centuries to assume that Paul is defending himself in the face of direct opposition, whether taken to be to his supposed Law-free gospel, authority as an apostle, alternately argued dependence or independence of the leaders of this coalition, or even his seemingly unique interpretations of Scripture. Yes, he is in a sense defending himself, but it is arguably by organizing his rhetoric to make an irresistible, offensive, preemptive strike. This measure is necessary unequivocably to convince the confused and wavering addressees. For they must try, if they are to obey Paul now, to take up a posture of resistance in the face of the compelling immediacy of the ostensible good news offered by the influencers; while perhaps at the same time Paul and his once compelling authority become more distant, and the power of their former desire to please him at all costs grows dim.

Paul begins this letter by dissociating his authority in these (for the interpreter) vague terms: he is an apostle "from God, not from humans [human agents] or by a human [agency]" (1:1; cf. 1:10-12; 1:13—2:21; 6:17). Once the resistance Paul calls for in this letter is announced, is it not likely that Paul is establishing his right to higher authority than these influential people but at the same time preparing the addressees to stand their ground, because they cannot control the outcome, being subordinate to the ones influencing them?[43] Whether this can be proven or not, it challenges sufficiently, combined with the criticisms of other interpreters, the identification of, or label for, those influencing the addressees as opponents. As such, it may prejudice the interpretation prematurely, before the letter has had a chance to be read. As J. L. Martyn aptly puts the methodological case for the weakness of the customary label *opponents:* "this appellation prejudices the matter we are investigating by implying that these people derive their identity from their opposition to Paul, and, therefore, that their work is a reaction to his."[44]

43. The implications of the allegory in 4:22-30 are apposite; for Paul comes out of this narrative with a call not to overthrow these people but to resist them (5:1-12). Similar is Vorster, "Dissociation," 302.

44. Martyn, "Law-Observant," 312. He calls the label *opponents* "somewhat reductionist" (*Galatians*, 117). At the same time, however, he states in n. 95 here that it is "possible," and his approach actually runs along this line, "that, in part, they came to Galatia in order to counter Paul's work." Thus, although he does not like the label, he does adopt the idea to which it refers.

Esler's attack on those who approach the question of their identity as opponents with circumspection, specifically noting Martyn and Lyons, is itself questionable.

Whether or not these people have opposed Paul prior to the writing of this letter, it is extremely likely that they will be opponents of Paul after it arrives, that is, if the resistance to themselves for which Paul calls in this letter is effected by the addressees. Thus, it seems plausible to imagine Paul writing with this reaction in view, to the degree that they might become aware of Paul as the instigator, the one who has opposed them and stirred up the resistance with which they are now, after the letter, confronted. Is he not correct to anticipate that they will become his opponents thereafter?

Agitators or Troublemakers

The use of such descriptions and labels as *agitators, troublemakers,* and a host of others is too common to attempt to attribute to specific interpreters. Paradoxically, their noticeable rise in popularity in recent works may be in part due to efforts to avoid or improve upon the weaknesses now more commonly recognized for the traditional label *Judaizers.* They derive from Paul's characterizations of these people, as traced above, and are extended by the variety of translations available in each case, especially of ταράσσω, most frequently translated as "agitators" and "troublemakers."

However, these descriptions and labels merely mimic Paul's value judgments in the context of his efforts to alter the opinion of the addressees about them; therefore, they are not very useful for getting

---

He has not proven that they have opposed Paul on the basis of his interpretation of 1:1 or 5:11. And advocacy of historical suspicion certainly does not render one's arguments anachronistic (contra *Galatians,* 71); quite the contrary. Just because that culture was agonistic (ours is of course to some degree also, as such notes from Esler and myself now exemplify), does not mean that these people opposed Paul, which presumes a knowledge of him, and position for themselves, that are not proven. Moreover, it overlooks the fundamental suspicion with which any agonistic rhetorical attack must be approached: whether constructed according to rhetorical theories, ancient or modern, they can be misleading on purpose. Note too Tyson in an article seeking to set out a "methodology for reaching a decision on the particular problem of the occasion for Galatians" bases three of the primary principles for identifying the (note) "opponents" on the prior conclusion that Paul is defending himself, and thus promotes the value of mirror-reading ("Opponents," 243–44, passim; similar is the approach of Gunther, *Opponents*). Yet Tyson admits (244; emphasis added) that the label, "opponent, should be used with a degree of caution, for it *presupposes* a group determined on the overthrow of Paul's authority and position, *while such a group is not to be assumed at the outset*"!

beyond limited polemical stereotyping for identifying those influencing them. In fact, they get in the way. Because these labels are used to undermine the motives and methods of those influencing the addressees, they do not clarify their identity for later interpreters but undermine their authority for the wayward recipients and are thus simply too imprecise and biased in unhelpful ways for the historical-critical task.

Clues taken from the surface level of Paul's accusations must be approached with appropriate suspicion of the rhetorical intent. One finds the rhetorical technique spelled out for classical oration by the author of *Rhetorica ad Herennium* thus (1.5/8):

> From the discussion of the person of our adversaries we shall secure goodwill by bringing them into *hatred*, unpopularity [*invidiam* = envy], or *contempt*. We shall force hatred upon them by adducing some *base, high-handed, treacherous, cruel, impudent, malicious*, or *shameful act* of theirs. We shall make our adversaries unpopular by setting forth their violent behaviour, their *dominance, factiousness*, wealth, lack of self-restraint, high birth, *clients, hospitality, club allegiance*, or marriage alliances, and by making clear that *they rely more upon these supports than the truth*. We shall bring our adversaries into contempt by presenting their idleness, *cowardice*, sloth, and luxurious habits.[45]

Paul seeks by employment of this language precisely to change the perception of the addressees about these other people, to undermine the motives and methods of those influencing his addressees in a direction that he not only considers different and wrong but one that he condemns as anathema, leading the addressees to inadvertently delegitimate the meaning of Christ for themselves.[46] But it is a recognized tendency of such polemic to proceed by the stereotyping of out-groups without concern to enunciate the nuances of distinction

45. I have emphasized aspects that are found or implied in Paul's rhetorical approach to the influencers in Galatians, although not a public speech, and in view of having already argued that although Paul approaches the influencers as his adversaries, this does not mean that they have approached Paul as such. Some are less clear but probable, e.g., their allegiances, which are implied in their insincere "courting" and avoidance of suffering "for the cross of Christ," that is, there is some allegiance that is more important than the addressees' interest in this matter and in their affiliations, from which the addressees' compliance would gain them honor (4:17; 6:12-13). Similar is Cicero, *Inv.* 1.16/22.

46. See also the discussion of Thurén, *Derhetorizing*, 58–72.

that would be of concern for describing other in-group members.[47] Thus, any labels taken directly from the surface of Paul's language perpetuate for interpreters the disadvantaged position that the polemical author intends; in fact, the interpreters thereby categorize themselves by internalizing the stereotyper's ideology and thus, by nature, inhibiting the consideration of critical alternatives, for example, contradictions and issues that do not fall within the narrowly circumscribed framework of the author.[48] The relevance of this insight is heightened to the degree that Paul's efforts are recognized as falling along the line of "social categorization" that may be described in contradistinction to the dominant group's "social mobility" solution that is offered by way of proselyte conversion. Paul calls instead for "social change," a solution that is predicated upon his assessment that the boundaries cannot be negotiated by the subordinate subgroup on the dominant group's terms (i.e., no proselyte conversion is permitted for the addressees), and thus a solution that seeks to provide alternative arrangements that will raise the self-image of the subordinate group (e.g., Paul's emphasis upon the addressees' already present status as children of Abraham, full heirs of God as righteous ones, apart from the influencers' terms).[49] Such an approach has as a central dynamic the negative stereotyping of the alternate solution and its representatives; hence, Paul describes them as ταράσσοντες.

Overall, these labels and others like them fail to help the interpreter imagine the fuller identity of these people, their affiliations, or their motives. They remain wooden, mere shadows whose enormous influence upon the Galatian addressees and the trustful embrace these influential people have received from them to date are thereby rendered almost unimaginable. Failure to take account of these rhetorical dynamics of Paul's accusations not only undermines any effort to expand the description of these people and their interests but will lead to conclusions that are suspect or worse, as history attests. It is unlikely and would surely have to be proven that these people see themselves, their message, or their interaction as agitating or troublemaking, or

47. The processes of stereotyping are set out by Hogg and Abrams, *Social Identifications,* 64–91; see esp. the discussions of the accentuation aspects of categorization, 68–78. See also A. Cohen, *Symbolic Construction,* 74–96.

48. Cf. Hogg and Abrams, *Social Identifications,* 78–84.

49. Cf. Hogg and Abrams, *Social Identifications,* nn. 26–29. See also the discussion, although to a different conclusion, in Esler, *Galatians,* 49–57.

would call themselves any such things. Is it not probable that they would describe the author of the letter in these ways after its arrival, assuming its message to resist themselves was obeyed?

Teachers

In a series of articles and a commentary on Galatians, J. L. Martyn has noted the weakness of many of the descriptions and labels under discussion. He has suggested that these influential people are better regarded and labeled as "the Teachers."[50] "Teachers" may be the best of the suggestions to date, because this label avoids the limiting value judgments inherent in the other choices and describes at least a significant part of their activity—and unlike the others, an identity with which they probably would agree; nevertheless, it is probably too restrictive for describing their role or interaction in relation to the addressees. For one, the role of teaching as the primary identifying description may infer that they have created the exigence—in Martyn's case it does—when the interpreter should remain open to the possibility that the exigence for these influential people was created first by the addressees—as a result of the teachings of Paul!—after the addressees have approached these people with their claim to a standing that was not established upon the basis of the influencers' controlling membership or reference group norms. Although their response may create the exigence from the addressees' and Paul's vantage point, it may not have been their action of teaching but their action of welcoming that triggered the complex mess that resulted thereby and to which both the addressees and Paul now variously respond.

And second, does *teachers* not limit the interpreters' hypotheses for these people to but one vocational aspect among the many probable ways in which they are exerting influence upon the addressees? In other words, might not their influence upon the addressees go beyond the formalities of the role usually associated with the task of teaching? Of course, some social interaction with students might be arguably implied for teachers, but it may be overlooked by the many readers who, unlike Martyn, have proven that they do not really consider these people with any depth of imagination. After all, these people do appear to manipulate in other ways as well, certainly as

50. Martyn, *Galatians,* 118, lists the following as explicit references to the Teachers: 1:6-9; 3:1-2, 5; 4:17; 5:7-12; 6:12-14.

Paul sees the case, accusing them of "persuasion," to be sure, but also of "unsettling," "excluding," "obstructing," "seducing," and "compelling." Moreover, it seems anachronistic to imagine that the nature of their influence or identity is confined to teaching within the way social networks appear to have functioned in their cultural world, with the kind of, for example, kinship and patronage dynamics that would obtain.

The Prevailing Descriptions of the Influencers

The prevailing portraits of the influencers share many features, and a clear consensus view is easily traced. Yet for every rule there are, to be sure, exceptions, and the consensus portrait is no exception to that rule, even if the exceptions are few. Listing some of these along with my own criticisms serves the purpose of bringing into question the appropriateness of allowing these widely held aspects of identity to direct the role of describing or labeling these people.

Prior to any investigation of the rhetoric itself, no matter how often repeated, the prevailing views represent not unquestionable facts but the conclusions of earlier interpreters, framed by their own interpretive lenses and interests. They thus should represent, for the next interpreter, merely working presuppositions. Thus, critical investigation of these descriptions as well as the labels just considered will help to clarify the landscape of this study, particularly in the interests of advancing historical-critical methodology for the interpreter of Galatians.

The issue before us may be posed in this way: given the limitation of not knowing their name(s) or an occupational title to identify them by, such as we call the writer "Paul," or a simple affiliation in epistolary terms, such as calling the recipients "addressees," what descriptions and labels can we imagine that these other people would be willing to accept from the interpreter as appropriate for identification of themselves?

We have just considered some of Martyn's analytical comments when mounting a critique of limitations of the prevailing labels, although noting that he did not always disagree with the dynamics to which they refer. Because he has done more than many other interpreters to imagine their identity, interests, message, and methods, his work provides a good platform for addressing a host of other identifications of these people. One will observe immediately, however, that his portrait of these people still articulates many of the almost universally held aspects of their identity and actions that have shaped and continue to shape the reading of this letter. The framework of this picture includes important features that are hardly argued, because they have been repeated often enough that apparently they seem certain. I will now set out a few comments at length so that the reader can see how the complex of connected initial decisions becomes the basis for the structure upon which not only the portrait of the influencers is built but the situation and message of the letter as well.

What portrait does Martyn provide then for these teachers? He lists fourteen aspects of their identification, but combining the most representative will serve the present purpose of outlining the consensus views: "the Teachers are *messianic Jews*, at home among Gentiles, in the sense of being able not only to live among them but also to make effective, apologetic contact with them."[51] This contact must not be taken to imply that the teachers are lax in their observance of Jewish religious life, which Martyn clearly states in the midst of another important building block: "the Teachers are in touch with—indeed, understand themselves to represent—*a powerful circle of Christian Jews in the Jerusalem church*, a group utterly *zealous* for the observance of the Law."[52] Thus they not only practice Torah observance but their understanding of the Law is defined by their relationship with the Jerusalem church, which they refer to as "their 'mother.'"[53] Comments made early in this work admit some concern with concluding that the teachers have come to Galatia from Jerusalem,[54] but overall, the following statement is programmatic:

> he [Paul] refers in Gal 4:25 to *the Jerusalem church that is being made present in Galatia* by the Teachers' claims (and probably on the basis of their relationship with the False Brothers). Thus, *to the degree* that, *under the sway of the False Brothers*, the Jerusalem church is offering *support* to the Teachers' work—thus reaching into the life of his churches as it earlier reached into the life of the Antioch church—Paul is sure that the Jerusalem congregation is itself producing Gentile churches that are enslaved.[55]

51. Martyn, *Galatians*, 118 (emphasis added).
52. Martyn, *Galatians*, 119 (emphasis added).
53. Martyn, *Galatians*, 126; see also 117 n. 95, and the references to other discussions listed there.
54. E.g., Martyn, *Galatians*, 126.
55. Martyn, *Galatians*, 464–65 (emphasis added).

They are not native to Galatia, but "outsiders": "Paul consistently differentiates the Teachers from the members of his Galatian congregations. He addresses the Galatians quite directly as 'you,' whereas he always refers to the Teachers by such terms as 'some person,' 'they,' 'these people.' The Teachers are *outsiders* who have only *recently* come into the Galatian churches."[56] Martyn summarizes their interests thus:

> It seems highly probable that Paul takes the path requiring self-correction because he *knows* that the Teachers are in *fact* referring to their message as "*the gospel.*" It follows that, no less than the apostle himself, the Teachers are in the proper sense of the term *evangelists*, probably finding their basic identity not as persons who struggle against Paul, but rather as those who preach "the good news of God's Messiah." *They are, then, Jews who have come into Galatia proclaiming what they call the gospel, God's good news.*[57]

These snippets culled from Martyn's commentary make no pretense to adequately represent the extensive research, nuanced discussion, or complete conclusions of his work, but they do capture his working assumptions in a summary useful for the present purpose of creating a sketch that is representative of his as well as the prevailing views. In fairness, at least the corroborating portrait of another important work should be introduced.

The summary of the discussion of these people in Richard Longenecker's commentary serves such a purpose. Noting that in the past 150 years various aspects of the identification of the influencers have been "both challenged and considerably refined," he observes: "the common, *almost uncontested* view during the patristic and Reformation periods was that Paul's opponents were *Jewish Christian Judaizers.*"[58] Today the interpreter may "more accurately" define these people as

56. Martyn, *Galatians*, 120 (emphasis added).

57. Martyn, *Galatians*, 121 (emphasis added).

58. R. Longenecker, *Galatians*, lxxxix (emphasis added). The history of interpretation is traced by Hawkins, "Opponents," who summarizes his own conclusion in the abstract to his dissertation thus: "it is apparent that Paul's opponents are not judaizing Gentile Christians (as many people today believe) but Jewish Christian judaizers, missionaries who have come into Paul's churches trying to induce the Gentile Christians to adopt the Law of Moses." Many of the exceptions will occupy discussion below, but the main lines are otherwise ubiquitous: cf. among studies of Paul, e.g., Sanders, *Paul, the Law*, 18–19; and Galatian commentators. The major lines are also well traced in Ellis, "Opponents"; Bruce, "Galatian Problems."

"Christian Jews—who came from the Jerusalem church to Paul's churches in Galatia."[59] Longenecker proceeds in his extensive commentary on the summary grounds that 1:6-7 and 6:12 "point conclusively to their being Christians."[60]

These influential people are taken by Martyn then, and with him the overwhelming consensus of interpreters ancient and modern, to fall into the following primary descriptive categories:

- Jewish people or groups;
- Christ-believers with a different gospel of Christ from Paul, his being ostensibly Law-free for all, whereas theirs combines faith in Christ with circumcision and Law-observance, so that Gentile Christ-believers must become proselytes or observant of Torah. They are usually labeled *Christians*, *Jewish Christians*, or *Christian Jews* (hereinafter not used but rather such descriptions as *Christ-believers*, or the adjectival *Christ-believing* or *in-Christ* Jews or Gentiles, etc., will be substituted);
- oriented toward a Jerusalem Christ-believing coalition.[61] That is, they do not function independently but rather in some way represent—although perhaps actually misrepresent, whether intentionally or not—the views and interests of the Jerusalem-based apostles. Even if not outright commissioned, then at least they function in a way that is understood to be sympathetic with the so-called pseudo-brethren who had been active in Jerusalem (2:1-10), and "the ones from James" as well as "the ones for circumcision" in Antioch (2:11-14). They are usually labeled "Jerusalem Christians" or "Palestinian Christians" or "Jewish Christians" or "Christian Jews"; in terms of "the Jerusalem church" or "Jewish Christianity" (hereafter referred to as the *Jerusalem Christ-believing coalition[s]*, etc.);
- "missionaries" or "proselytizers"; that is, evangelistic in purpose;
- and "outsiders" to the Galatian situations or at least "churches."

59. R. Longenecker, *Galatians*, xcv.

60. R. Longenecker, *Galatians*, xcv.

61. Cf. Boissevain, *Friends*, 170–205. Defining coalition as "a temporary alliance of distinct parties for a limited purpose" is useful, especially the emphasis on the temporariness implied in such groups in order to achieve a limited purpose, yet accumulating more tasks as time passes without yet achieving that purpose (171).

It is time to turn to investigating and challenging these constructions of the identity of those influencing the Galatian addressees, along with developing an alternative construction. Here, this evidence will be set out and evaluated relative to the immediate question of what descriptions should be granted in an investigation of this letter's situations and messages, more specifically, of the identity of the addressees and those influencing them. This must be done in order to limit as little as one can the possibilities for imagining their identity when engaging the rhetoric of the letter anew. The foundation of each of the following interpretations, although in many ways inextricably linked one to the other, will be briefly set out, along with some indications of their limitations, which show how, if accepted at the outset, they would unavoidably direct, if not entirely prejudice, the interpretive results.

Jewish People or Groups

Paul never actually calls these people or this group, or even possibly groups, Jewish. However, their advocacy of circumcision is implied in the rhetorical context, which is full of concern to oppose their influence by arguing for the addressees' present identification in such terms as their existing relationship to Abraham and God, yet not Torah. It is difficult to imagine that these advocates of circumcision for others are not themselves circumcised, and in this case understanding that to mean that they are themselves "complete" according to the norms of Jewish membership that are at issue in Paul's rhetorical response. At least one reference to these circumcision advocates arguably indicates that they are themselves circumcised (6:13; see discussion below in chapter 9), which renders them most likely, in this rhetorical context, Jewish people.

Yet a few interpreters have argued against this identification, or at least that it should be qualified as representing only some of the influential people at work among the addressees in ways that Paul, in this letter, seeks to undermine.

In the first direction, perhaps the work of Johannes Munck has been the most influential. He proposes, largely on the basis of the participle περιτεμνόμενοι in 6:13, that these influential people represent some of Paul's Gentile converts who have, on the basis of their former association with synagogues and present interaction with Scripture, had themselves circumcised; hence, he calls them "circumcised Gentiles."[62]

62. Munck, *Salvation*, 89, 129–34. Some interpreters have, quite differently than Munck, suggested that these are Gentiles, or at least some of them working along-

Circumcision would seem to render them proselytes and not Gentiles, although the way Munck ostensibly conceives of this identity outside of Jewish communal life makes for a possibly unique situation calling for a unique taxonomy; this inference will be challenged by a close examination of several aspects of his argument often overlooked.

In the second direction are the two-front theories of Wilhelm Lütgert and James Ropes.[63] This argument holds that, on the one front, there are Jewish advocates of a nomistic lifestyle (Baur's Judaizers), and thus it still retains a view of some of these people as Jewish.[64] But on the other front, they posit libertine enthusiasts, primarily in order to make sense of the parenetic material of chapters 5 and 6, where they take the language to imply the influence of an antinomistic party. The weakness of this view will be discussed below and in chapter 9, but this approach did not and does not convince many of the interpreters of Galatians.

In another vein, although still holding them to be Jewish, some have separated them from nomistic interests. Walther Schmithals in the sense of gnostics; Robert Jewett in the sense of political expediency. Schmithals makes much of the fact that Paul seems to say those influencing the addressees do not keep the Law (6:13), to support his thesis that they are Gnostics.[65] Thus while remaining Jews, they are not Jew-

---

side Jewish people too, who have come from outside as missionaries, but they are representatives of the Jewish churches of Jerusalem or Antioch and their interests (e.g., Hirsch, Michaelis); or, if the Gentiles are natives of Galatia, they are instruments of Jerusalem interests (Neander). Cf. Hawkins, "Opponents," 29–30.

63. Lütgert, *Gesetz*, 22–58, also argues that chapters 1 and 2 are often directed against the "freedom" advocates, and 4:8-9 holds the epistle together against both fronts of Law or return to paganism (67–88); Ropes, *Singular*. See also Enslin, *Christian Beginnings*, 216–24.

64. Ropes, *Singular*, 9, actually seems to be referring in some cases to non-Christ-believing Jewish people on the one front: "between Christian believers and unbelieving Jews there must be permanent opposition," which he follows by observing that this is one aspect that "reveals to us the situation in Galatia." But in his summary on 44–45, it becomes clear that the influencers are considered "certain Gentile Christians" who have "proved susceptible to the efforts of local synagogue Jews."

65. Schmithals, *Gnostics* 33–34, 39–43. On 18–19 he argues that Paul does not know much about them; working from hearsay, Paul misunderstands their comment about flesh to be against his bodily weakness. He wrongly thinks that his Jewish-style arguments will persuade the addressees, because Paul does not realize that their interest in circumcision is within Gnosticism. Only by the time later

ish in the sense of the nomistic practices usually associated with this identity, at least among the kind of Jewish people who would be active enough in religious nomistic lifestyle to be advocating proselyte conversion for the addressees. Jewett argues that the real objective of these influential people, who are Christ-believing Jews who have "convinced themselves that circumcision of Gentile Christians would thwart Zealot reprisals," is thus to travel from Judea to represent the interests of the Jerusalem churches.[66] They are still Jewish, but their interest in the addressees is not really the practice of Judaism.

Although most of these positions do not actually seek to refute these influential peoples' Jewishness (only Munck does), they are generally, when not categorically, dismissed in recent interpretive work.[67] But their existence in modern research represents a caution sign that should not be ignored for the interpreter seeking to avoid unnecessary limitations at the start of an investigation of their identity.

Christ-Believers with a Different Gospel of Christ

That these people are Christ-believers with a different gospel of Christ that combines Law with Christ-faith (i.e., Judaizers) is virtually unchallenged in the history of interpretation. The depth of antithetical bedrock presupposed between Paul and the other influential Jews who believed in Jesus is succinctly captured in James D. G. Dunn's summary for a distinguished 1994 symposium on Paul and the Mosaic Law: "The common ground we seek, therefore, is not first and foremost agreement among ourselves, but some measure of consensus on *the common ground* between Paul and his fellow *Christian* Jews *with whom he*

---

letters are written does Paul begin to understand them (also *Gnostics*, 245–53). See also Marxsen, *Introduction*, 45–58.

66. Jewett, "Agitators," 204–5; see also Harvey, "Opposition," 326–27.

67. Jewett's theory is an exception here, having influenced many recent interpreters to various degrees (e.g., R. Longenecker, *Galatians*, xciii–c), although Jewett does not actually question their identity as Jewish, or even their own behavior as Jewish, but only their interest in the addressees. Against Schmithals's view, which is largely predicated upon gnostic tendencies he detects being confronted in the Corinthian and other correspondence, much of it from later centuries, there simply are not sufficient gnostic traits implied in Galatians, quite the contrary, and we have insufficient evidence of Gnosticism among Jews at the time anyway. Moreover, these later developments are perhaps based upon later misreadings of Paul, see, e.g., H. Betz, *Galatians*, 7; Wilson, "Gnostics?"; Ellis, "Opponents."

was in dispute."[68] In other words, for these scholars, according to Dunn, it would seem that this aspect of F. C. Baur's interpretation is no longer questioned, for although many issues of Paul and the Law are still under discussion, prior knowledge includes the assumption as though a fact—"common ground"—that Paul's dispute was with his "fellow *Christian* Jews."[69]

Rare exceptions have ostensibly appeared recently in articles by Nikolaus Walter and John Muddiman, who have argued explicitly that those influencing the situation are non-Christ-believing Jews; as will be seen, however, these seem to constitute for them merely those who put pressure upon the Christ-believing influencers within the Galatian communities, thus these people represent another category of influencers.[70] Walter argues that the influencers are part of a wide-scale countermission against the Law-free gospel of Paul and the other leaders, and they offer "the opposite of a gospel of Christ: a gospel without Christ Jesus."[71] They intentionally call their message a "gospel," by which they echo Paul, as a "missionary 'trick'" in order to fool the Galatian addressees: "the opponents indeed stand outside the churches, outside any relationship with Christ, and they do not desire so much to invade the churches in particular; but rather, on the contrary, they want to undermine and obliterate by means of 'compelling' away from Christ toward Torah (cf. 6:12f.)."[72] Muddiman's comment seems to be

68. Dunn, "In Search," 309 (emphasis added).

69. Tyson, "Opponents," 252, differently notes that "they cannot be non-Christian Jews, for Jews would more likely denounce the entire Christian movement than attempt to influence it." This logic fails to consider, among other things, that it is only a few Gentiles somewhere in Galatia that are in view, not the "entire" movement. Moreover, it is not clear that they opposed the movement of whatever size and importance it was in Galatia or sought to influence anyone away from Christ.

70. Walter, "Gegner"; Muddiman, "Anatomy." Also Kosmala, *Hebräer*, 110–11, suggests that they are non-Christ-believing Essenes, based upon Acts 15:5, where Pharisaic believers are mentioned, but that they believe in Christ is not stated (from Hawkins, "Opponents," 44; differently Ellis, "Opponents," 293–95, has argued for the possibility of Essenes, but they are Christ-believing Judaizers). Baasland, "Persecution," 149 n. 30, in an undeveloped comment, recognizes that "since students largely have focused their attention on the confrontation between Paul and his opponents they have failed to ask if Paul is not attacking the argumentation of ordinary Jews. Historically, this is highly possible, and Gal. itself seems to suggest such an interference of outsiders."

71. Walter, "Gegner," 351 (translation mine).

72. Walter, "Gegner," 351, 355.

predicated upon a clear distinction between those who are "outside the Church" and those who are Christ-believers. These outsiders "are willing to use all the means of synagogue discipline, namely detention, fines, beatings and excommunication, to pressurize Jewish Christians into demanding that their fellow, non-Jewish, Christians accept circumcision."[73]

Both of these interpreters portray the influencers as representatives of non-Christ-believing Pharisaic Judaism, although for Muddiman such Judean Pharisees are once removed, because the actual influencers in Galatia are fellow members of the Christ-believing communities. It is not clear how the addressees are engaged by Walter's Pharisees, whom he has standing outside the communities of Christ-believers; thus, I will assume that he too has split the influencers into two groups: those outside and those inside the Christ-believing communities Paul addressed. Both draw strength for their points from the logic of Paul's appeal to the singular seed of Abraham, an approach that does not seem to be arguable to any person who believes in Jesus Christ, whatever else they might also believe. This argument, although suspect on the grounds of mirror-reading, seems to be an especially strong point against the consensus view.

Yet Muddiman's appeal is based upon a level of interest and authority for the Judean or even local synagogues that is without precedent and difficult to comprehend. How could they bring this kind of pressure to bear upon these go-betweens on behalf of Gentiles who have no identity with or in Jewish communal terms? The proposal follows a line of argument that shares some similarities with that made by Harvey and differently by Jewett. Such action on the part of Judean or any other representatives of Pharisaism is unattested. And it is also predicated upon an unattested notion of self-interest toward "righteous Gentiles," whom these "hostile Jewish authorities" and "zealous, exclusivist and persecuting Pharisee[s, as had been Paul himself]" are characterized as seeking to keep Paul from "siphoning off."[74] Finally, Muddiman's position is actually not consistent, bringing back in some way the role of the Jerusalem Christ-believing leaders and implying that the influencers in Galatia are Christ-believers who are themselves victims of outside pressure in a way that seems to reflect Jewett's basic thesis, for he also argues that "the agitators in Galatia must have

73. Muddiman, "Anatomy," 261.
74. Muddiman, "Anatomy," 268–70.

claimed that they had the highest authority, that of the Jerusalem apostles, for pragmatic compromise in face of persecution."[75]

Walter's brief article lacks some concrete social reality, for example, by arguing that the influencers stand outside the churches of Galatia; but one needs to explain their influence inside of them; moreover, it is not clear where Pharisees would be located or what their interest would be in separate Christ-believing groups of non-Jewish people. Would the addressees and their groups not be regarded as pagans? Would they not be members of the dominant society where power was concerned? What is the logic of a view that takes the social action to be motivated by the opposition set in the more theological terms of belief in Torah versus Christ? And why are non-Christ-believing Jewish Pharisees concerned with or in the position to compel such sectarian groups in such distant places, regardless of the hostility that might be attributed toward their rivalry with a past member among themselves like Paul? If his mission and communities are no longer Jewish and no longer in Judea among themselves, of what concern is it to Judean Pharisees? This view also seems to imply that the influencers are actually Christ-believers caught in the middle. The difference is that it is not the Jerusalem apostles but Judean Pharisees who do not believe in Christ that are on the other side applying the pressure, and their reach from Judea to Galatia again seems to follow the general line developed by Jewett.

Both portraits are in my view anachronistic, as well as dangerous in a way that does not seem to be anticipated: they create the impression that the line of definition and tension is between two religious institutions, Christianity and Judaism, much as they are sometimes portrayed later along monolithic lines, and this is heightened to the degree that they attribute to Jewish interests the kind of motives that have dominated later Christian Gentile stereotypes of Pharisees as selfish and greedy. Paul represents the new institution of Christianity, albeit one of two branches that have emerged, whereas these influential people represent Pharisaic Judaism in a way that has been often taken to signal presumed trends that are valued negatively by Christian interpreters in the stereotyping of later rabbinic Judaism.

In spite of my criticisms of these two proposals, they have at least argued against the consensus view, and scored a few points that need to be engaged in any investigation.

75. Muddiman, "Anatomy," 262.

What about their message as one of Christ plus Law? Martyn and almost all interpreters again are certain that this message is about both Christ and Law (Muddiman and Walter included, if I have rightly judged their implied influencers). For example, after examining the many methodological pitfalls of mirror-reading evident in the work of other interpreters of Galatians, which he rightly ties to the weaknesses inherent in this "extremely problematic" though necessary approach, John Barclay summarily maps out the "certain or virtually certain" results thus: "On the basis of Paul's reference to 'another gospel' (1.6-9) it seems clear that the opponents were Christians."[76]

Thus even in studies seeking to eliminate methodological weaknesses that characterize the state of research, with regard to the identity of these people and their message as another gospel of Christ, this assessment is virtually gospel itself. But is it really that clear?

This conclusion revolves around several assumptions, most importantly that these influential people in Galatia are connected in some way with Jerusalem Christ-believers or their interests and that Paul's reference to "another gospel"—note that its relationship to Christ is not mentioned—in the midst of delivering an ironic ridicule of the addressees, should be taken at face value to mean that they proclaimed a "gospel of Christ." This is predicated on the assumption that only a message in some way about Jesus Christ would have been called a gospel by Paul, regardless of the kind of rhetoric in which he is engaged. That is, regardless of whether it is recognized that Paul brings up this language in an ironic rebuke in the face of the failure of the addressees to realize that they have been relating to it inappropriately, as though it was as good for themselves as the one message of good in Christ they have received from Paul, it nevertheless must have been called a gospel in order for Paul to now do so. This decision involves another arguable interpretive move, concluding that the term *gospel* itself was not open to use by Paul, the addressees, or the influencers, outside of reference to the good news of Christ, but it was. As chapter 10 will show, it was a term widely used for other messages of good, not least political ones like announcement of victory or Caesar's birthday, mundane ones like the receipt of olives at a wedding, ironic ones like the death received by David's messenger upon delivery of the supposed good news of Saul's death, and perhaps, like it is to this day, for

76. Barclay, "Mirror-Reading," 263, 265. Similar appeal to this comment in 1:6-7 is made in virtually every commentary surveyed.

any ostensibly uncontestable message, such as the pun in the last paragraph was predicated upon.

Martyn joins many others who observe that calling this other message a gospel is the last thing that Paul would choose to do apart from the fact that it is what these influential people call their message.[77] I mention this matter here to indicate the weakness of adopting this view or forging any labels for these people on the basis of this conclusion prior to investigation of the letter independent of its assumptions: it is an interpretation that involves more than one prior interpretive move, not a fact, and far from clear.

As for whether these people proclaim the Law as their message of good, this virtual certainty, as usually conceived anyway,[78] is also suspect. If they were engaging Jewish people, such a message would make more sense, but why would they be proclaiming that which is obligatory for Jewish people to those who were not yet Jewish, on their own terms of definition?

There is a vast difference between proclaiming a message about identity transformation to Jewish identity, that is, about becoming a proselyte, and teaching someone who is already a proselyte how to live Jewishly, that is, observe Torah. Although proselyte candidates are certainly learning Torah-observant life during the ritual process, so that they are merely being in a sense confirmed by the community by the time of completion for a lifestyle that is virtually identical with that of other Jewish people, certainly with proselytes, this is not the same thing as many interpreters imply when they construe the issue in Galatia as one also of Torah observance rather than merely an issue of proselyte conversion. There is a discrepancy in terms of what Paul appears to be able to say toward undermining the addressees' interest in becoming people under the Law, for he implies that it is not Torah observance for proselytes but the gaining of proselyte identity that is in dispute.

Paul raises the suspicion that these people are not properly preparing the addressees for the lifestyle that will result upon completion, that they will then be "obliged to observe the whole Law" (5:3). Although this statement may be taken several ways, it at least throws into doubt the idea that the Torah was being proclaimed as "gospel"

77. Martyn, *Galatians*, 121.

78. Cf. Martyn, *Galatians*, 122–25, 134–35, 302–6: "in their christology, Christ is secondary to the Law" (124).

per se; Paul ridicules the addressees for their naïve failure to perceive the consequences of the choice they are contemplating as though it would make things easier for themselves to become accepted. Is it not rather the addressees' assumption of status as righteous ones, as though already acquired apart from proselyte conversion, that defines the dispute about circumcision as entrance requirement when the addressees are within the sphere of the influencers' norms? In other words, is not the exigence defined by whether the addressees have a legitimate status claim while remaining Gentiles, and not a concern (more appropriate for a Christ-believing proselyte anyway) for Torah observance *plus* faith in Christ?

Oriented toward a Jerusalem Christ-Believing Coalition

The long and widely held view that those influencing the Galatian addressees have something to do with the Jerusalem Christ-believing establishment under the leadership of the other apostles relies upon a premise that is remarkably slim.[79] Where their identity as Christ-believers, as just reviewed, hangs at least upon the appearance of an implication on the surface level of the situational discourse units of the text, this view has no such thread upon which to attach itself to the Galatian situations. The irony is easily illustrated. For example, Heinrich Schlier informs us, in the midst of arguing that precise identification of influencers as from the Jerusalem church is not very important but that only Paul's perspective is important, because Paul's view is based on such principles that Paul would not respond much differently if "another shade of a legalistic Jewish-Christianity showed up among the Christians in Galatia."[80] Thus he presupposes the identification to be precise on several points of identity, and this naturally guides his understanding of what Paul's "principled" position is.

79. Dunn, *Jesus, Paul,* 161–62, suggests an explicit Antioch connection is possible, in addition to maintaining a Jerusalem one (so too Taylor, *Paul,* 175). Dunn actually posits a direct connection anyway, for this demonstrates, if not the action "from Jerusalem," but rather Antioch, it is still "the decision of the church at Antioch to fall in line with the ruling or wishes of the men from James" (161). This is close to Bruce's conclusion that representatives from Jerusalem, after going to Antioch, decided to visit "Antioch's daughter-churches in Galatia" ("Galatian Problems," 270). Thus the methodological foundation for this view is subject to the same criticism.

80. Schlier, *Galater,* 24.

Several interpreters bring the general methodological problem into plain view. For example, D. W. B. Robinson signals the problem: "It is often assumed that they [his Judaizers] had come from Jerusalem, but the epistle is silent on this point."[81] And Peter Richardson makes a similar point that those who draw upon the Antioch material too strongly to construct the situations in Galatia may easily err: "There is a danger of reading more into the account than is warranted; and in the absence of clear evidence of outsiders in Galatia, we do well to maintain a *non liquet.* It seems better to work from the theory that the Galatian controversy is an internal problem."[82]

Ben Witherington observes that the point of these autobiographical examples is not to make statements of "identity" about the influencers in Galatia, but to construct "analogies" that will encourage the proper response of the addressees to those behaving in ways that corresponded with the players in those analogies; "analogies are not identity statements."[83] I have argued that these are not actually even analogies but historical examples, because no analogy with the Galatian addressees' situations is explicitly drawn, but rather, at least in the case of Jerusalem, a historical precedent is articulated as it applies to themselves (2:5).[84] The addressees would have to discern how it applied to their circumstance and Paul's situational discourse objectives. The Galatian addressees are to learn from these narratives that the call for resistance is continuous with this coalition's experiences in the past. But these narratives are not identity statements about the precise parties influencing the Galatian addressees.

One does find that some interpreters who predicate their interpretations to varying degrees upon this aspect of identification equivocate at certain points, admitting that the connection is not explicit but depends upon interpretive moves that may be questioned. Turning to the model case of Martyn, a comment made early in his commentary admits methodological concern. Whether or not "the Teachers have come to Galatia from Jerusalem," Martyn admits, "cannot" be said "with great confidence";[85] however, the extensive treatment in his comments nos. 45 and 46 (see the programmatic statement from pp. 464–65, cited

81. Robinson, "Distinction," 46; also Lyons, *Pauline Autobiography,* 79.

82. Richardson, *Israel,* 96; Lyons, *Pauline Autobiography,* 161.

83. Witherington, *Grace in Galatia,* 23. Note also Cosgrove, *Cross,* 31; Lyons, *Pauline Autobiography,* 163.

84. Sumney, "*Servants,*" 150, expresses a sympathetic view.

85. Martyn, *Galatians,* 126.

above), indicate no lack thereof.[86] This conviction is often observable in the midst of arguments in this and other works, and seems to grow in strength as the commentary unfolds.[87]

The data for this association is derived entirely from the autobiographical and allegorical material, not from the situational discourses.[88] Yet no explicit connection between the players in the narratives—which are constructed around different players in different earlier settings—and those in Galatia now, is ever drawn by Paul!

The stories are not comprehensive but constructed to support the points he is arguing in the situational discourse. It is not clear to the later interpreter what the addressees may have known about these matters from Paul or anyone else who is a part of this Christ-believing coalition, including perhaps those other "brethren" constituting the "we" with whom he now writes (1:2). What do his many references throughout the letter to the fact that he is reiterating (e.g., 1:9, 13; 3:1; 5:3, 21) and in an ironic ridiculing tone—in contrast to how he might approach them if time or space afforded direct interaction among them (4:19-20)—imply about the stories previously told?

The prevailing interpretations seem to proceed as though what is known has come from Paul's Jerusalem-oriented opponents and thus,

86. Martyn, *Galatians,* 122 n. 106, 126; idem, "Law-Observant," 322; idem, *Theological Issues,* 84 n. 19: "And the Teachers, not to mention their supporters in the Jerusalem church."

87. Note 106 on 122 (Martyn, *Galatians*) indicates little uncertainty before this comment either, but by page 218: "The Teachers' claim to represent the Jerusalem gospel implies a significant connection with a powerful part of the Jerusalem church"; and he contends that the Teachers' telling of a different version of the Jerusalem meeting (200) and the Antioch incident (240) to the addressees is essential to understanding Paul's need to redress these cases. He further ties them directly to the "False Brothers and their cohorts in the circumcision party, persons now possessing considerable power in the church of Jerusalem" (562). Martyn is joined by most interpreters in this basic move, some with reservations or at least taking measures to justify it, others quite boldly; e.g., Baur, *Paul,* passim, esp. 1.253, 256 (and the many who follow his lead); more recently, see F. Watson, *Paul,* 58–61; Lüdemann, *Opposition,* 35–36, 101–3; Goulder, *Two Missions;* Tarazi, *Galatians,* 10–13, 66; Esler, *Galatians,* 74–75, 137–40.

88. Note, e.g., R. Longenecker, *Galatians,* 292, who in interpreting 6:12-13, nevertheless finds it "difficult to believe" that the influencers in Galatia have no connection with "Jewish Christians in Jerusalem." Why? Because of "the polemic against Jerusalem influence that permeates the *narratio* from 1:17—2:10 and the parallel Antioch episode recounted in 2:11-14"; see also Witherington, *Grace in Galatia,* 448–49, and above note.

for example, depend upon circular reasoning at the very least for the assertion that Paul's authority is in question among the other apostles, or those who are supposed to now represent them, even if to misrepresent them, in Galatia. But all it would take for Paul's declarations of authority to be interpreted otherwise is for them to have learned from Paul and other representatives of this coalition that Paul was an apostle in good standing with the other apostles, his authority among themselves not in dispute, for the addressees to take his comments to signal another conflict entirely. And if the addressees' current conflict in Galatia is with those who maintain the traditional position that Gentiles should become proselytes of Israel in order to be considered members with full standing as righteous ones in the present age, and if they know that this was Paul's continued conflict with other Jewish interest groups that did not share the faith in Christ of himself and this coalition and its other apostles, in other words, if they know the politics implied to be intra- and inter-Jewish instead of intra- or inter-"Christian," then the implications of Paul's ethos appeals would turn upside down the consensus assumptions and the meaning of Paul's letter too. In fact, Paul's reference to what he has told the Galatian addressees before about these matters suggests just this to be the case.

In the case of the illustration Paul develops from the Antioch incident (2:11-14), it is clear that the problems include outsiders linked by Paul with James, and thus ostensibly with Jerusalem, who are Jewish, and that some of those present are believers in Christ.[89] How they are linked with James in particular, or even Jerusalem for that matter, is, however, much less certain than many interpreters appear to realize.[90]

More important for the moment is the question of whether the identity of these influential people in Galatia is in any way, directly or implied, related to the interests of anyone in Jerusalem in a way that has anything to do with developments among the addressees of this letter.[91] In other words, these common assumptions are debatable and do not represent a good starting place for the interpretive task.

89. Both 2:4-5 and 2:12-13 seem to indicate the possible involvement of Jews who do not believe in Christ in the various situations (so also noted by Richardson, *Israel*, 91–96).

90. Cf. Robinson, "Distinction," 46; Schmithals, *Paul and James*, 66–67; Wilson, "Gnostics?" 360, observes the possibilities are open.

91. Even the minimizing of Wilson, "Gnostics?" 360, still admits of "one or two people, especially if they were people of some standing or reputation," who seem to be linked with Jerusalem.

2:1-10

Paul makes one explicit comment associating the purpose of the telling of the Jerusalem meeting of 2:1-10, and that is in v. 5: "to them we did not yield by way of subjection even for a moment, so that the truth of the good news might be preserved for you," that is, for the Galatian addressees, who were not at this meeting in Jerusalem. Such is the reason for telling the story. What does it mean?

This resistance was to the pressure brought upon the coalition of leaders meeting together that could be described by Paul as having a freedom in Christ Jesus that would be compromised by the circumcision of Titus. The meeting was called because of a "revelation" Paul had, and the purpose was for Paul to lay before the other apostles, in private, the good news that Paul proclaimed among the nations or Gentiles (vv. 1-2). The critical data for interpreting the interests of the Christ-believing coalition in Jerusalem is bound up with identification of the "false brethren" who seek Titus's circumcision. Some interpreters go even further, arguing that these people actually express the interests of the leaders (apostles) other than Paul and Barnabas, but that is another matter altogether, another step removed from what the text provides and beyond the scope of this monograph.[92]

Paul describes these people as an interest group in a stereotypical fashion: the pressure to circumcise Titus was inappropriate to the private meeting Paul had sought "because," according to the NRSV translation, "of false believers secretly brought in, who slipped in to spy on the freedom we have in Christ Jesus, so that they might enslave us" (v. 4). But Paul does not draw any direct line between them and the influencers in Galatia; in fact, he does not use the language employed to describe them (i.e., παρεισάκτους, ψευδαδέλφους, παρεισῆλθον, or κατασκοπῆσαι) again in the letter. They are clearly distinguished from the other apostles who conclude the agreement with Paul and Barnabas. Who are they? What interests do they represent? How if at all does this reflect on the identity or interests of the influencers now in Galatia?

To begin with, the translation is inadequate for the task, and the proposed alternative helps to explore the political dynamics. There is insufficient space to discuss every aspect, but I propose the following translation of v. 4, which explains that Titus was not circumcised (v. 3), "in spite of the intruding pseudo-brethren, who came in alongside to

92. See Nanos, "Intruding 'Spies.'"

inspect the freedom of ours which we have in Christ Jesus, in order that they might enslave us."

This translation allows the technical possibilities latent in Paul's choice of κατασκοπῆσαι ("to spy out") to be magnified, for it both "carries the nuance of distrust"[93] as well as "inquiry with a claim to the right of supervision," which picks up the bureaucratic implications present in the wordplay on ἐπισκοπῆσαι ("to supervise").[94] This was perhaps the position or responsibility of those Paul called pseudo-brethren within Jerusalem Judaisms. Their role was to "investigate," maybe even to seek to prohibit any questionable or dangerous tendencies developing among these (or other) Jewish groups (as had Paul formerly!), thus Paul's accusation of their intrusive intentions for being present as "stealthily to destroy."[95] Paul's usage may include a value judgment of their investigative interests, namely, that they are "informants," hence the usual translation "spies."

Although their intrusive and harmful political intentions may be of a piece with the intentions and activities of spies to gather information for a hostile party, it is not the clandestine nature of their identity but the intrusiveness ("alien to the body into which they have come")[96] on false pretenses that is in view. If covertness, how could they have been identified precisely as spies by Paul even after this coalition meeting; or why were they admitted? Were some of the leaders of this coalition really spies? For whom? They are identified as "the intruding pseudo-brethren" who were seeking to "inspect" in order to "inform" on "our freedom." The threat is to the maintenance of Jewish honor within the occupied Jerusalem or minority diaspora Jewish communities represented by such disputable positions as, for example, the admission of Gentiles as equals (not just righteous Gentile associates) into the Jesus community or communities without proselytizing[97] (i.e., Titus), and

93. Fuchs, *TDNT* 7.417, who also notes that such spying "includes an element of suspicion."

94. Fuchs, *TDNT* 7.417 n. 1; cf. Fung, *Galatians*, 93; H. Betz, *Galatians*, 91 n. 307, notes Schlier's suggestion that "the opponents may claim a right to 'inspection.'"

95. Burton, *Galatians*, 83: "κατασκοπέω, 'to spy out,' with the associated idea of hostile intent, purpose to destroy . . . is here nearly equivalent to 'stealthily to destroy.'"

96. Burton, *Galatians*, 78.

97. Similarly Sanders, *Paul, the Law*, 290–92.

concomitant indiscriminate table fellowship with them (i.e., Antioch incident). These were arguably the very reasons for Paul's former opposition to the movement and that which he now calls "the freedom we have in Christ Jesus."

Perhaps the Jerusalem apostles had no choice about the presence of such investigators, that is, as long as they regarded themselves as a Judaism seeking a good reputation (honor) and legitimacy within the larger Jewish communities, they recognized their accountability to such authorities (guardians of honor and order). It is possible, indeed likely, that the Jerusalem apostles did not really desire the presence of such supervisory investigators, yet they found it necessary to tolerate their inspections in order to ensure their good standing. This in itself would seem to be a noble intention (even if debatable on any given point or at any particular time by others), as would be the concerns of these informants to ensure the compliance of these communities with prevailing intra- and intergroup norms for the protection of the rest of those under their social control, for a host of socioeconomic, political, and religious reasons.

The context of Paul's concern has suggested to many interpreters that the Jerusalem apostles were initially leaning toward compliance with the demands of these intruders.[98] Yet Paul says in this case "to them we [inclusive of the Jerusalem apostles] did not yield by way of subjection even for a moment [οἷς οὐδὲ πρὸς ὥραν εἴξαμεν τῇ ὑποταγῇ],[99] that the truth of the gospel might be preserved for you." The passive use of ἠναγκάσθη in v. 3 with regard to Titus "not *being compelled* to be circumcised" suggests that the apostles not only did not bring such pressure to bear[100] but that they would not have, any more than would have Paul; "but because of pseudo-brethren" who have arrived, unwelcome yet not without the authority to be present (because they have learned of the arrival of a Greek?), they are all experiencing social anxiety under such pressure.

98. Dunn, *Jesus, Paul,* 120; Burton, *Galatians,* 81; Lightfoot, *Galatians,* 105–6. This view turns on the assumption that it is Paul's independence from the Jerusalem apostles that is being emphasized here.

99. See Lake, "Galatians II.3-5," 236-45; Burton, *Galatians,* 75–82; H. Betz, *Galatians,* 88–91; R. Longenecker, *Galatians,* 49–50; Esler, "Making," 295, for discussions of variant textual readings that omit οἷς ουδέ as secondary and illogical.

100. See Burton, *Galatians,* 75–82, for discussion of the various interpretive possibilities for ἠναγκάσθη.

In other words, the purpose of Paul's visit and the laying out of his gospel to those of repute could have been private, as he intended. This would not have necessarily come to the attention of the informants or triggered their arrival on the scene—but the informants have learned of the presence of Titus! They thus "slipped [came] in alongside [παρεισῆλθον]"[101] to bring their opinion on this matter (the need to circumcise such Gentiles if they are to be present with indiscriminate status), which they regard within their proper jurisdiction, to bear. This suggests not opposition to this coalition per se but the right to come into this meeting to inquire, as well as some limitation of the rights of these informants to censorship and manipulative appeal (e.g., argument, accusation, shaming, censure).[102] The pseudo-brethren are the ones who throw down the challenge to honor on the matter of Titus, and they do so toward Paul and the other apostles as one. Paul and the apostles together then respond to this challenge: "to them [the pseudo-brethren] *we* did not yield submission even for a moment, that the truth of the gospel might be preserved for you [Galatians]" (v. 5).

What must be explored is the basis for calling them "pseudo-brethren"; what is pseudo about them? I suggest it is that their interests are misleading. There is no indication that they share the Christ-believing coalitions' belief in what Jesus Christ means for themselves, and especially on this matter of Titus being treated with full standing apart from completing proselyte conversion. What Paul is troubled by is their ability to gain entrance to a meeting that he had traveled there specifically to have with other leaders of this coalition; it was to be private. Here, there is space to merely trace the results of an extensive examination that yielded at least three ways to understand their identity and political interests from Paul's perspective as those of pseudo-brethren, not on the usually assumed (not generally argued, since taken to be self-evident) inter- or intra-Christian terms

101. Bauer, *Lexicon*, 424–25; Burton, *Galatians*, 83.

102. Paul accuses them of attempting in their role as informants of doing so in order "that they might bring us into bondage," which suggests more than just a reporting role but some authority to exercise social control, though it may be limited to censorship and manipulation. That is not to say that those to whom the informants reported did not have such power, and Acts 4:1-31; 5:17-42; 6:12; 8:1-3, for example, indicate such authorities to be operative concerning this Judaism. Swartz, Turner, and Tuden, *Political Anthropology*, 1–41, discuss the various means of social control short of coercive or violent force. See also Pitts and Etzioni, "Social Control," 381–402.

but in the inter- and intra-Jewish terms on which Paul represents them.[103]

1. The pseudo-brethren may have been seeking to take matters into their own hands without the authority to do so; in other words, they misrepresented their authority or the intentions of the authorities they professed to represent. In this case, they were in some fashion vigilantes who were seeking to step into a gap created by the tolerance of the authorities toward the Christ-believing coalition, a failure to exercise proper social control of this deviance that they felt must not be allowed to continue.[104]

2. Paul's point may have been rather to disclose that the intentions of the pseudo-brethren toward their coalition were suspect, that is, they misrepresented themselves to them, for example, by stating that their purpose was not to bring them into conformity ("bondage") but only to investigate so as to understand. In this case, they misrepresented the concerns and positions of the Jews in Christ to others in authority to whom they reported, although their presence as informants was well within their legitimate function as inspectors.

3. The crux of Paul's critique may not concern their present right to function as representatives in Jerusalem but the inherent illegitimacy of the present ruling class they represented and thus of themselves. In this case, their authority was based on the machinations of the Roman regime and not on Israel's, that is, on God's provision for the government of his people in the land.[105]

These possibilities should not be seen as excluding one another; they actually assume some overlap of political interests and activities in the dynamics of Jerusalem of this time. But they show that the Jewish brethren in Jerusalem may be characterized as false not in that they claim to believe in Christ but do not according to Paul's evaluation, but in that they do not believe in Christ yet represent themselves as agents having the authority to inspect (inspectors; but for Paul, they are rather informers) this matter within this Jewish coalition of Christ-believers. In doing so, they bring pressure to bear upon the Christ-believing

103. Cf. Nanos, "Intruding 'Spies.'" Schmithals, *Paul and James*, 107–8, also suggests the pseudo-brethren of Gal 2:1-10 were non-Christ-believing Jews; and Richardson, *Israel*, 91–94.

104. Cf. Rosenbaum and Sederberg, "Vigilantism," 4–12; Seland, *Violence*, 1–16, 83–85.

105. Cf. Goodman, *Ruling Class*.

coalition to comply with the prevailing membership and reference group norms of those agencies they represent, which are not Christ-believing, and find this practice of Gentiles being treated as though on a par with proselytes unacceptable. From Paul's perspective, they are false because they are "human agents" of "human agency," not "of God" according to the "revelation" of Jesus Christ, which has challenged the "traditional" interpretation "of the fathers" on this matter, now that the promise to Abraham of many nations has begun to be realized within the coalition of Christ-believers, God's new creation (cf. 1:1, 10-16; 3:6—4:7; 6:15).

The identification of these people and their interests is the critical matter for how they do or do not relate to any identification with the influencers in Galatia now. In order to challenge the prevailing readings as this investigation proceeds, even at the level of basic agreement on the terms for identification of the influencers in Galatia, it is necessary to reach a little ahead and explain how this works, and why I believe it legitimates dismissal of the connection with a Jerusalem, especially Christ-believing, orientation that the prevailing views all predicate important decisions upon.

On this reading, the inspectors correspond with the influencers' interests only in the sense that they bring pressure to bear upon the Christ-believing coalitions of Galatia to whom Paul writes, but they are in no way the same people in the two places, nor do they know of each other. The salient issue for the addressees is that the pressure that they are experiencing in distant Galatia, which I propose is also intra-Jewish (within the Jewish communities there), is not that different (on this matter) from the pressure experienced even by the leaders of this coalition in the intra-Jewish political climate of Jerusalem. Paul thus creates an inter-Jewish template (between Jewish interest groups) by which they may more properly reassess their own intra-Jewish context and thus understand what it means to walk straight toward the truth of the gospel of Christ on the matter of resisting proselyte conversion, for it would undermine for themselves the meaning of the death of Christ (cf. 2:5).

2:11-21

The second narrative unit from which the prevailing association of the influencers' interests and perhaps origins in terms of Jerusalem and the Christ-believing coalition there is assumed (again, not generally argued at length, because almost all agree on this point) is the so-called Antioch incident of 2:11-21 (some make a break at v. 14, 15, or elsewhere). Again, no direct link is made for the Galatian addressees, in this case not even any rhetorical aside to direct them, as had been supplied in v. 5 in the above narrative. Here as well, the limited concern of this study is the identification associations drawn, not the full interpretation of the incident or passage.[106]

Now, there is some explicit connection between the two narrative units themselves, because in vv. 11-12 Paul tells of Peter's coming to Antioch and then later of "certain ones from James," after whose arrival Peter "withdrew" from eating with the Antiochene Gentile Christ-believers and "separated himself." Why? Because he "feared the ones for circumcision."[107]

There are many loose connections here. Jerusalem is not named as the place from which either Peter or these certain ones from James have come, but it seems to be implied. More important is the question why both Peter and separately these certain ones from James have come. That is not supplied, and it is not clear what is implied. But even more problematic, while at the same time important, is that the reason for Peter's withdrawal is not directly linked to the certain ones from James, except by the coincidence of their arrival. Instead, a new interest group and label is introduced: "the ones for circumcision." Are they the same as the certain ones from James or local Antiochene interest groups stirred by this arrival? And are they stirred in agreement with the interests of these certain ones from James or perhaps in opposition to what their arrival makes no longer tolerable, so that they represent the last straw, one might say? And even more important for any connection to be made for the Galatian addressees is this: Is the group advocating the circumcision of the Antiochene Gentiles in any way linked with the coalition of James, or do they even share the faith in Christ of all of those Jewish Christ-believers who are so unsettled by them that they now withdraw along with Peter?

The answers are not clear, but the fact that the questions exist undermines the certainty of the prevailing views, not only for the interpretation of this incident in Antioch but for the construction of the players and situations in Galatia for which Paul relates it. For if the issue is again

106. See Nanos, *Mystery*, 337–71.

107. This translation takes the force of the ἐκ to be that they are "from" this interest group, that is, advocates of circumcision of these Gentiles, and thus "for circumcision"; see Cameron, "Exercise," 140.

a way to demonstrate the kind of intra- and inter-Jewish politics that are going on beyond the purview of the Galatian addressees in their various intra-Jewish settings, then this would again serve as a model for the call to resistance, at whatever price, for that is what faithfulness to the truth of the good news of Christ always involves. Thus here, Peter and the other members of the Christ-believing coalition who have withdrawn in the face of social pressure on this issue serve as an antimodel.

It is not easy, as the Galatian addressees now internalizing this message of proselyte conversion for themselves know only too well, to resist the attraction of social acceptance, especially by the dominant norm-setting and goods-holding group. This is more than just a psychological and religious need; it is sociopolitical to the core. It has resulted in temptation to compromise for even the most convinced leaders, even those who had walked with Jesus and met to hammer out the interpretation of these things, of Peter, James, John, Paul, and Barnabas. They too have suffered, some of them even capitulated at Antioch in view of this truth in the face of intense social pressure. But they were confronted, just as the Galatian addressees are in this letter, with a level of ridicule that may be mistaken for that of an enemy of their interests. There must be no compromise on this issue of Gentiles in Christ becoming proselytes as long as the present age persists. The cry thus goes on for the members of this coalition: how shall we then live!

3:6—4:7

The narrative midrash on Abraham from 3:6—4:7 contains little data upon which constructions of the influencers' identity rests.[108] It is, however, interesting to note that Paul's argument here is that Christ is the seed of Abraham.[109] If the influencers are also believers in Christ

108. Note, e.g., that Hays by choice does not discuss in any detail the situation or identity of the players in his extensive examination of how Paul uses this narrative; rather, his interest is in finding out what Paul brings with him when reacting to this (or any) situation (*Faith*, 1). Situational information simply does not emerge from there; however, I submit that elements of Hays's conclusion are nevertheless shaped by the situational issues that are supposed, not only when Paul was in Galatia previously, or to be taking place there at the time of Paul's writing, but also to be important in Paul's life before his arrival in Galatia and since, because this narrative, and not some other one, is related by Paul to accomplish a specific rhetorical task.

109. Walter, "Gegner." Sumney, "*Servants*," 154–55, notes Abraham's "absence in explicit statements and allusions," so that it is not evident that Abraham figured

and especially if linked with the apostles who draw their identity directly from their conviction that he is "the seed," why does Paul construct this argument as he does? Regardless of whatever else they might believe, if Paul is arguing against Christ-believers or those from the Jerusalem Christ-believing coalition (even by extension of their claims) who are the influencers in Galatia, it is hard to see how Paul imagined this point to score. The narrative supports the implied answers to Paul's ironic interrogation of 3:1-5, which is articulated in ironic ridicule again after this narrative unit in 4:8-11, 19-21; 5:1-5. That answer is that they are already members in full standing apart from becoming proselytes, that is, members of Israel, for the "new creation" community of God is the community of Israel and the nations: in Christ the awaited age has dawned.

4:22-30

The allegory of 4:22-30 is another step removed from providing reliable information apart from interpretive moves established elsewhere in the discourse and social reality known to the addressees, because that is the very nature of how allegory works. Any analogies drawn by the addressees depend entirely on what they know the identity of the influencers and the situations to be, which is what we do not know but are trying to find out. If they know that the influencers are from Jerusalem or appeal to Jerusalem for their authority, or anticipate that in response to Paul's argument they will do so, then this knowledge would determine the way in which they would interpret the allegory for themselves. But if the addressees know that the influencers do not come from Jerusalem, even if perhaps appealing to the authority of Jerusalem in some way in making their case, this would then determine how they interpret the allegory. The same problem exists with respect to whether the authority appealed to in Jerusalem, if this is the case, is the authority of the leaders of the Christ-believing coalition or some other interest group or groups. The later interpreter does not know what analogy is drawn where Paul does not explicitly draw one.

---

prominently in the influencers' arguments, and thus that Paul's use constitutes a response to these, but rather Paul "could well be the one who initiates discussion of Abraham." At the same time, Sumney recognizes that teaching drawing upon the Hebrew Scriptures would lead to an appreciation of the meaningfulness of Abraham for the addressees.

Some interpreters argue that a connection with Jerusalem is implied by Paul's comments, such as the issue of slavery in vv. 24-25, and thus that the influencers in Galatia are from Jerusalem or have appealed to the authority of Jerusalem. Moreover, some interpret this to refer to the apostles of the Christ-believers in Jerusalem as those who are enslaved. None of these inferences is clear in the allegory as Paul constructs it. No connection with the provenance of the influencers as from Jerusalem is made. Thus, even if the authority of some group in Jerusalem has been appealed to, the question remains: Whose authority in Jerusalem is in view? Is it not the place of authority for almost any Judaism of this period? If Paul is engaged in challenging or anticipating an appeal to traditional interpretation, it is not the apostles of the (presumably small and new) Christ-believing coalition but of other dominant and long-standing Jewish interest groups and policies that would most likely be in view. That is what is implied by way of the connection one might make with the Jerusalem meeting. For then representatives ("investigators") from a non-Christ-believing interest group had brought pressure to bear upon leaders of the Christ-believing coalition according to Paul's narrative in 2:1-10. Thus, it is natural to assume that it is the authorities of the Christ-believing coalition who represent the allegorical model of the heavenly Jerusalem of freedom and a non-Christ-believing interest group that would be allegorically illustrated as being "in slavery" to the policy of this present "evil" age by appeal to long-standing tradition of inclusion of Gentiles only by way of proselyte conversion, because this is the sole issue around which the allegory turns. That is the majority Jewish opinion of the period for any of the groups of which we are now aware, except for the Christ-believing coalition, according to Paul's own narrative in Gal 2:1-10.[110]

Moreover, is Paul defending against claims made about or in Jerusalem, or creating an allegory to score his own points, or perhaps in anticipation of the response and results his letter's call to resistance will precipitate, which because of the narratives just explored, relies itself upon the authority of those Christ-believers in Jerusalem who lead this coalition, and thus set the inter- and intra-Jewish terms of resistance? The answers cannot be derived solely from the narratives.

The rhetorical connections that are supplied at the beginning and ending of the allegory do challenge the prevailing views. Paul begins

110. But for one brief exception that is overruled (Acts 15), it is the way Luke tells the story in Acts as well (see Jervell, "Mighty Minority").

by ridiculing the failure of the addressees in Galatia to realize what "desiring" to become Jewish proselytes really involves for themselves (4:21). This indicates that he is approaching them as having internalized as good for themselves the influencers' message of the need to complete proselyte conversion to gain indisputable standing. But the allegory does not undermine the observance of the Law this would entail; rather, it undermines the challenge to their existence as children of promise, as was Isaac. The choice before them is similar to the one before Abraham: Will they trust in God's promise to bring about what they desire? Will they "wait for the hope of righteousness" (5:5), that is, undisputed standing as the righteous ones of God, which parallels Abraham's dilemma: Will he wait on God's promise to provide the arrival of his "promised" son? Or will they choose to employ the prevailing convention of the present age to gain what they desire in accordance with the expectation created by God: in their case proselyte conversion, in Abraham's case a concubine? If they choose the last, like Abraham's son by Hagar, they will find that they do not solve their problem but create a new one. In their case, that would be undermining the meaning of the cross of Christ for themselves, severing themselves from God's grace toward themselves as mere Gentiles as though the promised age had not begun; in Abraham's case, that will result in persecution of the awaited son when he is born.

When the allegory is coming to a close, many take Paul to indicate that the addressees are in a position to choose to throw out the influencers (cf. vv. 28-30). But actually when Paul turns back to address them directly he does not draw this inference out but quite the opposite. They are to "stand fast, therefore, and do not submit again to a yoke of slavery" (5:1). Paul calls for subordinate resistance! The following verses make it clear that what they are to resist is not the authority of the influencers per se but compliance with their identity norms for proselyte conversion.

What does this tell us about the influencers in Galatia? Like in Jerusalem or Antioch, to which Paul makes his ethos appeals to support the dissociating argument of this letter overall, there may be interest groups that have the position and power to bring pressure to conform on this matter to bear upon the Christ-believing coalition. They may even have the power to coerce compliance, but they must be resisted on this matter of Gentile conversion and the price of such resistance paid.

Summary

Paul's narratives are arguments to support the situational discourse, which suggests that the influencers in Galatia are in a position of authority where the membership and reference group norms by which the addressees' identity claims in Christ are in some important way measured. The influencers are the in-group in terms of these norms and their enforcement, but they are the out-group in terms of the addressees' identity reference and membership group norms shaped by the meaning of Christ for themselves, or Paul, that is, for this Christ-believing group, a "new creation" community of circumcised and uncircumcised, of representatives of Israel and the nations. By the influencers' standards, Christ and Paul are worthy of shame, whereas for the addressees they are, although marginalized as a crucified criminal or carrying the marks of this Jesus, worthy of the highest honor. Indeed, they had chosen to formally bless Paul when they had reason to fear him when among themselves, as a messenger of God, even as Christ Jesus himself (cf. 4:12-15).

These narrative units do not tell us that the influencers are either Christ-believers or in any way oriented toward the Christ-believing coalition or their leaders in Jerusalem. When these units are seamlessly mined for material to assess the context of the Galatian situations, the risks for interpretive error are extremely significant. Moreover, these methodological moves profoundly affect not only the analysis of Galatians but constructions of early church history.[111] For substantial decisions are necessarily spun around these few bits of data, because this is virtually the only firsthand source material for details about the earliest developments in Jerusalem and Antioch. That matter is, however, not the subject of this investigation, to which, on the basis of this analysis, I now return. Because of space limitations, this will be undertaken generally independent of concern to argue conclusions predicated upon a priori interpretations of the Galatian context, to the degree that they rely upon this narrative rather than the situational discourse units, or move back and forth without regard for such epistolary methodology in the analysis of this text.

111. See Sumney, "*Servants,*" 307–11, for agreement on the evidence of Galatians, but also the conclusion that none of the Pauline letters supports a Jerusalem-based anti-Pauline movement dogging his trail.

Missionaries or Proselytizers

Martyn calls these influential people missionaries, as do some others; yet other interpreters refer to them as proselytizers. This identification follows naturally and almost if not entirely from the association with Jerusalem or Antioch. But if they are not from there and if their message is not about Christ, or even so, if they are responding to the claims made by the addressees rather than initiating the contact to advance their own views, then it is a questionable identification indeed. They are then advocates of a position with which Paul strongly disagrees, at least for his Gentile addressees, but they are not best described or labeled as missionaries.

As for the second label, calling someone a proselytizer in the context of matters considered Christian appears to put a negative spin on their motives, perhaps in contrast to the christianizing evangelistic interests that the interpreters may themselves embrace. In view of the depreciating ideological views of things Jewish that are often implied if not intended in interpretations of the past, as well as the negative valence carried in such verbal endings,[112] this classification is also best left behind.

Outsiders

The influencers are considered to be outsiders, and usually called by this name, that is, other than permanent residents of this location, not Galatians. Even reserving the label *Galatians* for reference to the addressees betrays this conviction, implying yet that those influencing them are not Galatians as well. This is a logical result of the other conclusions about their provenance, interests, and activities. Although the argumentation for the outside identity of the influencers is generally slim, this aspect of their identity significantly limits the interpretive possibilities and must be addressed at some length.

A few interpreters challenge their identification as outsiders, although upon closer inspection the alternatives they propose often concede outside influence. After setting the major proposals out, I will engage the issues that arise, although on several points the full discussion will be postponed until chapter 9.

112. Note, not missionizer, Christianizer, or evangelizer.

Wilhelm Lütgert observes that it is difficult to explain what appeal a call by outsiders for circumcision among Gentiles would have and proposes instead that those on the Jewish front were local Jews ("Judaizers," i.e., Christ-believers) who objected to the Law-free claims of the addressees' churches, offering them protection as a *religio licita* as well, if they would become proselytes.[113] This is in part because he cannot imagine missionaries from Judea going to such a remote and non-Jewish place or how they could convince these Gentiles in Galatia to undergo the undesirable rite of circumcision by theological arguments or scriptural proofs.

Johannes Munck proposes that the influencers were Christ-believing Gentiles inside the Christ-believing congregations of Galatia that Paul addressed; at least that is how his construction is generally understood. Although Munck's argument is often cited and does have its sympathetic adherents on some points,[114] it has generally been dismissed. In addition to some comments upon this proposal below, the details will be set out and considered at length in chapter 9, when the issue of the Jewish nature of the influencers' identity is taken up directly. Most of his conclusions on the identity of these influencers and the situations in Galatia is guided by information derived from the narrative discourse units; in fact, consideration of this material takes up almost all of the forty-seven-page chapter concerned with this question![115]

Peter Richardson is one of those who develop Munck's thesis, although noting that the difference should be maintained between the Antioch example and the Galatian situation, concluding that the Galatian situation is both different and an internal affair.[116] Yet he proposes similarly that the influencers are "circumcised Gentile Christians, who are encouraging other Gentiles to become circumcised also, as a way of avoiding persecution from the Jews."[117] Moreover, he explains that

113. Lütgert, *Gesetz*, 16, 94–106; he is followed to various degrees by Ropes, *Singular*, 27, 44–45; Hirsch, "Zwei Fragen"; Dix, *Jew and Greek*, 41–42; Schoeps, *Paul*, 65; Enslin, *Christian Beginnings*, 216–24, esp. 220–21.

114. E.g., Gaston, *Paul*, 81, 90, 109, 221 n. 21.

115. Munck, *Salvation*, 87–134.

116. Richardson, *Israel*, 96: "In Antioch the opposition is from Jewish Christians from Jerusalem, together with the support (?) of the rest of the Jewish community. In Galatia, the opposition is primarily from Gentile Christians (who may have been circumcised as proselytes) encouraged by the intimidation of Jews."

117. Richardson, *Israel*, 90.

"they justify this position, which is psychologically quite understandable, as a necessity in order to be full Christians, and perhaps they cite Paul in their support. The real reason is a deep-seated desire to continue the relationship with Jews that came only as the result of a courageous decision."[118] He thus suggests that, while it is possible that Christ-believing Jewish "intruders" account for the Galatians' situation, "it does not seem necessary to postulate that extreme Jewish Christians went to Galatia to stir up trouble, on the analogy of Antioch. There is a danger of reading more into the account than is warranted; and in the absence of clear evidence of outsiders in Galatia, we do well to maintain a *non liquet*. It seems better to work from the theory that the Galatian controversy is an internal problem."[119] Yet by "internal," Richardson does not mean that the influencers are all part of the Christ-believing groups, but that they are not from outside Galatia: "Non-Christian Jews stand by as interested observers, threatening reprisals if Gentiles do not become circumcised. They bring pressure to bear upon their Jewish Christian friends to stop eating with uncircumcised Gentiles. Among the Jewish group are some Gentiles who, perhaps formerly, have become circumcised, and who are the most natural avenue for encouraging fellow Gentiles to submit to the rite."[120] Richardson thus sees a mix of insiders and outsiders, or better, out-group and in-group members, although all are from Galatia.

Gregory Dix anticipates several of the proposals under discussion, wherein the local situation as described by Paul is taken to suggest that the "agitation" is by the "local" Jewish Christ-believers to benefit themselves, that is, it is a response to their own difficult situation vis-à-vis the local non-Christ-believing Jews. The influencers thus seek to secure the circumcision of their fellow Gentile Christ-believers as a "concession of *expediency*," not of principle, "urging circumcision and some public conformity with the Law."[121] Dix makes this point against the view that the difficulties were the result of an organized campaign against Paul from Jewish Christians, because the "'troubler' is later identified as a single individual" (he notes Gal 5:10).[122] Yet he understands this individual to be an outsider to Galatia, having come from

118. Richardson, *Israel*, 90. See also 92, where the basis given is 1:6-7.
119. Richardson, *Israel*, 96.
120. Richardson, *Israel*, 97.
121. Dix, *Jew and Greek*, 41 (emphasis added).
122. Dix, *Jew and Greek*, 41.

elsewhere with news of the "results of a recent change of practice at Antioch," with the concern to show "to *non*-Christian Jews that conversion to Christianity does in fact *transfer Gentiles from the 'Greek' to the 'Jewish' cause.*"[123]

A. E. Harvey's position also argues for some interaction of the addressees with the local synagogues.[124] He suggests that the "pressure" on the Gentiles to "conform to the requirements of the synagogue" comes "ultimately from non-Christian Jews"; nevertheless, it "*might* be mediated by Jews or Gentiles within the church."[125] He sees the entire congregation of Gentiles under pressure from the local synagogue with respect to outward observances required, not their faith in Christ, so that "Paul's real opponents are those Christians in Galatia who are ready to yield to this pressure and are persuading others to do the same."[126] Thus, the ultimate pressure is from non-Christ-believing Jews outside the church, but the contact for Paul is with Christian insiders, whom Harvey regards as Galatian Gentiles who have already been circumcised. It is difficult to distinguish the influencers from the addressees at points in Harvey's argument, yet at the same time his proposal is predicated on a sharply drawn line between the congregations of Christians and the local synagogues, who are, in his view, interfering; thus, there are two groups of influencers: some are insiders, and some outsiders.

Joseph Tyson understands "Paul's opponents to be Jewish Christians native to Galatia" whose faith is the result not of Paul's work, but of earlier missionaries with connections to Palestine. Thus the reason for this development is that after these "Galatian Jews had become a part of the Christian community, some would inevitably have doubts about the validity of this new departure in which many gentiles remained uncircumcised."[127] In Galatia, there is thus "a confused Christianity with varying practices and imprecise doctrines. After Paul left, discussions among the native converts manifested this confusion, and some began to say that circumcision is necessary, that the apostles and Paul both required it."[128] He further proposes that "such

123. Dix, *Jew and Greek*, 41–42 (emphasis his).

124. Harvey, "Opposition," 326–27; see also Richardson, *Israel*, 90–97; Muddiman, "Anatomy," 260–61.

125. Harvey, "Opposition," 330 (emphasis his).

126. Harvey, "Opposition," 326–27.

127. Tyson, "Opponents," 252.

128. Tyson, "Opponents," 254.

doubts may have arisen spontaneously, or they may have been promoted by some of those Jews in Galatia who did not become Christians."[129]

Bruce Winter takes the pressure toward circumcision of the Gentiles of Galatia to be the result of concerns raised by the local Christ-believing Jews of the churches there.[130] Because their own legal rights to exemption from participation in the imperial cult were jeopardized by leaving the protection provided by the *religio licita* status of the local synagogues, which is now also the predicament of these Gentiles, it was necessary to take "evasive" action by giving the appearance of being "under a Jewish, as distinct from a synagogue, umbrella." This could be accomplished by circumcising the Gentiles, which would render them proselytes "in the eyes of the outside world," because the "social identification of Jews by the Gentile world was their observation of the law."[131]

Philip Esler explicitly refers to the influencers as outsiders,[132] understanding these influential people to be Christ-believing Jews with some kind of relationship to the Jerusalem church; yet he also includes among them local Jewish authorities with whom they are cooperating in order to accomplish the kind of compliance they seek to bring about among the addressees.[133] He thus, like several of these proposals, identifies as influencers both insiders and outsiders to Galatia.

These constructions indicate that the prevailing view of the influencers as outsiders to Galatia is not without its challengers, even if an outsider quality still generally governs the primary sphere of social identity for the influencers of these proposals, and in some cases is explicitly understood, perhaps along with others who might be considered insiders. In some of the constructions, the outside connection is made explicit somewhere along the way, although the argument seems otherwise to suggest insiders.[134] In other cases the outside nature of the

129. Tyson, "Opponents," 252.

130. Winter, *Seek the Welfare*, 133–43.

131. Winter, *Seek the Welfare*, 136.

132. Esler, *First Christians*, 9.

133. Esler, *First Christians*, 56; idem, *Galatians*, 88–92; for explicit connection to the Jerusalem coalition, see, e.g., *First Christians*, 60, 69; *Galatians*, 74–75, 137–40. Similar is Witherington, *Grace in Galatia*, 448–49.

134. Dix notes that the arrival of a Jewish Christian from Antioch with news of the "change of practice there" accounts for the "'anti-Pauline' tone the Jewish-Christian agitation had taken on" (*Jew and Greek*, 41; emphasis his). It seems then

influencers' identity is subtle but easily recognized upon inspection.[135] And in yet others, it takes evaluation of the implied social dynamics of their scenarios to clarify this implication. For the influencers' most important identity affiliation is taken to be with a community and its interests that are treated as though outside the Christ-believing community's meetings; rather, the influence the synagogue community's values and its social control agents are mediated by go-between Jewish believers in Christ who attend both. If the cultural climate of the place and time are given their proper due—for example, that they did not just attend synagogue or church meetings on certain occasions like modern individualists but were dyadic in personality and vitally linked in the expression of their religious life, which was embedded in the kinship

---

that the campaign is still similarly conceived as being against Paul and carried out by those who have now accepted the "Jewish-Christian" position, though they are from Antioch rather than Jerusalem. Dix explains the politics of this development in terms of the Antioch incident, by which he understands the problems to have arisen from the Jerusalem apostles (the messengers "from James"). They were not themselves extremists but rather concerned that the increasing rumors of fraternizing between Jews and Gentiles in Christ in Antioch and Galatia, which were putting the churches in Judea "in considerable jeopardy from *non*-Christian Jews," and thus Peter and the others simply sought to abate the danger by temporary modification (43; emphasis his). Thus the proposal of Dix is not really as locally contained as he initially states. Although he suggests the role of local influencers, including the Jewish Christ-believers and the non-Christ-believing Jews who were putting pressure on them to bring the Gentiles into compliance, he mixes the Galatian situation with the illustration from Antioch to suggest that the influence is both motivated by outsiders and transferred to Galatia by an outside agent. It is mediated by Antiochenes but with the ultimate influence coming from the pressure by Judean non-Christ-believers upon the Jerusalem Christ-believing apostles such as James.

Tyson, "Opponents," 252–54, admits of some background connection with Jerusalem interest groups, in addition to assuming the sectarian nature of the Christ-believing group, a matter arising in these proposals that is discussed below.

135. Munck's view still implies forces from outside the Galatian Christ-believers' communities to explain the desire "to avoid being persecuted as Christians," which he draws together with Paul's former activity as a Jewish persecutor of the Christ-believing congregations. Yet these were Jewish synagogues, and the discipline was carried out against Jewish members in the evidence we have. Thus, this parallel undermines Munck's thesis with its concern to detach the whole affair in Galatia from any involvement with Jewish communities, suggesting rather that Munck's view would belong with those who see the influencers as insiders but the pressure upon them from an outside agency and its agents, namely, the synagogue community (or communities) of Galatia or elsewhere.

and political worlds of their community—then this would suggest two highly differentiated communities. Thus, where Esler is explicit in associating the influencers in Galatia with Jerusalem and takes the community that Paul left behind in Galatia to be sectarian in nature, this being a defining characteristic of his portrait of Paul's mission already at this earlier time,[136] some of the other proposals considered implicitly appeal to similar social dynamics and thus suggest or imply that the influencers are in some way outsiders to the addressees' groups, if not to Galatia, and thus better defined as an out-group, or out-groups.[137]

136. A sect by definition opposes the forces that dominated their former group identity, according to B. Wilson's model (*Magic*, 9–69), which Esler explicitly applies; cf. Esler, *First Christians*, 62; cf. 13, 68–69; idem, *Galatians*, 122–26. Witherington, *Grace in Galatia*, 47, 270–76, follows Esler here. Similar also is the approach of F. Watson, *Paul*, 49–72.

137. E.g., for Lütgert they are outsiders to these supposed churches, but not to the area (so too Ropes, *Singular*, 45).

Richardson states at one point that "no absolute break is yet made between Jews and Christians" (*Israel*, 97), and in general follows this line of argument, but at some points he portrays the situation with a clear line between the Christ-believers and their interests and those of non-Christ-believing Jews, so that a sectarian scenario might be suggested (see citation above, also from 97). He sees two sets of influencers: some are non-Christ-believing Jews, whose reason for interest in bringing about this pressure is not clear, whereas others are Christ-believing Jews or proselytes who are receiving this pressure and then applying it to those Gentiles within their groups who have not yet become proselytes, in order to escape the persecution of all of this Christ-believing group's members. That the pressure is thus mediated suggests a separation in time and space on the basis of Christ-faith, and perhaps a sectarian model at work. Otherwise why are the non-Christ-believing Jews not applying this pressure directly upon these Christ-believing Gentiles?

Harvey's view helpfully recognizes that the issue is not so much theological as sociological, having to do with the practices of these congregations. But lacking is sufficient warrant for the synagogue's official concern for administering the practices of these congregations if they are already separate Christian churches or any historical examples of such behavior. Harvey's explanation appeals to examples of noncompliance among Jewish people, not Gentiles or those of other religious affiliations, so this hardly explains the persecution of non-Jewish Christian churches he proposes ("Opposition," 327). For example, the appeal to Justin's *Dialogue with Trypho*, chapter 10, cited on 328, does not work, as it is both much later and contextualized quite differently, being an apologetic constructed by a later Christian author. Most importantly, it does not demonstrate a desire to control or persecute a separate group or even an appeal for them to behave Jewishly but a criticism of the failure of Christians to observe the righteousness that would be expected on the basis of what they profess. This observation parallels that of Justin's chapter 8,

For various reasons, including failure of consistency, historicity, and lack of ability to explain the implied politics, these several alternate explanations have been generally dismissed. After consideration of some of these arguments, for example, Longenecker well summarizes the conclusion that still remains persuasive for most interpreters and, in fact, can still be observed at work in the assumptions guiding the alternative views just discussed:

> A . . . generally accepted point is that the opponents *were hardly indigenous to the situation*, for Paul repeatedly refers to them as distinguishable from the Galatian Christians (cf. 1:7-9; 3:1; 4:17; 5:7, 12; 6:12-13). Indeed, Paul seems not to have know them, either personally or by name. He refers to them generally as "some people" (τινές) and "anybody" (τις) in his opening statement of the problem (1:7-9); he asks during the course of his treatment such questions as "who has bewitched you?" (3:1 [citing further 5:7, 10]).[138]

In addition to these points Jewett also argues: "That they came from outside the congregation seems to be indicated by the fact that a sudden and unexpected shift of mind came over the Galatians (i.6) and that there was a struggle for the congregations's allegiance (iv. 17)."[139]

---

where he argues that it would be better to "abide in the philosophy of Plato, or of some other man, cultivating endurance, self-control, and moderation, rather than be deceived by false words, and follow the opinions of men of no reputation."

Sectarianism is implied in Winter's proposal of separate communities based on identity other than that established by Jewish norms, i.e., Christian as he conceives it. His churches have Jewish members, but their membership in those is a separate membership identity. It is difficult to imagine this does not involve awareness across the social networks of these people, as might be the case for an urban, minimally involved church attendee of our time. This does not account for the dynamics of community affiliation and the kinds of extensive networks among people of this time and place, even for the kinds of marginality that obtain with regard to the new as well as the old communal affiliations and identifications, especially at the boundaries that are created and negotiated by both the Jewish and Gentile members and those families and networks to whom they had and now belong (see A. Cohen, *Symbolic Construction*).

138. R. Longenecker, *Galatians*, xciv (emphasis added). This view is not as clear in the interpreters of the early centuries but is expressed by Luther and Calvin, then Baur (cf. Bruce, *Galatians*, 20–23). The consensus on this point has not changed substantially since Hawkins's 1971 comments, "Opponents," 12; note his brief rebuttals of those who question this matter (20, 99, 107–8). The commentaries are sometimes remarkably brief, e.g., Martyn, *Galatians*, 120.

139. Jewett, "Agitators," 204.

Further, Jewett argues that Paul must explain his relations with Jerusalem because the "agitators" had detailed information about these matters that the Galatian addressees do not: that they "dwelt on Paul's alleged dependency on Jerusalem" indicates their own "Jerusalem-oriented viewpoint." These fragments of evidence coupled with what Jewett takes to be Paul's polemic against Jerusalem in 4:25-31 and his reference to the Judean churches in 1:22 thus lead him to conclude that the origin of the Galatian "agitators" was Judea.[140]

Arguments for their association with Jerusalem have just been discussed, but this is further argued on the basis of the allegory of the slave versus the free women in 4:22-30. The suggestion is also made, on the basis of the language of casting out the children of the slave woman in the allegorical material, that the influencers are to be put out of the Galatian congregations, implying that they were to be returned outside, from where they had—it is assumed—come.

When the observations from both the situational and narrative discourses are combined, the intentions attributed to these outsiders range broadly from *benign:* concern to fill in details and complete processes that Paul has apparently overlooked or left unfinished (e.g., Howard); to *expedient:* seeking to stave off persecution from a non-Christ- or even Christ-believing group (e.g., Dix, Jewett, Harvey); to *venomous*: dogging Paul's trail to undo his work, perhaps in retaliation for his success against themselves in Jerusalem (that is, they are or represent the pseudo-brethren of 2:1-10), or the incident suffered during his confrontation with Peter in Antioch (2:11-21) (e.g., Lüdemann). Each of these arguments must be analyzed on its own terms, without assuming that the influencers in Galatia have any connection with those who are described in narratives, until this is itself investigated within the narratives themselves, and then applied to the findings from the situational discourse.

Many interpreters draw from the narrative discourse units in ways that fail to recognize how such units are distinguished from the Gala-

140. Similar are the arguments of Esler, *First Christians*, 59, who connects the problems in Galatia with "other people" who had come along after Paul and who are "almost certainly connected with Jerusalem" on the basis of Gal 4:25 (by which he means explicitly the Jerusalem "church" [*First Christians*, 60]), and connections made between the Galatian situation and the illustrations of the Jerusalem and especially the Antioch incidents (*First Christians*, 69; *Galatians*, 137–40).

tian situations themselves, providing earlier examples from other locations to which Paul appeals in establishing his own ethos, and that of this coalition, where these are in tension with the concerns of other interest groups, as is now the case in Galatia too. In the case of the Jerusalem example, whereas the inspectors or informants are identified in ways that suggest they are outsiders to the Christ-believing coalition, they are not identified as outsiders to Jerusalem. In Antioch, there appears to be pressure from a mixture of local and outside agents or perhaps the arrival of outside agents in some way precipitates a level of increased pressure from the local "ones for circumcision" leading to the eventual withdrawal of Peter and the rest of the Jewish members of this coalition from the indiscriminate table fellowship in which they had previously engaged. In such a case, it was not the purpose of these outsiders, at least of all of them, to interfere in the direction that results. Instead, it is, upon their arrival, their engaging in behavior in keeping with this coalition's that leads to increased pressure, because it now becomes clear that this is the principled behavior of this coalition not only in Antioch but in Jerusalem too. Thus, representatives of local interest groups who oppose such behavior are now moved to object more vigorously, to which Peter and the other Jewish members of this coalition respond.

It should be clear that the argument for the outside identity of the influencers cannot be established by appeal to these narratives. On this data alone, if anything can be inferred at this stage, it is that the influencers in Galatia, like the addressees, are not outsiders to Galatia but Galatians, even if they are outsiders to the coalition that Paul in this letter addressed as his own. If the influencers do not originate from outside Galatia yet would presumably not identify with the principles upon which the ethos appeals of these narratives depend, it would be better to describe the influencers, on this evidence anyway, not as outsiders but as representing an out-group.

When the situational material is cited, from which such constructions should draw, the observations upon which the outside agency of these influencers is based may be summarized as follows:

1. the change in voice: Paul's shift in pronouns from second person for the addressees to third for the influencers;
2. the interrogative references: his failure to name them, combined with his questioning of "who" is responsible for this trouble (3:1; 5:7, 10);

3. the expression of "surprise" at a "sudden" development: Paul's "surprise" that the exigence has presumably developed "so quickly" (1:6).

Let us consider each of these arguments of the prevailing view.

The Change in Voice

Despite the general agreement of interpreters, it does not follow that Paul's references to the Galatian addressees in the second person, as "you," but to the teachers in the third person as "some persons," "they," or "these people," demonstrate that they "are outsiders who have only lately come into the Galatian churches."[141] These merely tell us to whom Paul targeted this letter: not the influencers, about whom he writes, but rather those being influenced, to whom he addresses himself. Nevertheless, this line of reasoning has been pushed farther, to suggest that "it is possible that Paul deliberately distinguishes them in this way to drive a wedge between 'the agitators' and Galatian Christians who had not yet accepted circumcision."[142] In combination with Paul's anything but subtle expressions of disapproval—even to the point of rhetorical wishes for curses and castration—some such sentiment may be argued for every turn of phrase throughout this letter. Yet such negative sentiments are not reserved only for the influencers, as the ironic rebuke and accusation of foolishness, for example, are aimed squarely at the addressees as well.[143]

An interpreter should be careful not to make too much of such a basic shift in pronouns. On strictly grammatical grounds, this particular differentiation simply delineates, from the perspective of the author, the in-group being addressed (you or us) from the out-group in view in that address (he, she, it, or them). The change in pronouns does indicate that the letter is not directed to the influencers, even if it has been

141. Martyn, *Galatians*, 120; contra similar arguments by, e.g., Bruce, "Galatian Problems," 259; Jewett, "Agitators," 204; Hawkins, "Opponents," 20, citing 1:7, 10; 3:1; 4:17; 5:7, 10, 12; 6:12, 13; Dunn, *Theology of Galatians*, 8.

142. Barclay, *Obeying*, 43 n. 15.

143. Contra Lategan, "Levels," 173–75, who takes 3:1 to refer to the foolishness of the influencers, in an otherwise helpful description of the use of *pronomina* here to create textual space that is more inclusive with respect to the addressees and textual distance that is greater with respect to Paul and the addressees versus the influencers.

provoked by their influence.[144] But this does not tell us that the influencers cannot be among the addressees.[145] To be sure, this indicates that the influencers are an out-group from the perspective of Paul but not on the basis of their lack of "Galatianess."[146] The points made in the letter about "them," and the lack of suspicion of "them" of which the addressees ("you") are accused, do not tell us that they are outsiders or opponents but instead witness to the fact that the separation is not as oppositional from the viewpoint of the addressees as it is for Paul. On the rhetorical level, this simply informs us that they are not the target or implied audience: they are not the ones to whom Paul directs this address even if they are the ones about whom he writes.

Moreover, a similar distinction may be noted in additional sociological terms. Whether the influencers are present or not, where the addressees and Paul share a common in-group ethos, for example, of the necessity of avoiding behavior that will invalidate the meaning of Christ's death on their behalf, or the resultant experience of the Spirit (cf. 2:21—3:5), the influencers represent an out-group with their proposal of the necessity of completing the ritual of proselyte conversion. Might not they be an out-group precisely because they do not share this faith in Christ?

144. As Bitzer observes, "a rhetorical audience consists only of those persons who are capable of being influenced by discourse and of being mediators of change," even if others may be among the body of hearers or readers ("Rhetorical Situation," 7).

145. Contra Witherington, *Grace in Galatia*, 23, who "rules out" on the basis of these pronouns "that the agitators were in fact members of the Galatian churches." Walter, "Gegner," 355, argues that because Paul does not speak directly to the opponents and warns the Galatians with such strong language, the influencers must not be present in the assembling of the Galatian churches. He contrasts this case with the superapostles of 2 Cor 10–13, who are within the churches but want to revolutionize the situation. He also notes that Paul does not curse them in Corinth as he does these in Galatia, thus concluding that we must accept that the opponents stand outside the churches and outside of an actual relationship with Christ.

146. Gaston, *Paul*, 209 n. 8; Sumney, "*Servants*," 137–38, is notable because of the careful methodological aims of his work, yet he concludes that they are outsiders on the basis that Paul "distinguishes between the Galatians and the opponents," which shows the depth of circular reasoning, presupposing that the addressees are the only ones who are Galatians and then concluding that the influencers are outsiders because they are distinguished from the addressees. But where does Paul distinguish between them on the basis of their "Galatianess"?

An out-group identity is not necessarily the same as an outsider one. It may refer to a difference between two or more groups and thus to an intergroup phenomenon. It may also refer to a determination based upon group boundaries as viewed from the perspective of the various subgroupings within the boundaries of a larger group and thus to an intragroup phenomenon, even if functioning to distinguish between them. All such boundaries are constantly being negotiated, that is, they are by definition fluid markers of both the majority and minority group identities.[147] And the salience of this us-and-them distinction would be even more enhanced within or between groups if one or the other represents a minority or subordinate group. If the influencers represent the dominant in-group norms, then Paul's call to resistance is an appeal to a subordinate group that will suffer for this decision, which would make sense of the texture of his appeal, especially the later part of the letter calling for inner-group harmony and support in the face of marginality on the intra- or intergroup terms of the influencers. On the other side, from the in-group perspective of the influencers, the Gentile members of this Christ-believing subgroup need to be brought into conformity with the dominant membership and reference group norms.

Paul addresses the Gentile minority out-group as an in-group with respect to their membership among the people who profess faith in the good news of Jesus Christ, sharing a particular experience of God's mercy and spirit. On this matter, the influencers, even if the majority, are considered by Paul to be the out-group, being representatives of the dominant Jewish community's normative position toward the subgroup participants who are Gentiles, at least with regard to their need for circumcision if they are to be regarded as full members—even though these Jewish communities constitute minority groups themselves that are seeking to comply with the constraints of the dominant pagan communal norms. That is to say, against the usual conclusion that the influencers are not part of the community and represent a minority view that has suddenly been introduced into the groups addressed in Galatians, Paul's pronouns may be taken to indicate that the addressees (you) are a group marginalized by the dominant in-groups (them), even if they constitute minority groups in terms of the larger pagan society. What has changed is that now the addressees are tempted to conform, or at least comply with the wishes of "them" (the influencers) in order to gain acceptance by their group, for whom the

147. Cf. F. Barth, "Introduction."

influencers represent the prevailing norms. But why has this change of self-perception for this in-group of Christ-believing Gentiles now come about? The reasons could be several, including combinations of the following suggestions, which keep before us an in-group–out-group tension rather than suggesting the arrival of outsiders.

The level of distinction between this subgroup of Christ-believers and other Jewish groups may have become salient only over the course of time, not only within the larger Jewish communities but also within the larger pagan communities in which they dwell. It is entirely possible that new recruits into a community are unaware of the particularities or peccadilloes of the (sub)group to which they are first attracted or within which they now find themselves for any number of reasons.[148] It may be only with the passing of some time that they have become aware of the distinguishing marks of their subgroup identity, that is, that their own group is actually new and a subgroup, or that this subgroup is in some way marginalized because of its policies regarding themselves, a kind of out-group. This situation may have developed because of increased interaction with other groups within the larger whole, such as those not sharing their faith in Christ. In another direction, perhaps continued contact with the influencers would have lowered any defenses that had been based upon Paul's initial stereotyping of the distinguishing identity of this subgroup, thus the commonality of their lives as members of the larger communities would become more salient. At the same time, Paul's distance could work in the opposite direction, simultaneously accenting the differences distinguishing this subgroup and making more compelling the need now to address the problems that result.[149] Moreover, it may be, for the addressees, that it is the perceived closeness and importance of acceptance by those outside this coalition that has changed, or their

148. The networks of affiliation are of course many, and one cannot assume that every new member of these groups of believers in Christ (or any group) have come for specific theological reasons. For example, one should not overlook the kinship networks that would account for the presence of many family and household members who may not share or even understand the convictions of the patriarch or matriarch who has brought them into this group. And extensive research indicates that many new affiliates of groups choose this for a variety of reasons that may be only later grounded in the theological or other ideological positions of the group; see earlier discussion and Stark, *Rise*.

149. Cf. Tajfel, "Stereotypes"; Hogg and Abrams, *Social Identifications*, 64–91; Jenkins, *Social Identity*, 122–23; A. Cohen, *Symbolic Construction*.

increased pressure to comply with the prevailing norms for full acceptance, perhaps because of changes taking place among the influencers' own group or groups.[150] We should not overlook the possibility that changes within either the minority Jewish or dominant pagan communities, initially related or even unrelated to the Christ-believing groups, have effected an increase of pressure. Perhaps the pressure has reached a new level of intensity or taken a different, more persuasive or compelling course.

These suggestions incorporate an insight regarding the social construction of conformity: people seek to render interaction predictable in their social interaction, which is accented all the more at the margins of a group.[151] As these Gentiles interact initially within the coalition as their primary source of information and conform with the behavioral expectations, they would resolve uncertainty and gain an expectation of predictable results. But as they become more involved in the larger community this confidence may be undermined. In this way, any distinctions that involved negative assessments of themselves (e.g., being denied by the dominant community the honored identity propagated and experienced within their subgroup) would become more evident over the course of time, as a result of interaction with other influential people and ideas. The addressees then may be understood to be the "you" group in distinction from the influencers, "them."[152]

The boundary language Paul employs to divide "them" from "us" is subjective. It represents Paul's perspective projected from a partic-

150. Jenkins, *Social Identity*, 112, discussing Anthony Cohen's definition of community, notes that sequence should not be implied in words such as "response" or "defence": "They do not mean that communal identity, the shared sense of living in and as a community, is absent until, one moment, along comes the outside world to conjure it up. There will always have been an 'outside world,' even if only the next village. However, the outside world's salience, its power and size, and its perceived distance and difference from 'us,' may all change."

151. Jenkins, *Social Identity*, 121, 124.

152. F. Barth, "Introduction," 14, notes the role of shared values within an ethnic group identity, so that claiming this identity "implies being a certain kind of person, having that basic identity, it also implies a claim to be judged, and to judge oneself, by those standards that are relevant to that identity." Jenkins, *Social Identity*, 135, observes: "*Rights* may be what I expect of others as an aspect of my institutional identity, but they have no effect—they don't in fact exist—if those others don't recognise them. I cannot simply assert this or that 'right'; it has to be specified in a legitimate collective discourse about rights and about the entailment of rights in particular identifications" (emphasis his).

ular vantage point of a subgroup identity around a shared faith for "us" in Christ versus "them" who, it seems, do not share this bond. By Paul's standards, "you" or "us" are the in-group who must resist the influence of the out-group influencers, "them," even at the cost of being marginalized for failure to conform or comply with "them," even as have Christ (3:1) and Paul (6:17). At the same time, from the implied perspective of the influencers, Paul's addressees are rather the out-group, at least as long as they resist compliance with the influencers' norms, and this appears to be the perspective that the addressees have now begun to internalize. What makes the other message of good news so compelling is that such marginalization need no longer continue.

Thus, for the historical critic, although those able to embody such influence can be distinguished, they should not be objectified on this basis as merely outsiders or as so irrelevant to the self-identity of the addressees that they are but wooden figures: "them." In some way they are the "us" of the addressees' desires. In this way, we may make sense of Paul's accusation that the addressees are being attracted to the identity proposition of the influencers by such descriptions as "persuasion," and, for example, that they are being successfully manipulated to seek the influencers in response to being "shut out" of the communal identity, and thus access to goods, that they have been led to believe are already theirs in Christ.

As I see the case, this status as the out-group of the larger community—though the in-group as addressed by Paul within this subgroup identity as Christ-believers—is not determined by the pronouns, even as the prevailing view is not able to be based on this evidence. Rather, the rhetoric of Galatians suggests that the liminal and marginal nature of the addressees' status, as well as their options for response, are based upon the subordinate position of the addressees to the influencers' position of influence. Thus, Paul calls the addressees to "stand fast," to resist the pressure of the dominant group (cf. 5:1).

The Interrogative References

Does Paul's failure to name the influencers, combined with his questioning of who is responsible for this trouble (3:1; 5:7, 10), actually inform us that these people are unknown to Paul? To begin with, this evidence has been argued perceptively by Peter Richardson to the exact opposite purpose: that Paul's initially vague reference to "some [τινές] who trouble you" (1:7) infers that the troublers are Galatians, as it "should be sharpened if they are outsiders."[153] Is it not possible that the influencers were present when Paul was but not as involved with the Christ-believing subgroup, or at least not yet as influential with Paul's Gentiles when he was present? Perhaps they simply did not exert influence then in the ways that they do now or to the same degree, for in 5:7 Paul comments thus: "You were running well; who put an obstacle in the way of you obeying the truth?" Could that be the result of changes in the nature and scope of the groups addressed?

On this point, the dynamic nature of this new social movement is too often overlooked. In particular, if these Gentiles were newly introduced to the Jewish community through the Christ-believing subgroups or just distracted from the usual course of righteous Gentile interest in proselyte conversion (in the event that they were already righteous Gentiles before hearing the good news of Christ), then the change in the situations and the level of interest in the influencers' influence are understandable without supposing that they had not been present at all at an earlier time.

The rhetorical question "who" is, of course, no indication that one does not know the individual(s). As the indefinite relative clause in the subjunctive, ὅστις ἐὰν ᾖ ("whoever it might be") is used by Paul in this letter of ironic rebuke, it is a natural expression of disappointment that anyone would be accorded such influence when what they propose is in such direct opposition, from Paul's perspective, to the good news of Christ and the lifestyle that faith in it calls one to as it had been proclaimed by Paul—even if they were an angel from heaven!

The real target of this expression of disapproval is the Galatian addressees: "O foolish Galatians! Who has cast the evil eye upon *you*, before whose eyes . . . ?" (3:1); "*You* were running well, who put an obstacle in the way of *you* obeying the truth?" (5:7). This is clearest perhaps in the next expression: "I have confidence in the Lord that *you* will take no other view than mine; and the one who is unsettling you will bear his judgment, whoever he is" (5:10). Here, the rhetorical denunciation of the influencer is of a piece with the often useful put-down expressing exasperation toward one that the speaker probably knows quite well: "Who do you think you are!" or "Who do they think

153. Richardson, *Israel*, 92. This observation is weakened, however, by the use of τινάς (or τινά) in 2:12 for the ones from James, who are outsiders to Antioch, though even in this case they are identified more specifically as "from James," and they are not in Galatia.

they are!" Or in this case, actually: "Who do you think that they are!" And this is just the way parents often express disapproval of their children's peers when seeking to censure their influence. They do this whether or not they know the person in view and in spite of the fact that the parents of this other "who" person would probably see the context quite differently.

Ironic expressions of "who" do not suggest lack of knowledge of this person or group, or even of their name; rather, this expression of feigned ignorance is an ironic dig at the referents' own failure to rightly perceive who they are relative to the one(s) being undermined, or alternately, relative to the writer/speaker, to whom the addressees in some way belong. Precisely what drives home the rebuke for inappropriate behavior is their failure to act as they should in view of what they know.

The rhetorical victim of the expression of rebuke is not then the influencers but the Galatian addressees. Even if it is "cutting off" the influencers' influence that is the immediate rhetorical aim, it is the restoration of "running well" and "obeying the truth" by the Galatian addressees that is the ultimate goal, and this is the link with the autobiographical illustrations for Paul: walking straight toward the truth of the gospel.

To be sure, the influencers go unnamed, but they are not unknown to the addressees. The Galatian addressees remain anonymous too, and we do not thus conclude that Paul does not know to whom he writes. In fact, we do not learn the names of anyone in Galatia in this letter, yet surely Paul knows a great many of the names of those he has worked and lived among and to whom he now writes with such ironic and even sarcastic tones of rebuke. This phenomenon is actually not uncharacteristic of Paul's extant letters, which seldom name the addressees or those about which his concerns and instructions are expressed. Such stereotypical treatment is just as common for his comments calling for positive treatment of someone, for example, those who teach or lead, as it is for the negative ones.

Yet interpreters have offered a host of strategic rhetorical reasons for the failure to name the influencers. For example, Martyn suggests that failure to name the "Teachers" is "in order to indicate disdain," which he takes to also be the case for the "False Brothers" of the Jerusalem account, where Paul mentions only James, Cephas, and John.[154] Besides being insufficient evidence for such a claim, the mention of

154. Martyn, *Galatians,* 111, 121.

Barnabas as well as Peter in the Antioch incident may be considered a contradiction of this principle, as many understand the purpose of the illustration to be precisely to indicate such disdain for one or both of them. However the example is interpreted, surely Paul's honor confrontation with Peter is an important expression of disapproval in this letter yet one that includes the mention of his name. The evidence points to another reason entirely, that is, to the purpose of these narratives within the scope of the letter.

Paul names the other apostles of the movement to indicate that these well-known and powerful people are in agreement with Paul, even if they have arrived at their understandings of "the truth of the good news" independently yet with some problems from others who disagreed; likewise, even among themselves, it was necessary to work out the implications in the various circumstances encountered, sometimes not without some disagreement along the way.[155] One may even note that in the allegory of the free and slave women, that on the one hand, Sarah is not named while her son Isaac is, yet she is the example of freedom and the undisputed positive referent; on the other hand, Hagar is named while her son is not, although she is the example of slavery and the one who would be expected to remain unnamed on Martyn's argument. In addition, two allegorical mountains are named; what are we to make of this anomaly in terms of Paul's rhetorical strategy?

In another example of such explanations, Betz suggests that Paul is "avoiding the use of names and the providing of free publicity."[156] He notes that this is common and cites a later comment by Ignatius to confirm the practice. Betz concludes that this rhetorical strategy is intended to foster the impression that the influencers are few in number and that their names are unknown or just not worth mentioning, confirming the observation of Franz Mussner to this effect. Along this line, it may be argued that an author may employ a term such as τινές to avoid indicating more particularity, perhaps even that they cannot. Or it may carry a derisive connotation to intentionally suppress their names, by either deliberately belittling or blurring their identity.[157]

155. Titus and Barnabas are mentioned as though incidental yet notable because paradigmatic in the situations discussed.

156. H. Betz, *Galatians*, 49 n. 65; so too Martyn, "Law-Observant," 313–14.

157. Du Toit, "Vilification," 406–7.

All of this may be the case, but surely we cannot conclude that this applies on the basis of such possible wordplay, especially in the face of the observations made above about Paul's failure to name the Galatian addressees and many others to whom he writes. Vilification of someone is just as often accompanied by the clear mention of the person's name. So Philo explained: "I praise Flaccus, not because I have thought it right to laud an enemy, but to show his villainy in a clearer light."[158]

It should not need to be argued in the case of τις (1:9) and τινές (1:7) that such singular and plural indefinite pronouns like "someone(s)" and "something(s)" need not have any such negative implication, being essentially colorless grammatical expressions,[159] while at the same time, when used pejoratively, this common rhetorical device does not inform us that they are from outside. We have sufficient evidence elsewhere to know that Paul is upset about the influencers, but we do not know why he did not choose to name them or even whether this was a choice or necessity, rhetorical or otherwise. Paul does not even mention his fellow addressers to the Galatian addressees! Paul begins his argument with the reminder that, "As we have said before, so now I say again," which does suggest that this contrary good news, with its traditional approach to Gentile inclusion in the people of God by circumcision, had been a topic of concern when he was among them in the past (1:9-11).

In the discussion before us, namely, the identity of the influencers as outsiders, the specific historical evidence for constructing the identity of the influencers that has been derived from the stereotypical linguistic treatment of those who are influencing Paul's addressees against his intentions for them—in that he does not name them or refers to them as "someone," for example—has so far amounted to nothing more than conjecture. Paul's rhetoric is intended to influence his addressees against the aims of these other influencers, and where the vilification of them is obvious, he hopes to induce his addressees to share in his convictions regarding them.[160]

158. Philo, *Flaccus* 7; cf. du Toit, "Vilification," 403. The examples in Acts of naming those whom Luke certainly is not seeking to put in a positive light are several.

159. Used as positive referent, e.g., Rom 5:7-8; 11:14; Phil 1:15; 4:8.

160. Du Toit, "Vilification," 411.

The Expression of Surprise at a Sudden Development

Paul's expression of θαυμάζω ("surprise," "astonishment") in 1:6 is often taken to indicate that Paul did not anticipate this possible development since his departure. And the mention of its swiftness ("so quickly [οὕτως ταξέως]") furthers this understanding, for it is taken to indicate "that a sudden and unexpected shift of mind came over the Galatians (i.6)."[161] Dunn understands this surprise literally and thus to set the tone of the letter: "It denotes surprise or wonder at some unexpected and amazing utterance, or deed, or turn of events. . . . Paul's use of the word here, therefore, is probably an expression of the genuine sense of shock which the news from Galatia had brought him."[162]

Paul may in fact have been shocked by this news, but we certainly cannot deduce this on the basis of his exclamation of surprise (θαυμάζω). This whole line of thought is predicated upon a literal interpretation of words that may be employed for another purpose altogether: the subversive rhetorical function of rebuke in ironic terms, that is, by way of feigned ignorance, a move by which the ironists mask their hostile intentions by expressing an unflattering view of themselves. The declaration of feigned astonishment unmasks the naïveté of the addressee, though at the expense of the *eirōn* Paul, which constitutes the (ironic) signal at the heart of Socratic inversion. Even the pattern of Paul's exclamation follows that formally set out in epistolary handbooks and evident in many papyrus examples of letters of ironic rebuke. Thus, right on the surface level of the text, assuming that the addressees were familiar with this epistolary convention, they would be expected to regard this exclamation of ignorance or lack of anticipation as a stereotypical ploy. Of course, employment of irony in this way always runs the risk of misunderstanding, especially by those not in the situations addressed, which is obviously the case for the later interpreter. At the same time, this is part of irony's appeal for the original writer and audience; it is communal language from an in-group perspective not necessarily shared by anyone else, and though perhaps understood by the out-group, it will not be considered in the same positive way. The question the interpreter must ask is: Where is there any other evidence that Paul failed to anticipate this problem?

161. Jewett, "Agitators," 204; note also Lightfoot, *Galatians*, 75.

162. Dunn, *Galatians*, 39; note that he makes this comment while rejecting the rhetorical and epistolary terms of ironic rebuke, specifically citing disagreement with the arguments of H. D. Betz and Hansen.

Notably, the information that Paul has ostensibly just been surprised by is not a new possibility in Galatia at all, as his following comments make clear. That is, already in the past Paul has taught the Galatian addressees to avoid just this development (1:9; cf. 3:1-5; 4:19; 5:3, 7-10, 21): "As we have said *before*, so now I say *again*." In other words, it is arguably a development that Paul has anticipated. And why would he not? His gospel calls for a departure from the traditional interpretation for Gentile inclusion and legitimates this claim by appeal to the meaning of the death and resurrection of a Judean martyr of the Roman regime; it will not go undisputed. Anyone who upholds this view could anticipate being marginalized by the agents of the prevailing norms. Certainly, it is reasonable to expect these Gentiles to face status uncertainty and loss of resources if they do not ultimately comply with the prevailing norms. Moreover, proselyte conversion may seem attractive on its own terms, and certainly completion of communal rites of passage provides its own compelling logic. Would not Paul try to anticipate this problem and seek to create a new way to understand reality in terms of the good news of Christ long before he would try to set it out as he does in a letter of response, as we read herein?

What then do we know about Paul's anticipation of this development from a surface reading of 1:6 alone? Was he really surprised? In the sense of disappointment, yes. But in the sense of knowing this possibility, anticipating its reach or possible grip on the addressees, the likely answer is no. Paul's note of surprise here is loaded with a deeper meaning, though not a hidden one. The interpreter cannot take from the mention of astonishment or surprise in this ironic rebuke that Paul did not know the identity of the influencers or that they have come from outside after his departure. Such a conclusion misses the dimension of understatement for effect that underlines ancient irony. Instead, the interpreter is well served when understanding "I am surprised" as a rhetorical technique by which Paul shames the addressees, communicating by way of ironic inversion that "I am disappointed." What is at issue is not Paul's ignorance but the addressees' culpability; they ought to know better; after all, they have been told!

It is similarly possible that Paul's mention of this astonishing development "so quickly" indicates that this change of circumstance has occurred in a short period of time, as it would if taken at the literal level, but this conclusion is also not recommended in view of its employment in the epistolary rhetoric of ironic rebuke. Like the exclamation of astonishment, the mention of suddenness may serve a merely rhetorical role. It reflects, in fact, a stock term set out in the model syllogism for composing such a letter, which was to be further developed as appropriate to the specific social setting being addressed. Perhaps not coincidentally, the example of an ironic letter from Pseudo-Libanius discussed above includes both the expression of astonishment and suddenness within the same sentence: "I am greatly surprised at your sense of equity, that you have *so quickly* rushed. . . ."[163] In other words, this note of suddenness indicates the use of a standard rhetorical device employed to enhance a writer's ironic exclamation of surprise-disappointment, compounding the force of the ridicule.[164] It may indicate that this development was actually faster than one might expect, but it may not indicate any such thing. It might not at first seem to be as useful an approach if the development was actually very slow. But then again, irony can work in just this way as well. An ironic twist may accent the inappropriateness of this development after "so much" time has passed instead, regardless of what that length of time might actually be, thereby exposing naïveté, because it communicates with ironic force that the writer should have sufficient reason after all this time to expect otherwise.

If just such a development had seemed imminent when Paul had been among the addressees but had ostensibly been removed for some time as a result of his former teaching on this matter only now to surface again, then such an ironic twist might be contained in Paul's expression of suddenness. Therefore, while the translation "so readily" arguably gets the meaning just right,[165] it may sacrifice the sharp ironic edge delivered by the translation "so quickly." However this phrase is understood, it simply does not tell the later interpreter that the influencers are from outside, that they have suddenly or recently arrived, or that the addressees have been have been won over easily.[166]

If the speed implied in Paul's rebuke indicates anything, it is probably that the influencers were not sudden arrivals or strangers, the entrance of whom would be expected to raise suspicions and defensive measures from the start (xenophobia), a setting that might arouse the

163. *Epistolary Styles* [56], from Malherbe, *Theorists*, 74–75 (emphasis added).

164. Schlier, *Galater*, 36, suggests the reference is rhetorical and applies to the "rashness" of the Galatians' interest.

165. Winbery, "Gal. 1:6."

166. Ease is suggested by Thurén, *Derhetorizing*, 65, following Rohde; Thurén otherwise argues against those who seek by this comment some indication of time, noting the rhetorical nature of the expression.

fear of envy (evil eye), which was apparently the case for the addressees when they first met Paul (4:13-14).[167] Yet suspicion of the influencers' motives and the policies is precisely what continues to be missing among the Gentiles addressed, at least, as Paul puts the case by attacking their naïveté, including, in contrast to their initial expression of fear toward himself when arriving as a stranger, their implicit trust in the influencers (cf. 3:1; 4:12-20; 5:7-8). Not only would strangers be unlikely to receive a "quick" following, but this would remain the case after some time too, unless they came to be perceived not as rivals but as friends. Along this line, it is important to note that this strongly suggests that the influencers did not propose an overtly rival message in the perception of the addressees but one that could be safely regarded as complementary or helpful, for the kind of danger it held for them according to Paul is apparently unrealized. It may be that the influencers do not know of the perspective from which this direction is viewed as dangerous. Or if they did, perhaps they would not agree with or concern themselves with this matter in the same way; for example, if they do not share faith in Christ as the fundamental conviction that must not be compromised. To discussion of such implications we will soon turn.

Summary

All of the premises reviewed for concluding that the influencers are outsiders include other factors about their identity—such as Christ-belief and orientation toward the interests of the Jerusalem coalition of this persuasion, if not actually their point of origin as well, even if perhaps misrepresenting them in some way—which have been shown to be suspect. Against all of the arguments discussed, including the questionable usage of the narrative discourse units that is common to them, there are actually indications within the letter that the affair is not the result of outside agencies from Jerusalem, or even from other Jewish communities in the Galatian region (that is, when the Jewish communities are taken to be separated from the self-identity of the groups

167. Strangers could be feared as dangerous and thus would be in danger themselves; were they bearers of good or evil? Hospitality customs ensured their opportunity to assuage this fear; see Homer, *Od.* 7.32–33; Euripides, *Med.* 282–85; Herodotus, *Hist.* 5.72.3, 6.81; Servius, *ad Aen.* 8.269–70; van Gennep, *Rites,* 26–40; Bolchazy, *Hospitality,* 1–34, passim; L. Mitchell, *Gifts,* 16–18; Stählin, *TDNT* 5.1–19. The concern with envy or the evil eye on the part of a stranger is noted below.

Paul addressed so as to be labeled outsiders), ideas that include the implicit when not explicit conclusion that Paul's addressees are a part of sectarian communities, Christian churches. It will be argued instead that the influencers are from Galatia too, that they are indigenous to the addressees' social world, and that they represent the interests and norms of the majority or dominant Jewish communities (even though themselves minority groups within the Greco-Roman world of Galatia) within which the addressees' Christ-believing groups function as Jewish subgroups. The only stranger to the locations of the addressees and those influencing them appears to have been Paul! Thus, I have refrained from naming the addressees Galatians, referring to them as "addressees" or "recipients" or the "target audience," because these labels do not imply that the other players on the scene are not Galatians also.

Additional Factors for Identification of the Influencers

The consensus views have been clarified, and each of the descriptions and labels common to the interpretation of Galatians has shown itself to be worthy of suspicion. At the same time, there are several additional aspects to consider for the identity of the players that have not generally arisen in the interpretations reviewed. Some will be discussed as they naturally present themselves in the investigation of the text taken up in the following chapters, but a few warrant preliminary mention here.

How Many Groups of Influencers Are Implied?

The fact that this is a circular letter raises questions of the construction of the group as well as the number of players involved.[168] When taken to be outsiders on a mission, it is natural to imagine that they move among the various groups addressed, and thus there may appear to be little reason to consider this matter further.[169] But the circular nature of the letter, coupled with opening up the question of their origin as outsiders or intentions as missionaries, should also open up the question of whether these represent one seamless group.

Although Paul addresses the situations as though one exigence is in view, is it not possible that subtle differences or even large ones char-

168. Noted also by Hester, "Use," 394 n. 28.
169. Thus argues Lightfoot, *Galatians,* 29; also Tyson, "Opponents," 244.

acterize the situations and players of the communities addressed? Might not stereotyping the influencers in ways that make them seem to be the same serve Paul's rhetorical goals, including simplification? Is it not probable, if the influencers were in fact as indigenous to the location as the addressees, that different groups as well as individuals would be involved in each location? If so, did they communicate with each other or coordinate with each other?

To adumbrate our next topic of discussion, is it not possible that, for Paul, the problem turns around a single issue: that the exigence, as it is interpreted from his perspective, is singular, regardless of the complexities of the case(s) or players involved? Is it not likely that, to some degree, the addressees within these groups see the matter at dispute in his letter also in a singular way, if they are dealing with norms among the various influencers' communities that are essentially the same, even if administered by different people, and thus in different ways by different personalities? The addressees are wondering whether to complete the ritual process of circumcision; the others are advocating that they do; Paul is adamant that they must not. That constitutes a single issue but multiple exigencies when viewed from different perspectives by the various players.

The situations may appear similar in different locations as they revolve around this exigence, while at the same time they may be different and involve different individuals and groups as well as any number of particulars. Thus, the influencers' groups may be composed of different people in each location wherein the addressees' groups operate—especially if subgroups—yet they too may see the exigence in a singular way as far as the identity of the addressees is concerned: apart from completion of the ritual of proselyte conversion, the addressees' claims of full membership identity are without foundation, as are their expectations to be treated as though they were children of Abraham already because of faith in/of this Jewish martyr Jesus and the supposed meaning thereof.

How Many Individuals among the Influencers Are Implied? Possible Implications of Paul's Evil Eye Accusation and His Usage of Ταράσσω

In addition to not being clear how many interest groups of influential people might be involved, due to various locations of the addressees, it is also not clear how many individuals are implied. In some cases the referent is plural (1:7; 4:17; 5:12; 6:12-13), in some singular (e.g., 1:9; 3:1; 5:7-10; 6:17).[170] But there is good reason not to conclude that one individual is in view in 5:10, for example, while more than one in other sections of the letter.[171] Rhetorical aspects of each reference will need to be considered. Some examples, such as the use of the interrogative "who," which can be used for groups as well as individuals, have been discussed. Here, I want to introduce a new way to consider the data, which will take as its starting place a fuller consideration of Paul's usage of ταράσσω, the definition and translation of which is important even apart from this exercise.

The various nuances of this verb revolve around the basic sense of "stirring" or "shaking," as in when one stirs up water (cf. John 5:4), or the "motion" that is the result thereof.[172] On its own, the action of stirring settled water, for example, is a relatively value-free action. The value would be imparted if the position of being unstirred was considered its rightful state and stirring therefore inappropriate, as it is then "unsettled."

When it comes to figurative use, it seems to carry the sense of unsettling or being unsettled—"affected," one might say; the psychological sense of fear and panic that result from "turbulence"; or as Louw and Nida put the matter: it expresses "acute distress and great anxiety, with the additional possible implications of dismay and confusion" (cf. John 11:33; Acts 12:18; 1 Pet 3:14).[173] This psychological disturbance can be very intense, as in Polybius's usage in the singular for a soldier's dread, or for a group, for example, "sometimes a disorder affecting a flock."[174] It resonates also with the character of "fools" in a way interesting for the reader of Galatians: "Trouble takes on a pejorative moral meaning: 'The whole life of the fool is subject to convulsions, is agitated and shaken, is perpetual chaos and trouble; it retains no trace of authentic good' (Philo, *Confusion* 69)."[175] Moreover, it has a medical association

170. Dix, *Jew and Greek*, 41, argued on the basis of the move from plural to singular that one "troubler" was in view.

171. See, e.g., the grammatical solutions of R. Longenecker, *Galatians*, 232; Burton, *Galatians*, 285.

172. Louw and Nida, *Lexicon* 16.3–4.

173. Louw and Nida, *Lexicon* 25.243–44, 246.

174. Spicq, *Theological Lexicon*, "ταράσσω," 3.373 n. 3, citing Polybius 5.29.3 and 5.52.14; for flock: 5.13.4; 5.15.5; 5.25.4; 5.26.1.

175. Spicq, *Theological Lexicon*, "ταρασσω," 3.374 n. 6. Related to ταράσσω, the implications can be of stirring up as in a crowd, thus sedition, causing to riot, revolt,

with ill health (cf. Jer 14:19; Wis 17:8), a usage that is common in Hippocrates for "troubles and sicknesses."[176]

When these examples and definitions are augmented by the following information and placed alongside the data and dynamics of the implied Galatian situations, the association of this language with envy and evil eye beliefs arises, which bears directly on the present concern. Because this large topic will not be the subject of this project, I will give only a brief sketch here, as it may pertain to what is in view regarding the identity of those influencing the addressees.[177]

In view of the recognition that Paul accuses these people of having given the evil eye (envied) to the addressees (ἐβάσκανεν in 3:1) and additional evidence that Paul is dealing in this semantic domain at other places in the letter (cf. 4:12-14),[178] it is possible that ταράσσω may well resonate with this association when read or heard by the addressees. For example, Thucydides comments that: "certain ones were afraid that he would trouble [ταραχῄν] them in their success" (7.86.4).[179] Moreover, ταράσσω is explicitly combined with the powerful fear of the effects of envy by Herodotus; when Solon is taken to be slighting Croesus, he explains his calculated comment not to exalt them because the gods are always "envious [φθονερόν] and troubling [ταραχῶδες]" to humans (Herodotus 1.32.1; my translation). This association of envy with ταράσσειν is said by Dodds to be "regularly used of supernatural interference" (e.g., Aeschylus, *Libation Bearers* 289; Plato, *Laws* 865E).[180] And indeed Amasis tells a friend upon learning of his success: "But I do not like these great successes of yours; for I know the gods, how jealous [φθονερόν: envious!] they are" (Herodotus 3.40.2 [Persius translation]). Why? As Dodds put it: "the gods resent any success, any happiness, which might for

or rebel appear in usage of Acts 17:6; 21:38; cf. Lightfoot, *Galatians*, 208; Bruce, *Galatians*, 238; H. Betz, *Galatians*, 49, suggests this political language is used for causing confusion and turmoil ("disturb"); see also Acts 17: 8, 13. This has been taken to indicate opposition to Paul, but this kind of political implication may not be the desired result of the one doing the "stirring" (cf. Acts 16:19-20).

176. Spicq, *Theological Lexicon*, "ταράσσω," 3.374 n. 7.

177. Nanos, "O Foolish Galatians."

178. See J. H. Elliott, "Paul"; B. Longenecker, *Triumph*, 26, 153–57; idem, "'Until Christ'"; Nanos, "O Foolish Galatians."

179. Spicq, *Theological Lexicon*, "ταράσσω," 3.374 n. 7.

180. Dodds, *Irrational*, 51 n. 3.

a moment lift our mortality above its mortal status, and so encroach on their prerogative."[181]

Paul's descriptions of the influencers as "stirring up" the addressees in 1:7 and 5:10 (ταράσσοντες/ταράσσων; also related is ἀναστατοῦντες in 5:12) may well draw from this kind of semantic domain to include a resonance of Paul's ridiculing accusation in 3:1. Their "foolishness," he says, is because they have been "given the evil eye," that is, "affected" by the envious glance of those influencing them so that they are seeing things inappropriately. But Paul indicates that this development should not have occurred in view of what they have been taught and experienced, and would not have happened had they kept their eyes on the crucified Christ instead of the ostensible good that these other people offer them (cf. 1:6-9; 3:1-5; 4:12-20; 5:7-12; 6:12-13). They are behaving like ones who have been affected by an outside force—stirred up, disturbed, troubled, agitated, distressed, anxious, dismayed, confused, frightened, intimidated—unsettled by turbulence, and Paul names that force the evil eye of envy. For those who are shaped by this belief system, wherein such a gaze may be cause for loss of any good fortune possessed, whether the health of themselves or those in their care even to the point of death, or loss of goods and means of production, the phrase may echo in a powerful and effective way indeed. If the addressees were not or did not consider themselves victimized by these people before Paul's warning was sounded, they would certainly have cause to be anxious and unsettled thereafter.

Returning to the point with which this discussion began, it may be that the unresolved conundrum of Paul's seemingly inconsistent movement, from plural (e.g., 1:7; 4:17; 5:12; 6:12-13) to singular (e.g., 1:9; 3:1; 5:7-10; 6:17), when making comments to the addressees about those influencing them, is a function of the role played by the imagery of an evil eye accusation that resonates throughout the letter. They may be a group or groups, and consist in each location of different individuals constituting those groups, but in their response to and interaction with the addressees, it is singular, because such a gaze is singular in source: the anxiety springs from fear of the good of someone or group or even groups being seen by an envious eye. In this belief system, references are to the singular eye, not eyes, at least in the cultures with which this text dealt. It is perhaps a group or groups of influential people in view in each of the addressees' locations (e.g., 5:12; cf. 1:7; 4:17; 6:12-13), but

181. Dodds, *Irrational,* 29.

it is of *the* eye being cast toward themselves that is affecting them, according to Paul, so that the nature of this influence is related to envious rather than the helpful designs they have naïvely, to date, supposed (3:1; 5:7-10; 6:17).[182] The association might not have been drawn when the term was first used in 1:7, but by 5:7-10 it may have echoed with "dread"![183]

This does not mean that these influential people actually have envious designs or have "gazed" upon the addressees. These are aspects of Paul's rhetoric, designed to undermine the present implied trust of the addressees in these people and their other message of good. And this is consistent with the dynamics of this belief system, which is fueled by the gazee's and gazee detector's (i.e., Paul's) concern with the response of the other to their good, not by the gazer per se, who might in fact be an innocent victim of the fear or accusation.[184] The influencers have responded to the addressees' claims as inappropriate to their place and thus in need of being appropriately stirred up; but in terms of motives, it may be for the addressees' own good, as the influencers perceive things. That is, they have seen the confidence of the addressees in their new standing based upon the proclamation of Jesus Christ—for example, as already righteous ones, children of Abraham, heirs of God—in need of interaction, of stirring, of change. But the result for the addressees is motion where a settled state had been already assumed. In Paul's estimation, this glance was filled with envy.

This observation may provide another way to illuminate their identity, for Paul would presume that the warning, even if delivered as an accusation, was effective once made and was thus predicated upon a believable basis sufficient for the addressees to reconsider their previous view of the motives and methods of these people toward themselves. Rather than being stirred up appropriately, as they were believing themselves to be, that is, for their own good, perhaps they have been agitated instead, even affected by the dreaded eye, which would be unsettling indeed.

182. It is possible that while a group is or groups are involved, it is a single individual that is the ringleader or the caster of the eye. But this is not as likely in view of the circular nature of the letter and normal group dynamics that seem to otherwise be implied in the plural references and elsewhere throughout the letter.

183. Note that manuscript 075 has the variant ἐβάσκανε instead of ἐνέκοψεν in 5:7, which suggests that at least some copyist considered the possible allusion to be explicit (cf. Swanson, *NT Greek Manuscripts*, 67).

184. Cf. Nanos, "O Foolish Galatians"; Garrison and Arensberg, "Evil Eye," 292.

Are the Influencers Causing the Addressees to Suffer? Another Possible Implication of Paul's Evil Eye Accusation

Another possible source of information about the situations and these influential people may be supplied by Paul's comment in 3:4, which suggests that the addressees are in some way suffering: "Have you suffered [ἐπάθετε] so much in vain?—If it really is in vain?" Once again, the way one does or does not locate this language within the domain of Paul's evil eye accusation in 3:1 has a significant impact upon the interpretation. This may be translated "experiencing," but the accusation of the addressees having been affected by the eye in 3:1 gives the choice of "suffering" greater weight.[185] The force of the accusation hangs to some degree upon a recognizable loss that can be attributed to someone's envious gaze, in this case, a gaze cast by those whom the gazee had not suspected of such intentions.

This point shows the forceful edge to the irony with which Paul cuts the addressees, undermining their confidence in the interests of these other people and their proposed course for them. But still Paul's accusation may fail to convince if there is not a noticeable effect of suffering, once the addressees' attention is called to this victimization. But if they have in some way been suffering to date yet had not considered it as such, instead regarding their present condition of being shamed as an appropriate response to their inappropriate expectations of status, then this tactic may hit the mark.

In other words, the addressees had apparently accepted the identity proposition of Paul but discovered that it ran up against the longstanding official position of the alternate court of reputation that was in control of the larger situations in which they now found themselves by way of the influencers' influence—that is, traditional authority and authorities, or what Paul subversively refers to as human agency and agents—resulting in negative consequences for their self-esteem and access to goods. Why? Because the terms of the addressees' claims to legitimation were not accepted as conforming to the prevailing norms, as they had not yet acquired the status claimed on the terms dictated by these influential people as normal—traditional, scriptural, indisputable—at least in the present age!

Thus the addressees' own failure to comply with these other communal norms to date and the resultant suffering of shame and mar-

185. Note Paul's usage elsewhere: 1 Cor 12:26; 2 Cor 1:6; 12:26; Phil 1:29; 1 Thess 2:14. Cf. Baasland, "Persecution," 139–40.

ginalization have been deemed by themselves as appropriate to their current state. What Paul negatively evaluates by revealing as jealously sought by the influencers—not for the addressees' own good but rather in order to be excluded so as to cause them to be jealously motivated to seek what only the influencers seem to offer (4:17)—has not been regarded by the addressees as suffering. They have instead accepted these reactions as the proper responses to their own (now realized) hubris in assuming a place they have not yet earned. Such behavior toward themselves they had interpreted not as inappropriate but proper and even helpful—not as Paul now represents it negatively to be, when naming it as unsettling by way of purposeful obstruction, exclusion, persecution, seduction, compulsion—but as rather the appropriate response to their present preliminal or liminal state, as corrective discipline; although certainly unsettling, they rather represent unanticipated and troublesome delays along the way. But the addressees' own resultant behavior—like that of Peter's withdrawal at Antioch for fear of the ones advocating the circumcision of the Antiochene Gentiles in Christ—similarly masks hypocritically their own beliefs about the meaning of the death of Christ for themselves and thus manifests the lie at the source of their own retreat from walking straight toward the truth of the gospel of Christ.

The evil eye belief system involves a powerful paradox, and the exposition of the ambiguity this creates seems to be at the center of Paul's rhetorical move to enlighten the addressees about how things are instead of how they may appear. Public recognition is integral to the gaining of honor and is thus desirable; paradoxically, being seen makes one vulnerable to the deleterious effects of the envious gaze, the begrudging of the other of the very fortune that is at the heart of the recognizable honor. Thus, to expose oneself or to be exposed, especially among those perceived to be social equals, provokes a corresponding concern to protect oneself. There are two sides to the suspicious reflex this involves: on one side, the need to protect oneself or others in one's care from being affected where good fortune is recognizable; and on the other side, the tendency to attribute symptoms of harm or declining fortunes to an envious gaze and thus to seek healing and future protection from the envious source.

Paul's accusation presupposes both aspects of this system at work. However, ironically, his rhetorical approach suggests that the addressees have not perceived their present predicament in these terms, even though his comments make it clear that they are intimately familiar with the system and, in fact, had evaluated his own presence among them on the basis thereof (4:12-15).[186] Paul appeals to the perception of some good fortune among the addressees that is worthy of envy, namely, the receipt of the Spirit and the working of miracles among them (3:5). At the same time, he attributes their experience of suffering to social marginalization. The experience of suffering shame by having a claim to honor publicly refuted is not appropriate or for their own good. These policies have been enacted instead in the interests of the influencers' own good. The policies, Paul says, are the result of the influencers' pained response (i.e., envy) to the addressees actual acquisition of the goods being claimed.

The addressees' receipt of the Spirit of God and experience of miracles in their midst, developments in the addressees' lives that have occurred independently not only of proselyte status but even of any involvement on the part of the influencers themselves, have created envy, Paul's accusation assumes, the result of which is the casting of the evil eye and the manifestation of which is the present inappropriate suffering of the addressees for what God has graciously given them in Christ (3:1-5). Again, whether the accusation of Paul properly describes either the motives or actions of the influencers as envious or even explains the current state of the addressees is an open question for the historical critic. But the sharpness of the accusation may provide useful historical data.

"A Little Leaven Leavens the Whole Lump": Insider or Outsider Language?

It is also useful to consider Paul's proverbial maxim in 5:9: "A little leaven leavens the whole lump."[187] Here we are confronted not with outsider but insider language.[188] The contextual force of this comment has been generally overlooked by those who regard the influencers as outsiders on other grounds. But this passage falls in the midst of his argument against those persuading the addressees and offers a clue to their identity precisely as insiders (vv. 7-10): "You were running well; who put an obstacle in the way of you obeying the truth? This persuasion is not

186. Cf. J. H. Elliott, "Paul."

187. Found outside the NT only in Josephus (*Ant.* 3.252, 255). These cases are simply in explanation of priestly sacrifices, one for Shavuot or Pentecost with leaven and the other case of bread baked without leaven. There is no hint of Paul's usage here, in terms of either proverbial or polemical usage.

188. Richardson, *Israel,* 90.

from him who calls you. A little leaven leavens the whole lump. I have confidence in the Lord that you will take no other view than mine; and he who is unsettling you will bear his judgment, whoever he is."

The line of reasoning one finds in arguments regarding the leaven of 5:9, that the influencers are thus identified as a foreign element,[189] fails to recognize that leaven is a natural element, like flour, for making bread, though bread of a particular kind: leavened, that is, risen bread. If one seeks to make unleavened bread, then it is an ingredient that may not be used, for even a small amount will influence the final result, determining the nature of the bread as leavened. This quality is present in the way the noun for leaven (ζύμη) and the verb for what causes this effect of leavening or fermenting (ζέω) are related; the one necessarily gives rise to the other.

Without leaven, the bread will take a certain direction, in this case, Paul's (note the similar usage of the metaphor in 1 Cor 5:6-8). With leaven it will be affected to take another direction, in this analogy, that of the influencers. So the point is not its alien nature but the fact that even a trace of leaven will be influential in a way that ineluctably determines the final result.

The argument against this kind of understanding of the dynamic, for example, by those who take the image of leaven to refer to corruption or evil per se,[190] or to refer to a minority that has left the addressees' subgroup as heretics,[191] are expressions of conclusions reached apart from contextual application of the imagery of this passage. Paul is allowing for no compromise,[192] and in this way the point is similar to that of the curse- and castration-wishes, both of which are in fact found in the context. It is not that leaven is foreign or alien but that it is influential to the point of being determinative for the entire loaf: it only takes a little influence by certain ingredients such as leaven to affect the course that the whole loaf will take.

189. E.g., Sieffert, *Galater*, 16, is commonly cited.

190. E.g., Witherington, *Grace in Galatia*, 372. Although in the NT there are cases where leaven is used in polemical fashion (cf. Matt 16:6, 11-12; Mark 8:15; Luke 12:1), it was not so used in earlier Scriptures and is used also in the NT in a positive metaphor, like the mustard seed, of the mighty influence of something so small becoming so big in the context of a parable of the kingdom of God (Matt 13:33; Luke 13:21). Note also that in Matt 16:12, the point is that no concern is being expressed with the leaven of bread.

191. Hawkins, "Opponents," 100–101.

192. So too Dahl, "Galatians," 93.

CHAPTER 8

PROPOSING A NEW IDENTIFICATION: THE INFLUENCERS

I have imagined and described these "other" people as influential up to this point, and now I will explain why I have chosen to refer to these influential people in Galatia as the "influencers." Bearing in mind that "identity is always constructed from a point of *view*,"[1] my goal is to expand the way in which the interpreter may imagine, describe, and label, from a historical-critical perspective, those whom Paul accuses of affecting the addressees.

First, it will be helpful to define some terms that have been introduced in this discussion. The choice of *influencers* derives from the influence they have had, according to Paul, upon the addressees.[2] Paul's rhetoric implies that submitting themselves to this influence appears to the addressees like it will provide something good, the identity and resources that they believe themselves to need. In this sense the use of the term *influencers* reflects a primary meaning of influence: "to flow in."

The usage of the term with reference to those who are active among the addressees but in ways that Paul in this letter opposes provides the context for this description in terms of social influence. But how influence is evaluated, negatively, as Paul does, or positively, as most likely the influencers and to some degree the addressees do as well, is a matter of social perspective determined by where one stands on the appropriateness of that influence in the sphere of the addressees' lives.

Social influence may be understood, for example, as "characterized by argument, conflict and controversy in which individuals or groups try to change the thoughts, feelings and behaviours of others, by persuasion, argument, example, command, propaganda or force."[3] Within

1. Jenkins, *Social Identity*, 27.

2. Note Perelman and Olbrechts-Tyteca, *New Rhetoric*, 19.

3. Hogg and Vaughan, *Social Psychology*, 200; the following definitions draw especially from 200–232, and Hogg and Abrams, *Social Identifications*, 157–85, which well represent the prevailing views of the social psychological field. Another way to shape this discussion is provided in Malina, *Christian Origins*, 80–82.

such a context, a person or group may be influenced by their reference group (or groups; for brevity, I will use the singular form), that is, those who are psychologically significant for the influenced person's or group's attitudes and behavior. The norms of this reference group, that is, the normative attitudes and behaviors that characterize so as to define group membership and provide differentiation between groups, may be assessed either positively (one seeks to behave in accordance with those norms) or negatively (one resists or behaves in the opposite way). At the same time, a person or group has a more concrete affiliation with a group, which may be considered their membership group: that group to which the person or group belongs by the criteria of membership as defined by the consensus or social control agent(s) of that group.

These different groups and their different influences upon a person or (sub)group can overlap and conflict. A positive reference group will serve as a source of conforming behavior; because the person or group internalizes and validates the group's norms, they choose to behave in conformity with those norms. If the reference group is also the membership group, then the person's or group's conforming behavior will be positively validated by the membership group. But if it is not the person's or group's membership group but another reference group with which they conform, then the behavior may be negatively valued (as nonconforming) by their membership group. And if the reference group is negatively valued, and thus the norms not conformed with, but this group is also the person's or group's membership group, then coercive power to produce compliance may be applied. This compliance would constitute a change in expressed attitudes and behavior but not the internalization of the norms, so as to give merely the appearance of conformity to other members of the membership group, or perhaps only those considered to be agents of or sympathetic to the policies of coercion that have effected the compliance.

It seems that we can be certain, at least from the rhetorical perspective of Paul, that these other people are influencing the addressees, even if the degree to which compliance or conformity has been or is being actualized is less clear. Paul fears that the addressees' desires have been engaged to begin the alternate course of ritual proselyte conversion (μετατίθεσθε: 1:6; cf. 3:1-5; 5:1-12; 6:12-13), because he addresses them as though they have to some degree internalized as good for themselves this other message, that is, considered conforming with the values of this reference group in order to ensure compliance with membership norms. But his (present aspect) grammar throughout these passages and rhetorical purpose to dissuade from a course of action not yet completed—in fact one that he expresses confidence, albeit rhetorical, that they will successfully see themselves back from (5:10)—indicate that they have at this point only entertained starting down the alternate, seemingly complementary path (cf. 1:6-7; 3:1-5; 5:1-12; 6:12-13), and it is possible that some have already begun (cf. 6:1). So Paul's dissociating rhetoric seeks to convince the addressees to negatively value the influencers and their norms in terms of reference and see this present predicament as a misplaced call for compliance with membership norms that should themselves be modified in view of Christ's actions on their behalf.

Influencers is a label that can cover the various descriptions, including accusations of intentions and methods, that Paul explicitly makes throughout the letter. But it is itself relatively neutral. Like water when stirred, the value judgment "unsettled" or "turbulent" depends upon the view that its appropriate state is calm, and the action of stirring disruptive. A surfer or sailor might not agree with such an assessment of the value of water put into motion. Indeed, one can influence for good, as interpreters grant that Paul seeks to do in this letter.

Although he would probably not choose in the first instance to call himself an influencer, Paul would accept such a description of his intentions in this letter: he seeks to influence the addressees—they are within his membership group, and his rhetoric assumes that they are members of his reference group who seek positive evaluation therein.[4] He announces as much. And he has told them things in the past that should have influenced them to resist the influence of these other influential people and their other message of good, specifically to negatively value their opinion as a point of reference on the matter of membership norms. This letter actually is a message of refamiliarization with norms he now appeals to again in order to enhance the influence he hopes his message will finally successfully produce.[5] After all,

4. Note Paul's admission of seeking to persuade (πείθομεν) people in 2 Cor 5:11.

5. It is not clear whether the initial teaching of Paul was with people not affiliated or familiar with Jewish communal life, as would have been righteous Gentiles or God-fearers, and thus it is not clear if Paul's original teaching was defamiliarizing them with the prevailing understanding of reality or in the first instance familiarizing them with something that they were virtually if not entirely unfamiliar with as pagans.

besides the ironic ridicule that itself manifests his intention to bring them into conformity with the acknowledged norms for those who have confessed faith in Christ, Paul describes himself as a mother who is so upset by developments among her children that she wishes to bear them in the womb once again. And he expresses confidence that they will take "no other view than mine" (5:10).

There is no reason to presume any negative motive for these people or groups or their response to Paul's description of their interests toward the addressees at this time. They appear to seek to influence these Gentiles in conformity with the traditional membership and reference group norms that they have themselves internalized as good and thus as appropriate for directing these Gentiles in view of the claims they have themselves expressed: to be counted as full members among the righteous ones of God. This identification involves a boundary defining the normative interests of these influencers and the basis for reacting to the addressees' nonconformity to date with the norms for identification of membership, and further, for evaluating the legitimacy of those norms appealed to by the group of Christ-believers according to Paul's message of good. It may even be argued that initiation of the influencers' influence is merely the result of the influencers' own compliance, compelled by the insistence of the addressees of their need to acquire undisputed full membership status, even if that request by the addressees was itself in response to the perhaps congenial welcome as Gentile guests, albeit accompanying unexpected and painful denial of the validity of a claim to membership identity that the addressees have believed they already acquired, the assertion of which had begun the whole process. The attribution of influence as well as value judgments like "unsettling" have to do with who initiated the contact and on what terms, although they continue to extend to the various parties as the developments unfold.

If the addressees' interest in the influencers' group norms were merely referential, then the influence of the influencers would not be coercive, for the addressees would not and do not claim to be members, and thus obliged to comply with the prevailing norms for membership. If the addressees are not proselytes according to the communal norms of the influencers or as Gentiles placing themselves under their authority by choice, then they are not members in terms that would rightfully warrant coercive force, especially of pagans in a diaspora setting! The influencers would rather seek to alter the referential value of their communal norms for the addressees as Gentile guests seeking to convert to proselyte status, and their influence would be persuasive without coercion, to influence conformity with the entrance requirements of proselyte conversion that would allow the addressees the full membership that they seek. But if the addressees claim to be members of the influencers' group already, albeit not in compliance with the norms for acquisition of such membership, then coercive influence is invited, and compliance, if not conformity, would be considered essential.

Paul's rhetoric implies that, although no coercive force to be circumcised has been exercised toward the addressees, nevertheless, the claims of the addressees to full inclusion among the membership group of the historical righteous ones of God—that is, Jewish people, Israel—predicated upon their internalization of the Christ-believing group's norms established on Paul's influence when formerly among them, have put the addressees in a sphere of social life in which the influencers' perceived right to influence them seems legitimate. Thus, the influencers may consider their influence helpful and not coercive. They seek to provide the way for the addressees to negotiate the membership the addressees wish to acquire because of a positive evaluation of the influencers' reference or at least membership group norms (mistakenly having thought this was already accomplished). But they do so according to the norms of the influencers' reference and membership group, which the addressees must therefore now approach, wherein this claim is exposed as mistaken; they are shamed, but the way to redress the error is provided as well, so that honor is but a rite of passage away.

But Paul considers their influence harmful, destructive, anathema, because he does not grant any longer the legitimacy of the influencers' reference group norm for membership for Gentiles in Christ in view of the meaning of the good news of Christ as revealed to him and the other leaders of this coalition, which has modified the traditional interpretation of the fathers in view of the present dawning of the age to come. Like a parent seeking to distance his or her children from the worrisome results of conforming with peer-group norms that may endanger them far beyond what the children are at the moment apparently able to recognize as immediately of relevant equal value, Paul responds with stereotyping polemic that tells us more about his affection for his children than it does of the character of the peers. What the influencers may see as a genuine concern for conformity because of the expressed interests of the addressees in membership, Paul sees as compliance with the expressed norms of this other reference group instead.

This occurs because membership is already, in his view, granted by a higher norm than those to which they appeal, that of the revelation of God's fulfilled promise to Abraham for the awaited age by way of Christ. With the dawning of that age, Gentiles are granted membership in the reference group of Abraham's children according to promise, the righteous ones of God. On those terms the addressees have already conformed. So he characterizes the influence of the influencers upon his addressees as illegitimate and regards it as inappropriate coercion. The influencers, on the other hand, may see it as appropriate measures to bring conformity with the reference group norms to which the addressees seek to identify, along with compliance with the established norms for negotiating the entrance that the addressees appear to desire. But Paul's rhetoric implies that to date the influencers' perspective appears to have affected the perspective of the addressees; they are approached as internalizing this other message as good for themselves, so that it is conformity and not mere compliance from the addressees' point of view.

In other words, the influencers' interests in the addressees are not, from their own perspective, bad but good. Seeking to assert influence, to control the negotiation of the boundary presently preventing this identity claim and concomitant access to communal honor and goods is the responsible expression of their authority in the interests of the community bounded thereby, as well as those of these Gentiles. That is the matrix from which Paul's rhetorical interest works as well: the addressees face influential representatives of two membership groups; they must decide against the other alternative, because they cannot successfully conform to the norms governing referential and membership status for both, and the wrong choice would "sever them from Christ" (5:4)!

Ironically, after this letter has been received, the influencers may well regard the influence of Paul—his unsettling of the addressees—as wrongly motivated, or at least wrongheaded, in view of the long-standing communal norms, and manipulative, characterized, for example, as persuading, obstructing, subverting, jealously seeking, even compelling the addressees against their own earnest desires, not to mention best interests, that is, according to the influencers' internalized norms.[6]

6. Galatians 4:18 may certainly be taken to suggest such anticipation of the accusation of "jealous" interests toward the addressees on the part of Paul, once this charge might be made known to those influencing the addressees.

In the next section, I will develop two major new categories of description for the influencers. First is their identity in terms of Jewishness, proposing that they are not only Jewish but probably involved in the administration of the ritual conversion process, which explains their level of contact and influential involvement with the addressees in seeking indisputable status among the righteous ones. Moreover, the social dynamics in Galatia that Paul's rhetorical approach seeks to undermine may be accounted for even more precisely if some of the members of the influencers' group or groups are proselytes themselves. Second is their identity and affiliation with Christ and the Christ-believing coalition. I will argue that they are not Christ-believers or affiliated in any way, but that the social location and interests of the addressees (and Paul) bring out their influence, though not necessarily opposition to this coalition or the addressees' faith in Christ, as long as they are willing to conform with the norms for acquisition of that identity which they wish to claim for themselves. In discussing these topics, my construction of the situation and interpretation of the ironic message of Paul's letter will be articulated.

PART 3

A NEW CONSTRUCTION OF THE GALATIAN CONTEXTS

CHAPTER 9

THE LOCAL JEWISH AND PAGAN COMMUNAL CONTEXTS OF THE ADDRESSEES

Almost all interpreters regard the influencers in Galatia to be Jewish people, indeed, to be representatives of a Jewish interest group, because they promote circumcision. Yet this aspect of their identity is not considered on its own terms but with respect to additional interests. Interpreters inextricably combine the influencers' Jewish identification with their identity and interests as Christ-believers (thus usually labeled Judaizers and variously as Jewish Christians or Christian Jews), as well as outsiders, and in general, with connections to the Jerusalem apostles with whom Paul is supposed to be in conflict. Apparent exceptions to these identifying characteristics have already been shown to be just that, apparent, because they still include (at least imply) Christ-believing Jewish people mediating the pressure put upon the addressees, whether as a result of other local (e.g., separate Jewish communal) or distant (Jerusalem, Antioch) affiliations. And in addition, their identification is sometimes combined with other aspects of identity, such as, to varying degrees and for different reasons, Gnosticism, Pharisaism, or other such membership group or groups.

The work done to this point certainly supports a Jewish identity, whether of self, group, or groups, for the influencers, although it questions most of the other attributes just named. They are advocates of the circumcision of the addressees, after all: in 6:12, Paul accuses the influencers of being those who "would compel you to be circumcised," and in 6:13, as those who "desire to have you circumcised." And the influencers are here called by Paul οἱ περιτεμνόμενοι—although variously translated as the "ones for circumcision" or "ones receiving circumcision," among others—making it clear enough, even in spite of the lack of clarity of this participial phrase's meaning for the later reader, that the influencers are circumcised indeed, at least by the time that Paul writes.

Moreover, the exigence revolves around the issue of appropriate identity for these Gentiles seeking inclusion as equals among the righteous ones of God. Particularly significant is whether their present claim according to the norms of the Christ "good news" is legitimate in the face of the traditional "news of good," which involves proselyte conversion to acquire Israelite status, and their claim questions, if not entirely dismisses, their age-to-come status as operative for themselves in defining their current standing based upon a claim to be children of Abraham by promise. Thus, Paul interrogates the addressees Socratically in 3:1-5: will they seek "completion" in the flesh of an identity transformation already confirmed in the Spirit? Paul poses the matter in antithetical terms similar to those that define his own ministry (cf. 1:1; 1:10—2:21): Is it of divine sanction, or human, that is, according to the traditional interpretation of the fathers on the question of the truth of the gospel of Christ for Gentiles, or by direct revelation from God creating and confirming this realization?

The sarcastic wish in 5:12 that "those who subvert you would castrate [ἀποκόψονται: 'cut off'] themselves" implies not only that those influencing the addressees are circumcised but that they also represent the role of the circumciser, as would a *mohel* (מוהל). Here, Paul cuts his victim by arousing suspicion of those whom they must trust in a most delicate maneuver: instead of cutting the prepuce of these Gentiles, putting them in their "place" in traditional ritualized terms, Paul hopes the influencers will cut off their own members, consigning them to an undesirable end by the agency of their own "humanly" sanctioned hands. This graphic invective echoes the curses of 1:6-9 in a way that can stand on its own in the context of Paul's comments, although appealing perhaps to the extreme character of the castration rituals of the *galli*,[1] a common sight due to the presence of this pagan cult throughout Anatolia during this period, or maybe ambiguous eunuch status in Israelite terms. Regardless, the comment further indicates, along with the others just described, that the context of the influencers' concern for the circumcision of the addressees is to be understood in distinctively Jewish terms.

In spite of such polemic, we should remember that Paul's rhetoric develops the proposition of the addressees' identity as full members apart from circumcision (as representatives of the nations) by way of dissociating argument, that is, by the modification of existing Jewish

1. S. Elliott, "Choose," esp. 679; idem, "Anatolian," 419–503, 506–25; Neyrey, *Paul*, 191–92. If the influencers were themselves *galli*, however, the sarcasm would make no sense, because they are already "cut off" rather than circumcised. The point is that they are proud of their identity as circumcised circumcisers, and it is the subversion of this honored identity when it undermines the honored standing of the Gentile addressees in Christ that provides the force for Paul's critique.

(Israelite) terms and expectations. For example, he insists that the addressees as Gentiles are already children of Abraham, "sons" of God, full "heirs," righteous ones, members of "God's household" who await the reaping that will occur in the day of the Lord, of the One Creator God when he brings justice for all creation. Even their identification with Jesus Christ is put in terms of a uniquely Jewish worldview on the present order of this "evil" age: he was publicly crucified (3:1) and thus a Jewish martyr of the Roman regime. Yet this shameful way to die was a giving of himself "for our sins to deliver us from the present evil age, according to the will of our God and Father, to whom be glory in the age of ages," for he has "raised him from among the dead ones" (1:1-3). These are indeed terms of identity developed within a Jewish way of interpreting time and space.

Yes, it is safe to assume that the influencers' circumcision and advocacy thereof for the addressees are defined in traditional Jewish communal terms. And yes, it is safe to assume that the influencers are Jewish and represent Jewish communal interests. The issue is not merely a cut in the flesh but the completion of the ritual process of proselyte conversion into the community of the righteous ones, the Israel of God, that this action symbolizes.

The only substantial challenge to identifying them as Jewish people or groups has been Johannes Munck's proposal, which many have understood to maintain that the influencers are Christ-believing Gentiles whose interest in Jewish identity by way of circumcision is derived from Scripture independent of Jewish people or their direct influence. But Munck's argument paradoxically undermines the very basis of the identification that it seeks to uphold. For Munck, the influencers are Gentiles who have taken up Jewish identity concerns because of former experiences with synagogue life as righteous Gentiles (i.e., before Paul). Through these formerly acquired "Jewish spectacles," coupled with "a sympathetic picture of the whole Jewish Christian world" that they have because of Paul's own "sympathy and understanding" "about Jerusalem and the Judaean churches," the addressees have concluded wrongly that they should have themselves circumcised. That is, with "misunderstandings" because "newly converted," they thus "easily drop into habitual Jewish ways of thought," such as mistakenly continuing "to read the Old Testament as a Jewish book."[2]

2. Munck, *Salvation*, 89, 129–34. This composite includes what seem to me to be two paradoxical attitudes toward Judaism. It appears that the negative attitude

Thus, the influencers are for Munck a part of the Gentile addressees' membership group who have come to regard themselves as some kind of theoretical proselytes apart from continued participation in Jewish communal life, and they advocate that the same reference group norms be adopted by the addressees. It seems then that the reason assumed for those addressees who delay their own circumcision is their failure to have shared the same background, either in synagogues before Paul or by contact with him, and thus to lack enough exposure to and conviction of the reference group values that have shaped the course of those other Gentiles among themselves who are "in the present" being circumcised, according to Munck.

Although the influencers and the addressees might seem to be identified by Munck as Gentiles, for he calls them such, the distinction that arises in his argument is sharper. The influencers are understood to be Gentiles from among the all-Gentile addressees' membership group who have only recently become circumcised—Munck calls them "circumcised Gentiles"—which would seem to imply that they are (in some way theological) Jewish proselytes, but Munck does not so describe them.[3] Characterizing the influencers as "circumcised Gentiles" rather than proselytes does not really make sense in social terms framed Jewishly. They are no longer Gentiles once circumcised, even on Munck's own premises, which appeal to involvement in Jewish communal life, even if former, and the example of Paul, unless Munck is maintaining that this is like a disembodied group that does not have anything to do with other Jewish or even Christ-believing groups or movements of which we are aware, before, during, or after this time, an implication that is itself open to significant criticism as well and one that it does not seem that he actually intends to draw.[4] It seems safe

characterizes the influence of former association with specifically non-Christ-believing synagogue life, and the positive one is the exception reserved for Christ-believing Jewish life. These Jewish "church" members "made a practice of observing as many of the ordinances as was *necessary* in a Jewish milieu," so that from Paul's picture they did not conclude that "what was strange to them was of *inferior* quality" (131; emphases added). In other words, this infers that like Munck's Paul, these Jewish Christ-believers elsewhere did not judge living Jewish life essential in principle but rather merely expedient.

3. Also Gaston, *Paul*, 81, 90, 109, 221 n. 21; Richardson, *Israel*, 90, 96–97.

4. Maintaining this view would of course fail to make sense of different social processes, not least our knowledge of the existence, much less preservation, of this letter!

therefore, in spite of Munck's thesis, to assume that the influencers are Jewish, proselytes perhaps, and their advocacy of circumcision for the addressees is framed by traditional Jewish communal norms, to which they appeal.

Although the consensus is that the influencers are Jewish, which my own argument to this point supports as well, the dynamics of influence in terms that might make sense of their Jewishness, rather than those other attributes, have not really been explored.[5] This is naturally characteristic of the traditional approaches, which do not generally concern themselves with social (e.g., sociopolitical, social-psychological, sociological, even historical-critical or religious) or rhetorical criticism as much as matters theological, or with sympathetic engagement with Jewish religious life. But upon close inspection, this paucity of consideration is evident in perhaps unexpected places among modern alternative views that are concerned with social processes and rhetorical criticism. Let us consider two cases that represent that trend.

Current Trends in Interpretation

Consideration of political exigencies has arisen in the work of Robert Jewett and A. E. Harvey, whose theses (especially Jewett's) are probably influential on this matter because they seem to other interpreters to make better sense of the social dynamics, such as the ostensible marginality of the influencers based upon Paul's comments in 6:12-13, and the implied disregard for strict Law observance implied in his accusation there as measured by his statement of principle in 5:3. Yet even in these cases, the concern has really been not with the influencers as Jewish but with something and someone else: the interests of those who are imagined to have sent the influencers. In Jewett's case, the influencers as well as their senders are from Jerusalem;[6] in Harvey's case, the influencers are from local synagogues that exist separately

5. Contra Schütz, *Paul,* 124: "Insofar as there has been anything approaching a consensus about the origin and nature of the opposition Paul is countering with this letter, that agreement has focused on the Jewish nature of the opponents' interests."

6. Jewett, "Agitators," 204–5; followed by, e.g., R. Longenecker, *Galatians,* xci–xciv, 74–75. This thesis was anticipated by the work of, e.g., Dix, *Jew and Greek,* 42–44, who proposed a similar explanation for the Antioch incident but not the situation of the Galatian addressees per se and in various ways by those listed below with Harvey. See also discussion above on the issue of outsiders.

from the addressees' communities; they are Jewish members who also attend these "churches."[7]

Actually, these people and their interests are examined primarily as they are taken to reflect on what is behind the motives of the influencers' influencers, that is, those who send the influencers to bring pressure upon the addressees. In these constructions, the influencers seek to reduce the source of the pressure upon themselves by putting pressure upon the addressees. This motive and the concomitant actions are interpreted to be expressions of expedience on the part of the influencers, and even their senders, in the effort to avoid persecution from non-Christ-believing agencies that threaten them. Thus the lack of character demonstrated by the influencers' advocacy of the Galatian Gentile addressees' completion of proselyte conversion is emphasized, whereas their Jewish conviction consists essentially of self-serving political interests. This development is interpreted as a result of the zeal for the Law of those who send the influencers; thus, the senders fear zealous Jews.

In the view of Jewett, and those who follow his case, the influencers are sent in response to pressure brought upon the leaders of the Jerusalem Christ-believing coalition by Judean Zealots (although the formal existence of the Zealot party at this early date is a questionable proposition).[8] They thus are sent to the addressees in Galatia from Judea to seek "to *avert* the *suspicion* that they were in communion with lawless Gentiles" (emphasis added). They are not taken to be concerned with actual Law observance, with conformity on the basis of shared conviction but just with the appearance of compliance.[9] In Jewett's view,

7. Harvey, "Opposition," 326–27. Aspects of this essay were anticipated by, e.g., Lütgert, *Gesetz*, 16, 94–106; Ropes, *Singular*, 27, 44–45; Burton, *Galatians*, 349–50; Enslin, *Christian Beginnings*, 216–24; Tyson, "Opponents," 252. It is followed in various ways by the theses of, e.g., Richardson, *Israel*, 90–97; Winter, *Seek the Welfare*, 133–43; Muddiman, "Anatomy," 260–61; Esler, *First Christians*, 9, 56; idem, *Galatians*, 88–92. See also discussion above on the issue of outsiders.

8. Note the studies that have examined the issue since Jewett's article, especially Horsley and Hanson, *Bandits;* Horsley, *Spiral;* Donaldson, "Rural Bandits."

9. In social-psychological terms, conformity in general refers to an intragroup phenomenon wherein an individual expresses the norms of a group, and norms describe, evaluate, or prescribe the ideals that typify the beliefs, attitudes, and behavior of that group at a given moment. Social control agents or social influencers, such as parents, teachers, priests, and public officials, seek to ensure the conformity of its group's members to a set of group expectations, and successful execution of these roles is based on the power they are perceived to have to com-

those who send the influencers are themselves Christ-believers, as are the influencers, but they are still so aligned with Jewish communal (political) interests in Judea that the senders themselves are merely coerced representatives of the interests of non-Christ-believing Zealots. The Judean senders of the Galatian influencers must answer to non-Christ-believing Zealots for the failure (apparent noncompliance with reference group norms they have not actually shared until this point because of their faith in Christ) of their Christ-believing coalitions in Jerusalem to bring groups of Christ-believing Gentiles—even as far away as Galatia—into the fold as Jewish proselytes (according to presumably shared membership group norms). At the same time, the Judean senders of the Galatian influencers claim for themselves in Judea an ostensible Torah-observant lifestyle and thus harbor an expectation of political tolerance, if not privilege as well, for their Christ-believing communities in Judea (although this concern for Christ-believing must be merely theological in nature, because they seek by this expedient action to show that Christ believing has not altered the convictional values that guide their conformity with the membership or reference group norms of Zealots).

There are several significant problems with Jewett's thesis,[10] not least that it is not the Galatian influencers upon whom he focuses where Jewish interests are concerned but the proposed politically obsequious Jerusalem Christ-believing establishment of their senders and the senders' senders, as it were. The Zealots in Judea are supposedly interested in the compliance not only of the Jerusalem Christ-believers

---

pel conformity with those norms, whether by example or coercion (power: the ability to influence, which of course is relative, i.e., the perception of more or less power results in the ability to exert more or less influence or conformity). A further distinction for the term *conformity* is useful. When a member expresses merely the outward appearance of conformity without being entirely persuaded of the value of that norm, perhaps as a result of coercion, to gain approval, or for some other reason that makes the conforming behavior expedient for that member at that moment, it may be described as public compliance. This may be distinguished from an internalization of and identification with the norm, which represents true conformity. Hence, the interplay of compliance and conformity can be useful for teasing out the implied reference and membership groups and norms of each of the players under consideration. See Hogg and Vaughan, *Social Psychology*, 200–231; Hogg and Abrams, *Social Identifications*, 157–85; and chapter 8's discussion of norms.

10. See also the criticisms by Barclay, *Obeying*, 64–65 n. 81.

but of distant non-Jewish Galatians as well. Supposedly, the influencers are concerned enough to travel this great distance (Jewett puts them in the northern region of Galatia) to bring to bear coercive power on congregations composed, in his view, entirely of Gentiles—Celts actually. But how is it politically possible for Judeans to bring such power to bear on diaspora pagans, or why are such outposts of sufficient concern for Zealots in Judea? Are there not problems enough within the Christ-believing coalitions in Judea or surrounding regions like Damascus and Antioch to satisfy their concerns, if driven by a formal—or even informal—zealousness for strict Law observance in political, and by definition as Zealots, anti-Roman terms? Moreover, how do they even know about these supposed Celtic groups? Is it psychologically or religiously probable in political terms for this interest to extend to seeking circumcision of members of Galatian Jewish, much less Gentile, groups? If so, this case is a serious departure from the usual cautious, even discouraging Jewish attitudes and responses toward conversion, in that it represents a sometimes threatening or at least compromising proposition for a minority culture in a diaspora setting. And it makes little sense of the desire on the part of the Gentiles Paul addressed to seek Jewish identity through circumcision if it provided only such an implied hollow result for themselves.[11]

Jewett's proposition paradoxically attributes to the Galatian influencers, and implies for those in Jerusalem who sent them, at the same time failure to be willing to suffer for the cross of Christ, which has defined the context of the subgroup's existence they seek by this action to justify, and neglect of concern zealously to keep the Law. Because the Jerusalem Christ-believers are supposed to have undertaken this task to confirm their conformance with the zealous concern for Law observance according to the norms of the Zealots, who are by definition characterized by intense concern to expose and destroy imperialist syco-

11. Jewett, "Agitators," 207, does suggest some kind of perfectionism is imagined, but this is to explain the interest of the addressees in compliance because of their Hellenistic sensibilities, not the influencers, and is itself open to significant criticism (cf. Donaldson, "Gospel," 179). Although Donaldson's position is debatable (see e.g., Philo, *Spec. Laws* 1.1–11, 304–6; *Migration* 92; 1QS 5.5, 28), the problem remains for Jewett in that the Galatian influencers would need to exhibit such perfection in order for this interpretation of circumcision to be convincing, and they would need to be emphasizing this in order for the Galatian Gentiles to desire Jewish piety of the kind that would satisfy Zealot interests. But Jewett denies such interest in zeal for Law observance itself.

phants, this would imply that the Christ-believers have been considered zealous according to these norms to date, that they are norms they have internalized as their own. Such zeal for the Law is nevertheless not the real reason they are imagined to undertake this long trip (surely to many other communities as well). That is rather for expedient appearances rather than principle, "averting their suspicions," because they do not actually care about strict Law observance for themselves or those whom they now seek to circumcise but merely seek expedient compliance, not conformity from conviction. And thus even though the Judean senders of the Galatian influencers' level of Law observance has to date duped the Zealots in Judea, Paul thinks that he can undermine their base of moral authority by this one summary comment in 6:13, because neither the Christ-believing Judeans nor the influencers they have sent to Galatia are actually zealous for the Law in their pursuit of the circumcision of the addressees, as though it was a reflection of their own beliefs. They are merely seeking the outward appearance of compliance in an effort to relieve the tension they are experiencing in Judea from the Zealots who actually uphold these values. The logical conclusion is that the Galatian influencers and the Christ-believers in Jerusalem whom they represent are neither sincerely zealous for the Law nor willing to suffer for their faith in Jesus if this conviction would lead to policies with regard to the standing of Christ-believing Gentiles, not to mention themselves, that the Zealots would find objectionable.

In Harvey's proposal, the influencers instead represent nearby synagogue authorities in Galatia, who similarly seek to make the "Christian congregations . . . . conform to an outward pattern of Jewish observances." The influencers then "yield to the pressure and are persuading others to do the same." But sadly, the expedient motive is taken to be the Jewish community's selfishness, rather than inter-Jewish political concerns, because these Gentiles had been members of the local synagogues previously as "God-fearers": "reprisals were inevitable" unless compliance with circumcision was gained, because "the church had drawn away numerous supporters from the synagogue."[12]

Harvey's model is based upon a sectarian premise: "It may be assumed that when they [the addressees] first became Christians they had made a clean break from the Jewish community."[13] Although Harvey emphasizes that the concern among Jews is generally more practi-

12. Harvey, "Opposition," 323–32.
13. Harvey, "Opposition," 324.

cal than theological in orientation, his approach does not explain the influencers' Jewish interests as their concern to conform with reference group norms, which norms are moreover portrayed as selfish, but rather merely to comply with conflicting membership norms of two separated groups in response to coercive power from the Jewish group upon the "Christian" group, presumably if any of the members wishes to continue to also attend the synagogue.[14] The senders of the influencers are non-Christ-believing local Galatian synagogue social control agents who bring sufficient pressure to bear on "Jews or Gentiles within the church" that they comply and advocate the circumcision of the Gentiles.[15] Those troubling the addressees are identified more precisely by Harvey as those seeking to avoid "persecution by the synagogue," as "Gentiles who have only recently become Jewish proselytes, or who are still contemplating doing so," so that "Paul's real opponents are those Christians in Galatia who are ready to yield to this pressure [from the synagogue] and are persuading others to do the same."[16]

How synagogue authorities are able to bring pressure to bear directly upon Gentiles in a diaspora setting, whom Harvey argues have left their former synagogue community for a new and separate community known as "the church," he does not explain. The reason given does not provide the support required in political or religious terms: if Gentiles are outside the synagogue communal life by choice, then what right or interest do Jewish communal authorities have in the exercise of such control toward what would logically be considered, in Jewish as well as non-Jewish communal terms, a pagan affiliation? There is no evidence of any Jewish communities of the diaspora exerting pressure upon Gentiles to become proselytes apart from an expressed interest on the part of these Gentiles to undertake this status transformation within the context of Jewish communal life.[17] Even the evidence in Acts, to which Harvey appeals, does not justify this portrait, because in these

14. Although Harvey writes of conformity, he uses this in the sense defined herein as compliance, a concern with appearances and not with internalization of the norms in question. Nevertheless, his distinction between the tensions as observance-oriented rather than theological beliefs per se is useful.

15. Harvey, "Opposition," 330.

16. Harvey, "Opposition," 326, 324, 327.

17. Several other interpreters, who implicitly consider or explicitly state that the Christ-believing communities addressed no longer function as synagogue groups, appeal to the questionable and unattested notion of pressure from minority Jewish communities upon these groups in Galatia. For example, Ropes appeals to the later

brief sketches the political and religious interests are very differently portrayed: the synagogue authorities approached the pagan civic authorities, presumably because they did not have such rights or perhaps even interest in bringing pressure to bear upon Gentiles or in keeping them around should they choose to leave. They were concerned about the effects of these Jewish travelers upon matters within their own synagogues and towns (villages or cities), with their own Jewish members, not with a separate and thus pagan group's affairs. This is central Anatolia, not Judea, although even there such actions toward non-Jewish groups would run into problems with the imperial regime and any collaborating Jewish agents! Surely, consideration of the repercussions from nonsynagogal civic leaders in a diaspora setting would be sufficient reason to check any such supposed selfish ambitions toward other than synagogue groups before they are exercised, only to bring about their own harm from pagan, local, not to mention imperial, authorities in the end.

In these proposals and others like them, in addition to the more traditional approaches, it is really the influencers' identity as Christ-believers, marginalized Judeans, or those seeking to preserve local dual membership in synagogue and church that emerge as the most salient concern for the interpreter. The influencers have not really been considered in terms of Jewish identity, certainly not in terms of an honorable interest in observing the Law within traditional communal norms, especially in the matter of their interested interaction with the identity claims of the addressees or the nature of what the influencers consider for them a "message of good."[18]

Moreover, in addition to failing to make sense of Jewish religious sensibilities or political realities—which means they do not account for Roman or Hellenistic administrative political realities, in which Jewish

situation giving rise to Chrysostom's rhetoric in Antioch to suggest a similarity with the Galatian situation (*Singular*, 45). But Ropes fails to note that the situation of Chrysostom, if taken as a model, suggests not that the Jewish community was putting pressure upon the Christ-believing Gentiles of Antioch but instead that these Gentiles were themselves attracted to and chose to attend Jewish community meetings in addition to Christian ones. If anything, it may suggest that the lines between these communities were not as sharply drawn, even many years after Paul, as Chrysostom wished.

18. Martyn, *Galatians*, 117–36, proposes a sketch of the influencers' message, which is an advance, although many aspects of this sketch do not differ from the traditional Christian negative portrayal of Jewish interests, motives, or actions.

communal life is embedded—views such as these also do not have the power to explain the interest of these Gentile addressees in compliance, much less conformity, although such positive interest is clearly implied in Paul's rhetoric. Why would Jewett's distant Celts care about helping Judeans solve their political problems by the expedient submission of their members to the circumciser's knife? They might be coerced if they consider themselves members of the same group, which seems doubtful if Jewett's portrait of a Law-free (and thus sectarian) Paul has established and shaped their group membership and reference group identity in the first place, but such coercion is not what Paul's ironic style rebuke is invented—or at least structured—effectively to resist. And why would Harvey's "former" synagogue Gentiles, after having gained righteousness according to Paul's gospel, desire now to submit themselves again to selfish former membership and reference group authorities when they seek to extract a piece of flesh? After all, these Gentiles are presumed to have left in order to avoid just such circumcision and the ambiguous standing it offered compared to that of the separate Christian groups in the first place. Why are the addressees confused or torn; what about this other message or its messengers could appear good enough to themselves to warrant (re)consideration, when it involves such a clear departure from their previous choice to depart and the norms that Paul has established for their faith in Christ? Moreover, the sources of resistance probable in such a sectarian setting are not tapped by Paul's rhetorical approach. The addressees are rather urged to resist as though unavoidably subordinate to these authorities (cf. 5:1) and ineluctably subject to the results that will follow from continued noncompliance with their membership and reference group norms. They are to prepare themselves instead to suffer the disapproval and lack of support the resultant marginality will perpetuate rather than solve, to become like the marginalized Christ and Paul, which marginality is precisely on their behalf, and to help each other through this inescapable present "evil" period. They are not approached as sectarians but as a subordinate group.

On a positive note, what Jewett and Harvey do draw attention to in their efforts is the fact that we must make sense of the social setting in which Gentiles are responding to identity concerns of a Jewish nature. The issues are not merely theological but the pragmatic concerns of social identity. The kinds of social dynamics implied by Paul's response suggest matters of concern in Jewish socio- and religiopolitical contexts. The immediacy of the Jewish identity concerns with which the addressees are struggling suggests a continued intimacy of association, rather than distance and concomitant opposition to the membership and reference group norms at stake, such as would be expected of sectarian Christian groups, especially if populated by Celts or other Gentile populations who were not in contact with local Jewish communal life.[19]

I suggest that there is much to consider about the influencers in Jewish terms, including the nature of the constraints that they may have to negotiate as members of minority Jewish communities in larger pagan environments. That is, by avoiding the a priori conclusion that the influencers originate or represent distant or separate communal identities, or oppositional Christ-believing affiliations, one can gain much by considering the probable identity of the influencers on their own terms as advocates of the circumcision of the addressees. Admittedly, the information from which we must work does have its limits, for it is derived from Paul's oppositional rhetoric. Such a construction as Paul's considers only certain social aspects of their identity and in a rather stereotypical fashion. For example, the interpreter can assume that each and every influencer in each and every location is also a person. A variety of personalities, roles, interests, motives, and so on would be expected to characterize them as individuals as well as members of various social groups, including ways that are also independent of their relationship with the addressees. Thus, although the analysis of Paul's rhetoric here promises to offer a more complex portrait of the influencers in social terms, it still faces significant limits for constructing their identity in personal terms, or in social terms revolving around interests other than those associated with the addressees.

The nature of the influence Paul seeks to check is dynamic; it has motivated the addressees to reconsider who they are and who they want to become even after he has anticipated and sought to prevent such developments when among them (cf. 1:9, 13; 3:1; 4:19; 5:3, 21). We should look further into, for example, the implications of his par-

19. In this matter, many of those who have similar if not derivative explanations of the identity of the influencers in sectarian terms are similarly implicated; e.g., Martyn shares with Jewett the view that the addressee's groups are composed entirely of Gentiles in the northern Celtic region which had no contact with Jewish communal life (*Galatians*, 16).

ticipial phrase to describe the influencers in 6:13, the nature of their own vulnerability to suffering through failure to make the addressees comply with their own membership and reference group norms in vv. 12-13, and in these same verses their apparent quest for honor by way of gaining the compliance of the addressees. Likewise, we must consider what kind of authority they must have to be accused of such social control over the addressees, so as to "exclude" them in order to increase their persuasive appeal (4:17), "obstruct" them by way of persuasion sufficient to "unsettle" them and cause them to thus deviate from the course they were running well (5:7-12; cf. 1:6-7), or "compel" them to be circumcised (6:12).

In addition to the accusations of Paul throughout the letter, his rhetorical approach reveals a palpable need to so undermine the influencers' objectives, strategies, and tactics—their motives as well as actions—that the immense threat of their influence is unmasked. To this end, Paul goes so far as to seek to undermine the concern to observe the Law by those who seek to influence these Gentiles to put themselves under the Law (cf. 6:13) and thus become obliged to full observance. Moreover, this last implication for the addressees is—although first appearing at the end of the letter—not a new point but one that he makes for them "again" (5:3; 6:13).

Paul frames the case in this way: like leaven is to bread, necessarily influencing its leavened outcome (5:9), so the influence of these influencers, if it is not resisted entirely on this issue of identity for the addressees—regardless of the price that might be paid—will not be denied but will have incalculable effects. I suggest that the imagery of leavening the whole captures well the situations of the Christ-believers functioning as subgroups within the larger Jewish communities of Galatia, an intra- as well as inter-Jewish context. Although the influencers may represent minority groups in terms of the larger pagan communities of Galatia, they represent the majority as well as dominant in-groups in their interaction with the addressees. In terms of this relationship, the addressees represent minority as well as marginalized out-groups.

The cut in the flesh that is in question, although perhaps small (like leaven), is nevertheless enormously influential for transforming one's identity. One is either circumcised and belongs to the circumcised people, or is not, just as a loaf is either leavened and will rise, or not. The tension is not outside/inside but between two competing methods of bread making or identity formation (out-group/in-group), each with distinct results and symbolic importance. Any mixing of the one will have a decisive effect upon the result. From Paul's perspective, there is thus no place for allowing even a little influence in the matter at hand. The influencers may seem to offer "another" message that is complementary and that does not undo the good news of Christ, yet it is in fact not able to be observed "also": the one subverts the other in a way that the audience has not yet fully appreciated (cf. 5:17).

The Social Dynamics of 6:12-13

The social dynamics implied in 6:12-13 will be considered first, and then the interpretation of Paul's substantive participial reference to the influencers, because οἱ περιτεμνόμενοι is beyond certain translation, and its meaning will have to be determined by each interpreter on the basis of the interpretation of the context (I will use "the ones choosing circumcision" until argued; otherwise this translation is from the NRSV until the texts are discussed):

> It is those who want to make a good showing in the flesh that try to compel you to be circumcised—only in order that they may not be persecuted for the cross of Christ. For even the ones choosing circumcision [οἱ περιτεμνόμενοι] do not themselves obey the law, but they want you to be circumcised that they may boast about your flesh.

This accusation in the epistolary closing functions as a terse summary of the author's greatest concerns (6:11-17). Here, Paul seeks to undermine the influencers' effect upon the addressees by revealing the interests of their own group in gaining the compliance of the addressees. The main issue is the evaluation of the other message of good by way of proselyte conversion. Paul's charge is multidimensional, and it seeks in one final polemical burst to expose beyond question just how selfish the reasons are for the influencers wishing to "compel [ἀναγκάζουσιν]" the addressees "to be circumcised." The nature of the compulsion implied in Paul's comment communicates a value judgment that sums up all of the others we have traced throughout this letter, which negatively characterize the motives and actions of the influencers, to say the least.

As used here, and mitigated by those other descriptions of the influencers' motives and actions, Paul's accusation would seem to be concerned with subverting the evaluation of the compliance sought, probably in response to the addressees' own stated interests, and thus not likely best described as coercion or in a way implying physical force per se, but rather as persuasion, because the addressees have the option of noncompliance if they are willing to suffer the consequences of marginalization (rather than punishment) that may result.[20] The addressees are not members on the influencers' terms but in some way guests, who, because of their own expressed expectation of membership, have been presented with the options of proselyte conversion, completion of which will confirm this claim on terms acceptable to the influencers, or else they must cease making such claims, for they remain pagans, regardless of how welcome they may be as in some way righteous guests. The persuasive force at work is the result of an appeal to the prevailing norms, with which compliance is necessary to achieve the goal of the membership standing they thought that they already had by way of the subgroups' good news of Christ, on the majority groups' terms, and thus beyond dispute. The persuasive tactics and even argumentation may be insistent and may feel like persecution, as does being shamed or put in one's place, but the force involved seems to represent, stripped of polemic, the usual functions associated with the execution of social control pertaining to reference and membership group norms when there is a dispute at the boundaries. The structure of Paul's comment brings attention to five particular matters that will help us assess these dynamics as well as the identities of the players and situations in Galatia.

The Influencers Want to Make a Good Showing in the Flesh

Paul begins his charge by describing the influencers' interest in gaining the addressees' compliance as an effort to enhance the influencers' own status: "it is those who want to make a good showing [εὐπροσωπῆσαι] in the flesh" that seek this result. In other words, they literally want their "face to appear fair,"[21] that is, to gain or confirm their honor rating

20. The Greek word ἀναγκάζω has a breadth of usage determined by context. See, e.g., Acts 28:19, where it refers to the logical conclusion that Paul drew, compelled by the circumstance, but not actually coerced to make this particular choice; in fact, those bringing pressure upon Paul would have liked the outcome to take a different direction than he was "compelled" by his own interests to go; see also 2 Cor 12:11, where it refers to the response judged necessary because of the Corinthians' misguided views; and Gal 2:16, on my reading (cf. *Mystery*, 341–58). Yet it is used of coercion too, e.g., in Acts 26:11.

21. Cf. Lohse, *TDNT* 6.779.

by public recognition of a job well done. Reference to one's "face," or lack thereof, can indicate one's legal status, a sense found often in public inscriptions.[22] In this case, the status at issue is confirmed or gained by successfully accomplishing the task of bringing the Gentile addressees to completion of proselyte conversion. But who is the public or court of reputation that they seek to impress? By itself, this comment could refer either to the appearance they want to make with the addressees, with their peers, or with those to whom they answer for the execution of this task. The first possibility seems to be covered at the end of the next verse ("that they may boast about *your* flesh"), where it is likely referring to the glory that is gained from the addressees. The second, honor from peers, is not indicated directly, although it is a logical possibility, because relative change in honor rating is a most intense concern among those of the same group and engaged in the same task. The third one, enhanced honor rating or recognition of status or some other expression of approval from those to whom they answer for the successful persuasion of the addressees, is indicated by the balance of the concern expressed (they are seeking to avoid the results of dissatisfaction with those to whom they answer, i.e., "persecution for the cross of Christ"). The approval of those to whom they report on bringing this matter into compliance with prevailing norms appears to be the point of this language and that which Jewett's thesis seems to imply as well. Yet the interest in enhanced honor from their own peer group and the addressees could be indicated by this language as well, as it is more clearly in the balance of Paul's accusation. To this matter we will return.

The Influencers Try to Avoid Persecution for the Cross of Christ

The charge continues by providing the reason for the addressees' unsettling predicament: the purpose of the influencers seeking the addressees' circumcision is "only that they may not be persecuted [διώκωνται] for the cross of Christ." The ones that Paul accuses of fear-

22. See Winter, *Seek the Welfare*, 137–43, for discussion, including the observation that this language "sometimes had connotations of spuriousness," and thus he asks, "did Paul use this word as a *double entendre*" (139). Winter translates 6:12a thus to be: "As many as wish to give you secure legal status by means of flesh" (139); however, he applies the interest in gaining status here to the Gentile addressees rather than the influencers. Although that is clearly in view elsewhere in the letter, vv. 12-13 seek instead to undermine the influencers' interest in the addressees gaining proselyte status.

ing persecution for appealing to the meaning of Christ's death are not the addressees but the influencers themselves. This is an important aspect that is otherwise not clear in the letter until now and should not be obscured by the interpreter. The only group that had seemed to be marginalized was the addressees; now the marginality of the influencers is made known to us. They too are caught betwixt and between the articulation of two conflicting membership and reference group norms, two messages of good. The more important message of good in this instance is that of the reference group from whom the influencers fear persecution, and it would seem to follow from the desire for enhanced honor or status—because this is part of a continuous sentence and accusation of motives—that the influencers seek enhanced honor rating or status from those above them in this instance. But that is the "other" reference group and news of good, that message that Paul says is "not another," not the good news of Christ as proclaimed by Paul and believed in by these Gentile addressees.

As with Paul's self-description of his suffering for the truth of the good news of Christ for Gentile inclusion apart from proselyte conversion, the naming of this treatment as "persecution" indicates a negative subjective value judgment that would be disputed most likely by those who measure out the specific treatment (5:11).[23] From the persecuted one's perspective, it might be shaming, discipline, punishment, training, and so on, that was deemed inappropriate to the circumstance and by persons suffering the results thereof. The claim of persecution could indicate any expression of disapproval, beginning at the level of a simple facial expression, word, or action; for any suffering, especially for failure to successfully complete that for which one is responsible, such as when mitigating circumstances are not given their rightful consideration. That

23. Severe measures are sometimes implied in Paul's case, both as persecutor (1:13) and persecuted (2 Cor 11:16-33). This does not seem to be the addressees' case; they are simply told they have been such things as "unsettled," "excluded," "obstructed," "compelled," and perhaps worst of all, "evil eyed," but not punished, as though they were already members who transgressed those norms that they were by definition responsible to uphold. The addressees must be told that what they "suffer" (3:5) now from the influencers is inappropriate, for until Paul's letter arrives they do not seem to be evaluating the treatment they are receiving from the influencers as inappropriate suffering such as to view this as persecution, but rather as appropriate to their present standing as merely Gentile guests rather than full members, although they are surprised to learn that this is so and wish to negotiate the conflicting evaluations.

certainly can feel like persecution for the recipient, regardless of the precise nature or level of the actual suffering itself or measures taken.

It is probable that the influencers fear something more than a mere disapproving glance—after all, how persuasive for the addressees would such easily trivialized fear on the part of the influencers be in comparison with the more important cutting of the flesh that is at hand for themselves, or the results of exclusion instead? They may fear being shamed for this failure, which could then include even the slight expressed by a glance, but it is likely more explicit and might include fear of losing the position of influence with the addressees that they hold, to the degree that such position is formally conferred. This kind of fear would resonate with Paul's accusation of their motive not to be put in the position of explaining the mitigating circumstances that the addressees create for them by way of appeal to norms ("the cross of Christ" as the basis for not becoming proselytes) that neither the influencers nor those to whom they answer share. To further elaboration of this implication I will return.

Because what the influencers seek to avoid is described by Paul as persecution for the cross of Christ, interpreters have taken this to clarify the Christ-believing identity of the influencers. The influencers are understood to believe that they can only retain their attachment to Christ-believing identity without being persecuted if they get their fellow Christ-believing Gentiles circumcised. Based upon my reading of their identity to this point, in this case the influencers would thus be assumed by the prevailing interpretations to lack character in relation to the gospel of Christ, for they would deny what they believe the meaning of the death of Christ is for these Gentiles, namely, that these Gentiles are equal among the righteous ones of God apart from becoming proselytes, that without becoming Israelites they have become children of Abraham. But also it is implied that the influencers would deny what the cross of Christ means for themselves, as it is relegated to secondary status should suffering for it be in view.

The influencers' motives and actions have been variously described, but the focus for interpreters has been on their denial of the gospel of Christ when it comes up against whatever it is the interpreter has characterized this other message to be, and its messengers to hold more dear, usually in opposition to the so-called Law-free gospel of Paul, whether this means Jewish identity entirely, or just ritual or behavioral norms, argued to varying degrees. But how do these explanations make sense of the influencers' own concern to seek honor rating or legal status as measured by Jewish membership and reference group norms, or on the supposed Christ-believing norms either? Paul assumes he is providing a convincing explanation that will reverse the addressees' opinion of the influencers from one of trust to one of contempt. But how could he believe he had done so? Denial of the influencers' core faith in either Jewish life or Jesus would reduce the social realities of their status ambiguity but only at the apparently unimaginable expense of the very faith that is the source of both!

The logic of the prevailing interpretive solutions breaks down here, for they posit that the influencers are and represent Christ-believing Jews who transparently lack sufficient loyalty to the norms of the Christ-believing coalition so as to avoid suffering for what they believe in, the crucified Jesus, which conviction, at the same time, forms the basis for the concerted effort that the influencers make toward the addressees in order to preserve the interests of those who share this faith in the face of pressure from those who do not.[24] The interpreter should be careful not to internalize Paul's polemic with the outcome that the influencers are not regarded as sincere Christ-believers because they retain the value of Jewish identity and behavior, which results from the interpreter's identification of them as Christ-believers who would compromise their confession of the meaning of the cross of Christ for themselves in the face of pressure mounted against the

24. If we leave aside my arguments to this point, the importance of this issue is clear for the prevailing views, because Paul's accusation implies that the influencers seek to enhance their honor rating with the addressees (introduced above and discussed more below, especially indicated at the end of v. 13). Yet such honor rating for fellow Christ-believers, if the influencers are so identified, would not be gained if they are in fact compromising such a central issue around which their group identification with the addressees is based (even if received as representatives of the Jerusalem or Antioch Christ-believing coalition, for example, as most interpreters argue). They would not be honored by the addressees if they did in fact devalue the issue of the meaning of Christ's death. How could they expect to be? Thus, it must be maintained in these constructions that the influencers disagree with Paul about the meaning of Christ's death for Gentiles, from which the addressees have drawn, and do not present their views as complementing Paul's (as some interpreters have maintained), or if they have claimed this, do so in duplicity, which Paul's accusation is now aimed at unmasking. Would they not anticipate that their dishonorable conduct according to the reference group norms of expectation for fellow Christ-believers would eventually be revealed, either in compromising the meaning of Christ that they profess but put in secondary place, or in compromising their integrity by representing their position as complementing Paul's, which they know not to be true?

implications of that confession for their Gentile brothers and sisters. It is not necessary to conclude that the influencers lack the character of conviction in terms of their identity to make sense of the thrust of Paul's accusation. They need simply ascribe to a different view of reality and uphold a different set of norms than those that result from Jewish and Gentile Christ-believers' convictions of the meaning of the death of Jesus, which seems to be precisely Paul's point in this case. The influencers do not wish to suffer on behalf of the addressees for a conviction about the meaning of Christ that they do not share!

I suggest that what Paul is inferring is that these influencers do not want to grant legitimacy to the addressees' claims made on the basis of the meaning of "the cross of Christ," that is, predicated upon an appeal to the present end of ages meaning of a Judean martyr's purpose for themselves, because they do not share the addressees' belief in this meaning. The influencers thus do not want to have to answer for their failure to bring about compliance as though they accepted the legitimacy of this claim. If the influencers do not share this or any faith in the meaning of Jesus Christ for themselves, and if they must answer to other social control agents for the execution of compliance with traditional and nonnegotiable membership as well as reference group norms that prevail in the present age, then the problem is easily recognizable. In addition to their own probably internalized positive evaluation of those norms, given that they are in this role, and negative evaluation of the addressees' resistance legitimized by their persistent claims to have already acquired what this ritual promises Gentiles apart from completion thereof—the dynamic implied for the influencers' motives in the letter heretofore—another powerful force at work for the influencers is now revealed. It is not difficult to grasp why they do not want to fail to successfully carry out these responsibilities in terms of honor and concomitant rights and privileges within their group, but it is even less difficult to imagine why they would not be willing to represent the case of the addressees' resistance to those to whom they answer as though they shared the basis of that claim to legitimacy—if they do not!

This proposal may be simply put: the influencers do not want to suffer status disapproval and loss of the legal rights and privileges that they have gained, which they believe would be required of them if they represent to those to whom they answer what these Gentiles claim as though legitimate, because these claims are based upon a faith in Christ that the influencers and those to whom they answer do not share. The addressees' disputable appeal has been based upon the meaning they attribute to the death of a martyr of the Roman regime for themselves, that is, the cross of Christ, by which appeal the addressees claim not to need to thus complete the ritual process of circumcision in order to gain full membership among the influencers' community, according to the truth proclaimed in Paul's gospel of Christ. Because the influencers do not share the addressees' faith in the meaning of this death, the legitimacy of the addressees' appeal rests upon a non sequitur, that is, in terms of the norms that control the influencers' own identity and interests, and thus it fails to concern them as representing a claim for which they should suffer. But instead of mere rejection, they offer the addressees good news based upon tradition and beyond dispute among themselves and those to whom they answer: these Gentiles need but complete the ritual process of conversion to gain what they seek, standing as full members among the people of God! This interpretive solution is in sharp contrast to moving this failure of logical connection to the center of the influencers' own modus operandi itself, as do the prevailing interpretations. They instead identify the influencers' zealous concerns toward the addressees with their shared Christ-faith but allow to stand—as Paul puts the matter—an accusation that this is of a secondary nature, which the influencers are willing to compromise. The new possibility raised here in seeking to make sense of Paul's rhetoric, that the influencers and those to whom they answer do not share the addressees' faith in Jesus as Christ, will occupy the next chapter.

Those Who Wish to Glorify Themselves in Your Flesh

Verse 13, which has the participial phrase that will be taken up shortly, contains two accusations; the second will occupy us first, the first will be the subject of the next section. Paul states what may be an additional reason for the influencers' "desire to have you circumcised": "that they in your flesh may glorify themselves [καυχήσωνται]." Again, the matter of flesh concerns circumcision, which is symbolic for the completion of proselyte conversion; word arrangement according to the Greek, slightly awkward in English, helps to bear this meaning out.

Paul here ironically employs the graphic image of circumcised flesh, much as he has done with language in general throughout the letter and circumcision in particular (cf. 5:12!). But this time a different ambition of the influencers is Paul's target. They are accused not only of seeking to enhance their honor rating or legal standing and avoid persecution from those to whom they answer, as set out in v. 12, but also of wishing to glorify or boast in or for themselves, as the verb καυχήσωνται brings out when used in the middle subjunctive form. Paul seems to reveal here the idea that the addressees' circumcised flesh will function for the influencers as a symbol of honor, of victorious completion of their task. At the same time, he does so in order to subvert the meaning of this as entirely self- (group) seeking, ethnocentrically protective of the identity of righteous ones in the present age, as was appropriate until the age to come has dawned with the meaning of Christ's death. But now to deny this to the representatives of the nations called by God in Christ is a failure to observe the Law: "for even the ones receiving circumcision do not guard/keep the Law" (6:13).

Paul's accusation rests upon the premise that trust in the circumciser symbolizes subordination to the circumciser's successful execution of communal norms and thus to his construal of reality, of what is really real. The boasting in view is not something that is done for oneself alone but in the context of those who grant the honor and confirm the legal result. It seems that Paul wants to undermine a natural aspect of any ritualized approach to identity such as is undertaken in the rite of proselyte conversion: the hierarchical implications for the addressees of subordinating themselves to participation in the ritual process that will culminate with this symbolic gesture. If so, Paul is attacking a dynamic that is observed by anthropologists of ritual over and over again across a wide spectrum of societies around the world: discrimination is inferred within the structure of the hierarchy of ritual identity![25] Indeed, it is clear that where there is any kind of status distinction, there will discrimination be found.[26] And in an honor-shame culture such as this letter represents, ritualized differentiation of identity obviously promotes an agonistic environment of great consequence for the addressees and thus makes sense of Paul's employment of this rhetorical tactic to achieve his subversive goal. This is the case even if the same point could be made against Paul's approach too, in that he appeals to the ritual of baptism, which is, in the present "evil" age, an entrance requirement that must be administered to initiates who undertake a new way of life, thus producing hierarchy and discrimination of the same nature as that to which he objects.

25. Cf. Kertzer, *Ritual;* Leach, "Ritual," 524.
26. Cf. Hogg and Abrams, *Social Identifications*.

The Influencers Do Not Themselves Guard the Law

The last point ties into the accusation that the influencers, although they "are receiving circumcision" and advocating it, "do not themselves guard/keep/observe [φυλάσσουσιν] the Law" (6:13). Much ink has been spilled over this polemical accusation, especially because of Paul's comment in 5:3: "I testify again to every man who receives circumcision [περιτεμνομένῳ] that he is indebted [ὀφειλέτης] to do [ποιῆσαι] the whole Law."

It would likely stray too far from the approach to the topic taken here to review the traditional and alternative interpretations for the purpose of demonstrating their weaknesses. In my view, interpreters often do not listen to or judge either Judaism or Paul on its or his own terms. The traditional approaches misjudge and condemn Jewish identity and the purpose of Torah thereby, as well as missing the point of Paul's critique, flaws that have been explored in many of the other views of the last half-century. Many of the alternative views continue to misunderstand Jews and Judaism too, continuing many of the negative stereotypes of Jewish interests, impulses, policies, and actions; and even within the updated portrait of Judaism they provide, they still fail to make sense of Paul as Jewish. Overall, the rhetorical character that derives from the distance between the vantage point of Paul and the influencers, not to mention the addressees, is not given sufficient consideration, and interpreters' negative characterizations of Jews and Judaism are attributed to Paul's voice, derived from interpretations of the context and his response that are herein challenged.[27] For if Paul was a Torah-observant Jew and did not suggest that it should be otherwise for Jewish believers in Christ, and if the situations and perspectives on what constitutes the exigence in Galatia and elsewhere are as I have suggested, for each of the parties, the criticism of the influencers in Law terms takes on a very different meaning.

Where the identity of the influencers and dynamics of the Galatian situations are concerned, the negative stereotypical assessments of the influencers' motives and lifestyle as merely outward, as though they did not actually internalize as good for themselves or the addressees

27. Ironically, for example, the legalistic motive traditionally attributed to the influencers fails to make sense of Paul's accusation that they do not keep the Law or inform the addressees that this is why they should become proselytes! See also Thurén, *Derhetorizing*, 68–69.

the observance of the Torah, fail to make sense of their interest in or appeal to the addressees in Galatia, so that they now internalize as good for themselves this message of proselyte conversion. In view of the prevailing readings of this comment, it is little wonder that the influencers are usually not investigated at any length, much less their Jewishness. I will simply set out my own proposal.

In this summary section of the letter, Paul is taking a last stab at undermining the powerful influence that these influencers have had upon the addressees. As has been described at length, Paul senses and fears that the addressees have begun to internalize as good for themselves this other path as though it was a welcome complement to their faith in Christ. However, Paul is certain that it is an obstruction that will sever them from what they have gained in Christ, for it inherently denies that Christ has brought the dawning of the age to come, treating all things—as represented in their own identity—as though it had not. When the motives of self-service (in intra- and intergroup terms) that Paul seeks to bring to the surface are considered in the context of this comment, combined with the epistolary nature of the letter as ironic rebuke, what Paul seems to be doing is arguing in dissociating terms. He seeks to undermine the influencers' interests according to the motives that should be at the heart of Torah observance, for these are the norms to which the influencers now appeal for the circumcision of the addressees. Their interest in the proselyte conversion of the addressees suggests that they are those who uphold Torah as of paramount importance. Yet, as Paul sees things since the revelation of Jesus Christ to him, instead of upholding the Law, which the addressees should and apparently do assume to be represented in the lives of the influencers, the influencers violate that Law, because the addressees are themselves being violated by the underlying self-serving motives of the influencers' group or groups, where the expressed interests of the addressees, on the basis of their appeal legitimated by faith in Jesus according to Paul's gospel, are concerned.

The influencers are circumcised (6:13) and thus bound already to this code of honor (5:3), but their "unsettling" approach to the addressees in order to persuade them of their message by putting them in their place as liminals or mere guests and not full members—shaming and manipulating them so that they will comply—has not been what it has to the addressees seemed, that is, good for the addressees as Christ-believers. Really, Paul informs them, the influencers' own interests are being served. The policies and behavior that the addressees have begun to accept as appropriate, if they would now value their own prior expectations based upon the good news of Christ as inappropriate, undermine the good that they already have in Christ and that which has led to their interest in what the influencers now seem to offer them in the first place, inclusion among the righteous ones of Israel's God. After all, the influencers are now obstructing the course upon which the addressees were running toward the good; they are, however, turning upside down the notion of what is good for themselves according to the good news of Christ.

In view of Paul's traditional declaration that the center of a Torah-observant life is love of one's neighbors, to which even the addressees as Gentiles in Christ not under the Law are called (5:14), Paul seeks to undermine the very foundation of the moral authority to which the influencers appeal. Paul writes that the influencers seek not the welfare of the addressees but their own, which is accomplished by stating that they do not themselves keep and guard the Law. But—and this is the point, I think—the influencers should exemplify in their relationship with the addressees as Gentiles precisely this central tenet of the Law! The different evaluation between Paul and the influencers regarding what exemplifies Torah observance for the Gentile addressees arises from the difference of opinion about what Christ means for them and thus about what behavior appropriately exemplifies the love of God that is the very aim of Torah. If the influencers are unwilling to stand up for what Paul has made clear to be in the best interests of the addressees, then from Paul's vantage point, it is because the influencers put the priority on their own concerns, including conformity with the constraints derived from traditional notions of what is expected of pagans seeking incorporation as righteous ones. These constraints likely include prevailing pagan communal as well as Jewish norms that do not express the addressees' profession of an altered reality based upon the meaning of Jesus. In other words, Paul's critique of the influencers' lawlessness is based upon his own interested view in response to his understanding of Jesus as the Christ of Israel and Savior of the nations.

The influencers already have ascribed or acquired legal and moral standing as righteous ones of God, and, unlike the addressees at the moment, the influencers have this status on the communal terms that render their standing and access to concomitant goods indisputable. They should thus be concerned with the welfare of these Gentiles seeking association, in Paul's view, by recognizing that the demonstration of God's holy and righteous Spirit in the lives of these Gentiles demands thinking about their claims in terms outside of those traditionally agreed ones that define identity in the present age and instead in terms of those that will define identity in the age to come. They are turning entirely to the worship of Israel's God as the One God of all of the nations. And they are not doing so as Gentile guests or benefactors might, continuing their civic and familial duties of idolatry, as would be expected according to the conventions of the present age wherein one's standing is in Jewish communal terms either as Jewish or pagan. These Gentiles are really between two differently bounded human communities and two ages too. In the face of the addressees' uncertain standing by the traditional norms, yet obvious righteousness and expression of Spirit life in nontraditional ways for Gentiles who are mere guests or liminals engaged in the process of conversion, they now, according to Paul, should be considered as fully incorporated outside of completion of this ritual. But instead, in violation of the very principles of Torah identity to which the influencers appeal, these Gentiles, Paul's accusations assert, are instead envied and shut out. The approach stands within the prophetic tradition; it is an internal critique based upon appeal to the true nature of Israel's relationship with God and Torah.

The influencers are thus in violation of the spirit of Torah by seeking their own honor at the addressees' expense—"they do not themselves guard the Law, but they desire to have you circumcised so that they may receive honor by putting you in your place" (6:13)—when, by Paul's reckoning, they should be reconsidering their norms in the face of the demonstration of God's Spirit at work among these Gentiles. For Paul, the norms of the influencers necessitate that they recognize the age to come has dawned indeed, just as these Gentiles claim by way of appeal to the meaning of the cross of Christ for themselves. What separates Paul and the influencers is not their high evaluation of Torah but their relative evaluation of the meaning of Christ for these Gentiles and for themselves, so that what constitutes appropriate Torah behavior toward these Gentiles is valued from an entirely different point of view. Thus, the issue becomes one of which party is doing the Law lawfully in the inclusion of these Gentiles—in view of the dawning of the age to come in Jesus Christ!

This interpretation is confirmed by way of Paul's continued argumentation in the following verses (14-17). In contrast to that of which he accuses the influencers, Paul appeals to his own self as not seeking honor (καυχάομαι: as defined in context above, the right to boast in the face of the addressees although they are Gentiles and thus not

Israelites). In fact, Paul declares that his present way of differentiating who are God's righteous ones apart from discriminating between Jew and Gentile has been profoundly altered precisely because of the cross of Christ; he has been "crucified" to the standards of judgment of this "cosmos [κόσμος]" (the "humanly" understood structure of reality, to which the influencers—according to Paul's argument throughout—appeal). Moreover, Paul's way of life serves as the model. The terms for defining this identity are thus no longer to be applied to assessment of these Gentiles according to the terms of definition of the present age—by circumcised status or not. This is for Paul a rule, principle, canon, or limit (κανόνι), in other words, a redefinition of the boundary by which the righteous ones of God should now exist (στοιχήσουσιν) in the present age based upon the dawning of the age to come.[28]

This message is the good news that Paul proclaims in the face of the "other good news which is not another": on the basis of the meaning of Christ's death, and not proselyte conversion, the assessment of the addressees' standing in the new community of God (i.e., "new creation [καινὴ κτίσις]") has forever changed. I propose that Paul is here insisting that this is the standard to which he holds the influencers: to the degree that they are in a position to and actively involved in influencing his Gentiles, precisely because they are οἱ περιτεμνόμενοι, the influencers are accountable. For Paul, because of the influencers' own identity claims in the context of their interest in persuading the addressees, they are responsible to recognize the age-to-come community that God is now forming in the midst of the "present evil age." This is confirmed by the demonstration of God's Spirit—according to the proclamation of the meaning of the death of Christ—in the lives of these Gentiles (3:5). They are thereby to be recognized as representatives of the nations turning to the One God of Israel as the One God of all humankind, as bearing witness that in Christ the end of the ages has dawned.

Even if the influencers do not themselves share these Gentiles' faith in Christ, because by definition they are seeking to define the boundaries of communal identity for these Gentile Christ-believers according to the norms for the historical righteous ones—indeed "the Israel of God"[29]—they are thus held accountable. That is why Paul denigrates the basis of the influencers' authority as merely human: they insist

28. See too Nanos, *Mystery,* 362–67, on the implications of Romans 7.

29. Cf. Richardson, *Israel;* W. Campbell, *Intercultural Context,* 74–75.

upon the traditional interpretation of reality even when confronted by incontrovertible evidence provided by God's present revelation in Christ and the demonstration of God's Spirit in their midst in the lives of these mere Gentiles. Thus, he justifies his characterizing of the influencers so roughly, even to the extreme of castration and curse wishes. The addressees represent the nations turning to worship the God of Israel as the God of all creation, all the nations of the humanly perceived cosmos. They are not Israelites or candidates to so become; if they were, then the end of the ages has not dawned in Christ, when all of humankind becomes one, as God is One.

By way of caveat, however, it is not clear that apart from their involvement with the addressees any such judgment of culpability need be implied from Paul's letter, toward Jews or Judaism in general. The context of his rhetoric is definable within situations involving the interests of Paul and the Christ-believing Gentile converts in his (sub)groups where they come into conflict with other communal norms according to the interpretation and concomitant actions of the influencers. Apart from the historical anomaly within Jewish (Israelite) social space for which Paul argues—Gentiles as full members without becoming proselytes because of the actions of God in Jesus Christ—the tensions that arise between grace and Law or works and faith do not arise. These are not questions that arise for Jewish people about Jews, whether Christ-believers or not, or even about Gentiles per se, but they concern the status of these particular Gentiles only because of the claims being made by Jews such as Paul. Otherwise, no tension need be assumed between such complementary terms. Again, it is a dissociation that arises because of the particular claims being made and denied, both sides able to appeal to tradition and revelation.

Thus, while the addressees are not themselves Israelites, Paul holds that this does not invalidate their claim, because Israelite status—that is, circumcised—is not the only measure of identity as righteous ones. That status is ultimately to be defined by way of the fulfillment of the promise made to Israel apart from circumcised identity, by promise to Abraham when he believed before he was circumcised (3:8), a promise that was on behalf of all of the nations, thus Israel (circumcised) and the rest (uncircumcised). Thus, Paul declares himself free of this world's (including now, in view of the revelation of Christ, Israel's other traditional) conceptions of community definition between the nations—in this case circumcised or uncircumcised, Israel or the nations. This is because of the meaning of the death of Christ, his public dishonor on a cross by the authority of the Roman rulers of this "evil" age, which shattered by way of his public shame the pretensions to honor acquired in terms of the human cosmos. Thus, he undermines the kind of honor and legal status gained naturally by way of hierarchical differentiation, whether intended or not, the appeal to which in this undermining phrase he accuses the influencers of seeking by way of putting the addressees in their merely guest or even liminal (proselyte candidate) instead of their already incorporated (as full children of Abraham) place. Paul has been "crucified" to this measure of discrimination; honor and shame according to the definitions of the current merely human authorities (i.e., the κόσμος) have been rendered invalid for the relative status of himself and the Christ-believing addressees. He may thus suffer persecution, but he will not comply (5:11).

Although the consensus views have not been articulated at any length, they fail to logically explain this passage in view of the addressees' interest in the influencers' message and methods of persuasion to date. For example, it is highly unlikely that pagan men of this Roman, probably Greek or Celtic culture, would be tempted to proselyte circumcision who were not intending to zealously pursue a Jewish lifestyle, drawn to this radical decision by those in Galatia who were so inclined themselves, and setting a desirable example. If the influencers are not actually making a good showing in the flesh, seeking honor on Jewish terms defined by observance of the Torah, regardless of how the halakic details are articulated among this community, it is difficult to understand how Paul could anticipate his approach would be convincing.[30] Paul does not explain Pharisaic halakot, and there is no reason to believe that the non-Jewish Galatian addressees were familiar with the details of the various interpretations that existed between the many Jewish interpretive movements, especially in Judea. Thus, why would the addressees in Galatia think that it is according to Paul's former Pharisaic measure of Torah observance, and not that of the influencers' communal interpretation of Torah, or Paul's own practices when among them, that are being here critiqued? The prevailing interpretations rely upon the later interpreters' knowledge of such internal disputes about Torah within and between the various Judaisms, but Paul does not in this letter indicate any such knowledge exists among the addressees; rather, he indicates the addressees' naïve failure even to recognize the level of Torah observance that would be

30. Contra Jewett, "Agitators," 207–8.

required of them by the influencers' communal norms—should they become proselytes (5:3).[31]

From a rhetorical standpoint, if the influencers were overtly compromising Law observance according to their own Galatian communal norms, Paul has missed the single most effective weapon for rendering ineffective their influence toward Law identification for the Gentiles. This passing comment in v. 13 notwithstanding, Paul could have specifically cited the occasion(s) of their failure to observe Torah, thereby discrediting their "news of good" and exposing their hypocrisy with a deciding blow—as he had Peter at Antioch, when he failed to conform with the norms to which he ascribed. But Paul approaches his addressees with the "surprising" dissociating accusation that while these influencers, who seem to generously offer inclusion through proselyte identity, may appear to be role models with regard to Torah (which defines the righteous ones in the present age), their motives are really at odds with the intentions of Torah.[32]

31. Social identity research indicates that while the different subgroups and individual perspectives may be familiar to those of the group, this is often not the case with respect to an out-group, where stereotypical notions of the other are common, and less awareness of the variety within and between those groups is recognized, or of concern (cf. Hogg and Vaughan, *Social Psychology*, 370–71, who refer to this as "relative homogeneity effect"). Later interpreters of Paul represent a different situation, especially since the rise of historical criticism, because they are specifically familiarizing themselves with historical groups other than their own (even if they have their own interested perspectives, and may draw conclusions that are not charitable to those historical [out-]groups whom they continue to view stereotypically as the "other"; e.g., the negative stereotyping of Pharisaic norms and motives, in this case, even painting Paul with this broad stroke to the degree that he is understood to base his supposed arrogant evaluation of the influencers' observance upon those norms). While the Gentile addressees might have learned something about differences between Jewish group practices in their own locations, it is unlikely that they are familiar with the nuances that these groups are aware of, and certainly unlikely that they know or care about the differences between Jewish groups from elsewhere. The issue at hand is the need to be careful in projecting the knowledge gained from later critical study onto the addressees about (out-) groups and the (in- and out-)group differentiations among them that the addressees' groups were unlikely to know in the same way as the participants of those groups, to the degree that they are not a part of those groups and their identity-forming concerns.

32. Similarly Howard, *Crisis*, 15.

Οἱ Περιτεμνόμενοι: Interpreting Paul's Substantive Participle

This brings us to the last element to be considered now in this passage, namely, the proposed meaning and translation of the controversial participial reference to these influencers as οἱ περιτεμνόμενοι. Tracing the main lines of argument provides the following meanings and translations from which to work:

- Present middle causative, thus emphasis on the influencers' advocacy of circumcision of the addressees is the focus: "those who cause to be circumcised," "the ones causing receipt of circumcision," or simply, "the advocates of circumcision."[33]
- Present middle reflexive, emphasizing the active aspect of the middle with the focus on self-motivation: "those who get themselves circumcised," "those who choose to be circumcised," or "those who circumcise themselves."[34]
- Present middle permissive, which highlights the present sense of the action with a passive twist; thus it could be translated as "those who receive circumcision," "those presently getting circumcised themselves," or "those who let themselves be circumcised."[35]
- Present middle habitual[36] would signify a temporal habitual force at work, "those who customarily circumcise," "those who are customarily circumcising," or "those who customarily get themselves circumcised."
- Present middle concessive,[37] would focus upon the connection by accentuating the exception that it involves, bringing to bear the opening οὐδέ: "even the ones who are circumcised," "even the ones who circumcise," or "even the ones who get themselves circumcised."
- Present middle circumstances attendant[38] brings out the action of the main verb, in this case, the accusation following that focuses upon the connection between their identity by way of this substantive participle and the undermining "revelation" that the

33. So argue, e.g., Lightfoot, *Galatians*, 222; Jewett, "Agitators," 202–3; Bruce, *Galatians*, 270; Witherington, *Grace in Galatia*, 449.
34. Harvey, "Opposition," 324; Conrad, "HOI ΠERITEMNOMENOI."
35. So Munck, *Salvation*, 89.
36. Cf. Voelz, *Grammar*, 135.
37. Cf. Voelz, *Grammar*, 135.
38. Cf. Voelz, *Grammar*, 135–36.

influencers do not themselves "keep" or "guard" the Law, thus: "the ones who are circumcising," "the ones circumcising," or "the ones who get circumcised" do not "keep" or "guard" that which they would be expected to hold most dear.

- Present passive, thus emphasizing the influencers' own receipt of circumcision. This may be translated as "the ones who receive circumcision." Burton argued that it referred to a subgroup of the addressees that had been circumcised, a problematic proposal already discussed.[39] Fung suggests that it instead refers to "those who do receive circumcision," a group of Jewish advocates of circumcision to be distinguished from non-Jewish advocates of circumcision whom he imagines to be a part of the composite group of influencers, and thus he argues that it is to the same end as taking the participle in the middle causative sense, as "the advocates of circumcision."[40]
- Perfect passive, or οἱ περιτετμημένοι, a variant construction actually attested in a few important manuscripts (including P^{46}), focuses on the condition that results from a previous action and would translate "those who have been circumcised" or "those in the state of circumcision."[41] This might also be translated as perfect middle, and if reflexive, for example, then "those who have chosen to be circumcised."

All of the proposed translations could be argued in various ways to support the proposal I believe follows from the above arguments pertaining to the context in which this phrase is used.[42] Therefore, I have put this consideration after discussion of the context because the explanatory value of any decision on this substantive participle must

39. Burton, *Galatians*, 351–53; Hawkins, "Opponents," 94–95, likes it grammatically, but then on 107–8 concludes that it does not make sense of the context; Tarazi, *Galatians*, 322–23. See criticisms by Howard, *Crisis*, 17–18.

40. Fung, *Galatians*, 302–4; Beker, *Paul*, 45, 52; Martyn, *Galatians*, 563; cf. also discussion in Lightfoot, *Galatians*, 222–23; this construction seems to also be R. Longenecker's view (*Galatians*, 292).

41. Cf. Swanson, *Galatians*, 127; and discussions in Hawkins, "Opponents," 87–89; Richardson, *Israel*, 86–87, although not adopted in their conclusions.

42. Respecting the view that this kind of variety makes it clear that it cannot be settled unambiguously on strictly grammatical grounds, see, e.g., H. Betz, *Galatians*, 316, who opts for "the circumcised" but concludes that a "decision on this problem is impossible"; similar is Howard, *Crisis*, 18–19.

make sense of its verbal aspect, that is, its relationship to the circumstances under which the verbal action of the main verb takes place.[43]

The central thrust of Paul's turn of phrase is designed to emphasize the influencers' culpability: they have a duty to recognize the place of the addressees as Gentiles yet righteous ones of God on equal terms with proselytes. The Gentiles are included on the basis of the meaning of Christ's death, to which the addressees have appealed, and should no longer be regarded as mere liminals, as those not entitled to full membership standing until they have completed proselyte conversion, and they are certainly not mere guests.

Regardless of how the influencers may regard the addressees' other beliefs in the meaning of a historical martyr of the Roman regime, that is, whether they care to dispute the addressees' overall convictions in Jesus, this premise has not been accepted by them as the legitimate basis for an appeal to full and equal standing among the historical people of God. The influencers' Jewish communities and their norms for membership and associated rights and privileges, which the influencers serve in some role as guardians thereof, do not accept the addressees' appeal to other norms. The addressees must gain proselyte status to satisfy their claims: the men must be circumcised. That decision is unacceptable to Paul. And the main verb rings clear; these influencers who advocate the addressees' circumcision are themselves circumcised, of course, but, in Paul's opinion, they violate the very standard to which they appeal, for they "do not themselves guard/keep/observe [φυλάσσουσιν] the Law." Moreover, his accusation continues, what they really "only" desire is "to have you circumcised in order that they may attain honor thereby."

If this participle is interpreted as present active in the middle voice, the emphasis clearly falls upon the influencers' own decision on the matter at hand, regardless of the fact that they have not invented the norm, the tradition, or the immediate application in Galatia: concerning circumcision of the addressees, they are actively involved in the advocacy and facilitation, and they are thus culpable. The middle voice is preferred grammatically when it makes sense, yet there is a certain redundancy to this point if taken as causative, because the point that they advocate circumcision is already made explicitly apart from this participle. Of course, that may argue precisely for it as the best choice, as does Jewett. If that is the point, then why not οἱ περιτέμνοντες?

43. Cf. Porter, *Idioms*, 181–93.

The middle active form can also infer reflexive action. Carl Conrad has repeatedly suggested that the passive is not really a distinct form in Greek but rather another usage of the middle, so that a middle passive form indicates an intensification, either an investment of him- or herself in the action, or, less often, as receiving the action.[44] In this case, the point is not redundant, as in advocating circumcision for the addressees, but rather that the influencers who advocate the addressees' circumcision have chosen circumcision for themselves: they are thus proselytes, formerly Gentiles, just as the addressees are still.

The alternative reflexive translation is doubtful in view of the fact that one does not circumcise oneself; this is an action of identification with a community. This consideration serves as a good transitional point by which to turn to the possible interpretations, considering them not so much exclusive of one another but perhaps as in some way part of a larger inference that would be salient for the addressees, given what they know about the influencers, but have not considered in the way Paul now seeks to undermine as mere appearance.

If taken as present middle but in the permissive, the culpability of the influencers remains central, but the emphasis shifts to their receipt of circumcision and thus would seem to also imply that they are themselves proselytes. This could be taken to indicate that they were circumcised, whether they actively wanted or chose to be, or it could still carry the sense of having been circumcised by choice and in this sense virtually the same as the middle reflexive.[45] It could still arguably refer to Jews from birth, because they too "received" circumcision, even though it is through their parents' observance, according to Scripture and tradition, but of course they do not actually choose this for themselves. This leaves open whether the person or persons have been circumcised as natural-born Jews, that is, by their parents' choice, although in general not a matter of deliberation but of habitual ritual observance of an unquestioned communal norm, or the result of proselyte conversion, whether by personal adult choice or as a member of a household group that has undertaken this status transformation by the norms of household identity that may apply to them (e.g., as children or slaves of one who converts, and thus obliged to do what the father deems appropriate for the household). And George Howard is surely

44. Conrad, "HOI ΠERITEMNOMENOI." See also Bligh, *Galatians*, 218.

45. This seems to have guided Schoeps's identification (*Paul*, 65, 77) and is an implication noted by Lightfoot (*Galatians*, 223).

correct to point out that Munck's approach "presses the contemporaneity of a verb which denotes a one time event" to the point of trivializing it:[46] the circumcision in view cannot still be "in the present" when Paul learns of it, when he writes, and when the letter is read.

Three forms of the present middle that might be considered do not resolve the difference that is signified by the causative, reflexive, or permissive, that is, whether it is the action of circumcising, choosing circumcision, or having been circumcised that is in view. But each of them does bring an aspect of the verbal function into consideration of the contextual meaning in a useful way. In fact, each of them emphasizes the connection with other elements in Paul's accusation that are important for interpretation. The habitual aspect may put the emphasis upon their customary role as circumcisers, thus in some way symbolically associated with the function of *mohelim* (although it is highly unlikely that they were all in fact such specialists),[47] which makes their failure to guard the Law unexpected, and in this way the same emphasis gained by the aspect of attendant circumstances. The ones who are involved in the rites of passage culminating in the circumcising of others would certainly be expected to be concerned with observing and guarding the Law. But especially attendant circumstances could emphasize that they are culpable because they are circumcised themselves, either by reflexive choice to have been circumcised or, less so, with the permissive result of being circumcised. Present middle concessive would focus upon the connection of the exceptive opening, "even," and thus also result in accentuating the accusation of the influencers' failure to keep or guard the Law. This choice seems to bring out the possibility emphasized in the reflexive and inherent in the permissive: the influencers' own receipt of circumcision should have precluded this inappropriate result of not observing the Torah while seeking to bring others to identity as Torah people. Thus each of these aspects of the active middle form could serve Paul's purpose, by way of this substantive participle, to undermine the connection between the influencers' interest in circumcising these Gentiles and their failure to be concerned with the most important aspect of the state that will result for the addressees, not to mention of the influencers' own ascribed or achieved standing as circumcised ones, their

46. Howard, *Crisis*, 17.

47. This may account for the shift to the singular referent for the one unsettling the addressees.

identity with the Law itself, which they should above all keep and guard from violation.

It appears then that this participial phrase, if taken in the present tense in middle voice, refers most naturally to ones who have chosen to have themselves circumcised—proselytes. All it would take for this aspect to be unquestionable for the addressees is knowing the state of the influencers as proselytes. Because we do not know this, the possibility that it refers to those advocating the circumcision of the Galatian addressees must remain open, even if the need for such an inference seems to be questionable, given the explicit construction of the overall letter and its summary, wherein their advocacy of the addressees' circumcision is already clearly central and outright challenged. Still, this does not alter the force of the overall interpretation of the surrounding context that has been or could be offered; it just blunts an additional aspect that Paul could have undermined, had he chosen otherwise, in his effort to cut through appearances, in his estimation, that were leading the addressees to misjudge realities, especially if the influencers were in fact proselytes themselves. It can still carry the inference that they "received for themselves circumcision" and thus in some way refer to their choice or state if causative, habitual, concessive, or circumstances attendant, but this aspect is brought out more clearly in the present middle reflexive or permissive (and to a lesser degree also in the concessive), where it implies that these people are former Gentiles who have themselves in the past (just when in terms of time is not inferred) decided to become proselyte Jews, just as they now advocate for the addressees.

If interpreted in the present passive voice instead, then the emphasis is clearly directed to the influencers' own receipt of circumcision, and the implications would seem also to be along the line of the present middle reflexive, permissive, and concessive: the influencers are themselves former Gentiles who have undertaken proselyte conversion by way of completion of the ritual process they now advocate for the addressees. As already argued, this does not imply that they are themselves Paul's addressees; quite the contrary, Paul writes to dissuade those who have not completed this rite. But it could include some Gentiles formerly associated with the group to which he writes, perhaps still associated; nevertheless, they would no longer be his target audience when the letter was written, or if they have completed this rite between writing and arrival, at least when it is read. This same sense is captured, although not quite as unambiguously, if translated "the ones who are receiving circumcision," because it is a reference to the influencers' choice that is still in view, and perhaps with a sense of the recentness of their own completion of the status that is now in dispute, but this is a time inference of the verbal tense that is itself a questionable aspect.

If the influencers had been circumcised as children, one way to take the passive or some aspects of the middle sense of their "receiving circumcision," they would thereby, now by choice, have identified themselves by those norms that apply to the circumcised and thus be held accountable to do the Law, to love their neighbors instead of seeking to gain honor at their expense. The weakness of this choice, besides the argument for the preference of middle reflexive form when possible, is that Paul has in this letter, and elsewhere in his correspondence, along with the usage attested by other authors of this time, described Jewish people instead merely in unambiguous terms as "circumcised ones" in contrast to those who are instead "foreskinned ones."

If this participle is taken in such a passive sense, it may imply that the influencers are proselytes themselves. This is not because the present participle cannot have the sense of reference to one circumcised by birth, as when Simon attacks Peter and Paul in the *Acts of Peter and Paul* with the statement: οὗτοι οἱ περιτεμνόμενοι πανουργοί εἰσιν, which is a single and later example that confirms the atemporal character of the present participle.[48] But this example is the exception, and Paul refers in this letter to natural-born Jews and advocates of circumcision otherwise—"the circumcised [τῆς περιτομῆς]," with reference to the apostles and those to whom they will go when relating the Jerusalem conference (2:7-8), and probably "the ones for/from circumcision [τούς ἐκ περιτομῆς]" who were active in Antioch (2:12)—in keeping with usages common for designating people in a Jewish state as signified by their circumcision; indeed, "those who receive circumcision" is a strange way to refer to Jews, who are rather "the circumcised ones." Nevertheless, this exception does bring out an important caution with respect to interpretation of this participle when it is taken as present passive (or present middle permissive): although the circumcision has taken place, it does not necessarily tell us when.

But the important point is, here this participle, like the middle or passive participle of 5:3, is employed to undermine the confidence of the Gentile addressees in their understanding of what was actually involved in turning to this other message: "I testify again to every man

48. Hawkins, "Opponents," 90–93.

who *chooses* [or *receives*] *circumcision* [περιτεμνομένῳ].” Thus, the emphasis is on undermining that, by way of attention to the influencers’ own identity concerns, the addressees will really understand what is at stake. Anyway, this is surely a strange construction for describing natural-born Jews, especially from the direct hand of one who shares this identity from birth, unless it is some other aspect of their identity that is in view in this instance.

Although modern commentators have uniformly rejected the manuscript variation of perfect passive and do not seem to consider the middle voice, the grounds for their conclusions depend upon different interpretations of the context of Paul’s comments about both the meaning of the feared suffering for the cross of Christ as well as the subversive nature of Paul’s accusation about their failure to uphold the Law as they should, because the influencers are those who are or have chosen to be circumcised.[49] It seems to follow that “those in the state identified by circumcision,” who now advocate the same for the addressees, especially if middle reflexive, emphasizing that this is the result of their own choice, would be most obliged to uphold the principles of the Law itself. But their insistence upon the proselyte conversion of the addressees after the addressees’ stated appeal to standing legitimated (i.e., justified) by the meaning of Christ’s death, Paul takes to be the seeking of self- and group honor. Instead, by the Torah to which the influencers are bound by their own circumcision to observe, and in view of the demonstration of the Spirit among these Gentiles as would be expected when the age to come dawns, the influencers should be reconsidering the truth of their claims and welcoming the addressees as full members indeed. In Paul’s book, that is doing Torah with their neighbors, Paul’s addressees.

In conclusion, whether it is the influencers’ own choice to gain this status (“the ones who choose circumcision”), perhaps with a more passive sense (“the ones who receive circumcision”), or simply their advocacy of circumcision (“the ones circumcising”) that is in view in this participial phrase, it is precisely the influencers’ identification with the importance of circumcision for defining the righteous ones, while at the same time not guarding the Law as Paul believes they should, that is in view. Likewise, the perfect passive or middle of some manuscripts, “those in the state of circumcision” or “those who

49. E.g., Jewett, “Agitators,” 202; Richardson, *Israel*, 86–89; Tarazi, *Galatians*, 321–22.

have chosen circumcision," still carry this same inference. For this commitment is itself undermined by their failure to keep before themselves the very aim of the status they have received—whether ascribed or achieved—to live according to Torah, which upholds the interests of the neighbor above those of oneself (family or political subgroup of Israelites). In the end, whatever choice is made about this substantive participle, these influencers are Jewish, whether natural-born or proselytes, and thus in Paul's judgment "indebted to do the whole Law" (5:3). This identification invites further consideration.

Are the Influencers Agents of Ritual Conversion?

The above argument about the influencers' identity leads to the conclusion that they are in some way involved with Gentiles at the boundaries of communal identity and interaction. More specifically, it seems that they are facilitators of the ritual of proselyte conversion, responsible for the various aspects of this process; "gatekeepers," one might say,[50] those whom some anthropologists might label as "ritual elders."[51] This would make sense of many of Paul's characterizations, such as their ability to "exclude" the addressees from what they seek with the purpose of enhancing the addressees' desire for it, and of course their ability to persuade and manipulate to compliance, more than that, to conformity, because the addressees are approached by Paul as though they had internalized this message of proselyte conversion as good for themselves. It appears likely that in their role in the community they welcome Gentile guests and oversee the communication of communal norms to Gentiles who seek association at various levels. And when interest in conversion from guest to proselyte status is expressed or necessitated (e.g., if wishing to marry a Jewish member), they would conduct the process that ensues.

Thus, the different perspectives on the addressees' identity of Paul (fully incorporated) and the influencers (liminals or even guests who have not begun) has led to the uncertainty that the addresses now seek to resolve. While the addressees seek to escape this unexpected or perhaps more intensified marginalized situation and the influencers to manage the implications the addressees' claims have made for themselves, Paul also seeks to influence the situations and writes this letter

50. E.g., Martyn, *Galatians*, 124.
51. Turner, *Forest*, 93–111; idem, *Ritual Process*.

calling for perpetuating this state of status ambiguity where the influencers are concerned, on the basis of his understanding of God's perspective that their status is secure already by way of Christ.

Paul's concern appears to be with opposing the specific identity transformation completed by the rite of circumcision that the addressees have been considering, reminding them that they have begun, not down the road of proselyte conversion, but instead down another (even if in many ways parallel) track toward worship of the One God of Israel, yet remaining Gentiles, representatives of the nations turning to the One God of all humankind, and "waiting for the hope of righteousness" (5:5). Within the scope of his response and the anticipation of how it will be received, we are confronted with the dynamics of ritual identification. This topic will provide much to consider about the explicitly Jewish nature of the exigence and of the players.

To the degree that Paul's rhetoric indicates that the struggle in Galatia is along such lines of social control, it is useful to discuss how "ritual operates as an *emblème* of membership."[52] Jesse Pitts generalized the dynamics thus: "ritual does act as a reinforcer of conforming motivation. It makes the actor feel part of an all-enveloping group that shares his attitudes and with which he can think of himself as standing in a primary-type relationship. The actor's good standing in such a group depends upon his continued commitment to the symbolic system evoked by the ritual."[53] It is just these kinds of dynamics that make sense of Paul's all-out attack, as exemplified by the parental nature of his ironic rebuke; he knows what he is up against intuitively, perhaps even having been on the other side of this divide himself (implied in 5:11).

These Gentiles are being tempted to become proselytes in order to gain the honor of Jewish identity that the influencers broker by their method, which was the prevailing interpretation of the traditions of the fathers for Paul's Jewish contemporaries, and would ensure these Gentiles the social and emotional as well as religious satisfaction and security that they desire among the people of God. In other words, they were being persuaded that as long as they remained merely pagans in status—regardless of whether labeled righteous or God-fearing or in some other way—they were excluded from the position of equality with proselytes or Jews as the children of God; they would not receive

52. Pitts, "Social Control." 386.
53. Pitts, "Social Control," 386.

the full acceptance they so earnestly sought. They may have thought that they were sons and daughters of Abraham on the teaching of Paul, but they were not; they had either misunderstood Paul or been misinformed by him. Although they may have stood their ground securely for a while on the level of ideas, they have been consumed by the emotional fires of public censure—they have been shamed.

Ritual Theory and the Galatian Social Dynamics

We have seen that the tensions addressed in this letter have to do with matters of identity in terms of Jewish communal and personal boundary markers, most clearly, of proselyte conversion, which included circumcision of male candidates at or near the completion of the ritual process.[54] It is thus important to sketch out the basic players and activities of this reidentification process or rite of passage that provide the means for non-Jewish people to negotiate the boundary defining group membership.

It will be helpful to apply the framework for explaining rituals associated with identity transformation that occurs in such rites of passage as proselyte conversion in general anthropological terms. Specialists have provided a helpful way to analyze the order of the ritual dynamics that generally accompany a ceremonial passage from one social standing to another. These characteristic patterns, or rites of passage, have been associated with spatial passage, as though one is passing through a boundary or a threshold (limen). The transitions within these rites are subdivided into rites of separation (preliminality), transition rites (liminality or marginality), and rites of incorporation (postliminality or aggregation).[55] Although in theory a rite of passage may be expected to include each of these three phases, one or another tends to be more characteristic of any given rite depending upon the people involved and the ceremonial situation, which is not necessarily uniform in practice.

Viewing proselyte conversion in such spatial or time-oriented language is helpful for keeping in mind the fact that we are dealing not with a sudden and complete change in the instant of initial decision making but with a process, and a ritualized one at that, which—while

54. Unfortunately, we know little of the features of this ritual predating the rabbinic literature; see Hoffman, *Covenant of Blood*.

55. Van Gennep, *Rites*, 10–11, 21; Turner, *Ritual Process*.

no doubt different in some ways for different people, communities, situations, and periods—takes place over an extended period of time and involves many dimensions of religious and psychological experience, which are embedded in sociopolitical life.[56] And this dynamic is not only the case when dealing with Jewish proselyte conversion but, as Thomas Finn states in his monograph on the topic: "Conversion in Greco-Roman religion, whether Pagan, Jewish, or Christian, was an extended ritual process that combined teaching and symbolic enactment—the cognitive and the performative—and yielded commitment and transformation."[57]

The ritual of proselyte conversion is initiated by a decision to turn from pagan identity and practices to those of the Jewish community. The liminal stage characterizes the time of transition, when one is no longer a pagan but not yet Jewish, not having completed the ritual process, and in most cases, the training that would be expected to occupy the proselyte candidate in the meantime. Candidates may suffer marginalization in terms not only of their past pagan network of associations but also in terms of their new chosen identity, that is, they are not entitled to full membership privileges and rights until the new identity as proselytes is fully attained. That takes place at the completion of the ritual process, when they become proselytes, confirming the community's acceptance of them. Yet in a way this merely marks a transition that is by then already very real in the lifestyle of the convert and community. For he or she—more likely them, as it would usually be a family affair in antiquity—would have already undergone many of the psychological and social changes involved in turning from pagan to Jewish identity, from former networks and patterns to new ones, including most if not all of the practices of Jewish life, even if the legal requirements may not be fully assessed until the passage is confirmed in the final integrating stage of the process. So too the Jewish community will have incorporated them to a certain degree into their communal life, varying, for example, as required by the level of displacement experienced in their former pagan networks while undertaking this transition.

56. Cf. Rambo, *Understanding Religious Conversion;* Finn, *From Death.*

57. Finn, *From Death,* 9. See also Segal, *Paul,* 72–114; Zaidman and Pantel, *Religion,* esp. 63–79; Beard, North, and Price, *Religions of Rome.* Failure to account for these dynamics leads to trivializing the issue in Galatians, as though a mere snip of the flesh, found in many interpretations, but even, e.g., in Martin, "Apostasy," remarkable because he otherwise emphasizes the social dynamics.

The stages of this ritual process are adumbrated in Judith 14:10, a late second-century B.C.E. account of Achior's conversion, an Ammonite commander whose response to Judith's successful saving of Israel was put thus: "When Achior saw all that the God of Israel had done, he believed firmly in God. So he was circumcised, and joined the house of Israel, remaining so to this day."

In the context of these first-century dyadic people, the issues are sharpened. In addition to identity concerns that may be considered psychological, for example, status dislocation and the accompanying lack of honor on either community's terms, many practical issues arise. If their lives are no longer intimately networked in pagan social structures but are not yet completely networked in Jewish familial and community structures, how will they provide for themselves and their families while in this liminal state? For those on the path to proselyte identity, this liminality is a temporary condition, with attainment of communal integration in the Jewish community in full view. Liminal persons are "neither here nor there; they are betwixt and between the positions assigned and arrayed by law, custom, convention, and ceremonial."[58] But it is to be expected that any community making such passage possible has the disposition and policies to make manageable the marginality that would be naturally suffered, and the mechanisms for expressing approval or disapproval of the candidates, which will effectively console and manipulate them along the way. But what if the addressees have not even entered into this liminal category according to the communal norms guarded by the influencers and thus into the obligations and privileges that obtain for candidates rather than those considered guests?

If the communities to which Paul wrote Galatians were and represented themselves as members of local Jewish communities, albeit differentiated as subgroups by their faith in Jesus Christ, then there is no reason to suppose that newly introduced non-Jewish people would be aware of intragroup differences within the larger Jewish communities, even if those differences may be quite evident to members of the groups themselves. The ritual of conversion forges connections within the overall community of the Jewish people—past, present, and future, and any subgroup disputing its validity or function would be eventually recognized and engaged, a fact with which the addressees have apparently only now become powerfully aware. In this case, the views now mediated by different significant others involved in their social-

58. Turner, *Ritual Process*, 95.

ization within the same larger communities—which are based on two different understandings of the present reality of the addressees' identity—lead to conflicting results for them.[59]

Here, it may be useful to note that specialists observe that potential converts evaluate their alternatives by consideration of several factors. As Lewis Rambo puts it, the perceived rewards of conversion are evaluated on the basis of "the person's own life experience and values as well as those of friends and relatives. In addition, the potential convert weighs the social rewards (consisting of approval, respect, love, relief of fear and tension) and the cognitive benefits (ultimate meaning and solutions to practical problems). Decision making is thus not entirely an internal process but an experience of social interaction with friends."[60]

Within a community, the "plausibility structure" for the interpretation of reality is self-evident.[61] Central to the conversion process is the reconstruction of the interpretation of reality based upon the views of the new group, which are supported by self-evident assumptions.[62] The new interpretation of reality is learned and sustained in community and mediated by significant others who guide the convert.[63] The transformation to this new reality must be legitimated, an aspect that is grounded in the legitimation of the process for conversion itself.[64] It involves reinterpretation of the perception of the world within the legitimating apparatus of the new reality. The convert is vulnerable to any legitimate suggestion that threatens the certainty or plausibility of his or her new reality. If this Christ-believing group is defined within Jewish communal and thought structures and not against them, then the dissonance that would be encountered by those formerly not part of the community would be salient. If the influencers are representatives of the traditional communal norms, then their understanding of reality is unavoidably important in the process of the addressees' new construction of reality.[65] There cannot be two realities. This is not the way reality was explained by Paul. The addressees are confused.

59. Cf. Berger and Luckmann, *Social Construction*, 163–70.

60. Rambo, *Understanding Religious Conversion*, 126–27.

61. Berger and Luckmann, *Social Construction*, 154–63.

62. See Segal, *Paul*, 74–75.

63. Cf. Berger and Luckmann, *Social Construction*, 157–59.

64. Cf. Bourdieu, *Language*, 115.

65. Hogg and Abrams, *Social Identifications*, 170: "The power of consensus to reduce uncertainty resides precisely in its implication that others have disambiguated reality: that they have valid knowledge."

Even in our more individualistic culture, initial participation in a new religious group "is often facilitated by the existence or establishment of emotional bonds between a potential convert and the advocate and/or the group. It appears that a person's decision whether to make a long-term commitment to a group may largely be determined by the degree of connection the person feels with the new group, as opposed to the degree of emotional connection he or she feels outside the group."[66] Studies have shown that even the belief system, such as the perspectives and language required to describe a new way of looking at the world and their life experiences, are probably only learned adequately after participating in the new group and likely by means of participation in the rituals at that.[67] But even more important, "the major factor ultimately influencing an individual's commitment to the group was not the level of belief, but whether the person had stronger relationships with people in the group than he or she had with people outside the movement."[68] To the degree that the more dyadic culture of those in the setting being investigated is recognized, the significance of these observations is increased.

It is understandable that the addressees are surprised by this response to their expectations of status and want to find a way to escape the results of finding themselves regarded as merely liminals, or preliminals. They are probably extremely vulnerable to any social approval or disapproval processes, emotional as well as legal. When dealing with conversion, which involves people, groups, and processes, change is natural and extends to motivations as well, especially as perceived advantages may appear to change.[69] Moreover, to the degree that they have surrendered themselves to a new group and way of understanding the world, they have yielded some self-control to the authority of the group leaders and traditions.[70] As former pagans, they are likely open to self-surrender, to compliance with the group norms different from those they know. If in this state, they are caught in a

66. Rambo, *Understanding Religious Conversion*, 127. The sources of much sociological research are summarized and applied in various ways in Stark, *Rise*.

67. Rambo, *Understanding Religious Conversion*, 118–23, 127; Stark, *Rise*, 15–23; Snow and Machalek, "Convert"; note the observations by Staples and Mauss, "Conversion or Commitment?" Also Berger and Luckmann, *Social Construction*, 157–61.

68. Rambo, *Understanding Religious Conversion*, 127.

69. Rambo, *Understanding Religious Conversion*, 139–41.

70. Cf. Rambo, *Understanding Religious Conversion*, 132–37.

dilemma, desiring the new yet wishing to avoid the insecurity that may accompany loss of control; they are vulnerable to resolving this tension by "giving in," what has been labeled a "leap of faith," which promises relief and freedom.[71] Instead of public honor based upon their conformity with the Christ-believing (sub)groups' membership and reference group norms, they find themselves shamed for "inappropriate" expectations in relation to the norms of the dominant in-groups represented by the influencers. They want to reduce this dissonance, cognitive and social. What options are available to them?

The Influencers as Agents for Interaction with Gentiles

Although Paul's exclamation of surprise may be an expression of ironic dissatisfaction rather than lack of anticipation, I suggest that it is likely that the influencers and the addressees are actually even more surprised in their encounter with each other's expectations than is Paul at the result. The question at hand for both groups is how to resolve the conflicting understandings of how identity works, of what is really real.

To put this another way, the function of the influencers' appeal to this completion ritual may not be so much to "set the order" of social life, but in this case it may represent the ability of ritual's appeal to "restore order" when it has been threatened or lost. Victor Turner described this dynamic in terms of "social dramas."[72] These are initiated by a "breach" of social custom, law, or ritual propriety. The breach indicates that the ritual self-ordering of this society has failed to maintain the order of things, which provokes a "crisis" for those entrusted with its maintenance. They will initiate procedures designed to "redress" the situation. The drama is resolved eventually either through the reintegration of those responsible for the breach or by the public recognition and legitimation of a social schism between the parties involved.

Applied to the situations Paul addresses in Galatians, the breach is generated by the expectations and claims of the addressees to identity as fully righteous ones, and thus to treatment as equal members of the community based on the truth of the gospel. The influencers, functioning as social control agents, in some sense as ritual elders oversee-

71. Rambo, *Understanding Religious Conversion*, 133.
72. See Driver, *Magic of Ritual*, 137.

ing the processes of proselyte conversion for any Gentiles wishing to become full members, respond to the crisis of this unanticipated challenge to the truth of the traditional order of things. They seek to redress the situation by persuading the addressees that they are welcome to gain the desired identity that they now claim, but that they are misinformed if they think that this has already been achieved apart from completion of the appropriate ritual for such conversion: the status at issue is not granted arbitrarily, which may be their view of the addressees' appeal to their already having gained full membership status without undertaking this rite.[73]

Paul's rhetoric implies that the influencers' techniques include the obvious persuasive forms of communication such as teaching and explaining the Scriptures and the customs of the community. Techniques of shaming that will communicate at the emotional and psychological level that the addressees should take their proper place are also employed. The point is that their approach includes the demonstrative power of ritual itself—a power that can be just as powerful as the authoritative command.[74] That this is what is taking place is indicated in Galatians by the fact that Paul accuses them of various ways of trying to put the addressees in their place, to manipulate them by, for example, unsettling, excluding, and persuading them, but they do so in order to compel the addressees to understand themselves as defined by this rite and thus to complete it to achieve their goal. In order to gain the group acceptance they seek on undisputed terms, the addressees now wish to comply, no, conform with the influencers' appeal to this other message as good, because they identify with that group and its norms as being the same as their own, which suggests it is the same identity that they had been led to believe was their own already: righteous ones of the community of God. But the expectation that this identity would be confirmed has not been realized; instead, they have been welcomed on different terms. The addressees' appeal to "another message" about the meaning of Christ for themselves already has become an obstacle instead of a solution and brought upon them pres-

73. Cf. Kertzer, *Ritual,* 51; Bourdieu, *Language,* 117. This aspect is useful for considering the issues in Galatia in another way. The influencers are still approaching the addressees as though they have not yet undertaken completion of this rite, which suggests that the influencers have not been informed of the ultimate level of resistance this letter now makes clear.

74. Cf. Leach, "Ritual"; Driver, *Magic of Ritual,* 173.

sure, if they wish to continue to claim such identity, to conform with the prevailing norms to complete this status transformation.[75]

Here, we might explore one of the windows into the possible psychological motives of the influencers that emerge from his description of their method of shaming in 4:17: "They are jealous [ζηλοῦσιν] for you not for [your] good; they want to exclude you [ἐκκλεῖσαι ὑμᾶς] in order that you would be jealous [ζηλοῦτε] for them."

The influencers exclude Paul's Gentiles from the indiscriminate inclusion they seek as equal coparticipants among the children of God. Instead of honor and security, they find themselves shamed for the mistaken notion of having completed the process of conversion: they are still in the pre- or initial liminal stage of the ritual process and they have not yet realized what they have sought for themselves among the people of God through their faith in Jesus. Worse yet, they may not be regarded by the influencers as even having decided to begin this process based upon their assumptions of identity according to Paul's gospel!

Nevertheless, the influencers' attraction is variously defined as being "jealous for," "earnestly courting," or "zealous for" them; that is, the influencers do not dismiss the addressees as unimportant, nor in view of this comment is it likely that they have begun any policies that might be considered stigmatizing them as deviants. Rather, they are engaged in putting the addressees in their place as nonproselytes, perhaps even just guests (not yet liminals), in spite of their unusual claims to be already members of equal and full standing with those who have completed the rite. They keep an eye on the addressees, one might say. And this combines well with Paul's accusation of envy: from Paul's perspective, their desire for the addressees is not for the addressees' good, it is not emulative jealousy, but for bad; it is rather envy and should be avoided and protected against. There is nothing wrong in principle with being jealously sought or seen when it is for good; in such a way Paul is willing to accept his own interest in the addressees (v. 18), for that is a complement to having good that others wish to gain as well. But it is to be feared when that jealousy is envious, thereby begrudging one the good that one has gained, it is this of which the influencers are accused.[76]

75. Cf. Hogg and Abrams, *Social Identifications*, 174–75.

76. The differences between envy and jealousy are explained in Nanos, "O Foolish Galatians"; see also discussion immediately below. Simply put, jealousy is wanting what is regarded as your own, or what another has that you wish to

Whether the influencers genuinely care for the interests of Paul's Gentiles or in some way empathize with their situation, which seems natural enough to assume, these righteous Gentiles are important to the influencers, because the addressees' presence naturally involves comparative evaluation, and their claims are an inherent judgment of the influencers' own understanding of reality, their own claims to status, in terms of honor and goods. The perceived threat to the integrity of communal identity leads to intensification or reassertion of circumcision, which symbolizes the historical people of God.[77] The addressees are significant politically, because their conformity with the communal norms is important to the influencers themselves and those whom they represent, both their community and family, as well as the social control agents to whom they report. They also offer the means for enhancing the influencers' own recognition and honor by successfully demonstrating their zeal and commitment to the norms that obtain. But apart from Paul's rhetoric, is it not also probable that the influencers, considered on their own terms, have noble interests and intentions as well?

To the degree that the addressees are responding positively to the influencers before this letter arrives, the drama is unfolding in a way that will eventually resolve itself with the integration of the addressees as proselyte candidates, liminals, and then proselytes, after the completion of the conversion ritual. They are beginning to regard the influencers' message as good, their interests as one with the addressees' own.[78] Paul's letter calling for their resistance to this solution will disrupt the process, causing another breach. The drama is not yet finished, but the way in which it has unfolded as implied by the approach of Paul's rhetoric in this letter would seem to imply that it does not yet involve schism but rather precedes any such notion on the part of

have, whereas envy is begrudging what another has or gains. Whether you have it or not, or even wish to have it or not, you are pained at the good that someone else has or gains.

77. Cf. A. Cohen, *Symbolic Construction*, 28, passim.

78. Hogg and Abrams, *Social Identifications*, 171, follow up their point that "all one's beliefs rest directly or indirectly upon social consensus for their subjective validity," by stating: "While the agreement of others confers certainty, so disagreement, social conflict, or dissensus produce uncertainty. However, it is only disagreement with others with whom one expects to agree which has this effect—that is, with others who are categorized as identical to self as regards the attributes relevant to making a sound judgement of the specific stimulus being judged."

either the addressees or the influencers, who are negotiating identity after being surprised by their different understandings of who they presently are.[79] However, after Paul's letter, to the extent that the addressees act upon it anyway, social developments are likely to take a different course. I suggest that Paul did not recognize the sectarian possibilities that his call to resistance might initiate; these came to fruition in later centuries in spite of, in my view, what was originally the dissociating argument of a reformer responding urgently to an unsettling situation among subgroups of this coalition in its larger communal context when he could not immediately reach them in person to reiterate the implications of the reality of which he was convinced.

The Internal Communal Politics of the Influencers' Identity

The salience of some of Paul's accusations can be understood on internal Jewish communal terms. For example, the addressees' claims would undermine the present order of entrance, of distribution of identity, honor, and goods that had been negotiated in the past on the basis of Scripture and tradition by way of proselyte conversion. Paul's own comment in 5:3 bears witness to the concern for full Torah observance that obtains for Jewish people and extends to those who complete proselyte conversion. The claims of these Gentiles and Paul threaten these lines and would be justification enough to precipitate a protective response. But the social dynamics are probably not so confined.

The influencers function somewhere between the Gentiles Paul addresses and other social control agents, either of their own minority Jewish communities or perhaps as representatives of Jewish communi-

79. Hogg and Abrams, *Social Identifications*, 174–75, in noting the distinction between compliance and conformity, observe: "In the absence of coercion, people conform to a group with which they identify, remain independent from one with which they simply do not identify, and express anti- and counter-conformity if the group is one from which they actively wish to dissociate themselves." They write here not of dissociation in Perelman's sense, as I have been using the term, but in the sense of seeking to separate themselves from this group, sectarianism. The addressees' positive response to norms that are different than those they have internalized with Paul suggests that they do not know Paul or themselves in a sectarian way vis-à-vis the influencers but as sharing identity instead. Likewise, the essentially benevolent aims and techniques of the influencers seem to be employed toward misguided subgroups instead of former and now antagonistic separatist groups.

ties who answer for them to those who represent the dominant pagan society. This dynamic of organizational social control is explained by Amitai Etzioni thus: "Normative power [the use of symbols for control purposes] is exercised by those in higher ranks to control the lower ranks directly; normative/social power is more commonly used indirectly—for instance, when the higher in rank use an individual's peer group to control him, as a teacher might do in a classroom."[80] Their successful influence is recognized no doubt in terms of honor and socioeconomic as well as religious opportunity, not to mention emotional satisfaction or legal requirements that may be fulfilled. It does appear that the influencers themselves are in some kind of marginal state by which their successful persuasion of these Gentiles to complete the ritual process of conversion by circumcision serves their own purposes of recognition with those to whom they answer; or, more properly considered, that the influencers' interests could now be portrayed at least along this line by Paul in seeking to undermine them.

For the interpreter, the identity of the influencers is inextricably tied to analysis of Paul's rhetoric, which was not written to them but to the addressees. The identity of the influencers and their message of good is thereby further enhanced by consideration of the dynamics of the addressees' own concerns. The addressees have trusted these influencers as guides and begun to internalize their message as good for themselves.

By acceptance of the assessment of the influencers for themselves as Gentiles—guests or liminals instead of already aggregated members—the addressees would accept stepping down to the place as appropriate for themselves that the various techniques—for example, instruction combined with shaming and other forms of manipulation—were designed to get them to move to in the first place: under the influencers in terms of the hierarchical distinctions that govern a community bounded by circumcision. Thus, Paul seeks to communicate that in this way the influencers will gain honor or boast in the addressees' flesh, in the addressees taking a place below themselves, and only moving to the place that they claim for themselves by way of the meaning of Christ if they complete the ritual process of conversion. The benefit of relative honor rating will be evident immediately, and it may well be expected to continue to always signify the greater honor of the influencers vis-à-vis the addressees, all the more so as those who have

80. Etzioni, "Social Control," 396.

helped them to safely negotiate that crossing and gain in undisputed terms that for which the addressees longed. Completion of this rite demonstrates that the influencers are right about what is good for the addressees after all.

This approach accounts for the fact that the addressees are new to understanding their own identity in Jewish terms—sharpened immeasurably to the degree that we may take them to represent dyadic cultural psychological concerns for knowing themselves by way of the others' assessment of them according to communal norms. If so, then the addressees would be highly sensitive to any feedback from the influencers, intuitively aware of the dishonorable implications of having taken a seat reserved for someone of higher status than themselves, and open thereby to judging the message of how to overcome this distance by way of completion of proselyte conversion. This "other" message would then indeed represent welcome "good news"!

The reaction of the addressees implied by Paul's rhetoric indicates that they are responding to the normative power of shaming. This suggests that they have not yet been labeled deviants or schismatics, for such people and groups become unconcerned with acceptance by those who represent the norms and values of the group of which they are now "formally" members, instead looking to gain honor within their new court of reputation.[81] Paul seems to anticipate in his ironic ridiculing approach the foolishness of the addressees, perhaps intuitively aware that one of the persuasive forces of ritual is the way it discourages critical thinking, presenting a clearly defined course of action that promises to resolve their problems.[82]

To the degree that the addressees have begun, prior to Paul's letter, to understand themselves as liminals or even preliminal guests, they would need to negotiate the ambiguity of this situation. They are thus vulnerable to the persuasive case made by the influencers: the addressees may negotiate their present marginality by the traditional and long-standing means available to them, which have successfully set this Jewish group apart as the righteous ones on legal as well as moral grounds,[83] because these Gentiles have already initiated this process when they turned from paganism to the worship of the One God. They can do this by simply completing the ritual process of pros-

81. See Braithwaite, *Reintegration*.
82. Cf. Kertzer, *Ritual*, 85.
83. Cf. Bell, *Ritual Theory*, 121.

elyte conversion, wherein they can now imagine their own interests are served, even if it is the ideology of that very system that has marginalized them.[84]

Like rhetoric, ritual has a built-in logic; the very form of the presentation leads them to believe in the message put forth.[85] This is an attractive option with much to recommend it. It is after all legitimated by the same Scriptures from which Paul works and likely at the level of real conviction for the influencers who are engaged in its promotion among the addressees, who believe this ritual is the way that God has provided for incorporating non-Israelites into status as Abraham's children, providing for themselves a symbolic identification within this community.[86] This tradition is grounded in the very revelation of God, from whom Abraham received this commandment.[87] And it is, presumably, recognized to alter the standing of Gentiles by the larger pagan society in which the Jewish communities operate. All in all, it works, as the influencers (especially if proselytes) know experientially, in solving the precise problem of identity and the concomitant concerns for acceptance, both psychological and physical, within the larger community.[88] Why do the addressees hesitate?

The addressees must adapt to their new circumstances but following Paul's teaching have not met with the success they had hoped. Instead, they have met with rejection. That is why the shame administered by the influencers has affected them so deeply and why they now seek integration in the community (or communities) through Jewish status on the terms of the influencers; that is, through completion of the ritual of conversion by circumcision they will avoid further shaming and marginalization and instead gain the desired honorable status with all the rights, security, and obligations that follow.

84. Cf. Bell, *Ritual Theory*, 192.

85. Cf. Kertzer, *Ritual*, 101. Ritual "makes desirable what is socially necessary by establishing a right relationship between involuntary sentiments and the requirements of social structure. People are induced to do what they must do" (100, citing V. Turner).

86. Cf. Kertzer, *Ritual*, 13–24.

87. Cf. Bell, *Ritual Theory*, 193–223; Kertzer, *Ritual*, 40, quotes Bloch.

88. It is important not to get caught in the functionalist trap of thinking that the only reason the influencers emphasize this ritual is to conserve the status quo or resist change; cf. Driver, *Magic of Ritual*.

The External Politics of the Influencers' Identity, Including Pagan Communal Constraints

It is now clearer why the identity of the influencers can be characterized by Paul as marginal and thus give him a place to attack their own self-serving need to ensure the addressees' compliance. The influencers answer to the community, but more specifically to the social control agents who have entrusted them with the overseeing of this important communal task, for the successful execution of their responsibilities.

Those to whom the influencers answer would seem on the surface to be other leaders of the Jewish community they represent, but this strictly inner- and intracommunal dimension need not be the only politics at work. The influencers could themselves be the highest communal leaders, but the marginality might instead be the result of their responsibility to answer for the communal norms of the non-Jewish population and its social control agents. Of course, this concern could apply by extension to any member or lower-level social agent of the community. Even though the point of tension addressed in Galatians is intra-Jewish for the addressees—because the exigence arises from the clash of the prevailing Jewish norms that shape the influencers' view of reality with those of this Jewish subgroup—the seeds of the influencers' concerns to unyieldingly assert the necessity of the addressees' compliance with the traditional norm of proselyte conversion may be much more intercommunal, expressing the insecure situation of their minority communities within the larger civic pagan world in which they are embedded and their own need to comply with the status quo.[89] Concern to maintain the appearance of the *pax Romana* would

89. The use of the label *pagan* is problematic, but the options of Greek, Greco-Roman, or polytheist, for example, are too. Polytheist may put too much emphasis on the religious dimension for the modern reader, whereas other aspects of ethnicity were likely salient, because religion was embedded in politics. We are not certain whether the addressees are Greeks, Romans, Celts, or Phrygians, thus limiting the usefulness of these labels. And it is also a problem to label them Greeks or Greco-Romans because of the implication for the Jewish players, accentuating a difference that may also be misleading, because these Jewish people are likely Greeks and Greco-Romans in significant ways as well, with lively interaction and investment in the local so-called pagan political communities. Moreover, care must be taken to avoid association for the modern reader with the later forced separation of Jewish communities into ghettos. See discussion below.

logically be shared by local elites, including those representing the interests of local Jewish communities.[90]

These intercommunal politics might account for the intensity of the boundary maintenance concerns of the influencers in the context of those to whom they report, both inside and outside the Jewish communities themselves. Paul characterizes the motives of the influencers as selfishly seeking to avoid the threatening results of the addressees' claims in Christ: "and only that they may not be persecuted for the cross of Christ." This kind of concern on the part of the influencers might arise if, to discuss but one example, the addressees were claiming protection under the synagogue exemption from participation in the imperial cult (or other local cult) practices of their pagan family and social network, while not yet Jewish proselytes or even formal candidates.[91] This would implicate the entire Jewish community, and perhaps jeopardize the legitimation to which it appeals for exemption, which was probably a matter of some debate even apart from such apparent infractions. Especially to the degree that the Jewish communities of Galatia were themselves minority groups with associated concerns, any pagan guests would represent in some way the dominant pagan society's interests. Great care must be taken to manage the misunderstanding that could easily arise with dire consequences. These addressees are vitally attached to pagan networks with interests that are threatened by the new claims of the addressees, including familial and commercial interests, even superstitious beliefs that the entire network would be expected to hold.[92] Their claims thus represent a potential threat to the interests of the Jewish communities, which function as minority communities constrained by the concerns of their pagan neighbors.

90. See also Fredriksen, *From Jesus*, 154–56; Goodman, *Roman World*, 102–3, 325.

91. On the subject of the imperial cult, see especially Price, *Rituals* (with a focus on Asia Minor); Fishwick, *Cult* (with a focus on the western side of the Roman empire); Bowersock, "Imperial Cult"; and the collection of essays in Horsley, *Empire*.

92. See Price, *Rituals*, passim, who, e.g., on 101–32, discusses many facets of imperial cult festivities, including their importance for the whole community and not just the elite, and how the significance of this institution was not merely formal but extended to many areas of civic life. E. A. Judge has argued that violation of the "decrees of Caesar," the charge brought against Jason in Thessalonica according to Luke (Acts 17:7), refers to the personal loyalty to Caesar sworn by local magistrates and thus acceptance of the responsibility to prevent any activities in the community that might appear to threaten the faithful performance of that oath ("Decrees"). See also Zaidman and Pantel, *Religion*.

It appears that Jewish communities were understood in this period as in some way voluntary associations (collegia) of ancient foundation.[93] Collegia were generally permitted some degree of self-government independent of the Roman or other local governments' control; yet, as Sandra Walker-Ramisch summarizes, this "in no way absolved the citizen member from participating in public worship, sacrifices, and festivals, and in general honoring (*eusebeia/pietas*) the state gods and ancestral customs; nor did it exempt her or him from showing honor and respect for the council and people (*philotimia*)."[94] Although collegia were "an integral and integrating part of the socio-political life of the city-states," they were not sectarian, that is, they did not reject the dominant social order, but rather they tended to "mirror the municipal organization and public cult of the *polis*."[95] Such collegia exist within a system in which "*pietas* and *philotimia* were the 'glue' of the empire."[96]

The public worship of the civic gods constituted both the expression of religious conviction and political solidarity, for it constituted the traditional expression of civic patriotism; indeed, the embedded nature of religious identity and practice is particularly salient when dealing with such social implications.[97] S. R. F. Price summarizes the conclusions of his study of the imperial cult in Asia Minor thus: "The cult was a major part of the web of power that formed the fabric of society. The imperial cult stabilized the religious order of the world. The system of ritual was carefully structured; the symbolism evoked a picture of the relationship between the emperor and the gods. The ritual was also structuring; it imposed a definition of the world. The imperial cult, along with politics and diplomacy, constructed the reality of the Roman empire."[98] In such a context, the following observation gives clarity to the social tensions that might arise for pagans, who to some degree understand their lives and interests, personal and communal, as intimately connected with the expression of the imperial cult: "*pietas* and

93. Cf. Kloppenborg and Wilson, eds., *Voluntary Associations*.

94. Walker-Ramisch, "Graeco-Roman Voluntary Associations," 133–34.

95. Note Philo, *Spec. Laws* 1.51.

96. Walker-Ramisch, "Graeco-Roman Voluntary Associations," 133–34.

97. For the interface of religious and political interests and those of both Romans and Greeks that were represented by adaptation of traditional Hellenistic beliefs and practices into the institution of the imperial cult, see Price, *Rituals*, passim; e.g., on public versus private, see 117–21; and for a summary, see the conclusions of 234–48.

98. Price, *Rituals*, 248.

philotimia were considered the sacred duty of every citizen and their observance an act of loyalty to the empire and an affirmation of the social order. To fail in this duty was *asebeia* (*impietas*) and this could mean exile, or even death."[99]

According to Josephus (*Ant.* 14.185–267), Julius Caesar's public declaration of Jewish communal rights as a *religio licita* was delivered in letters to cities around the republic, many in Asia Minor (e.g., Parium, Ephesus, Sardis, Kos, Laodicia, Tralles, Miletus, Pergamum). They justified exclusion from such expressions of civic piety as the worship of gods other than their own, because of their ancient foundation.[100] These rulings and actions contrast sharply with the policies forbidding other collegia that were reiterated by Caesar (Josephus, *Ant.* 14.216). He was followed on this policy as well, although to varying degrees, sometimes ruthlessly (e.g., Tiberius, 14–37 C.E., including Egyptian and Jewish; Claudius, 41–54 C.E.; Nero, 54–68 C.E.), although some rulers were more respectful than others (e.g., Augustus, 28–14 B.C.E.), usually toward those that could claim ancient foundation (*Ant.* 16.162–73). Although some interpreters have argued that these decrees should not be considered a kind of Magna Carta always in force everywhere,[101] it is nonetheless the case that they were extended to many communities throughout Anatolia according to Josephus and that according to Roman law of this period Caesar's rulings had established a precedent that obliged future rulers to recognize the legitimacy of Jewish ancestral religion, regardless of the precise legal definitions of their voluntary associations in each civic context.[102]

That the special rights of Jewish communities were at times resented and even challenged in various communities is clear in the accounts from Josephus. The kinds of tensions that might have been developing in Galatia bring out just how these things might evolve and what internal actions might be taken to protect vital interests from being threatened, in this case, by faith claims on the part of non-Jewish people that the leaders of the larger, albeit still minority Jewish com-

99. Walker-Ramisch, "Graeco-Roman Voluntary Associations," 134; see also Goodman, *Roman World*, 299–301.

100. Cf. Cotter, "Collegia and Roman Law"; also Nanos, *Mystery*, 43–46.

101. Cf. Rajak, "Charter." Sanders, "Common Judaism," argues against such minimizing of the available evidence.

102. Note too the extreme appreciation of Caesar evident in the exceptional degree of mourning expressed by the Jewish community upon his death (Suetonius, *Lives* 1.1.84).

munities did not share. It was one thing for pagans to associate as guests or even benefactors and still carry on their lives independent of Jewish identity, that is, continue to engage in, for example, the idolatrous practices of local and imperial cults. This was to be expected; they were not proselytes or even candidates to the degree that righteousness might pertain for them as well at various points along the way. This may be illustrated by the case of the donor Julia Severa.[103]

According to an inscription from Acmonia of Phrygia, immediately west of Galatia, Julia Severa built or gave the Jewish community a house or hall of prayer. Yet this mid-first-century C.E. friend of the Jewish community was most likely not a Jewess or even a proselyte candidate, for she was also recognized by the senate at Acmonia as a high priestess of the house of the divine emperors and also as president of the competitive games.[104] She is thus in some way likely to be regarded as a special kind of pagan or Gentile guest or friend but yet not held accountable to lead a Jewish life. This suggests a distinct communal identity for this Jewish community but at the same time a respect for their role within the collective processes of the civic community of which they are a part. Like other collegia and private or voluntary associations, the Jewish community seems to in some way echo the functions of the polis in which it exists; it is an organic part of the larger whole, and its own concerns for local patriotism should not be overlooked.[105] Tessa Rajak offers the following explanation of the evidence for Jewish communities of Asia Minor functioning as an organic part of the larger pagan society: "Judaism could be incorporated into the civic context through the inclusion of a synagogal community into the workings of the polis. So the character of that community would inevitably be dictated by the Greco-Roman polis norms. In this way, I would suggest, the Greek political system permanently shaped the evolution of Diaspora Judaism."[106]

Therefore, I suggest that since it is logical to assume in the communities in Galatia that the Jewish communities were probably exempt from participation in the local citizen expressions of worship, not least the imperial cult—a central and powerful symbol with great conse-

103. Cf. Rajak, "Synagogue."

104. Rajak, "Synagogue," 166–69.

105. See Trebilco, *Jewish Communities*, 167–85; and essays in Jones and Pearce, *Local Patriotism*.

106. Rajak, "Synagogue," 165.

quences for the self-interests and expressions of an Anatolian community or communities, which practice is widely attested for the region in villages as well as cities—that this would be sufficient "difference" to lead to concern not to offend the local pagan population with whom mutual interests were at work.[107] It is likely that the fit was not entirely comfortable in this area. The interests of the local population are intimately tied up with cultic expressions of various kinds that the Jewish communities presumably eschew; their cultic activity is confined to Jerusalem and its Temple. They may appeal to Roman legislative precedent that permits this otherwise seemingly "antisocial" behavior for Jewish communities as voluntary associations or special "collegia" of the diaspora, to whatever degree these may be understood or not as *politeumata* in any given location.[108] And at the same time, they may appeal to the civic solidarity witnessed in the dedications made to the emperor in the Temple at Jerusalem, even if not the standard offerings of cult.[109]

107. Evidence of imperial cult activity is not confined to the cities, although an important Roman colony such as Pisidian Antioch yields much (and, e.g., a Roman colony coexisted with the hellenized polis at Iconium; cf. Mitchell, *Anatolia,* 1.77, 91) but is attested in villages of Asia Minor as well, which were self-conscious of their need for recognition. Note that villages and cities of an area had vested interests in each other's cult activities; cf. Price, *Rituals,* 78–90. Price even notes an example such as the promotion of the imperial cult "on the imperial estates of Choria Considiana in Galatia, where communal organization had probably not advanced far" (86). In addition, many other cult expressions are attested, such as Cybele and other deities, and nonparticipation in these unifying social activities would also be notable; moreover, these may incorporate imperial cult and thus involve communal culpability at several levels (91–100). Price notes what he calls an exceptional example that is of interest for a study of Galatians. A large and highly organized association with its center about twenty kilometers north of Pisidian Antioch, the *Xenoi Tekmoreioi,* which drew members from some two hundred places, mainly obscure villages, was dedicated to worship of Artemis, yet four extant documents of the society open with a dedication to the emperor (98). In general, in Galatia, "under Rome, the [local] cults continued to be prestigious, but the communities were transformed into Greek-style city-states and the priesthoods tended to become multiple and to be held (annually) by the local hellenized aristocracy" (Beard, North, and Price, *Religions of Rome,* 1.341). See also the inscription from Priene (Lewis and Reinhold, *Roman Civilization,* 1.624–25). See discussion in Mitchell, *Anatolia,* 1.101–17.

108. Smallwood, *Jews under Roman Rule,* 225; Kasher, "Civic Status"; Lüderitz, "Politeuma?"; Barclay, *Diaspora,* 25 n. 18, 60–71.

109. In addition to any prayers that may have been offered for the emperor, and honors expressed, for example, in dedications, daily sacrifice was made in

It is logical to imagine that the synagogue's social control agents would be on guard to ensure that their practices conformed to the policies governing this nonconformist behavior.[110] Otherwise, their lack of civic piety might be cause for alarm, if not social pressure, even interference from their pagan neighbors, especially if some misfortune befell them or their village, town, or city, arousing superstitious fears of retribution for impiety among their own citizens.[111] They constitute, after all, local minority groups granted special privileges by Roman rulers that by nature undermine the beliefs and interests of the dominant local communities (e.g., Greek, Roman, or Celtic), sufficient cause for envy and resentment, for example, apart from aggravating the perhaps fragile status quo that has been gained to date by suddenly supporting a subversive policy, such as would be the case if they sought to justify the exemption of Paul's pagan addressees from their proper pagan social obligations.

Jerusalem on behalf of the emperor, which may have functioned in lieu of participation in imperial cult. This sacrifice was apparently funded from the collection of the temple tax from throughout the diaspora (Josephus, *Ant.* 14.110–13; 16.160–78; *J.W.* 2.195–98; *Ag. Ap.* 2.65–77, esp. 77; Philo, *Embassy* 133, 152–61, esp. 157, 355–73; Tacitus, *Hist.* 5.4–5, esp. 5.5.1; Cicero, *Flac.* 66–69). See also discussions in Horbury, "Tax"; North, "Development of Religious Pluralism"; Rajak, "Synagogue," 164–66; Trebilco, *Jewish Communities*, 167–85; Borgen, "Participation"; Kloppenborg and Wilson, eds., *Voluntary Associations.*

110. See Goodman, *Roman World,* esp. 102–3, 325, for the political concerns of local elites, including compliance with the exceptions granted by Rome to Jewish minority populations among them.

111. Luke tells of the pertinent example of Demetrius, the silversmith of Ephesus, and the concern expressed in terms of both his trade and the reputation of the temple of Artemis, with whose honor and worship the city's reputation was linked, in reaction to Paul's winning of converts from among pagans to his Jewish subgroup (Acts 19:23-41). Note that Alexander was going to represent the voice of the local minority Jewish community in response to the riot but was unable to do so over the crowd noise, so eventually the town clerk stepped in to assure the crowd that things were not as they had been led to believe, presumably with some sympathy for the plight of Alexander and the Jewish community's interests. It seems that the larger local Jewish community did not intend to upset the status quo and would have criticized Paul's activities among the pagans or argued either that those activities had been misunderstood or did not represent the views of the local Jewish community. See Tacitus, *Ann.* 4.36; Dodds, *Greeks,* 32; Finn, *From Death,* 48; Price, *Rituals,* 60–61, 66; Beard, North, and Price, *Religions of Rome,* 1.134–49 and 1.313–63; North, "Development of Religious Pluralism," 177–79; Garnsey and Saller, *Empire,* 175.

Within these kinds of dynamic social settings, Paul's Gentiles seek association within the Jewish communities and consider themselves, because of his earlier teaching, equal members, children of Abraham, righteous ones of God, although they are not proselytes traditionally granted such legal identity and attendant rights. They no longer regard themselves as pagans for whom it is still appropriate to engage in such idolatry, and they likely appeal to the practices and protection of the Jewish communities for legitimating their withdrawal from participation. The need for negotiating access to resources would logically be precipitated by such withdrawal from the fabric of family and village or city life, and it is likely that some expectations were expressed, if not requests made, based upon the addressees' new understanding of their identity. The pagan networks of support into which they were born and raised would begin to break down as their intentions became known, bringing shame and fear, creating the need to provide for themselves and any family members in their trust by appeal to the new network of those whom they perceive to share in this new identity.

While such gestures of solidarity might have been respected by the Jewish communities' members and appreciated in many ways, they might also have endangered their own rights and privileges, which at any given time might be suspect even apart from such new considerations, as special privileges not shared by others often are. Would they have the right to guard such Gentiles under the authority that their voluntary association or synagogue communities were granted? Would they or should they have been willing to suffer and risk bringing upon the entire Jewish community the consequences that might be required by the pagan neighbors of these guests, not to mention those of the dominant pagan society's control agents?

This kind of complexity would surely arise in some diaspora cities; of civic tensions along such lines as this we have ample evidence, regardless of accommodations made, and appeals to examples of good citizenship, such as dedications to the emperor or other significant figures.[112] We do not know if any such tensions are characteristic of the precise locations of Paul's Galatian addressees, independent of their concerns, or because of them. Yet the letter does clearly suggest, granted in the context of Paul's polemical effort to undermine their group motives as selfish, that those influencing the addressees are themselves

112. See discussion above, and Josephus, *Ant.* 14.185–267; 19.299–306; *J.W.* 2.285–308; Philo, *Embassy* 132–34.

in some way in a precarious position because of the nonconforming behavior of the addressees to date, that is, their noncircumcised identity. After all, Paul says that the influencers as a group do not want to be "persecuted for the cross of Christ," that this is why they want the addressees circumcised and bring pressure to bear (6:12).

Would they or should they be willing to suffer, still less possibly to involve the entire Jewish community in suffering, for a faith claim that the influencers and larger community do not share, when there is a traditional and unequivocal way to legally negotiate the addressees' identity so as to remove this pressure? To put this another way, according to the perspective of both the Jewish and pagan people of the time, in the context of Jewish identity, for example, the world is bifurcated: unless they actually become Jews, the addressees are pagans, non-Jews on both Jewish and pagan terms.[113] A case like Julia Severa seems to confirm that just such a distinction could be successfully negotiated to the satisfaction of both communities by someone remaining a pagan while also a friend or guest of the local Jewish community. But a claim of equal and full rights with Jewish people from Gentile associates who have not negotiated proselyte identity by the means available for doing so puts them, as Gentiles, not only in a marginalized situation vis-à-vis their association with the Jewish community but also and perhaps more dangerously in a precarious place legally and morally from the perspective of, for example, their pagan families, neighbors, and the social control agents of the community who still hold them accountable, "as pagans," to their values and norms.[114] Indeed, the problem of their marginality is increased to the degree that it impinges upon the interests of the groups on either side, because this claim to identity is outside the norms of either community, Jewish or pagan, and thus, if accommodated, may marginalize these people and groups on the terms of the other people or groups. The eventual consequence is witnessed later in the first century and thereafter when Christians were clearly distinguished from Jews and pagans, without *religio licita*, and thus called to suffer for failure to participate in their obligations to the imperial cult.[115]

113. Naturally, other group differentiations would characterize perspectives derived from other group identities, e.g., between Romans and Greeks, between Greeks and barbarians, etc. (cf. J. Hall, *Ethnic;* Stanley, "Neither").

114. Philo, *Spec. Laws* 1.52, 308–9; *Virt.* 103–4; MacMullen, *Paganism,* 62; North, "Development of Religious Pluralism," 185–86; Mitchell, *Anatolia,* 2.10.

115. Consider the response of Trajan to Pliny the Younger when governor of Bithynia (ca. 110–12) in *Letter* 10.97, where someone denounced as a Christian may

Both pagan and Jewish people and groups, especially their respective social control agents, have an interest in maintaining the traditional norms and their enforcement. They constrain their response to the claims of these Gentiles of a new social reality. On the non-Jewish side, the imperial claims are undermined, just as they are on the Jewish side, because the traditional understanding of communal identity for inclusion of non-Jews is now made by means of an appeal to modifications based upon the disputed meaning attributed to the death of a Judean martyr of the Roman regime. The most vulnerable group affiliation is naturally the one that represents the minority, in this case the Jewish community, and this is a situation that is underlined to the degree that any special privileges granted by the dominant community may be particularly troublesome in the current pagan as well as Jewish intra- and intercommunal relationships. Thus, it is understandable that the Galatian Gentiles, if making claims to identity that threaten the status and interests of the Jewish minority, would meet with resistance to those claims.

Interestingly enough, it appears that the influencers have expressed neither outrage nor exclusion; at least that is not suggested by the Gentile addressees' implied positive response. No deviance labeling is implied. Rather, they respond to the various techniques of persuasion and manipulation, including shaming, with the desire to be accepted, to gain oneness. They not only trust the influencers, they wish to comply, even conform, much to Paul's dismay, by taking up the ritual process of conversion that will render them fully acceptable on the influencers' terms; indeed, they want to be under the Law, to become proselytes.

If pagans are sheltering under the synagogue authority from the execution of their responsibilities as pagans, whether on Roman, Greek, or indigenous (e.g., Celtic or Phrygian) terms, it is not surprising that the social control agents of the Jewish community at various levels and of various interest group affiliations would be expected to explain or justify this infraction of accepted and traditional social

escape punishment "by worshipping our gods" (cf. Whittaker, *Jews*, 152–53); or the case of Polycarp, the Christian bishop of Smyrna in the mid-second century (Whittaker, *Jews*, 154–60). Cf. Schürer, *History*, 3/1.124–25 (although the appeal to Eusebius, *Hist. Eccl.* 6.2 in n. 81 is rather weak to support the point); de Ste. Croix, "Why?"; Price, *Rituals*, 123–26; Winter, "Imperial Cult"; Brent, *Imperial Cult*, 73–139; Garnsey and Saller, *Empire*, 174–77.

norms within their own community as well. This is heightened if the offending parties have already explained their behavior as legitimate because of their belief in "the cross of Christ." At every level of authority within the Jewish community, among those who do not share this conviction, there would be aversion to supporting this claim and certainly of suffering for it. It may be that the developments that Paul attacks among the addressees in 4:8-11 are related to just this kind of realpolitik.

In this case, Paul ridicules the addressees as former idolaters: "turn back again [ἐπιστρέφετε][116] to the weak and beggarly elements [στοιχεῖα], of which you again want to be slaves. You observe days, and months, and seasons, and years" (4:10). Troy Martin has argued, against the consensus, that what the addressees are turning back to are not Jewish practices but pagan ones.[117] I find his case convincing, and it is useful for evaluating the matter at hand. Stephen Mitchell makes an observation that sharpens the point, although not specifically discussing this verse, and writing instead of that "which stood in the way of the progress of Christianity": "the force which would have drawn new adherents back to conformity with the prevailing paganism, was the public worship of the emperor. The packed calendar of the ruler cult dragooned the citizens of Antioch into observing days, months, seasons, and years which it laid down for special recognition and celebration."[118] Simon R. F. Price argues persuasively for not only the importance of the imperial cult to the life of the city or village population as well as the elites, that it was celebrated not only in the sanctuaries but in all the civic centers including the fields for competitive games, and that it served not only as a vehicle for demonstrating prestige within a community but also between them, but in sympathy with the above comments he also observes that: "time itself was changed by the imperial cult."[119]

116. The echo of 1:6-7 should not be overlooked.

117. Martin, "Apostasy"; idem, "Pagan and Judeo-Christian Time-Keeping."

118. Mitchell, *Anatolia*, 2.10; his observation would not need to be different if writing about a Christ-believing Jewish subgroup (Winter, "Imperial Cult," 101–3, makes a similar observation in discussing Acts 18:12-17, noting that Gallio's ruling implies the recognition in Corinth that "Christianity was a sect within Judaism and therefore *religio licita*"). Mitchell's reference here to Pisidian Antioch provides an excellent example, as would also a reference to Iconium (1.104), although the imperial cult is widely attested in Galatia and throughout Asia Minor (1.100–102), even in villages, as noted above. See further Price, *Rituals*, 78–100.

119. Price, *Rituals*, 106–7.

This interpretation of Paul's reference to pagan timekeeping schemes related to the observation of local and imperial cults makes sense of the fact that Paul has identified the addressees as former idolaters in this context, not former righteous Gentiles or Jews. However, Martin has taken this to mean that the addressees have decided on the basis of the persuasive case of the influencers that circumcision was necessary to become part of the Christ-group, which they do not wish to undertake, and thus that the addressees have decided to abandon the Christ-group and return to pagan life. This conclusion strikes me as virtually impossible. It runs against the grain of Paul's argument, which assumes that the addressees have begun, if not to internalize the message of proselyte conversion as good for themselves, to consider it as the more desirable option to reduce the dissonance. Paul's argument also assumes at its stasis, the rhetorical device to which Martin appeals, that they would not turn to this course if they understood that it undermined the meaning of the death of Christ for themselves, which by way of this letter Paul anticipates and clarifies, even expressing his confidence that they will now get back on the course they had been running so well.

I suggest that Martin has gotten right that the addressees are in some way beginning to return (or at least contemplate returning) to pagan public cult practices that they had abandoned completely as inappropriate to their standing as righteous ones according to Paul's gospel but that he has missed what this signifies. They are not doing so because they do not want to become proselytes because of the Hellenistic sensibilities Martin attributes to them (while paradoxically also reducing the communal significance of this identity process by trivializing it as a mere snip of the flesh). Rather, the addressees are responding to the status ambiguity that has resulted from the response of the influencers to their claims to identity in the absence of proselyte conversion, in fact, without an expression of intention to begin the process at all. The addressees are thus informed that they are not protected from their pagan civic responsibilities by the authority of Jewish communal identity because they are not proselytes or candidates. The influencers do not want to suffer for the cross of Christ, which they do not believe legitimates the addressees' claim to aggregated identity, and thus to the rights and privileges of Jewish communal life, in this case exclusion from civic cultic practices, although surely many other issues might be at stake too.

Thus, the addressees have begun to turn back "again" to those practices necessary to avoid the undesirable consequences of their marginalized identity on both the Jewish and pagan communal sides; or perhaps it may be at this point a more rhetorical point that Paul is making, because they are taking seriously the need to consider this course, because it is being recommended by all those of influence in Galatia, both the Jewish influencers who recommend proselyte conversion to escape this accommodation and pagan family and neighbors, if not yet communal authorities too. Therefore, Paul ironically rebukes the addressees, in effect undermining their trust in the influencers' authority to determine how they know or do not know God presently: Do they not realize that they are already a part of God's new creation within the boundaries of Israelite righteousness? Although not Israelites, they are "known" as full heirs and children of Abraham by God!

In this way, we can understand the seeming paradox of Paul's ironic rebuke, at the same time accusing the addressees (in 1:6-7; 3:1-5; 4:21—5:4) of desiring to become proselytes, having internalized this as good for themselves—the fear of which echoes throughout the letter—and at the same time ridiculing them for desiring to return to civic pagan practices (4:8-11; 5:1). This accounts nicely for the ambiguity of identity for those to whom the influencers answer most directly, regardless of the exact rank of the social control agents of the Jewish communities with whom the addressees interact, because it provides a way to account for the probability that the ultimate pressure at least includes concern with the interests of the pagan civic communities within which their minority Jewish communities must coexist, indeed, in which they participate in significant ways. It need not be the case that the civic authorities have as yet become aware of these developments, as the policies might be objectionable on this justification without outside pressure having actually yet materialized; just the influencers' anticipation of it or the complaint of one of the addressees' more immediate kin could be enough to provoke this preventive action. Such constraints the minority Jewish communities had to accept in order to ensure that their own special freedoms according to the prevailing status quo were not jeopardized, and it is not difficult to imagine that claims made by subgoups within their communities which might threaten such interests would be challenged immediately, even before the leaders of the larger pagan communities might learn of them.[120]

120. See also the discussion of Winter, "Imperial Cult," 101–3, who notes that since Gallio recognizes the Christ-believers as a Jewish sect in Corinth, they would be protected from participation in the imperial cult.

A further significant result of this proposal is the explanatory power it holds for understanding the level of Paul's opposition to the influencers' influence upon these Gentile addressees in Christ, even to the point of curses and castration wishes. The addressees are unsettled. The path they had been "running" toward "obeying the truth" has been "obstructed," with ominous results, in Paul's view. They are considering a course that will undermine not only the meaning of Christ for themselves, the gospel, the Spirit, and Paul but their very knowledge of God, or rather God's knowledge of them as other than idolaters. If this is what the politics of the situations are producing, then Paul has cause to be frightened and angry, at least understandably from his own perspective, which reaction in my view the prevailing views have not yet sufficiently explained. He is indignant that the vulnerable situation of his converts is being exploited by the pressure and appeal of the traditional ordering of reality. And it would make sense of his call to freedom from a former ("and do not submit again") "yoke of slavery" (5:1), which for these former pagans is not Jewish Law observance but observance of pagan practices such as are expressed by participation in the imperial cult and other idolatrous festivities that are part of pagan civic life, which these influencers themselves are free from, yet ironically, support as appropriate for the addressees in their present pagan state![121] Of such "human" constraints in the "present *evil* age" the addressees have been "freed" by way of the good news of Christ, even if not by way of human conventions. Like Paul, they should be crucified to the "cosmos," and the "cosmos" to themselves (6:14), for they are now members of the community of the God of Israel's reign, that new community of Israel and the nations worshiping the One God in the midst of this age on age-to-come terms, so that, even if not Israelites, they should live appropriately (6:15-16; restating the message of 5:1—6:10).

Thus, we can see that, if the addressees wish to escape the necessity of complying with the dominant pagan communal expectations, they face pressure to comply with identification according to the minority Jewish communal expectations for transfer to their sphere of responsibility, which is accomplished by becoming proselytes. The addressees' present claims have put the Gentile members of these subgroups of

121. In imperial cult terms, the goddess of freedom (*libertas*) symbolized the political freedom of the empire, and in later years, "after the deaths of despotic rulers like Nero and Domitian, she was exalted and given the cognomen Augusta" (Axtell, *Deification*, 23–24).

the minority Jewish communities in a compromising position with respect to their identification with Jesus Christ as the agent of their transfer from pagan identity to righteousness. They are told by Paul that they must resist the compulsion to seek indisputable identification as righteous ones in the Jewish sphere of their new life by way of proselyte conversion and at the same time not accept the yoke of slavery to the obligations that are incumbent upon pagans within the pagan sphere of their old identification, for either choice would in essence render meaningless the action of God in Christ toward themselves as representatives of the nations in the dawning of the age to come in the midst of the present age. They are now members of the new creation community of God, marginalized as it may be from both sides (according to the Jewish-versus-pagan paradigm of dissociating argument) of the prevailing powers of the present interpretations of what is real in the present age, that is, according to the authorities of the cosmos to which they have now in Christ been crucified. And thus Paul's instructions follow in the balance of the letter. In short, the message of Galatians chapters 5 and 6 is that the addressees must pull together as a suffering minority group to succeed in this seemingly impossible task, as they together "wait for the hope of righteousness (5:5)."

Understanding the influencers in these terms has the additional benefit of providing a probable basis for understanding how the various communities addressed in this letter might be engaging situations and persons similar enough in outlook, message, and methods to be stereotyped by Paul as though undifferentiated. It is not necessary to presume that an outside interest group is moving simultaneously and in precisely the same ways among the several groups or to speculate how they could succeed in such a scenario to provoke precisely the same response from the various communities of addressees.

The Influencers' Own Concerns

In addition to such political expediencies, it is desirable to consider the influencers on their own terms. It bears repeating that it is logical to assume that the norms that the influencers seek to uphold shape their own understanding of reality and thus of what is legally and morally right in regard to these Gentiles and their newly developed notions of identity and expression of interest in full membership. Paul does not attack their exemplification of these norms except where their unsettling of the addressees is in view. This charge does not emerge until Paul's summary comments, and there it is not against the appearance of Torah-led lives. Rather, Paul accuses the influencers in the style of the prophets, condemning the spirit of their interests as selfish. They should do the Law lawfully, that is, with the interests of the other paramount.

In addition to simply expressing conformity with their own understanding of what is right for these Gentiles, what else might Paul's rhetoric imply about the influencers in Jewish communal terms? At least three impulses can be detected that might be expected of influencers functioning in the mediating role according to this construction of the Galatian situations, in addition to those that arise if the influencers are themselves proselytes. In general terms, as a stereotypical group, the influencers would have likely been concerned to:

1. successfully complete their task, for both God and their communities, which is implied in their persuasive ability (1:6-9; 4:21; 5:7-12) as well as their zeal (4:17). They are in pursuit of enhanced honor rating, both among those to whom they answer (5:10-12; 6:12) and the Gentile addressees (6:13); it would be shameless to do otherwise;[122]
2. obey authority, whether God's word as it has been traditionally interpreted or those human authorities to whom they answer. These are powerful psychological forces for those in mediating roles, even in modern cultures;[123]

122. The seeking of enhanced evaluation of self and group, i.e., positive self- and group esteem, is at the heart of human motives that are explored in social identity theory (cf. Hogg and Abrams, *Social Identifications*) and in discussions of this honor-shame culture (cf. Gouldner, *Enter Plato*, 42–58, 78–106; Pitt-Rivers, "Honor"; idem, "Honour and Social Status," 19–77; Malina, *Social World*). Note that Paul calls the addressees to reject seeking honor from one another in these agonistic or contest-oriented honor-shame terms, and toward the norms of Spirit-led lives, norms embodied in Torah, that is, to loving and serving rather than challenging or envying the neighbor (e.g., 5:13-15, 26).

123. Cf. Milgram, *Obedience*. We should not overlook the possibility that some of the influencers suffered some level of strain in their role of bringing the addressees to compliance (153–64), and we do not know the outcome, whether some withdrew from this activity or were persuaded to see the situation differently in the end. And we should not overlook the fact that Milgram's study brings to light the many different kinds and levels of response within a person and between people, and that responses can change with the changing of situations, players, commands, and the passage of time.

3. avoid shame and discomfort, not only of their current standing but also of their current role, and even the good standing and privileges of the community interests that they represent. The consequences for failure to properly complete their responsibilities because of the claims of these noncompliant Gentiles that are, moreover, based upon a faith in Christ that the influencers do not appear to share, as chapter 10 indicates, would provide powerful motivation. This would explain the basis of Paul's undermining comment that they are seeking to avoid persecution for the cross of Christ (6:12) and provides another explanation for their willingness to employ the kind of manipulative tactics that would render Paul's accusation salient, even if they would probably value them quite differently than does Paul (1:6-9; 3:1-5; 4:12-21; 5:1-12; 6:9, 12-13, 17).

Paul's argument is dissociating throughout, calling for a modification of the norms while subverting the authority of their keepers, in view of the change of aeons. Before this summary comment, he challenges those who appeal to tradition when it runs against the evidence of modification with the coming of Christ, as manifest in the life of the Spirit among these Gentiles, which confirms his revelation that the age to come has dawned, and calls all of Israel to recognize this news as good, for Israel and the nations. Paul does not then attack ritual or ritualized identity but only how these Gentiles are to be judged.

It seems that the influencers are simply living according to norms of Jewish life, which they have internalized as good, and seek to share with these pagans who approach them with an interest in full membership among the righteous ones, or rather with the surprising expectation that this identity they have already gained independent of them or the traditions that they uphold. The differences between the influencers' group identity and that of the addressees are accentuated in the very ways that social identity theorists would suggest, that is, according to the operative in-group prototype of the ones assessing or categorizing themselves in terms of their group identity. "Social consensus or agreement, then, is an intrinsic property of the social group, and disagreement or dissensus is unexpected and creates pressures for conformity, or the recognition of disjunctive category membership in order to explain disagreements. Consensus both resolves subjective uncertainty and confers objective validity upon opinions, perceptions, and conduct because it permits external attributions to be made."[124] This results in the influencers exaggerating the intergroup differences between the circumcised and the uncircumcised in the question of identity as the righteous ones of God, just as, for Paul, it leads to exaggerating the in-group boundary of this coalition apart from circumcision, but instead based upon what he and the addressees together believe the meaning of the death of Christ to be for uncircumcised as well as circumcised, thus making the influencers an out-group, who have appeared to the addressees as the desirable in-group members from whom they seek acceptance.[125]

Social identity involves a process of constructing and negotiating perceived communal boundaries—which are not uniform but vary, for example, in meaning and importance from person to person, from time to time, and among both the insiders and outsiders about each other and even themselves—especially when long-standing norms that have served to symbolize and differentiate a group are understood to be threatened. Moreover, the tendency toward conformity with the expectations of significant keepers of the norms of one's group, in-group behavior, is a powerful and yet normal dynamic of social life.[126] Hogg and Abrams call the social influence responsible for conformity to group norms leading to intragroup consensus, agreement, and uniformity "referent informational influence": "This process occurs in three stages; first, people categorize and define themselves as members of a distinct social category or assign themselves a social identity; second, they form or learn the stereotypic norms of that category; and third, they assign these norms to themselves and thus their behaviour becomes more normative as their category membership becomes salient."[127]

Recognition of these kinds of social dynamics should lead to fuller and more sympathetic historical-critical consideration of the influ-

124. Hogg and Abrams, *Social Identifications*, 173.

125. See, e.g., Hogg and Abrams, *Social Identifications*, 19–30, 68–84, 171, 187, on accentuation effects and categorization.

126. In addition to the measured conclusions of social identity theorists concerning the evidence of minimal group studies, which can suffer from limitations of contrived experiments (cf. Hogg and Abrams, *Social Identifications*, 157–85), the tendency toward conformity can be frequently observed in everyday life, e.g., among academics (cf. Hamilton, *Social Misconstruction*, 9–20, passim).

127. Hogg and Abrams, *Social Identifications*, 172. It should be noted that they are developing these conclusions with respect to modern Euro-American subjects; it is highly probable that these kinds of social aspects of identity apply all the more to the lives of first-century people and groups, often described as dyadic (twinned).

encers, at least in group (or stereotypical) terms and to new insights into Paul and the addressees as well, especially in matters such as Paul's boundary maintenance and the addressees' temptation to conform. There is no reason to believe that the influencers' appeal to Torah, tradition, or consensus is based upon values other than the grace of God and love of neighbor, the norms of Jewish identity and life; the communal boundary at dispute is rather drawn at the place where the meaning of the revelation of Christ for Gentiles in the present age has been introduced by this subgroup. But it is the rhetorical approach of a champion of this position trying to dramatize the stakes for the unsettled of this group that provides the information from which we work. Paul seeks to dissociate these values now in the face of their identity crisis and thereby draws a more rigid boundary for this (sub)group than it has recognized from his teaching when among them. The later interpreter must proceed with care. We cannot know what price the influencers may have paid, will pay, or why. The same goes for the addressees. Lack of nobility of purpose should not be presumed.

This proposal assumes that Gentiles expressing interest in associating with Jewish communities—in terms of the various levels of social contact with Jewish communities that obtain—would be generally welcomed, although naturally varying given the personalities, times, places, and circumstances involved. Indeed, evidence suggests that Gentiles were encouraged at times by certain Jews to worship Israel's God or adapt at least some positive perspective that would fall within the various classifications of righteous Gentiles (e.g., Josephus, *Ant.* 20.34–48 for Ananias with Izates; *Ant.* 8.117 for Solomon building the Temple to persuade all men to serve God; *J.W.* 7.45 for those bringing in the Antiochenes; and the witness of the New Testament).[128] But as long as the people or groups in view are Gentiles—not proselytes or candidates involved in this ritual process—there is no indication that they would be expected to believe or behave as though Jews.[129] Josephus distinguishes between the veneration of God by Izates in Adiabene, when Torah is studied by this non-Jew but not yet fully observed, and after completion of circumcision, when the observation of his Jewish practices by the people may be expected to have dire con-

128. Cf. Goodman, *Mission*, 87.

129. Implied as well in Josephus, *Ag. Ap.* 2.123, writing about those Greeks who have adopted Jewish Law but "lacking the necessary endurance, have again seceded."

sequences (*Ant.* 20.17, 34–35, 38–41, 49–53, 75). In *Against Apion* 2.210, Josephus understands Moses' community to welcome those not only born into the family but also aliens adopting "the rules of life" (τοῦ βίου νομίζων), a kind of inclusion to the "intimacies of our daily life" that is distinguished from that granted the "casual visitor."

In summary, several aspects of the Jewishness of the influencers' personal and communal identity, in addition to attention to their humanity, make sense of the rhetorical situation implied in Paul's letter. For the purpose of differentiating positions within a network of status relationships, "ritual serves to reaffirm what these status differences are," for "ritual serves to remind the congregation just where each member stands in relation to every other and in relation to a larger system."[130] In this case, it is not difficult to see that the status aspirations of the influencers are in some way tied up with their facilitation of the ritual processes of conversion. They work at the boundaries of communal identity, where ambiguity and danger lurk. And this dynamic would apply all the more if the influencers, or at least some of them, are themselves proselytes. Although proselytes have completed the initiation rituals and gained full standing, they would likely remain fully aware of their own ambiguous status among natural-born Jews, and even other righteous Gentiles at various stages of affiliation and commitment, not to mention other proselytes. If so, it is easy to understand them to be now engaged in advancing their own honor (legal or moral communal standing) by pressing the point of circumcision for pagan guests expecting equality outside of the completion of such ritual processes or the other sacrifices such full commitment necessarily entails.

The addressees' claims involve a veiled threat to the influencers' own legitimacy and imply a culpability to commit themselves to the route that is available for those seeking to gain this standing. They also threaten the community's standing with the civic authorities, and the social control agents of both have a vested interest in keeping the peace. Such guests need to be put in their place.

At the same time, it is important to keep in view that, as those who are defined by these rites, the influencers most likely truly believe in their efficacy and appropriateness, and have perhaps even suffered for

130. Cf. Leach, "Ritual," 524.

them.[131] As A. Cohen concludes: "the reality of community lies in its members' perception of the vitality of its culture. People construct community symbolically, making it a resource and repository of meaning, and a referent of their identity."[132]

Are the Influencers Proselytes?

There have been indications throughout this chapter that the social dynamics imply that the influencers might be proselytes. Paul's accusation assumes the influencers are marginalized and involved in the marginalization of the Gentile addressees, which places their interaction at the margins of the community's identity concerns. Paul places their own intentions on the honor-shame axis along with those of the Gentiles he addresses, that is, agonistically defined in terms of the prevailing Jewish communal norms for Gentiles who seek to be honored as belonging among the people of God. They have been able to win the trust of the addressees, although not yet their complete commitment.

Yet the influencers' own fate seems to be in some vital way tied to their ability to persuade the addressees to complete proselyte conversion in order to gain the identity they seek on indisputable terms. The failure to gain the addressees' compliance will somehow adversely affect their own ranking or at least not enhance it as they desire. Paul claims further that they fear persecution will result. Moreover, Paul accuses the influencers of having reacted to the good acquired by the addressees with envy, which indicates a level of comparative association. Interestingly enough, many observers of social interaction have noted that the finer the differences between groups, the stronger the commitment to differentiation and protection.[133]

Whether Paul has rightly judged them and their motives, the identity of the influencers as proselytes seeking to complete their assigned task in keeping with their own convictions of what is right is certainly implied. And it is not difficult to imagine that if proselytes they would be zealous in such matters; indeed, the zeal of converts is widely enough recognized to be proverbial, whether the motive is entirely in the interest of the other to find this great advance or related to the need

131. Cf. Turner, *Forest*, 99–100.

132. A. Cohen, *Symbolic Construction*, 118.

133. E.g., A. Cohen, *Symbolic Construction*, 110–14 (citing also Pitt-Rivers); Hogg and Abrams, *Social Identifications*, 23, 74; Coser, *Conflict*.

to enhance their own self-esteem for the step they have themselves already taken, as social identity theorists suggest.[134] This is also easily understood if the resistance of those in the preconversion condition threatened in some way either their own situation or the communal values to which they now subscribe.

In addition to such social dynamics, Paul's employment of the substantive participle οἱ περιτεμνόμενοι to describe them in terms of circumcision may undermine by implication the influencers' own decision to have undertaken this rite.[135] For Paul uses it to undermine their moral authority, if they are not going to live according to the principles of behavior toward their neighbor to which they are thereby obliged. They clearly advocate circumcision of the addressees apart from usage of this participle in the middle causal sense, and its use here seems rather to indicate that they have themselves "chosen" (middle reflexive) or "received" (middle permissive or passive) circumcision, so that they are in such a state (also if perfect middle or passive).[136] However it is translated, Paul regards them as responsible to uphold the Law with a special concern for those whom they now seek to bring within its sphere, making them vulnerable to his attack on their integrity if they should have their own and not the addressees' interests in view. This seems to imply that Paul is by this phrasing accentuating the hypocrisy of their interest in these Gentiles' completion of proselyte conversion, themselves having been in the same situation but now failing to live up to the life they have chosen: "for even οἱ περιτεμνόμενοι do not themselves guard/keep the Law, but. . . ."

134. Hogg and Abrams, *Social Identifications;* note too Segal, *Paul,* 206. Also, consideration of the dynamics of honor comparison attributed to Greco-Roman culture should not be overlooked, as when Epicharmus declared: "It is obvious that a man who is not envied is of no account" (from Gouldner, *Enter Plato,* 43, 55–58; see too discussion of evil eye or envy elsewhere in this monograph, and Nanos, "O Foolish Galatians").

135. See also Harvey, "Opposition," 324.

136. Some interpreters have noted the possibility that Paul's language in 6:13 may be taken to indicate that proselytes were involved (e.g., Lightfoot, *Galatians,* 223; Harvey, "Opposition," 324; others say they were circumcised Gentiles but do not call them proselytes, e.g., Munck, *Salvation,* 89, 129–34; Gaston, *Paul,* 81, 90, 109, 221 n. 21; Richardson, *Israel,* 90, 96–97).

Some Identity Implications of Paul's Evil Eye Warning

The implications of Paul's accusation that the influencers have "cast an evil eye" upon the Gentile addressees (3:1) are interesting to consider. For example, this rhetorical approach implies that the relative standing of the influencers and addressees is close, and thus the probability of proselyte status is increased. Even a brief discussion of this belief system and Paul's application provide an important entrée into the social dynamics, especially in terms of the relative social position of the influencers vis-à-vis the addressees.[137]

Fear of such a gaze is an indication that the envious designs of the gazer are suspected of bringing loss toward some good that the gazee possesses. Those of near social standing, including neighbors and extended kin—anyone of similar ascribed or previously acquired standing—are highly suspected by the one suffering some misfortune. In a limited good context where the gain of another or their family involves the threat of loss for oneself or family, this fear is powerful indeed. The concern is increased if the good was recently gained, perhaps even more pertinent if the one fearing the gaze is in the process of gaining the good, such as in rites of passage. This is the vantage point of the influencers: they treat the addressees as liminals in need of completing the ritual process of proselyte conversion. To the degree that the addressees have come to see themselves in this light, they should consider themselves particularly vulnerable to envious glances; but the strange thing is, they have not so feared the influencers, an anomaly that Paul's evil eye warning exploits.

In the context of Paul's accusation, the good at risk is indicated, for Paul appeals to the implied disregard of the addressees' "receipt of the Spirit" and experiencing of "miracles" that would be involved in compliance with the influencers' message of their need to "complete" proselyte conversion (3:5). At the same time, Paul indicates that the addressees in some way presently "suffer" (v. 4). Thus Paul "surprisingly" reveals by way of ironic rebuke that the addressees have failed

137. See earlier discussion and Nanos, "O Foolish Galatians," where the details of this system are discussed; among the many other sources drawn on for this argument, see Aristotle, *Rhet.* 2.10; Plutarch, *Moralia* 7.1–7; 8.5.7; Walcot, *Envy;* Gouldner, *Enter Plato;* Schoeck, *Envy;* Foster, "Limited Good"; idem, "Anatomy of Envy"; Elworthy, *Evil Eye;* Dundes, *Evil Eye;* J. H. Elliott, "Paul"; B. Longenecker, "Until Christ."

to suspect that their present unsettled state, in which they have foolishly considered this other way of gaining full standing as righteous ones, is not the result of the influencers' helpful guidance, as they have supposed. Rather, it is the result of the influencers' envy of the good already gained but apart from completion of the rite of passage deemed by the influencers necessary for the acquisition of such good. They thus begrudge this good, by way of the Johnny-come-lately effect, instead of honoring it. Why have the addressees failed to suspect that this envious force was what was causing them to be so confused?

Although envy may be feared from those of higher standing, whether ascribed or acquired—for example, from the gods—Paul's protective warning implies the usual social dimensions of this fear, that is, among those of similarly ascribed standing and social proximity, thus rendering the comparative gaze of the other salient. Aristotle articulated the dynamics of envy in just such terms, and they are repeated in a straight line from classical to modern circum-Mediterranean cultures, interchangeably applied to envy and the evil eye.[138]

Thus, it seems probable that the salience of Paul's accusation, warning really, of unsuspected envious motives on the part of the influencers, whether correct or not, would make sense in contexts in which the influencers share ascribed status with the addressees and also close social proximity, in spite of their newly acquired status within the Jewish communities. They have acquired higher standing by completion of proselyte conversion, and with it honor and associated rights and privileges. At the same time, they carry the identity of being former Gentiles. No matter how much this might prepare them to identify with the plight of these addressees, they regard them nevertheless as Gentiles who need to accept their place according to the approved communal norms of membership. It was good enough for them, so who do these Gentiles think they are![139]

The Influencers' Empathy and the Addressees' Trust

If the influencers are former righteous Gentiles, they can thus empathize with the plight of the righteous Gentile addressees. In fact, from their perspective, far from trying to be troublemakers, agitators, or

138. Cf. above note 137, and Garrison and Arensberg, "Evil Eye"; Murdock, *Theories of Illness*.

139. See also Richardson, *Israel*, 97.

opponents, they are trying to be helpful toward the addressees: like Paul, their influence is directed toward what they believe to be for the addressees' good.

The influencers' genuine concern combined with the ability to relate sympathetically with the addressees' plight would explain the trust they have gained to date and the lack of suspicion, because they seem to offer a helpful hand to gain the good that the addressees have apparently not acquired. The authority of tradition mixed with the power of personal witness to the successful results of completing this other course, rather than suffering the marginality that the present course and claims of the addressees will only perpetuate, would be a compelling combination indeed. Conformity is certainly increased to the degree that the influencers' identity is both salient and paradigmatic: the very persuasive force to which Paul seeks to ground his own appeal.[140]

The addressees have been thereby convinced by these sympathetic and paradigmatic guides that they have (mis)judged their introduction to standing as righteous ones, as though it afforded the standing gained only at the completion of this course; only then would they have equal rights with the influencers to the desired good. They are thus considering if not already beginning to become candidates, liminals, and vulnerable indeed, and they naturally trust those who will guide them through this passage. And that is just where Paul's ironic approach strikes, revealing "realities," undermining the mere "appearance" of good things.

Although these several proposed features of the influencers' identification within dynamic intra-Jewish communal terms (whether proselytes or not) do not necessitate that the influencers are not Christ-believers or are from outside synagogues or even distant places like Jerusalem, the explanatory power is increased measurably if they are not.[141] These leaders have a vested interest in resolving the situation according to the traditional interpretation of the fathers, that is,

140. Cf. Hogg and Abrams, *Social Identifications*, 174–75.

141. E.g., although not the direction he chooses to follow, R. Longenecker (*Galatians*, 292) notes: "Taken on their own, the subjects of both v 12 and v 13 [chap. 6] could be understood as Gentile 'Judaizers' who had no connections with Jewish Christians at Jerusalem."

that circumcision is required to achieve equal Jewish status for Gentile males regardless of their faith claims about Jesus, a concern that is difficult to make sense of if these Gentiles are part of Christian communities separated from synagogue authority, as many interpreters maintain, rather than minority subgroups under the jurisdiction of the synagogues.[142]

The influencers are seeking to gain approval and security by orchestrating the compliance of Paul's Gentiles with prevailing traditions for ritual conversion within the dominant Jewish communities, that is, for those who do not share their faith in Christ, regardless of the Galatian Gentiles' faith claims for full membership on the basis of their belief in Jesus.[143] The influencers are thus set against the gospel of Christ from Paul's vantage point. This makes sense of the fact that, from Paul's perspective, they are proponents of a rival method for the incorporation of Gentiles into the people of God that is not really a message of good news at all. This antithesis is captured in Paul's introductory comments, for example, in the distinction between the agency of humans and their "traditional" conventions when these come up against the new revelation of God (1:1-16).

In addition to what has been proposed, for example, in terms of their wishing to avoid suffering for the cross of Christ if they do not share this faith, there are other indications that the influencers are not Christ-believers. And this identification would have many benefits for further identifying the Jewish aspects of the influencers' identity. An intra- and inter-Jewish way of interpreting the conflict, rather than intra- or inter-Christ-believing one, would also help interpreters escape the seemingly ineluctable conclusion that Paul denigrated Jewish identity and behavior in view of the meaning of Christ, an implication that persists even when they seek to resist this aspect of the argumentative force of their reading. It would allow Paul's rhetoric to exhibit dissociating argumentation entirely within the context of the Jewish communal concerns that result from his understanding of what God is doing within and through Israel for all of the nations, apart from any

142. Cf. the discussion of majority influence in Nemeth, "Intergroup Relations," 229–43; Hogg and Abrams, *Social Identifications,* 157–85.

143. Differently, arguing for a sectarian communal situation and a Christ-believing identity for the influencers, Esler (*First Christians,* 55) recognizes that logically the influencers are not so much against "being a Christian itself" as "allowing the Gentile members of the communities to be uncircumcised."

later sectarian or separate communal identity that developed and became Christianity instead, perhaps even as an unanticipated result of this very letter. It is thus time to turn to another aspect of identity that emerges as questionable from this discussion: Are the influencers Christ-believers?

CHAPTER 10

PAUL'S "GOOD NEWS OF CHRIST" VERSUS THE INFLUENCERS' "NEWS OF GOOD"

The prevailing identifications of the influencers as Christ-believers have been based primarily upon two aspects drawn from the situational discourse, combined with the prevailing interpretations of the narrative discourse units. However, the narratives do not provide primary data for the identity of the influencers in Galatia, do not confirm that Christ-believers provide the parallel reference group for the influencers in Galatian, and offer no unambiguous evidence that those present in Galatia have any connection or concern with Jerusalem, much less the Christ-believing coalitions or their leaders. Not one of these connections is made in the situational discourse; I have argued that none is even implied. In view of the argument that the situational discourse should be primary for evaluation of the Galatian situation and the above discussions of the range of possibilities for interpreting the situations and players involved in the narrative units, as well as the limitations for drawing analogies until the situational units have been thoroughly examined, those units will not be the subject of this phase of the investigation of the identity of the influencers in Galatia.[1]

One of the situational passages, Paul's accusation that the influencers seek to avoid persecution for the cross of Christ by persuading the addressees to complete proselyte conversion (6:12), has been discussed. It was found not to support the assumption that the influencers are Christ-believers but rather to imply quite the opposite. They do not want to suffer for the addressees' appeal to the meaning of the death of a Jewish martyr of the Roman regime in order to legitimate their resistance to completing circumcision. The influencers and those to whom they answer do not appear to share the addressees' conviction about the value of the cross of Jesus in the present age, around which the addressees' identity claims turn.

The other situational passage, wherein Paul puts the message of the influencers into direct conflict with the message of Christ (1:6-7), will

1. See discussions in chapters 4 and 7, and my "Intruding 'Spies'"; a full treatment of the autobiographical narrative is under way in a forthcoming project.

occupy most of this chapter. The consensus views this "other" message as "good news [εὐαγγέλιον]" that is different from Paul's "good news [εὐαγγέλιον]" yet still a gospel of Christ, which logically implies that the influencers are Christ-believers. They are understood to hold a different view of what the good news of Christ means in relation to the circumcision of these Gentiles, at the very least. Often, it is argued that they regard the place of Jewish identity and observance of Torah differently from Paul overall, as applicable to both Jew and Gentile who believe in Christ.

Commentators sense the need to argue this point to varying degrees, although none finds it necessary to go to any great lengths. In other words, this conclusion is apparently self-evident.[2] James Dunn's approach is representative: "The fact that Paul uses the Christian technical term for 'the gospel' also is clear indication that those whom he was about to attack were also Christian missionaries. He calls their message '*another* gospel' because it was significantly different from his own; but he calls it '*gospel*' because that was the term they no doubt also used in their capacity as missionaries like Paul."[3]

J. Louis Martyn emphasizes the point that Paul did not choose to call their message good news except that this is what the Teachers referred to it as, raising the rhetorical issue in a manner that is interesting: "Does Paul take the route that requires self-correction only for the sake of rhetorical emphasis? Probably not. . . . It seems highly probable that Paul takes the path requiring self-correction because he knows that the Teachers are in fact referring to their message as 'the gospel.'"[4]

Paul certainly juxtaposed his previously proclaimed good news (εὐαγγέλιον) of Christ with the "different good news which is not another" of the influencers. But I suggest that the more probable conclusion is that this other message was not about Christ in any manner and that its messengers were not Christ-believers. I will argue that the consensus view has dulled the force of Paul's ironic employment of the

2. Departing from the consensus are the articles by Walter, "Gegner," 351–56; Muddiman, "Anatomy," 264, 267–70.

3. Dunn, *Galatians*, 41–42 (emphasis his). I believe that this view represents every commentary consulted. See earlier discussion, esp. Barclay, "Mirror-Reading," 263 (cf. 265); cf. Bruce, "Galatian Problems"; Vos, "Argumentation," 2; Lyons, *Pauline Autobiography*, 127; Howard, *Crisis*, 9.

4. Martyn, *Galatians*, 121; cf. 109. Walter, "Gegner," maintains that the influencers call it a gospel as a "missionary 'trick'" by which they intentionally echo Paul (351–52).

label εὐαγγέλιον, which has profoundly affected the way that the influencers are identified as well as the entire construal of the situations of the addressees, and thus the way to read Paul's response. The full text upon which the issue turns is in 1:6-7:

> I am surprised [Θαυμάζω] that you are so quickly defecting [μετατίθεσθε][5] from him who called you in [the] grace [of Christ] for a different [ἕτερον] good news [εὐαγγέλιον], which is not another [ἄλλο], except [in the sense] that [εἰ μή] there are some who unsettle you [ταράσσοντες ὑμᾶς] and want to undermine [μεταστρέψαι][6] the good news [εὐαγγέλιον] of Christ.

Several factors are involved in reaching any conclusion. First, the notion that because Paul used the label "good news [εὐαγγέλιον]" for this "other" message, interpreters can be certain that this message was a message of Christ, the term εὐαγγέλιον presumably confined by Paul and others of this movement, as well as others who interacted with them, to the proclamation of a Christ-message. I will soon discuss the broader use of this label by both Paul and others of the period and also investigate the adjective ἕτερον/ἄλλο used to describe the εὐαγγέλιον of the influencers as "another" or not. In addition, I will assess the exceptive (εἰ μή) clause, which defines the sense in which Paul refers to this other message as εὐαγγέλιον and will note some generally

5. Bauer, *Lexicon,* 515, defines this middle usage as to "change one's mind, turn away, desert, turn apostate," and includes an example of the accusation of "turncoat [ὁ μεταθέμενος]" for Dionysius of Heraclea because of his desertion from the doctrines of the Stoa to go over to Epicurus. See also Josephus, *Ant.* 20.38; Burton, *Galatians,* 20; H. Betz, *Galatians,* 45–47; Maurer, *TDNT* 8.161.

6. The usage of μεταστρέψαι here is contextually value laden, though the verb need not mean anything more than "turn," "transfer," "twist," "alter," or "to change from one thing or state to another," often its opposite. It can have a positive sense, e.g., Exod 14:5; Ps 66:6; 1 Esdras 7:15; Plato, *Resp.* 7.518d; or a negative one, Ps 78:44, 57; Joel 2:31 (MT 3:4); Amos 8:10; 1 Macc 9:41; *Test. Asher* 1.8; Acts 2:20; James 4:9; (cf. Bertram, *TDNT* 7.729; Bauer, *Lexicon,* 513; Burton, *Galatians,* 25). Especially pertinent is Sirach 11:31: "turning good into evil, and to worthy actions they attach blame." Some translate as "pervert." The translations "undermine" or "subvert" are often appropriate, which seems to be the case here. For example, H. Betz, *Galatians,* 50, translates as "turn things upside down" and notes that originally this term was "political and suggests revolutionary activities." See also Martyn, *Galatians,* 112; Morland, *Rhetoric of Curse,* 144.

unrecognized ironic elements of the usage as well as the situation of the interpreter.

The prevailing interpretations fail to adequately consider the development of irony communicated in this θαυμάζω clause: in the same breath drawn to express his "surprise [θαυμάζω]" at their desertion for "another good news," Paul actually denies that this other "good news" should rightfully be considered "another." Paul does not exactly say with F. F. Bruce that it is "no gospel,"[7] but he gets thereby at the sense of Paul's usage, for Paul does reverse himself in calling it that "which is not another," and he wishes a curse upon the influencers for their message in a manner that suggests that Paul, at least, may not consider these influencers to be his brethren in Christ nor their message a "good news of Christ" (v. 7). Rather, it is παρ' ("alongside" or "contrary to") the good news of Christ (vv. 8-9) that the messengers "desire to twist," but which for the addressees results in "turning upside down the good news of Christ" thereby emptying the good news of its "truth" for them. It is news, to be sure, but not "good," at least not for the addressees, from Paul's point of view.

It is my view that Paul is addressing an intra-Jewish context with the label εὐαγγέλιον chosen precisely for the unexpected inter-Jewish rhetorical emphasis it provides. Thus, what we are confronted with is not the rhetoric of self-correction, as though Paul is compelled to adopt the language of the influencers, but the introduction of an unexpected comparison delivered through the uniquely disarming effect of irony. In other words, Paul is the one on the offensive, not the influencers, by introducing this shocking association of the influencers' message with the εὐαγγέλιον of Christ as though it were "another." But I maintain that he makes this association only for rhetorical effect: he disqualifies its value as "good" in comparative terms; he confronts the addressees' reaction to it as inappropriate and unacceptable; and he judges as malicious the intentions of its proponents toward the "good news of Christ."[8]

Paul gives it this label, then takes it away. His ironic point is that this other message has no standing as good news except to the degree that

7. Bruce, "Galatian Problems," 271.

8. Similarly Morland, *Rhetoric of Curse*, 144, notes: "It seems obvious that the opponents themselves never openly intended to pervert the Galatians, nor was it a hidden strategy of theirs. Again we have an instance of Amplification: Paul points to a consequence of their teaching, and by presenting it as their intention, he amplifies their activity as especially cruel."

the addressees foolishly respond to it as though it were. If ironic, neither the addressees nor the influencers may have attributed the label εὐαγγέλιον to it, at least not as though it were another way to proclaim the news of Christ.

The Usage of *Good News* (Εὐαγγέλιον) in Paul's Period

The good news (εὐαγγέλιον) of Jesus Christ is the centerpiece of Paul's life and work.[9] But the issue for identifying the influencers and their relationship with Jesus Christ is whether Paul's use of εὐαγγέλιον must be limited to the lips of believers in Jesus or even to a declaration about Jesus in the formal sense that it has come to have in the Christian tradition, with the results then applied to exegesis of Gal 1:6-7, as the conclusions of the prevailing views assume. Are the terms εὐαγγέλιον and its cognates limited to usage by believers in Jesus Christ at this time and in these locations so that it could not be employed by Paul to refer to competing proclamations seeking to influence his converts, either on the part of competing Jewish movements or interests, or even pagan ones, but without reference on their part or Paul's to matters pertaining to Jesus Christ? Could not other competing messages from the Jewish or even pagan communities of good news for Paul's Gentiles be in view? Furthermore, if this is the case, could not Paul employ this label ironically, that is, without intending it to be taken literally to describe the content of this other message or imply that it was actually called by anyone else (the influencers or addressees) good news of Christ?

In these cases, although Paul may see it as a competing message, those influencing the Galatian Gentiles may see their good news message as not competing but rather complementing, or existing independently and without comparison. In fact, the influencers may even have little or no knowledge of Paul's message or rival point of view and absolutely no concern to deal with it. However, even if they did view their message as competing with Paul's, they might see this as necessary in view of the incomplete or misguided nature of any message that would lead these Gentile addressees into (mis)understanding their place so egregiously. In fact, they might have the best interests of the Galatian Gentiles in mind in believing that Paul, or whomever it is they attribute these notions to, has failed them.

9. Cf. Rom 1:1-6; 1 Cor 1:17; 15:1; Gal 1:16. See Hays, *Faith*.

Translating the adjectival noun εὐαγγέλιον (from εὐαγγέλος) into English as "gospel," or the verb εὐαγγελίζω (middle voice: εὐαγγελίζουαι) as "to announce or proclaim the gospel" is, to begin with, problematic. Because *gospel* is and has been for a long time used as a uniquely Christian term, it is anachronistic for our investigation, having lost the more fluid sense of good news or announcement or message of good originally communicated, and its verbal cognate is further limited by the lack of an English verbal form of "gospel" (i.e., "to gospel"), thus the translation "announcing" or "proclaiming the gospel." The limitation is especially evident when used together as in Galatians 1:11, where the much richer dynamic interplay of the terms in their original language is evident: τὸ εὐαγγέλιον τὸ εὐαγγελισθὲν ὑπ' ἐμοῦ ὅτι οὐκ ἔστιν κατά ἄνθρωπον [lit.: "the gospel that was gospeled by me is not according to a human.]" I will generally use "good news" and "to proclaim good news": thus rendering this sentence "the good news which was proclaimed [as good news] by me is not according to a human agent or agency."[10]

Εὐαγγέλιον derives from ἄγγελος, "messenger" or "one sent," and the verbal forms of εὐαγγελίζω from ἀγγέλλω, "to tell" or "to announce," from which we also derive our word *angel*.[11] An εὐαγγέλος brings a message of victory or other news that causes joy.[12] It is sometimes political, but need not be, as it could refer to news of a personal nature such as a wedding, even by Aristophanes (*Eq.* 656) for the εὐαγγέλιον that anchovies had become cheaper![13] Εὐαγγελίζομαι refers to the bearing or proclaiming of this glad news. Εὐαγγέλιον refers to the message itself bringing joy and also functions in the Greek

10. The tension being developed is not divine versus human in a dualistic sense, for Paul did not necessarily regard traditions held by humans to be opposed to divine (cf. 1 Corinthians 15), but it is between Paul and the prevailing interpretation of the traditions of the fathers by other human agents or their agencies when they did not account for the "revealed" meaning of Jesus Christ (Gal 1:13-16).

11. Other sources will be noted, but the following definition of terms draws especially from Friedrich, *TDNT* 2.707–37; Becker, "Gospel, Evangelize, Evangelist," *NIDNTT* 2.107–15.

12. In the LXX always εὐαγγελιζόμενος, which appears to be a literal translation of מבשׂר (Friedrich, *TDNT* 2.712).

13. Friedrich, *TDNT* 2.722. P.Oxy. 3313 is a second-century C.E. papyrus example of usage for the announcement of good news of a wedding (cited by Judge, *Rank and Status*, 24–25). Judge finds this odd and suggests that this person must not be familiar with "the distinctively Christian sense of the word" to have "used it in a private connection" (25)!

world as a technical term for the particular "news of victory." This meaning is likewise carried in the Hebrew term בשׂר (e.g., 1 Sam 4:17; 1 Kgs 1:42; Jer 20:15). It can also refer to the reward the messenger of victory receives in gratitude from the recipients (Homer, *Odyssey* 14.152–53, 166–67) or to the sacrifice made in response to the god who caused this good.[14] This word is closely connected with the sense of promise. It is common in oracles, where it refers to news before the event itself has been realized for those to whom it is announced.

In Paul's period, the plural εὐαγγέλια functioned in the imperial cult for the announcement of significant events concerning the divine ruler: birth, coming of age, enthronement, speeches, decrees, and actions are "glad tidings" of happiness and peace now realized in him. Such declarations provide assurance of being brought under the "benevolent wings of empire."[15] The addressees live in the world of this imperial ideology in addition to the world of the general usage of this term.[16]

The prophetic development of the heralding of good news is most important for understanding the usage in Jewish literature of the period and in the New Testament. Quintessential is Isaiah's dramatic announcement of the return of Israel from exile to the long-awaited reign of God witnessed by all of creation (Isa 52:7-10, NRSV):

> How beautiful upon the mountains
> are the feet of the messenger who announces
> peace [εὐαγγελιζομένου ἀκοήν εἰρήνης],
> who brings good news [εὐαγγελιζομένος ἀγαθά],
> who announces salvation,
> who says to Zion, "Your God reigns."[17]

This expectation continued among Jewish groups in our period as witnessed, for example, in the *Psalms of Solomon* 11.1 (ca. first century B.C.E.): "Sound in Zion the signal trumpet of the sanctuary; announce

14. 2 Samuel 4:10 exemplifies the Hebrew usage as both good news (cf. 18:20, 25, 27; 2 Kgs 7:9) and the reward for good news (cf. 2 Sam 18:22) embodied in בשׂרה: "Good fortune is contained in good news, and therefore he deserves a reward" (Friedrich, *TDNT* 2.721).

15. N. Elliott, "Paul and Politics," 37.

16. So too Martyn, *Galatians,* 127. The inscription found in Priene in Asia west of Galatia from 9 B.C.E., declaring "the birthday of the god [Augustus] was for the world the beginning of the *glad tidings* (line 41) which have gone forth because of him" (Martyn, 128), attests to the language of the period and area.

17. Cf. Isa 40:9; 60:6; 61:1; Ps 40:9 [MT 10]; 68:11 [MT 12]; 96:2.

in Jerusalem the voice of one bringing good news [εὐαγγελιζομένου]"; in Qumran texts 1QH 18.14-15;[18] 11QMelch 2.15-24; 4Q 521.12; CD 2.12; in the Gospels;[19] Acts 10:36-38;[20] and in Paul.[21]

The explicit development of this citation from Isaiah in Romans 10:15 and the surrounding context provides Paul with an argument for the mission to the Gentiles based on the faithfulness of Israel's God to Israel first and then also through her to the nations, for "the same Lord is Lord of all" (10:12).[22] In this way, Paul's usage is explicitly linked with his assertion of the Gentile mission in the context of the One God of Israel now reconciling all of the nations also in Christ; it is an affirmation of his faith in the One God of Israel as the One God of all of the creation, for God is One, in concert with his application of the confession of the Shema.[23]

There is no need to bifurcate the influence on the New Testament development of εὐαγγέλιον to either imperial proclamation or Isaianic announcement, for they combine powerfully in the expectations of those Jewish people and groups who awaited the rule of the One God that would necessarily unmask the pretensions of all other gods and empires: "The all-embracing royal and religious claims of Caesar are directly challenged by the equally all-embracing claim of Israel's god. To announce that YHWH is king is to announce that Caesar is not."[24] Taken to its logical conclusion, this combination provides the following important insight: "*The more Jewish we make Paul's 'gospel,' the more it confronts directly the pretensions of the Imperial cult, and indeed all other paganisms whether 'religious' or 'secular.'* It is because of Jewish monotheism that there can be 'no king but god.'"[25]

18. Collins, *Scepter*, 132 n. 89, suggests that the prophecy of Isa 61:1 is applied in 1QH 18.14 to the hymnist himself.

19. The term is attributed to Jesus in Mark 1:15; 8:35; 10:29; 13:10; 14:9; 16:15; Matt 4:23; 9:35; 24:14; 26:13; and the context of Isaiah echoes in Matt 11:5-6; Luke 4:16-21; 7:22.

20. Dunn, *Theology of Paul*, 168 n. 24, observes the allusion to Isa 52:7 and 61:1 in sequence.

21. Additional echoes include Eph 2:17; 6:15; Rev 1:6; 5:10.

22. O. Betz, "Jesus' Gospel," 68, suggests that Paul's noun usage of εὐαγγέλιον is derived from the Targum on Isa 53:1 ("But who believes our gospel?"). In this case, the Aramaic equivalent of εὐαγγέλιον, בסורתנא, from the verb בשׂר, renders the Hebrew שמועתנן ("report").

23. Gal 3:20, 28; Rom 3:29-30; see Nanos *Mystery*.

24. Wright, "Gospel," 228. Similarly N. Elliott, "Paul and Politics."

25. Wright, "Gospel," 228 (emphasis his). Note Spallek, "Origin," 180–81.

It should be clear by now that I do not intend to suggest that the usage of εὐαγγέλιον in its various forms for the message or proclamation of the good news of Jesus Christ by Paul generally represented anything other than messianic eschatology, but at the same time I want to make it clear that this was not the only way in which it could be or was used by Paul or his Jewish or pagan contemporaries, to which I now turn.

Josephus provides an example of the politically charged sense in *Jewish War* 4.618, where the "good news" of Vespasian's gaining of the government of Egypt and turning his sights on Rome was proclaimed abroad and celebrated with sacrifices and oblations. Yet significantly, in this same work we find Josephus using εὐαγγέλιον in the informative sense without any imperial or messianic connotations, in fact, in ironic wordplay. The treacherous news brought to Florus by the ambassadors of the ruling elite, who invited him to come into the city for fear of the seditious groups gaining ground, is described by Josephus thus: "Now this terrible message was good news [εὐαγγέλιον] to Florus" (*J.W.* 2.420). Similar ironical inversion is attested in Greek literature[26] and later in rabbinic puns.[27] But most importantly we find a similar wordplay on the meaning of the news in the rare noun usage of εὐαγγέλιον in the Septuagint.[28] That instance (2 Sam 4:10; 2 Kgdms 4:10 in LXX) also constituted an ironic twist on the double meaning of εὐαγγέλιον (though in the plural): the messenger thought that he was "bringing" David "good news [εὐαγγελιζόμενος]" about the death of Saul, only to be killed, for the value of the news was perceived differently by David than the messenger had expected. David explains his action of killing the messenger with this chilling irony: "which was the reward I gave him for his news [ᾧ ἔδει με δοῦναι εὐαγγέλια]."[29]

26. Friedrich, *TDNT* 2.711. On 715, Friedrich notes that the announcement of victory came to be treated with suspicion as "false stories of victory are circulated to boost the morale of tired soldiers." Thus, the term picked up an ironic dimension in some cases, such as when Nero, who wanted his mother killed, receives from his mother the good news of her deliverance. The messenger bringing this bitter news thought to be good is killed by the recipient, Nero (Dio Cassius 61.13.4).

27. Friedrich, *TDNT* 2.726–27; Martyn, *Galatians,* 134; O. Betz, "Jesus' Gospel," 55.

28. Friedrich, *TDNT* 2.721, 725.

29. See also LXX 2 Kgdms 18:19-27, where again the εὐαγγέλια brought to David of victory is not unequivocally good because it is mixed with the sorrowful news that Absalom has been killed.

Consider too Philo's telling of biblical stories such as the good news of finding Joseph (*Jos.* 245) and the arrival of his brothers (*Jos.* 250), a use common to Josephus also, interestingly enough, even when not found in the Septuagint itself (*Ant.* 5.24, 277; 11.65).

The flexibility of usage is thus demonstrated from many sources, but most significant perhaps for my point is the varied usage of Paul himself. Of course, Paul uses the verb often for "to announce," "to proclaim" (1 Cor 9:16, 18; Gal 1:16, 23; 4:13; 1 Thess 3:6) and "to preach the good news" (Rom 1:15; 15:20; 1 Cor 1:17; 2 Cor 10:16; Gal 1:8-9), and he can develop emphasis by combination with the noun (Gal 1:11; cf. 1 Cor 15:1; 2 Cor 11:7).[30] Yet Paul is not limited to this verb; he also uses other equivalent verbs for the activity of proclaiming the good news, such as κηρύσσειν ("to proclaim": Rom 10:8, 14, 15; 1 Cor 1:23; 9:27; 15:11; Gal 2:2; 1 Thess 2:9), καταγγέλλειν ("to announce": 1 Cor 2:1; 9:14; 11:26; Phil 1:17-18), and λαλεῖν ("to speak": Phil 1:14; 1 Thess 2:2, 4, 16).[31] In Phil 1:14-17 alone, he uses three different verbs side by side with regard to proclaiming the good news about Jesus, although in this case the application includes those who speak of the good news in order to cause Paul affliction.

In 1 Cor 15:1-11 (and Rom 1:1-6), core events and their interpretation are embedded in Paul's use of εὐαγγέλιον in a formulaic fashion. Moreover, he refers to this as a tradition handed down, an observation quite at odds with the vitriolic denial of the nature of the "good news" he opposes in Galatians. Yet as Helmut Koester observes: "Neither the formula quoted in 1 Cor 15, nor any other formulaic statement of the gospel in Paul is ever repeated."[32] For Paul, neither the content of the "good news" nor the exact points emphasized in its proclamation represent a fixed formula.[33] In each case, various aspects of the acts of Jesus and the meaning considered may be different. The summary comment of Michael Winger is well put: "If we grant simply that the

30. Koester, "Kerygma-Gospel," 362.

31. Harnack, *Constitution*, 301–2, 321–24, 326–28, notes that Paul never states explicitly an antithesis between "good news" and "Law" ("when he [Paul] speaks of the Gospel he is not thinking of the Law but of the fulfilment of the promise"; 326); also Stuhlmacher, "Pauline Gospel," 167–68.

32. Koester, "Kerygma-Gospel," 362.

33. Koester, "Kerygma-Gospel," 361–62. See also Hughes, "Gospel," 221; Schütz, *Paul,* 119; also 35–83, esp. 54, where he wonders that since "tradition is specific content," whether "gospel" and "tradition" are synonyms. See also Spallek, "Origin," 184–88, for discussion of the formula and the active sense in Paul's use.

gospel is something which has happened, then it seems that there is in principle no limit to the number of different ways in which this might be announced or described or discussed."[34]

Another important aspect of Paul's application of the broader semantic field of εὐαγγέλιον comes to the front when we consider his usage of this language with regard to the figure of Abraham. Paul appeals to "the good news proclaimed beforehand [προευηγγελίσατο]" to Abraham (i.e., before his circumcision). The content of this good news was that "'In you shall all the nations be blessed'" (3:8). This good news was obviously proclaimed before Jesus or any message could be directly attributed to him or his followers; for that matter, before any kind of message had developed that should be considered or called messianic by later definitions. It is thus logical to deduce that this Scripture reference was not limited in usage to the εὐαγγέλιον of Jesus Christ or to Paul's proclamation alone. Such a meaning would obviously not have been the case for other Judaisms of Paul's period when interpreting or citing this passage. It could be argued that this statement was developed by Paul precisely because it was central to the message of the influencers: "the Teachers are 'first cousins' of those Jews who pursue among Gentiles the proselytizing mission referred to in the Gospel of Matthew (23.15)."[35] Moreover, the association of the declaration to Abraham of the promise of a son with the label *good news* continued in the rabbinic tradition on Genesis, though obviously with no association with Jesus: Gen 18:1-15; *b. Baba Meṣia* 86b; *Mekilta*, Pischa 14; cf. Fragment Targum to Gen 21:7 and *Gen. Rabbah* 50:2.[36]

Along a similar line, the rabbinic *Midrash on Psalms* offers a view of the giving of the Torah as the good news that was brought by many bearers of the news to the nations, so that all of the world would know the word of the Lord: "'The Lord gave the word [i.e., the Torah]; great was the company of those who bore the tidings.' When the Holy One, blessed be He, . . . gave forth the divine word, the voice divided itself into seven voices, and from the seven voices passed into seventy languages of the seventy nations, so that everyone understood it. Hence it is said, 'Great was the company of those who bore the tiding.'"[37] Again,

34. Winger, "Tradition," 77.

35. Martyn, "Law-Observant," 317. See Goodman, *Mission*, 69–74; Stowers, *Rereading*, 166–71.

36. Cf. Martyn, *Galatians*, 135 n. 147; Stuhlmacher, *Evangelium*, 130, 138.

37. From Martyn's adaptation of Braude, *Midrash*, 1.541 (*Galatians*, 134; see also *t. Soṭa* 8:6; *b. Shabbat* 88b; Stuhlmacher, *Evangelium*, 150).

this announcement of good news is independent of a message of Jesus Christ or any other clear messianic figure; rather, in this case, it is a message of the giving of the Torah by the Lord, and through his messengers this good news was proclaimed to all of the nations.

At least one case makes it completely clear that for Paul the semantic field of εὐαγγέλιον is not specifically limited to the announcement of the good news of Jesus Christ: "But now that Timothy has come to us from you, and has brought us the good news [εὐαγγελισαμένου] of your faith and love and reported that you always remember us kindly and long to see us, as we long to see you" (1 Thess 3:6). Surely there are other ways to describe the good news brought (εὐαγγελισαμένου) by Timothy of the Thessalonians' faith and love if εὐαγγελίζομαι was reserved exclusively by Paul and others to the announcement of the messianic victory (or of Jesus specifically), yet Paul employs just this participial phrase. In this case, he follows the common nonchristological usage for the bringing of good news noted among other first-century Jewish authors of the Hellenistic world. We have already investigated some cases in Josephus, and this was the way εὐαγγελίζεσθαι was employed by Philo as well.[38] In other words, the semantic field was broader among Jews, as it was among Greeks, than the christological or even messianic purpose to which it was being primarily put by Paul and the other believers in Jesus as Christ in describing the fulfillment of the Abrahamic promise in Jesus Christ.

The identity of the influencers and the nature of their good news message simply cannot be concluded confidently on usage of the term εὐαγγέλιον alone, thus undermining the current almost unanimous assertion that in Galatians it must refer to the good news about Jesus Christ or those who proclaim him.[39] According to my analysis, however, the term allows at least the possibility that the influencers, if they used it, need not have applied it to a message about Jesus and thus that they need not have been believers in him. It just does not carry the christological weight it has been assigned.[40] Now we must consider the

38. E.g., Philo, *Moses* 2.186: "a welcome promise [εὐαγγελιζομένη] of a plentiful crop of fruit," which is announced by the blossoming of the almond tree; see also *Creation* 34; *Names* 158; *Abraham* 153.

39. Sympathy with this view is expressed by Muddiman, "Anatomy," 264.

40. Note the ideological disappointment expressed by G. Friedrich in his revealing conclusion that εὐαγγελίζομαι does not contain the messianic implications he would like to find: "The result for the NT is quite negative. Yet the inquiry is not superfluous, since it helps us to see how Jewish writers think and

contextual dynamics of εὐαγγέλιον, the way the term is applied in Paul's argument.[41]

The Ironic Nature of Paul's Rebuke in 1:6-9

The "Different" Good News Which Is "Not Another, Except"

What the influencers may proclaim as a message of good for the Gala–tian Gentiles in their marginal situation, even if (although not necessarily) by expression of the very term εὐαγγέλιον, Paul denounces as anything but good news in the light of the message of good in Christ. Even if a "different [ἕτερον] good news," it is, in a word, ἄλλο ("not another"), and those who unsettle the Galatian Gentiles with this message are worthy of being cursed.

---

speak under the influence of Hellenism. The NT maintained its independence of Hellenism" (*TDNT* 2.714).

41. Martyn, *Galatians*, 130–32, contends that the singular use of εὐαγγέλιον (lit. "glad tiding" or "good new" [*sic*]) is uniquely attributed to Paul and would have been a noticeable change from the plural εὐαγγέλια (glad tiding*s* or good new*s*) of the imperial announcements, which continued to come throughout an emperor's life and then again with the next one, versus the singular announcement of the one-time event of Christ.

However, I have noted evidence of use of the singular form outside of the announcement of Christ in this period: in Josephus (*J.W.* 2.420); Philo, in n. 38 above; and in Paul, in Thessalonians. While indeed rare in extant literature prior to or contemporary with Paul, the singular εὐαγγέλιον is attested in Homer's *Odyssey* (14.152, 166). See also examples in Plutarch, *Demetrius* 17.6.7, for the reward for a message of victory; cf. *Agesilaus* 33.5.1.

The Galatians may not be expected to know any of these literary references, but they do indicate that the semantic range is not as limited to the plural as suggested; the message of the other groups and its announcement may be referred to as εὐαγγέλιον without necessarily containing any suggestion of such theologically loaded finality or concern with the message about Jesus or another messianic figure. Moreover, Martyn's approach fails to explain how the Galatian Gentiles could have been open to another glad tiding (also singular) since Paul's departure, that is, after they had already heard and responded to the glad tiding of Paul when among them, if it was presented, per Martyn, in such explicitly rival or non-Pauline Torah-priority terms. In addition, it would seem that this singular expression would have been coined by the Jerusalem believers in Jesus before Paul, such as Peter, not imitated by them (cf. Gal 1:22-23; 2:2, 7-8; 1 Cor 15:1-11). Cf. Acts 10:36-43 with 15:7, drawing on Isa 52:7; the link with Peter for earlier traditional use is argued thus by Stuhlmacher, "The Theme," 21–22; idem, "Pauline Gospel," 171–72; also 163–65; see also Harnack, *Constitution*, 294–95.

In addition to the conclusions drawn from Paul's employment of "good news" as decisive for identifying the other message and its proponents as a supposed Christian phenomenon, the consensus among interpreters is that Paul's explicit declaration of the ἕτερον εὐαγγέλιον (other, different, another good news) further guarantees that the influencers proclaim a message of Jesus Christ differently (e.g., faith plus circumcision) and that they call it as such good news of Christ, and thus that the Galatians addressed understand it to be good news of Christ.[42]

The often-repeated lexical argument that Paul used ἕτερος to indicate that the other (different) good news was of a different kind, while using ἄλλος when enumerating the difference, to indicate that this other good news was not of the same kind, can be argued to be supportive of my interpretation, but it remains too uncertain a grammatical premise upon which to build argumentation.[43] But if it is granted that ἕτερος signifies a classification that separates on the basis of difference of kind, whereas ἄλλος signifies another element classified within the set of the same kind, the question remains, Along what line does the difference run?

The common proposal that the element of difference conveys that what is proclaimed by this other message is *in addition to* the good news of Christ (e.g., Christ plus Law) remains merely one of several options, although this logical limitation does not seem to have been considered. The relevant classification of kind may concern the differences that exist between the elements of any messages of good (the valuation of the good arising from the different kinds of messages, such as imperial declarations, the declaration of Jesus as Christ, and any other declarations of welcome news, such as the declining price of anchovies, or in the case being argued, of how to successfully negotiate the current identity boundary that these Gentiles face), not merely among those subclassified as messages of good having to do with Jesus Christ. The classification of the referent, and thus of the difference, cannot be assumed a priori by the interpreter who was not present to know what good this other message contained.

42. E.g., Burton, *Galatians,* 22; Dunn, *Galatians,* 41–42; Martyn, *Galatians,* 110. Walter, "Gegner," 351–56, is the exception.

43. For the contrary view, see, e.g., J. K. Elliott, "Use." I have discussed this debate in detail; see Nanos, "ΑΛΛΟΝ & HETERON." For the various arguments, see Bauer, *Lexicon,* 315 γ; Ramsay, *Galatians,* 262; Burton, *Galatians,* 24, 421–22; R. Longenecker, *Galatians,* 15; H. Betz, *Galatians,* 49 n. 60; Bruce, *Galatians,* 81; Hansen, *Abraham,* 235 n. 51; Silva, *Explorations,* 55; Lambert, "Another."

The grammatical differentiation between these uses of εὐαγγέλιον in 1:6-7a is made by Paul apart from reference to Christ, thus the salient difference may be whether the messages do or do not concern Christ, whatever other good they may contain, such as how they both claim to offer these Gentiles the good news of righteous identity, which is the effect of the following argument. The contrast is drawn between two different messages of good, not two different messages of Christ, and even Paul's authority is subordinate to the message of good in Christ (1:8-9).

So although this grammatical decision might be useful for making my case, I am not convinced that it is warranted by the evidence and will refrain from any argumentation built upon it.[44] There are plenty of cases in which the use of both words simply breaks up an otherwise monotonous or repetitious style, as in "one and another" instead of "another and another" (e.g., 1 Cor 10:29; 12:8-10; 15:39-40; John 4:37; Acts 2:12; Aristotle, *Politics* 4.1291b19ff.; 1300b20ff.). Lexically, ἕτερον and ἄλλος, like εὐαγγέλιον, simply do not seem able to carry the interpretive weight they are asked to bear. They need not. They are present to play their semantically different yet synonymous part in the delivery of Paul's ironic rebuke.

Ironic Anomaly: The Purpose of Paul's "Except That [εἰ μή]"

Having earlier set Paul's letter within the specific context of ancient letters of ironic rebuke, it is time now to discuss how the nature of Paul's exception clause in v. 7b (εἰ μή: "except that"), unlike the literal explanations of his prior statement in v. 7a regarding "another good news which is not another," is not taken by interpreters at face value, "except in the sense" that it is; thus, revealing the "ironic anomaly" in their own clarifications.[45] For these interpreters assume that Paul, the addressees, and the influencers all must speak of this other message as εὐαγγέλιον of Christ. This assumption is followed by the ostensibly logical deduction that they must believe in Christ and thus that they are believers in Christ plus some kind of Jewish identity or behavior by which they have corrupted this belief and message in some way now opposed by Paul. Yet at the same time many observe that Paul's

44. See Nanos, "ΑΛΛΟΝ & HETERON."

45. Of course, even the so-called literal or surface meaning of a text is the product of interpretive decision, which is determined by the assumptions at work on the part of the interpreter (cf. Fish, "Short People," 195).

idiomatic use of εἰ μή "suggests no one would even think of calling the Judaizers' message a 'gospel' *except* with the intention of confusing the Christians of Galatia."[46] Interpreters have thus paradoxically observed that this other message is not the good news of Christ yet mirror-read as though it was.

I rather suggest that Paul is the first one to think of calling the influencers' message "good news" in the formal sense associated with faith in Christ, except his intention is not to confuse the Galatian addressees but to awaken them.

Attention to Paul's use of irony heightens the prospect that neither the influencers nor the addressees have conceived of or called their message a εὐαγγέλιον of Christ. By dissociating the usage of εὐαγγέλιον, that is, modifying the traditional usage in view of the declaration of Christ-faith, Paul demonstrates in a striking manner just how dangerous is their present situation. In this way, he will shock the addressees into realizing that the consequences of their present course are irreconcilable with their faith in Christ. The addressees' negligence and naïveté are in view, and Paul employs a strategic yet stereotypical rhetorical approach for confronting such foolishness that instantly shames them, not harshly so as to destroy but by communal rhetoric that aims to restore. Through irony, he is calling something that is not being recognized clearly for what it is—as witnessed by their inappropriate positive response to it—what it is "in effect" for them because of their response.[47] By declaring a message "another εὐαγγέλιον" that is

46. R. Longenecker, *Galatians,* 16 (emphasis his). Calvin, *Commentaries,* 31, with direct reference to Paul's use of ἄλλος, notes: it "is a correction of the language he had used about *another gospel.* He declares that it is not a gospel, but a mere disturbance" (emphasis his). Lightfoot, *Galatians,* 76, offers this paraphrase on the basis of its exceptive quality: "Only in this sense it is another gospel, in that it is an attempt to pervert the one true Gospel." Burton, *Galatians,* 22–24, concludes that Paul's intention is to exclude the possibility of misunderstanding him: "The clause [ὅ οὐκ ἔστιν ἄλλο, εἰ μή] is thus a qualification of the preceding statement, intended to exclude the possible implication that that which the Galatians were urged to accept was really a gospel which might legitimately be substituted for that which Paul preached." Bruce, *Galatians,* 82, concludes: "No one would think of calling this substitute message a 'gospel,' Paul implies, except with the intention of confusing the minds of believers. Gospel it is not; it is a message of bondage, not of freedom"; so also H. Betz, *Galatians,* 49; Dunn, *Galatians,* 42; Martyn, *Galatians,* 135–36.

47. Cf. Bourdieu, *Language,* 116: "The symbolic efficacy of words is exercised only in so far as the person subjected to it recognizes the person who exercises

"not" another εὐαγγέλιον, in order to make it clear that it should not be treated as though it is one—because it is not a εὐαγγέλιον of Christ—he has exposed the addressees' foolish response to this message to date.

Following the juxtaposition of the other good news with that which is not another, Paul continues the sentence to further clarify his point. The translation of the conjunctive εἰ μή in v. 7b, by which he joins the next part of the sentence, has been the focus of much discussion. Although εἰ μή may be read adversatively as "but," the consensus view is that it is better to read this as "except that." In the rest of the sentence, Paul provides the reason for this exception.

Martyn concludes his discussion of this section in a way that is representative of a long line of commentators who recognize that Paul is in some way constructing this oppositional statement to deny to this other message the status of gospel: "Given these developments, Paul opens the body of his letter by differentiating the Teachers' counterfeit gospel from the true gospel of Christ (1:6-9). Thereafter, he displays the contrast between the two messages through the entire letter, consistently *denying* that the Teachers' message *is in any sense the glad tiding of Christ.* There is only one gospel, and it is the one Paul brought to the Galatians at the beginning."[48]

Interpreters consistently recognize that in some way the only sense in which this other message is being called good news is with regard to the effect it has had on the addressees of unsettling them and on the gospel of Christ, twisting so as to undermine its meaning for the addressees. Except for these senses, it is not another.[49] Its ability to unsettle the Galatian Gentiles unmasks their regard for it as inappropriately high. In effect, they treat a message that is not on the same level as the message of Christ as though it were on the same level, thereby twisting or turning upside down the meaning of the one message by the other, in effect, thus unconsciously emptying the news of good based on Christ by way of attributing to this other message good apart from Christ. They will become, to the degree that they continue

---

it as authorized to do so, or, what amounts to the same thing, only in so far as he fails to realize that, in submitting to it, he himself has contributed, through his recognition, to its establishment."

48. Martyn, *Galatians*, 135–36 (emphasis added).

49. Holmstrand, *Markers*, 149 n. 21.

on this course, accomplices in depriving the εὐαγγέλιον of Christ of its meaning or of rendering the death of Christ gratuitous (2:21) and negating their prior faith and experience of the Spirit (3:1-5). Although they are confronted for being in the process of "turning to another good news," the defection they are accused of is "from him who called you in [the] grace [of Christ]."[50] The point of this good news is that it declares God's grace toward them while still Gentiles, apart from identity as proselytes or candidates undergoing this ritual process. The complete undermining of this message of Christ by the other message rather than its support is something Paul is certain that the addressees have not realized and will not intend to be any part of once it is now brought to their attention in this letter (cf. 5:10).[51] Even if Paul (or an angel) were to proclaim good news other than the good news of Christ, he would be accursed (1:8-9)! The good news of Christ, not Paul's version of it, is the final authority for judging news for these Gentiles as good or not.

Do not these interpreters exhibit in their very conclusions one of the palpable qualities of the kind of irony with which Paul confronts the Galatian addressees here? "Is not a source of irony's attraction and repellence alike that it may plausibly be taken literally, invites us to take it literally, makes a certain sense when taken literally? Yet a nagging doubt hints at a meaning hidden behind the mask."[52] These interpreters grapple with and finally manifest in their clarifications of Paul's meaning that they are caught in the "irony of situation," which may be defined as follows: "the reader is made to perceive, usually by indirection, two meanings in the form of a contrast, like a reality hidden

50. S. Williams, *Galatians,* 38, makes the important observation that it is not a "changing from one understanding of the gospel to another. Rather, he [Paul] says, they are deserting 'the one who called you.'"

51. The proposal of Walter, "Gegner," 351–56, that the "opponents" are proclaiming their message explicitly as good news but not about Christ, rather against the good news of Christ in a directly competitive way, does not make sense of this aspect of the Galatians' current failure to realize their predicament or of Paul's response. It is clear that the Galatians agree with Paul and would not want to be associated with nullifying the death of Christ; they have but failed to realize this was the implicit result if they accept the other message. This is also a shortcoming in T. Martin's proposal that the Galatians were explicitly turning back to paganism because they rejected the message of circumcision, which they saw as the legitimate Christian gospel but to which they declined to submit ("Apostasy," 441–42).

52. Good, *Irony in the OT,* 22.

behind appearances, or a difference between what should be in a situation and what is."[53]

Interpreters recognize Paul's use of wordplay here, even if that was not their explicit understanding of what their interpretation described, in their own way testifying to the unique ability of irony to hover over its victim, who remains aware of its force, even if unable to capture its full potential or bring down its undivided meaning—of its cutting edge, its lasting bite, its power to manifest the obvious side by side with the unstated. For each of these interpretations of εἰ μή suggests that Paul's intention in the situation dwells not on the literal level of his statement: it is not to communicate a lack of anticipation on his part (surprise) or to accurately describe the content of the other message as a message of Christ but to express disapproval by feigning ignorance that belittles the addressees' inappropriate esteem for this other message as "good" (rebuke). In this way, Paul discredits and distances this other message from the good news of Christ, which it, ironically, works not for but against.

Paul is "surprised" that they have not realized that this other message is not just another message of good news that they can respond to in addition to the message of good news in Christ, which appears to be the addressees' supposition or at least what they would like to convince themselves to be the case. But of course the interpreter, like the Galatian addressees, is meeting not just an astonished Paul but a disappointed and perhaps frightened one, and an admonition that takes the form of rebuke. The addressees are affectionately shamed by this careful statement of rhetorical surprise by Paul at developments among them, but this wonder is inextricably and paradoxically mixed with instant judgment: "Is this so" with "This cannot—must not!—be." How could they miss the meaning(s), or we?

The ironic edge to the rebuke instantly cuts, making the addressees painfully aware of their error. Paul employs irony to bring from between the two poles of meaning (that this other message appears to be good news, yet it is not good news of Christ) the shocking third meaning: what it is for the influencers (good news), it is not for the addressees, except in the sense that the addressees' response to it has made it seem to be such, with the result of allowing the good news of Christ to be changed, distorted, turned upside down, emptied of significance, undermined, or subverted.

53. Tibbetts, *Strategies of Rhetoric*, 250.

The addressees would immediately realize that by letting this message unsettle them in this way they have (unintentionally and unexpectedly) taken the dangerous first step (captured in the present tense aspect of the accusation) toward foolishly treating this other message on a par with that of Christ, although it is not. At the same moment, they would be struck by the reality that this is so only because they have made it so—in that they have imputed to it comparable significance. Moreover, they would be simultaneously awakened to realize the consequences. Although unintended, yet perhaps not entirely unanticipated (to the degree they may be aware they are pushing beyond what they should), they are beginning the process of deserting Christ. In effect, they are beginning to turn to another way to access the grace of God that effectively empties of significance the message of Christ, which divergence is, from Paul's perspective, the unmistakable commencement of defection that will result in conversion to a different way of standing before God and the community of his people as the righteous ones. Once this light is tripped, Paul's declaration of surprise suddenly pales compared to their own. Will they turn to a message of good other than in/of Christ?

Ironically perhaps, the ironic force is realized implicitly by interpreters in the excepting clause of this passage. The grammatical cues are so strong that they bring a certain harmony to the interpretive conclusions in spite of varied arguments along the way. Surprisingly, this agreement has been achieved without explicit recognition of the ironic development of Paul's language.[54] But at a price: Paul's use of the reference to the other message as εὐαγγέλιον has been mirror-read literally to provide the basis for identifying the influencers and their message. Because this is woodenly confined in meaning to a message about Jesus Christ, even if it was differently put, the conclusion drawn is that something must be added or subtracted to this other message—not Christ, because it is about him, but Jewish identity (circumcision) or observance (Law). These are contrasted with grace for some interpreters, as though Jewish identity and behavior were based on something else. But the choice is rather between a Christ and not-Christ message to gain the good that they seek, the hope of righteousness.

Paul's use of the exceptive clause (εἰ μή) after the negating "which is not another," in a statement begun with the ironic note of surprise, provides a clear grammatical cue for the addressees that Paul is calling

54. Some do note the ironic element, e.g., Oepke, *Galater*, 47.

this other message a εὐαγγέλιον in an ironic sense. And the balance of the sentence that follows this exceptive conjunction clarifies further that the apparent meaning of the words is subverted by the real meaning of the situation. Interpreters outside the original addressees' context, and thus outside the primary location for "getting" irony, also understand Paul's subversive meaning here because of this lexical intensifier, even if they take the first half of the sentence literally based on their understanding of the situation, that is, that there is no reason to question whether the influencers did proclaim a εὐαγγέλιον of Christ.[55] Those addressed in the original situation should have gotten it without this key, that is, if the influencers did not proclaim a εὐαγγέλιον of Christ but rather another message (perhaps, but not necessarily, by the label εὐαγγέλιον); however, with this indicator, they cannot be expected to miss the ironic twist on εὐαγγέλιον that follows the rhetorical exclamation of surprise with which he opened.

Paul's Ironic Rebuke and the Reading of 1:6-9

What conclusions may we draw from the irony in Paul's language in 1:6-9?

Three stylistic markers have been explored thus far. First, the letter style of θαυμάζω (surprise), a socially agreed formal marker for expressing rebuke ironically that is witnessed in ancient letters and explained in rhetorical handbooks, indicates that Paul is employing irony to undermine the attraction of this other message.[56] Furthermore, the negative or excluding clause, "which is not another," func-

55. See Cronjé, "Defamiliarization," 217–19, for a discussion of Paul's techniques of defamiliarization in which he shifts expectancies in figures of speech. Cronjé observes that 1:6 represents the device of "Paradox," with a "seemingly contradictory expression," noting the use of this clause (another good news that is not another): "Now, if one could talk about retarded perceptions, intensified perception due to distortion of some kind, due to deautomatization, estrangement, this is one place where it most certainly would have occurred" (222). He concludes that the usual translations miss the direction Paul points: "There is no other Gospel than the one the Galatians received by Paul" (222).

56. This conclusion respects L. Hutcheon's warning that even the most agreed-upon indicators of irony may be disputed, for nothing is an "irony signal in and of itself," that is, "its existence as a successful 'marker' will always be dependent upon a discursive community to recognize it, in the first place, and then to activate an ironic interpretation in a particular shared context" (*Irony's Edge*, 159).

tions to indicate that an unmistakable inversion of meaning is present in the text: Paul does not mean that this other message is a εὐαγγέλιον, even if he has employed the label to denote it. Finally, the qualifying εἰ μή ("except [in the sense] that") functions so effectively as a marker that it is able to steer interpreters into the world of ironic inversion without explicit recognition of the phenomenon, for it is a εὐαγγέλιον only in the sense that it is wrongly given parallel importance with the good news of Christ by the twisting of the influencers and the anxious response of the addressees. Independent of whether anyone in Galatia had called this other message εὐαγγέλιον, at least in any sense as good news of Christ, these markers indicate that we are dealing with "overt irony" in 1:6-9. Such irony is meant to be understood at once by "tone of voice (or its stylistic equivalent) which directs us to disregard the ostensible meaning or indicates the real meaning."[57]

Additional features for disclosing and analyzing irony move this observation in the direction of my proposition that Paul's employment of irony in this case suggests that no one had in fact considered this other message a εὐαγγέλιον of Christ and thus that the situations addressed in Galatians should be thoroughly reconsidered. Quintilian's three indicators for recognition of irony in *Institutio oratorio* 8.6.54 merit discussion, even if oversimplified for orations (emphasis added): "This is made evident to the understanding either by the delivery, the character of the speaker or the nature of the subject. For if any one of these three is out of keeping with the words, it at once becomes clear that the intention of the speaker is other than what he actually says."[58]

These stylistic markers obviously fall under Quintilian's first category of delivery. These indicate the presence of irony, so that they do not disclose that Paul was to any degree actually surprised; rather, they provide a vehicle for rebuke. As Paul is not present in person to make it clear that he is employing irony by inflection and gesture, he uses the straightforward letter style of θαυμάζω,[59] the immediately negating clause, and the judgment rendering exception clause, so that it is unmistakable to those addressed that this other message, which he has

57. Muecke, *Compass,* 54; farther, "What makes irony overt is a blatancy in the ironic contradiction or incongruity."

58. See Booth, *Rhetoric of Irony,* 49; Muecke, *Compass,* 57–58.

59. This also corresponds with Booth's first category (*Rhetoric of Irony,* 53–57).

labeled another εὐαγγέλιον, is in his opinion—just as he had stated before when among them! (1:9)—nothing of the sort.[60]

The argument for irony at work at this level finds further support in the expansion of Quintilian's insight by, for example, Wayne Booth, who notes that an ironic marker is evident when something is brought up initially only to be contradicted in the discourse.[61] Within Paul's statement and throughout the letter, he contradicts what he ascribes to the other message at the outset: he calls it good news only to deny that it is good news or should be called such. Also, Booth demonstrates that an exaggerated change in style alerts one to the presence of irony.[62] There is a clear clash of style in this opening comment, in that where one would expect the usual statement of thanksgiving for the recipients of the letter, a style present in many papyrus examples and all of Paul's other extant correspondence, the Galatian addressees are greeted instead by this terse rebuke.

Without the clear presence of the first marker of irony, the second device for detection, the character of the speaker, as well as the third, the nature of the subject, are topics that cannot render certainty for the later interpreter, though they would have been salient categories for the original addressees who knew Paul, as well as how the message was being proclaimed and labeled, for "irony cannot be used if there is uncertainty about the speaker's opinions."[63] The problem for the later interpreter is simply that our construction of Paul's character or the nature of the subject at hand in Galatia biases the way we do or do not make the case for irony here, yielding a circular course, for it is "only by having some idea of the beliefs held within certain social environments [that we can] guess whether or not a given text is ironical or not."[64] If the consensus view is correct that this other message was a message of Christ that was called a εὐαγγέλιον, then apart from the epistolary "surprise" and lexical indicators discussed, neither the subject nor the speaker need be ironic in using it as Paul does, even if he goes on to criticize it for departing from the good news of Christ by Paul's stan-

60. Knox, *The Word Irony*, 149–50, extends Quintilian's three to four in a way that also takes in the εἰ μή clause, that is, when a figure makes a pretense followed by a qualifying "but." See also Booth, *Rhetoric of Irony*, 49–57, for the aspects of written rather than oral "delivery" that signify irony.

61. Booth, *Rhetoric of Irony*, 61–67.

62. Booth, *Rhetoric of Irony*, 67–73.

63. Perelman and Olbrechts-Tyteca, *New Rhetoric*, 208.

64. Perelman and Olbrechts-Tyteca, *New Rhetoric*, 208.

dard of definition. But if the other message was not called εὐαγγέλιον of Christ, then Paul's use of this label runs counter to both the nature of the subject and of Paul's character in elevating it so, thus revealing irony. Therefore, while the first socially agreed upon marker can be recognized by comparison with ancient letters and their articulation in handbooks, the interpreter's prior view (e.g., ideologies, beliefs, assumptions, and conclusions about the context) dictates the recognition level of irony by these two other means, because we are removed from the original discursive community.[65]

Having said this, however, so that I admit this does not prove the case but can only support it, I suggest that the other markers are present to the degree that we give attention to the communal dimension of the usage of irony in the case that we have already firmly established by the first indicator. For the presence of any one of the three suggests that Paul is using irony here to instruct the addressees, and we have seen that it is an overt expression of irony at that; thus we might logically expect to find the other two markers operating here as well.[66]

On the one hand, irony creates community in the sense that those who "get it" now share a viewpoint over against those who do not. Irony creates or intensifies a boundary marking the in-group (who share the view once realized) from the out-group (who do not share the view or who reject it). On the other hand, it takes a shared or communal context for irony to take place; it is a renewal or an intensification of a value already known and shared. This is foundational for the dissociating argument.

Linda Hutcheon has made the case that "discursive communities make irony possible in the first place. . . . the more the shared context, the fewer and the less obvious the markers needed to attribute—or signal—irony."[67] One who does not know the situation or the ironist may

65. Cf. Hutcheon, *Irony's Edge*, 97–98, who observes: "There have been many explanations offered for why people 'misunderstand' ironies. . . . But perhaps what is called ignorance (and even lack of practice or context) is simply a question of the ironist and the interpreter belonging to different discursive communities which do not intersect or overlap sufficiently for the comprehension of an utterance as ironic to occur."

66. Cf. Booth, *Rhetoric of Irony*, 41: "The initial act of judgment, uniquely forceful in irony, will thus work strongly to support or weaken the second judgment, one which the reader of ironies shares with all other readers: where, really, does this author stand?"

67. Hutcheon, *Irony's Edge*, 18; cf. 89–115, esp. 95–97.

not recognize anything less than overt irony. For example, if one knows nothing of the nature of Bolingbroke, then one may not consider the statement, "Bolingbroke was a holy man," to be ironic. Of course, if one is familiar with the story of Bolingbroke, then the ironic intent would be immediately recognized. But even someone who knows nothing of Bolingbroke, when encountering it as a classic dictionary entry for illustrating irony, is thus oriented to recognize it as such, and appreciate that there is an overt ironic play being made on the statement.[68] In fact, in this case, one can be certain that the author did not intend the literal meaning to stand alone, however differently that literal meaning may be interpreted.[69] In other words, within the context of irony expressed overtly, one can infer that Bolingbroke was less than holy from the perspective of the ironist without knowing Bolingbroke or anything about him. The metapropositional base in this case is provided by the explicit listing in the dictionary under irony.

Ironic construction depends on a shared set of assumptions. Otherwise, the response of those addressed may be of a piece with what we might expect in response from the influencers, if Paul's irony had been directed at themselves. That is, they may have been able to affirm the surface statement. They may have been able to reply, "yes, our message is good news and you should not be surprised by this defection; it is for the best, for good news that is superior." An ironist assumes that the surface statement will not be greeted so, that the persons addressed will recognize the pretense and consider applicable the criticism; they will dwell with the author on another level that involves a shared rejection of the lower one, a shared norm.[70]

I thus suggest Quintilian's third indicator is operative (what is said is contrary to the nature of the subject), following from the presence of irony by the first marker, θαυμάζω, which functions as a metapropositional base for their reading/hearing, in that it explicitly instructs the addressees how they are to understand the proposition, how they are to assess the author's attitude throughout the clause,[71] that is, ironically, in an expression of disapproval. In addition, the nature of the subject, this other message to which the addressees are giving place, is not called a εὐαγγέλιον "of Christ" but "not another"; nor is it regarded intention-

68. Booth, *Rhetoric of Irony*, 18.
69. Cf. Fish, "Short People," 185.
70. Booth, *Rhetoric of Irony*, 34–37, 53.
71. Holmstrand, *Markers*, 25, 148.

ally by the addressees on the level of the εὐαγγέλιον of Christ they have received from Paul. This is indicated in that Paul states the negating and excepting comments immediately, and follows with a reminder that when he formerly taught them the good news of Christ, he had warned them against any such contrary one, which indicates that he is undermining the initial use of the label in a way that he believes they will understand and share. If such a comparison of the εὐαγγέλιον of Christ with this other message expresses an obvious misrepresentation of what the nature of this other message is or claims to be, they would have a clear level of indication that the intention of the speaker is out of keeping with the words on the subject and thus that Paul's intention was ironic.[72] A shared value is at work, even if they are considering another competing value (from Paul's viewpoint, even if not initially from their own).

Moreover, if this is the case, then the second indicator is functioning as well, for they would know that it was against Paul's character to give this other message such an honored distinction, having already taught against this other message in the past, perhaps even associating it with a curse (1:9). In fact, they would know that such an attribution expressed anything but his character![73] In addition, they would realize that Paul was not surprised by this development in the sense of being without anticipation or information, as though he did not recognize the threat was real and present among them. They would thus recognize that the ironic depreciation inherent in this self-disclosure was intended to reveal disapproval of this other message and of themselves.

"What Am I, Your Maid?": A Contemporary Example of Ironic Rebuke

I wish to develop for clarification an example of the exegetical process being discussed here. If we were to read Paul writing: "What am I, your maid?" would we begin with the assumption that Paul is talking about his activities in a way that exemplifies those of a maid of the period? Would we examine the many features and activities of a maid and even of the variety of maids, with the hope of locating which kind of maid

72. See Booth, *Rhetoric of Irony*, 57–61, on a known error proclaimed as a signal of irony; 67–72, on clashes of style.

73. Cf. Booth, *Rhetoric of Irony*, 73–76, for discussion of the dynamic that "we are alerted whenever we notice an unmistakable conflict between the beliefs expressed and beliefs we hold *and suspect the author of holding*" (73; emphasis his).

Paul had in mind? Then would we argue that because Paul would rather be understood as anything but a maid in his service, that he must have been explicitly accused of being a maid by someone, a charge that he now confronts? And so on.

Those of us who have had this language of rebuke directed toward ourselves, for example, by a parent, or directed it ourselves, for example, toward a child, realize that it is useful for drawing an analogy the listener does not expect but not just on the cognitive level. The ironic exposing of the way that the speaker understands the implications of how the addressee is treating the speaker is intended to shock and shame the addressee, to make that person realize that the comment or behavior is inappropriate and has at its center a disrespect (arrogance or ingratitude), perhaps even unintended, that once exposed will cause the addressee to deliver a contrite apology for the inappropriate attitude formerly implied. The effect of this feigned identity is entirely changed, obviously, if the person saying it actually is their maid or blunted considerably if the speaker has previously been wrongfully accused of being the maid. In other words, it would be a poor choice for effecting the desired result.

The ability of such ironic rebuke to cut the victim is located precisely in the unexpected comparison, which surprises the inappropriately unaware recipients and dissuades them from foolish comment or action that might even so much as imply this in the future; or at least it should! Moreover, it is likely to elicit an apology for having so missed the mark. It is surely not to solicit an answer to the opening surface question "What am I?" or "What do you think I am?" nor would it be expected to lead to a discussion of maids.

In the same way, we should consider Paul's introductory exclamation of so-called surprise a rhetorical gambit, with the result that it is unlikely that anyone—the addressees or the influencers—were calling this other message formally by the label εὐαγγέλιον, that is, not good news in the same sense as they would refer to the good news of Christ. Paul is the first to make the explicit comparison in order to shock them into realizing the inappropriate value that they have been granting this other message to date and thereby to dissuade them from such foolish thinking or behavior in the future. The implication is that they did not explicitly mean to treat this other message this way and had not realized that such was implied by their comments or behavior (or at least they had tried to convince themselves that this was not the case). And if so, then the influencers have neither called this message a εὐαγγέλιον in the same way (with the label or with reference to Christ) nor represented their message in opposition to Paul's.

Why Did Paul Introduce the Label Εὐαγγέλιον If It Was Avoidable?

The skeptical reader may ask at this point: If Paul doesn't regard the message of the influencers as good news in the received sense of "the message about Christ," though "another," that is, mixed with other elements by which it is fatally flawed, then why didn't he simply write: "another *message*, which is not the good news of Christ"?[74] This is a good question, but the answer emerges in the very asking, for it loses the rhetorical force of unexpected comparison, the irony that cuts the feet out from under one, or as Søren Kierkegaard put it, the "secret trap door through which one is suddenly hurled downward."[75] Interestingly, this same rhetorical attraction is evident in the very interpreters cited, for although they regard the other message as good news and note that Paul does not actually call it a "not" or "no good news," they find the wordplay appealing.

Karl Plank makes an important point pertinent to our case. He draws from Robert Tannehill's observation: "plain speech is good for communication within established interpretations of the world but it bypasses the imagination and so has little power to change these fundamental interpretations. . . . The communication of plain speech will be accepted as an 'idea' and placed in the pigeonhole where it will least disturb our basic vision of self and world."[76]

If Paul deals at the level of plain speech in confronting this other message "again," he will play into the agreed denotations at the expense of the connotative differentiation he needs to emphasize in a new way in order to dissuade them from the present course forevermore. Indirect speech can offer an advantage through its unique ability to challenge a system of values and generate a response at the level of immediacy rather than mere calculation: "symbolic speech is experienced before interpreted."[77] Unexpected juxtaposition of labels, as Paul employs here, has the effect of jolting them out of the zone in which they have been able to comfortably reconcile two messages,

74. Martyn, *Galatians*, 109–10, 121, poses just this question.
75. Kierkegaard, *Concept of Irony*, 64.
76. From Plank, *Affliction*, 76.
77. Plank, *Affliction*, 76–77.

which by Paul's standards are not compatible in this way. They have heard this message at the level of plain speech before, but the force of it has somehow not been realized. Paul cannot let the present system of valuation continue unchecked and so subverts the categories through indirect speech, by ironic rebuke.

The value of indirect language to avoid the defensive response of direct accusations or harsh interrogative ones has been mentioned already. This may be used to soften the level of shame created, as it allows for the victim to save face. It implies that they have been foolish but not defiant, wayward but not deliberately malignant. And of course it is the nature of irony to introduce a degree of levity, of humor, that limits anxiety and permits the dissipation of hostility while building a bridge for reconciliation. It allows for the defense that things may appear other than they really are. The victim need but admit to folly and make the appropriate changes sought; the need for self-defense is lessened and no separation need occur.

The Galatian Gentiles know that this is another or different message that appears to be good for themselves, one that Paul did not teach them—that is implied and even stated throughout the letter—yet somehow they did not seem to realize that this message was so dangerously undermining the good news message of Paul about Jesus. Or perhaps they just did not want to admit to themselves that they knew better, or at least that Paul had sought to communicate this in the past, a common repressive response to social anxiety (cf. Peter at Antioch).[78] The rhetorical use of εὐαγγέλιον for their message sets up the antithesis, sharpening the depth of the compromise inherent in hearing or observing it. The use of εὐαγγέλιον provides the force of the deep meaning to the opening rebuke of astonishment, increasing the shock value: "don't you realize that your quick interest in conforming with the desires of the influencers will turn upside down the good news of Christ, that you thereby defect from the grace of Christ and nullify the meaning of his death?" (cf. 1:6-7; 2:21). So much more is at stake than they seem to realize: the truth of "*the* good news" is being compromised for the comfort of acceptance—of wanting to be just like everybody else, to put it in the language of the adolescent compulsion for conformity above principle. The weight of theological truth must penetrate the powerful drive toward social belonging, and just such word-

78. See Nanos, *Mystery*, 337–71; for a psychological profile of this behavior in contemporary society, see Leary and Kowalski, *Social Anxiety*.

plays are often called upon to stop the victims in their tracks and awaken them to radical reconsideration of the cost, of the principle they will surely violate, of the reality that the means are the ends in the making.

The fact that Paul can appeal to the importance of the meaning of Christ's death for themselves as a bedrock conviction shared with the addressees is enormously important. This illuminates the observation that the rhetorical force of the contrast is christological, not because they are seeking to reject Christ or somehow modify their belief in him but precisely because they have failed to realize this inherent compromise of their profession of faith in Jesus Christ is at stake. But once they do, Paul is certain that they will be compelled to reconsider the seriousness of their present course and change directions. And thus the addressees are rebuked through irony, which provides the unmatchable cutting force of unexpected comparison.

The addressees have been thinking and acting on a level driven by social concern for honor and associated advantages within the community. Thus, Paul strikes by way of dissociation, modifying their (mis)understanding of the situation because they have failed to realize what the deeper issues are, striking at their failure to recognize the theological compromise inherent in the path being offered by this ostensibly "good" news, by which they become accomplices in altering the truly good news of Christ. To which court of reputation (assurance of standing before God and within the community as children of Abraham, of God) will they subscribe? Will they remain with the one accessed by faith in the good news of Christ, which offers full standing while they yet remain Gentiles, although leaving them vulnerable to being regarded as mere guests by those who do not share this viewpoint based on faith in/of Christ; or will they "sever" themselves from Christ by turning to the one accessed by adopting the message of the influencers to complete the ritual process of conversion, which offers full standing as proselytes regardless of their convictions about Christ, and thus escape from the limitations or sufferings of marginal status before the influencers?

Reading Paul's Rebuke Ironically

Paul calls this other message *εὐαγγέλιον* in Galatians in the sense that it is a message that by its very nature competes with the good news of Jesus Christ as Paul proclaims it. And he does so precisely in order to emphasize that it must not be responded to in the manner the addressees are beginning to do so, in order to deny that it is a εὐαγγέλιον, and to make it clear that so regarding it is a direct affront to the εὐαγγέλιον of Christ to which its proposal is "contrary," so that turning toward it constitutes desertion from him who called them, whether they have managed to perceive this fact or not. Surely, Paul is within his rights to be distraught that the addressees could have failed to realize this—after all, they have both his teaching (1:9, 13; 3:1; 5:3, 21) and the witness of the Spirit (3:2-5). To be sure, after reading this dissociating letter—though it is of course possible to reject it—they will never regard this message or its messengers in the same way. If they believe that the age to come has dawned in the midst of the present age in Christ, they will never again be able naïvely to regard that "different" or "other" as "another" message of good news compatible with the εὐαγγέλιον of Christ, to which they can give allegiance without denying the effective meaning of the death of Jesus for themselves, that is, without compromising forever their confession of faith in "the good news of Christ."

That is not to say that the influencers did not regard their message as good news for these Gentiles. I think they did. Nor is it to deny the possibility that they would have used εὐαγγέλιον to describe their welcome news for these marginalized Gentiles—though this is much less certain. We have seen that the semantic field of usage was wide enough to apply this language to a message of good news about matters other than Jesus as Christ, so that the good news of including Gentiles as full members of the people of God may have been denoted by just such a label; nevertheless, if this was the case, the ironic twist is weakened. And we must not rule out the possibility of ironic usage by the influencers—though I am not suggesting this was the case—as they would have seen the bad news implicit in a good news of Christ by which these Gentiles were trapped in their current marginal state but with the expectation of being regarded on a par with proselytes.

In the same way, this is not to say the Galatian Gentiles did not receive this other message as good news—it appears that they most certainly did! Nor is it to deny the possibility that they described it by the term εὐαγγέλιον. Although the use of this term by the Galatian addressees would not rule out the ironic inversion, it does blunt the point. The language of εὐαγγέλιον can be used to refer to the imperial cult, to the practice of which the addressees have been asked to return if they are intending to remain pagans on the influencers' (and pagan society's) terms, rather than become proselytes, and this association may also be at play in Paul's ironic rebuke. But in this sense it is likely that the addressees have already assessed any such alleged good news as bad for themselves, thus rendering this meaning, if at work, to a secondary place behind the attractive alternative, the good news of proselyte conversion that promises them escape from such constraints as this, which apply to mere pagan guests.

If one has been in the habit of calling someone a maid, the dramatic impact of the question "What am I, your maid?" is blunted. It is the shock of being accused of behaving in a way that was not perhaps being realized on the conscious level; once exposed from the viewpoint of the one being inappropriately treated, the unexpected irony revealed in the question accomplishes the rebuke that gives a dissociating argument its clarifying and unforgettable edge. The view argued herein is that the matter of faith in Jesus Christ (or not) is simply not the influencers' active concern: they do not believe that the death of a Judean martyr of the Roman regime, to whom the addressees appeal to legitimate (on the basis of the proclamation of Christ) their present status as righteous ones independent of completion of the normal rite of conversion, is of any consequence for themselves. If the addressees do, fine, as long as the implications do not impinge upon themselves. But of course they do, given the proclamation of Paul's gospel to which the addressees appeal to legitimate their resistance to returning to the practices of pagan life, such as observance of the imperial cult.

If the addressees heed Paul's calling to "walk straight toward the truth of the good news of Christ," a conflict between the traditional and prevailing norms that guide both the Jewish and pagan communities and the newly revealed norms proclaimed in Jesus Christ is certain. It is in the hope of provoking the addressees to hold true to this call and the suffering its adherence may require that Paul's letter was written. Paul's seemingly defensive concerns are not reactions to present developments concerning outright opposition to himself but rather to the undermining of the principal truths and implications of their profession of faith in the meaning of Jesus Christ for themselves, which his message of the good news has proclaimed. His argument is constructed in anticipation of the addressees' compliance with the call to resistance and of the influencers' probable response to the exigence that this choice will create. Thus, in the final chapters, Paul instructs the addressees to give to each other the acceptance and support required to sustain the bad that may come their way in the present "evil" age, because they will not win this from the influencers while they hold fast to the claim of the dawning of the good of the age to come in the meaning of the death of Jesus, a Judean martyr of the Roman regime, just as does Paul, who suffers the same. They must "become as he is," those who together "wait for the hope of righteousness," serving each other as they "walk straight toward the truth of the good news of Christ."

CONCLUSION: THE IRONY OF GALATIANS

This reevaluation of the evidence suggests that the Galatian influencers were not believers in Jesus Christ, nor was their message good news of Christ. Their concerns did not arise from an inter-Christian opposition to Paul or his supposed Law-free gospel, and they did not arrive suddenly from outside Galatia. All of these would have raised a level of suspicion among the addressees that is not indicated in Paul's rhetoric. The naïve response of the addressees to the intentions, methods, and message of the influencers to date as good for themselves, along with their rationalizing of their offer as complementary to the message of Christ they had learned from their patron Paul—both of which are suggested by Paul's response, by analysis of his accusations, and of his approach to them in the style of ironic rebuke—tell against these traditional characterizations. Before reading/hearing Paul's polemical assault, the influencers appeared very differently to those he now addresses in Galatia, as trusted guides, likely even friends, who had their best interests in mind. Rather, I suggest that the influencers represented Jewish communities in Galatia that were concerned about the integration of these particular Gentiles, who were, through their involvement in the (still Jewish) Jesus subgroups, an integral part of the larger Jewish communities at this time. But their appeal to traditional norms maintained in the present age apart from Christ to modify the identity expectations of Paul's children in Christ threatened the addressees' interests in ways that neither the influencers nor the addressees perceived accurately—according to their parent, Paul. We have only his response.

This response implies that these Gentiles declared themselves to be identified with the Jewish communities in a new and disputable way, as righteous ones apart from proselyte conversion. This claim brought to the fore their identity as friendly guests to be sure but also their as yet pagan standing and thus the immediacy of the influencers' own minority communal concerns. Because the addressees were seeking full and equal status within larger (and largely non-Jesus believing) Jewish communities, the influencers were led initially to regard them as more than merely welcome guests but instead as potential proselyte candidates. The influencers thus expected them to initiate and complete the usual process for acquiring such status, the rite of proselyte conversion, which for males included circumcision. In the meantime, and especially to the degree that the addressees have resisted this course, the addressees were told that they must understand themselves as members of the pagan world and not yet members of the righteous ones. They were not entitled to the protection of the Jewish community as though they were proselytes or even candidates. And they were not obliged to observe Torah beyond the norms for such guest association either. They were welcome but by their own choice as pagan guests. They should not expect that the Jewish (minority) communal leaders would suffer the consequences of breaking with long-standing intercommunal norms in order to facilitate an identity claim that they did not themselves find legitimate by way of appeal to the death of a Judean martyr of the Roman regime.

This approach to the Galatian situation recognizes that within intra-Jewish contexts it was entirely plausible that Jewish communal groups without affiliation with Jesus Christ could assert that it was possible for Gentiles to be included among the righteous people of God now—these Gentiles needed but to complete the ritual process of conversion that provided proselyte Jewish status—and as such, these influencers might be regarded by the Galatian Gentiles as helpful proclaimers of inclusive good news. The proclaimers of this "other" message for righteous Gentiles seeking full inclusion might not have known much or for that matter anything about Paul or his good news, although it was likely that they had some knowledge of these matters. Assuming that Paul declared this news within these diaspora communities, they would be quite aware of him and his message and thus of the subgroups of his founding but not necessarily of the specific issues that would arise with the way the Gentiles within these subgroups were being taught to understand themselves. Nevertheless, as soon as the social control agents of these Galatian Jewish communities became aware of the compromising implications that were emerging among these coalitions of followers of Jesus, they did not approve of the radical conclusions being drawn by these Pauline pagans in Galatia, namely, the expectation of full inclusion now without circumcision—that is, without proselyte status—as Gentile righteous ones, by faith in Christ. In this sense, the influencers would have rightly understood but disagreed with the message that Paul refers to succinctly as "the truth of the gospel," that he has preserved for the addressees during earlier confrontations in Jerusalem (2:5) and Antioch (2:14), that he has previously taught among them in person (1:6-13; 3:1-5, 27; 4:12-20; 5:3, 7), and that he now underscores throughout this letter. It is the positive attraction of Paul's Gentiles to this other news as good that is confronted in Paul's undermining turn of phrase.

Galatians exemplifies the characteristics of a letter of ironic rebuke: the ironic nature of the letter is present on the very surface of Paul's language. I have argued that the implications for identifying the influencers, the nature of the social situations in Galatia, as well as the interpretation of Galatians, are many. But another aspect of taking seriously this epistolary characteristic of Paul's argument is recognizing how it undermines confidence in the interpretive history of this text as well. This should come as no surprise to the critics availing themselves of tools not applied in the past, in addition to recently developing awareness and commitment to taking "the other" on its own terms, including, for the later Christian interpreter, the Jewish people and religious life of those with whom Paul was interacting.

It is now widely agreed that the conventions that prepare and shape interpreters' expectations for the message of the text are in force when they begin, in fact, before they begin, to read the text. If approached as a theological tractate or an oration in a court of law, for example, or as a polemical attack on Jewish identity and Law observance as Galatians has often been read, then an entirely different set of expectations shapes the interpretive process than those suggested herein. But if Galatians exemplifies a letter of ironic rebuke designed to address Gentile members of a Jewish coalition who have begun to depart from the course they had been running when confident that their understanding of the meaning of Christ was legitimate—rightly so according to Paul's revealed good news—then the guardians of the majority or dominant communities, who are guided in their sensibilities and responsibilities by long-standing membership and reference group norms, will no doubt consider it their rightful duty to obstruct such a course. This would especially be the case for Jewish communities in diaspora settings, which, although dominant among such new subgroups of believers in Jesus, are themselves minority groups, with all the social constraints this would imply.

It appears that both the confused Galatian addressees and those who are influencing them are seeking to reduce the dissonance that has resulted from the addressees internalizing as good for themselves Paul's message of Christ for Gentiles in the present age. It is the addressees' assertions of identity that create the exigence for the influencers, and it is the influencers' response that creates a new exigence for the addressees. The influencers resist the addressees' claims to fully integrated status while remaining Gentiles, but they welcome the intention to gain the standing of righteous ones. The traditional good news to which the influencers appeal maintains that the desired identity may be negotiated only by completion of the rite of proselyte conversion. This generous and inclusive response has taken the addressees by surprise, and they have therefore begun also to internalize this as another message of good. Along with their convictions about Jesus Christ, which do not seem to concern the influencers except as they threaten communal boundaries and norms, the addressees see the way to combine these seemingly disparate messages, to eat their cake and have it too.

Paul is not amused. His response may be likened to that of a parent who has caught his or her teenager in a compromising turn justified by the powerful urge of acceptance by the youth's peers, the immediacy of this seeming good too strong to resist, the persuasive power of its logic overwhelming. Paul launches not into a cool reasoned case. He has already explained the facts in the past. So Paul turns to rebuke and ridicule by way of ironic dissociation. Such rhetoric is designed to undermine their confidence, to turn seemingly certain realities into certainly real appearances.

But although Paul's ironic turn of phrase had a uniquely qualified clarifying effect for the addressees, it has instead obscured the analysis of this text for later interpreters (including interpretive communities), who do not share the communal knowledge of the author and addressees in their historical situation. What was clear on the surface level of the text as the force of irony cut through the addressees' confidence, drawing them closer to the realization of truth, has had the opposite effect thereafter, rendering mere appearances into seeming realities. It has, ironically, made the surface meaning appear obvious, so that many aspects of the prevailing constructions have continued virtually without dispute, even without the need for substantial argument. Should the interpreter be certain of negatively stereotyping the influencers' motives, methods, and messages, when these were so uncertain to those who knew them, those to whom Paul wrote to effect just such an inversion? Should the powerful forces of social attraction implied by the addressees' interest and Paul's uncompromising parental response be so easily dismissed? Should not the recognition of these dynamics now give the interpreter reason to pause, to approach this text anew?

Historical-critical interpretation of Paul's letters depends invariably upon the context imagined for his choice of language. This reading of Galatians implies that Paul's ironic approach to this rebuke, although clear and persuasive for his own children in Galatia—who recognized the epistolary delivery of this irony and knew the character of the speaker and the nature of the subject to be out of keeping with his words, and thus the intentions of the writer to be other than what he actually said—has actually obscured the identity of the players and the situations, when read apart from this consideration, ever since. Although beyond the scope of this project to articulate further, if so, then the meaning Paul's message held for the original audience has ever since likely been hidden too.

APPENDIX

SOME PROBLEMS WITH RHETORICAL CLASSIFICATION OF GALATIANS

Classical Oration?

Recent study of Galatians has intensified the quest to classify the discourse contained in this letter within one of the three species (genres) of classical rhetoric as defined in Greco-Roman handbooks.[1] In fact, this is where the Galatians debate has most often focused since the introduction of Hans Dieter Betz's Hermeneia commentary in 1979.[2] These approaches to oratory were set out by Aristotle in *Rhetoric* 1.3, under the categories of judicial, deliberative, and epideictic, depending upon the situation of the intended audience, and were developed or modified over many centuries.[3] Oversimplified, they focus on particular

1. This is not to suggest that concern with the rhetorical nature of the letter is an entirely new development but to emphasize the intensity of this concern since H. D. Betz's work. For this consideration within earlier interpreters as well as its recent course of development, see variously Kennedy, *Classical Rhetoric;* Fairweather, "Rhetoric: Parts 1 & 2"; Anderson, *Ancient Rhetorical Theory,* 13–28; Mack, *Rhetoric and the NT,* 10–12; Classen, "St. Paul's Epistles"; Cooper, "Victorinus." Kern, *Rhetoric,* 43–89, 167–203, 204–55, argues that in the history of interpretation of Galatians, and for that matter Paul's other letters, seldom has anyone believed Paul engaged in classical handbook rhetoric, and many have rather noted his lack thereof.

2. The modern debate arguably began with Betz's article in 1975, although Classen has clarified that this matter was the subject of interpretive concern in earlier times ("St. Paul's Epistles"); see also Cooper, "Victorinus." This debate on rhetoric and Galatians will be one of the central issues in my forthcoming book, *Galatians Debate.*

3. Aristotle's *Rhetoric* (cf. 1.3; passim) apparently influenced the development of these three categories (e.g., the unsigned works *Rhet. Alex.* 1 [ca. 300 B.C.E.] and *Rhet. Her.* 1.2.2 [ca. 85 B.C.E.]; Cicero, *Inv.* 1.5.7 [ca. 90 B.C.E.]; Quintilian, *Inst.* 3.4.6–8 [ca. 90 C.E.]), even though it was not originally published and may have been unavailable from the third until perhaps the early first century B.C.E., and contained some views that differed with the works most influential in Paul's time; see discussion in Kennedy, *New History,* 62–63, 80, 87–88; Anderson, *Ancient Rhetorical Theory,* 38–43. For discussion of the diversity of rhetoric among the various authors, see Kern, *Rhetoric,* 39–43, 167–203. Overall with application to the NT, see Kennedy, *NT Interpretation,* 19; idem, *Classical Rhetoric,* 72–75. For developments of

approaches to various occasions for which the orator hopes to offer a persuasive speech. By consideration of the occasion and audience, as well as the message or goal of the intended persuasion, the orator selects (invents) one of these three rhetorical approaches in order to elicit the desired response.

Judicial or forensic (δικανικόν; *iudiciale*) rhetoric is best suited for accusation or defense characteristic of a legal situation such as a court of law, with its natural focus upon judging events that have occurred in the past (*Rhet.* 1.3, 10–15). The goal of such oration may be measured in the concern to establish justice or injustice, although the topics central to the other two species may be accessory points of appeal as well. Although an act may be admitted, the justice of the act or lack of it will still be in view. It is in the context of this concern that stasis theory will later provide a highly technical methodology for clarifying and arguing a case.

Deliberative (συμβουλευτικόν; *deliberativum*) is the genre of choice for exhortation or dissuasion, such as in the political assembly or in the giving of advice privately, with a concern for what direction to take in the future (cf. *Rhet.* 1.3–8). The goal of such rhetoric is the setting out of the advantage, the course of action recommended as better, or the harmful, the course from which they seek to dissuade the audience as worse. Within this persuasive purpose, the elements characteristic of the other two species may be incorporated, such as concern for justice and injustice (forensic), or honor and disgrace (epideictic). The emphasis is upon the self-interests of the audience; this genre is thus especially suited to a call to the expedient or useful course, such as the declaration of war or the making of slaves, even if, for example, the concern for justice (in terms of those who will incur the resultant loss) may be subordinated or subverted thereby. Thus, what will be deliberated about is not just the end but the means to the end, what is good for the audience as well as expedient.[4]

---

new rhetoric, especially of epideictic, see Perelman and Olbrechts-Tyteca, *New Rhetoric,* 47–52, 193–95, 261–63, 350, 411–15, passim; Kraftchick, "Why Do the Rhetoricians Rage?" 67–71.

4. Aristotle, *Rhet.* 1.6. Note Quintilian took issue with the emphasis upon expediency if taken in the direction of supporting a dishonorable course in the interests of expediency alone, rather emphasizing that it is the right course for themselves that is in view (*Inst.* 3.8.1–3), and he referred the reader to Cicero, *De or.* 2.82.

Epideictic, demonstrative, or panegyric (ἐπιδεικτόν; *demonstrativum*) rhetoric is especially appropriate to the matters of honor, for which one is praised, and disgrace (shamelessness), for which one is blamed (*Rhet.* 1.3, 9; 3.12). These topics occur, for example, in funeral orations and tend to focus upon the present or existing condition they wish to be held or affirmed, perhaps recalling the past or anticipating the future as well as in making a point. It is suited to inculcating or challenging a value without necessarily calling for a course of action thereby. Within this genre, like each of the others, the topics of the other species may be considered but are subordinated to the concern for honor or disgrace. This genre is thus particularly suited to a call to take up an honorable course, such as loyalty to a friend, even if it may be less expedient or perhaps result in disadvantageous or undesirable consequences as well: "For example, they praise Achilles because he went to the aid of his comrade Patroclus, knowing that he was fated to die, although he might have lived. To him such a death was more honourable, although life was more expedient" (Aristotle, *Rhetoric* 1.3.6). The functional aspects of this rhetoric were expanded upon by Perelman and Olbrechts-Tyteca by emphasizing its application to argument that seeks to enhance adherence to a set of values and the concomitant course of action that should follow, which may take many shapes depending upon the elements considered necessary, including the incorporation of elements of forensic or deliberative rhetoric.[5] It is the intensification of adherence that is the goal of such argumentation, although it may emphasize either association (from shared premise to specific conclusion) or dissociation (separation of language or tradition previously held together) in order to prevail in the face of a rival set of values.[6]

Currently, there are proponents of each of the three classifications for Galatians. Particularly strong lines have been drawn between those who classify it as judicial or deliberative, but there are proponents of epideictic as well.[7] It is quite clear that one must proceed

5. Perelman and Olbrechts-Tyteca, *New Rhetoric,* 47–51.

6. Perelman and Olbrechts-Tyteca, *New Rhetoric,* 193–95, 261–63, 350, 411–15. Note especially the emphasis that "the purpose of epidictic [*sic*] speech is to increase the intensity of adherence to values held in common by the audience and the speaker" (52). See Kraftchick, "Why Do the Rhetoricians Rage?" 67–71.

7. Proponents of forensic classification include H. D. Betz, *Galatians;* idem, "Literary Composition"; followed by Brinsmead, *Dialogical Response;* Hester,

with caution in the face of the many positions now being taken on the topic by various scholars, each equipped with examples and theories, both modern and antique, that allow them to make a sophisticated case. In addition, concern with the varieties of definitions of these classifications in the different handbooks of the time, whether Greek or Roman, and over a period of many years, as well as their application to orations and not letters, introduce the need for extreme care in embracing any particular methodology or in its application to this text.[8] Even ostensible parallels must be approached with suspicion: Does Paul draw from them? Are they commonplaces? Or are they merely coincidental, indicative of the similar forms likely to be adopted by one engaged in persuasive communication? Care must be taken to differentiate diachronic efforts relating the letter to ancient classification and influence (formal similarities) from synchronic analysis (functional similarities), however helpful both may prove to be in analysis of Galatians. That is, because a text exhibits aspects of one or

---

"Rhetorical Structure"; idem, "Use"; Martin, "Apostasy." Criticism of this classification is generally in the works of those who argue for the alternative ones, on various grounds, see, e.g., Kennedy, *NT Interpretation,* 144–52; Aune, "Review"; Meeks, "Review"; R. Hall, "Rhetorical Outline"; Lyons, *Pauline Autobiography,* 112–19; Smit, "Letter"; Fairweather, "Rhetoric: Parts 1 & 2"; Classen, "St. Paul's Epistles"; Cooper, "Victorinus"; and commentators, e.g., R. Longenecker, *Galatians,* cix–cxiii; Esler, *Galatians,* 60–61; Witherington, *Grace in Galatia,* 27–31.

Proponents of deliberative classification include Kennedy, *NT Interpretation,* 144–52; Lyons, *Pauline Autobiography,* 119–20, 136, 173–75; R. Hall, "Rhetorical Outline"; Smit, "Letter"; Russell, "Rhetorical Analysis"; Fairweather, "Rhetoric: Part 3," 219, 240, though with caveat; Cosgrove, *Cross,* 25–30; Aune, *NT in Its Literary Environment,* 206–8; and commentators, e.g., Matera, *Galatians,* 11; Esler, *Galatians,* 61, 137; and especially Witherington, *Grace in Galatia,* 25–41, passim. Important too is M. Mitchell, *Reconciliation,* 22–23, although dealing directly with classification of Corinthians.

Proponents of epideictic classification include Hester, "Placing the Blame"; Kraftchick, "Why Do the Rhetoricians Rage?" 67–71; J. White, "Apostolic Mission," 159–61, although he argues more from epistolary features and functions.

Extensive criticism of each of these classifications is available in Anderson, *Ancient Rhetorical Theory;* Kern, *Rhetoric,* and others listed in many of the notes that follow below. Also see Nanos and Elliott, eds., *Galatians Debate,* forthcoming.

8. Hester has argued the case for formal classification of Galatians according to classical as well as new rhetoric differently in several publications and now proposes a more functionalist and integrated approach to the enterprise (cf. "Composition").

more species of handbook rhetoric, the question remains whether it conforms to the classification as would the speech of one seeking to employ these methods according to the handbooks.[9]

One must judge any decision regarding the rhetoric of Galatians by its interpretive value, which, for all the work that has been done, still leaves much room for consideration. Conclusions to date have generally supported existing interpretive directions, giving one or another viewpoint additional ammunition in support of a case, but they have seldom revealed new directions for interpretation or seriously questioned the consensus views, for example, on the issue of the identity of the addressees, the influencers, or the nature of the situations, the matters that concern this study. These approaches actually yield less information than one might hope for constructing the situations or exigencies in Galatia as Paul perceives it, and thus the purpose and message of this letter. I will not seek here to critique the details of the present views, which can be found at length in the arguments of proponents of the competing classifications, as well as in the works of critics of the process, both of which are indicated in my notes, but offer the following general conclusions.

The results of rhetorical analyses to date have largely been confined to determining the structure of the letter: how it breaks down so that a helpful outline may be generated. A review of the introductory remarks of the interpreters applying rhetorical criticism will show that the process of attributing one of the rhetorical species to Galatians begins with a prior assessment of the situations among the audience being addressed as well as the intention of the author; thus naturally this interpretive assessment is brought to the exercise rather than derived from it. They then proceed to try and match these interpretive assumptions to the species considered most appropriate for a message addressing such a case. This is in some ways appropriate, of course, and to be expected of the exercise, as such rhetorical theory (e.g., invention and arrangement) was focused on selecting and developing the means to communicate, rather than on interpretation per se.[10] But the extant literature does not analyze or deconstruct in the direction that inter-

9. This is the thrust of the suspicion evident in Anderson's (*Ancient Rhetorical Theory*) and Kern's (*Rhetoric*) extensive treatments and concluding dismissals of these approaches for failing to demonstrate that Galatians falls within the classical classifications of the handbooks; see also Fairweather, "Rhetoric: Part 3."

10. Cicero, *Inv.* 1.7/9; cf. Weima, "What?" 458–68.

preters must take, without knowledge of the situation or the rhetorical intention, but only in the other direction, from this knowledge to choosing the appropriate classification and fashioning the speech considered most likely to persuade.[11] The exercise is further flawed by the fact that we are dealing in this backward manner not with orations developed for a court of law or public gathering, for which the handbooks provided these rules, but only with the text of a letter sent to several gatherings of Christ-believers, about whom, apart from this letter, we know very little.[12] As Berchman observes, if the genre of rhetoric is not even clear enough to be agreed upon, "then surely the more complex aspects of rhetorical criticism such as the definition of Paul's mode of topical arrangement, his forms of syllogistic argumentation, and the speech parts employed to frame his speech act, appear beyond description and definition."[13]

Thus, while categorization of Paul's letter within such rhetorical types developed to differentiate orations may prove helpful for the interpreter, offering heuristic benefits, for Paul was surely involved in writing a letter fashioned to affect the addressees and thus with rhetoric in the broader sense as communication strategically crafted to persuade, I join those who remain skeptical of making too much of any final categorization of Galatians along this line, as though it was the conscious intention of Paul. We are dealing with a letter and not an oration,[14] even

11. Anderson, *Ancient Rhetorical Theory,* 90–92, 256; Kern, *Rhetoric,* 27–30; Bitzer, "Rhetorical Situation," 2.

12. Cf. Kern, *Rhetoric,* 22–23 (note Plato, *Gorgias* 454a–b). This weakness may be mitigated to some degree by grounding the letter's reception, e.g., either in a law-court setting for forensic (so H. D. Betz), a political gathering (*ekklēsia*) for deliberative, or epideictic for public celebration of civic-religious occasions.

13. Berchman, "Rhetoric," 2.

14. See Malherbe, *Theorists,* 2–3, for both sides of the argument; on the one hand, Demetrius, *On Style,* applies rhetorical terms to letters (so too Cicero, *De or.* 2.11.49–50, may be taken this way), but on the other, he notes that there does not seem to have been "an entire theoretical system." Urging caution or even dismissal of connection between letter writing and classical rhetoric or handbooks are Aune, *NT in Its Literary Environment,* 158–59; Classen, "St. Paul's Epistles," 269–70, 280–91; Anderson, *Ancient Rhetorical Theory,* 93–109, 111–23, 141, 165–67, and esp. 34, 100, 103; Stowers, *Letter Writing,* 27, 51–52, 56; Porter, "Theoretical Justification," 100–122; idem, "Paul of Tarsus," 533–85, esp. 539–47, 562–67; idem, "Ancient Rhetorical Analysis"; Weima, "What?"; D. Watson, "Rhetorical Criticism," 22–24; Reed, "Epistle," 171–93; idem, "Using Ancient Rhetorical Categories"; Kern, *Rhetoric,* 30–34, passim. Among those working specifically on Galatians, note the various levels of concern, e.g., Dahl, "Galatians"; Hansen, *Gala-*

if perhaps acted out upon delivery,[15] and a letter that exemplifies the epistolary category of ironic rebuke.[16]

I respect the fact that such categories were understood to be somewhat artificial and overlapping, and the line between letters and oral discourse arguably not sharply drawn, being somewhat independent traditions;[17] however, the enormous variety of outlines along each of the formal rhetorical paths tells against this application. Moreover, they are not convincing when applied to the structure of Galatians,[18] which follows more naturally the structure of a letter of ironic rebuke—similar to that of a disappointed parent to his or her children—than an oration for one's fellow citizens. Both letters and speeches do share the concern to persuade, but Paul's letters are more speech and sermon, such as one might expect in a synagogue meeting.[19] Moreover, as Cicero noted, speeches whose object was, for example, rebuke, did not

---

tians, 22–24 (emphasis upon letter of rebuke-request but finds forensic characteristics in 1:6—4.11; after 4:12 deliberative; see also idem, *Abraham,* 55–71); R. Longenecker, *Galatians,* ci–cxix; Cosgrove, *Cross,* 23–31; Dunn, *Galatians,* 20; Williams, *Galatians,* 28–31; Martyn, *Galatians,* 20–23; Esler, *Galatians,* 18–19, 59–61.

15. Botha, "Letter Writing"; idem, "Verbal Art"; Loubser, "Orality."

16. Fairweather's playing down of the rebuke aspect of the letter in classifying it as deliberative is perhaps telling ("Rhetoric: Part 3," 219; noted by Anderson, *Ancient Rhetorical Theory,* 123, also 141).

17. See discussions in Stowers, *Letter Writing,* 51–57; Aune, *NT in Its Literary Environment,* 197–99; M. Mitchell, *Reconciliation,* 22–23; Hughes, *Early Christian Rhetoric,* 47–50; and opposite views of Kern, *Rhetoric,* 30–34; Anderson, *Ancient Rhetorical Theory,* 100–104, as well as suggestions on 104–9.

18. See Fairweather, "Rhetoric: Part 3," 220–21, 226–27; Anderson, *Ancient Rhetorical Theory,* 124–25, 165–67; Kern, *Rhetoric,* 120–66.

19. See Anderson, *Ancient Rhetorical Theory,* 102; J. White, "Saint Paul," 439; idem, "NT Epistolary Literature," 1743. See, e.g., Philo, *Spec. Laws* 2.61–63; *Moses* 2.214–16; *Hypothetica* 7.12–13; *Contempl. Life* 28–31 (for practices of the Therapeutae); Luke 4:16-29; Acts 13:15-49; for discussion of sermons, education, and discipline, see Levine, *Ancient Synagogue,* 144–47, 367–81; for comparison with approaches of the later rabbis, see Lemmer, "Why?"; Thyen, *Der Stil;* for Greco-Roman approaches, see Malherbe, *Moral Exhortation.* N. Elliott, "Paul and Politics," 27–33, discusses also the challenge of accounting for the political persuasion and coercion that classical rhetoric served for the ruling elites of the Roman Empire when seeking to coordinate these sources with the interests expressed in Paul's letters.

logically fit within this threefold rhetorical system (*De or.* 2.15.50, 64). He thus elsewhere states: "For what does a letter have in common with a speech in court or in an assembly?"[20]

In the end, each of these classifications may be applied functionally to the letter of Paul to the Galatians, within the limitations noted, with varying success, and without certainty that any were explicitly in view for Paul as he fashioned his argument. For the present study, focused upon the identity of the players and the nature of the situations provoking the letter, the immediate value is limited. Nevertheless, attention to the functional aspects of these rhetorical theories may be useful in seeking to articulate Paul's message after the situations provoking it has been first investigated by other means.

For example, the deeply communal nature of irony, and even more so of ironic rebuke, are more suggestive of a family setting, of the parental role of exhortation and discipline, even manipulation by way of shaming and punishment. The strategic value of irony is not in setting out a case or option as much as reinforcing an already shared value. It is a call to live within the insights of the past as the reality still shining, for those who can see it, in the face of the mere pretense located in the appearances of the present. In this sense, it is an engagement in subverting the culture of the other by appeal to one's own.

Although not conforming to any of the three genres of classical rhetoric in terms of form, in terms of essential functionality, the findings of this study suggest that at the center of Paul's rhetoric is not recounting of the past in order to defend himself (i.e., forensic) or setting out a new option for the addressees to consider (i.e., deliberative) as much as calling for them to continue to adhere to the norms that they have already embraced in the face of a rival orientation, even at the price of some present disadvantage (i.e., epideictic). In this sense, an epideictic rhetorical quality is present in this letter, at least as this classification

20. Cicero, *Fam.* 9.21.1; from translation by Anderson, *Ancient Rhetorical Theory,* 101. This concern for the differences may also be noted in Demetrius, *On Style* 223–35 (text in Malherbe, *Theorists,* 17–19). Among Demetrius's many interesting comments on this point, note, e.g., the following: "There should be a certain degree of freedom in the structure of a letter. It is absurd to build up periods, as if you were writing not a letter but a speech for the law courts. And such laboured letter writing is not merely absurd; it does not even obey the laws of friends, which demand that we should 'call a spade a spade,' as the proverb has it" (229). In this letter, Paul certainly seems to do just as Demetrius recommends!

has been expanded in functional scope by the advocates of so-called new rhetoric.[21]

Ironically, in this case Paul's is not exactly a new message of good news, because he has proclaimed it in the past to the addressees. In one sense, it is the other message that is rather newly elevated to its competitive place by the response of the influencers and the considered acquiescence of those Galatians he addresses. However, the other message may be older—it can, after all, appeal to tradition—but its significance for the addressees as compared to the message of Christ that they have already embraced is a new development, one that appears to define the exigence for the inventor of this text.

21. Cf. Perelman and Olbrechts-Tyteca, *New Rhetoric.* There is an epideictic quality that comes through, for Paul appeals to "values that are beyond question" for the addressees, as would a teacher or parent (140).

Sympathetic seems to be the evaluation of Anderson, *Ancient Rhetorical Theory,* 166: "Against both forms of rhetorical genre it must be reiterated that Paul is not simply trying to persuade his audience, he is giving them a solemn rebuke! . . . But all things considered, in this letter Paul is better likened to a philosopher whose pupils have departed from his doctrines than to a defendant on trial, a prosecutor in court, or a politician in an assembly. Indication of this may be seen in the fact that attacking the convictions of the audience (as Paul surely does!) was in rhetorical theory regarded as a faulty method of argumentation (cf. *Rhet. Her.* 2.43; Cicero, *Inv.* 1.92; *De or.* 2.304–305)." See further discussion in chapter 3 above and Aristotle, *Rhet.* 3.1.7; 3.12.6; also discussion of epideictic quality in Stowers, *Letter Writing,* 27–28, 51–52; idem, "Social Typification," 84–85; Hester, "Placing the Blame"; J. White, "Apostolic Mission"; for new rhetoric, see Kraftchick, "Why Do the Rhetoricians Rage?" 67–71.

BIBLIOGRAPHY

Primary Sources

Braude, William G., trans. *The Midrash on Psalms.* 2 vols. New Haven: Yale Univ. Press, 1959.

Charlesworth, James H., ed. *The Old Testament Pseudepigrapha.* 2 vols. Garden City, N.Y.: Doubleday, 1983–85.

Feldman, Louis H., and Reinhold Meyer, eds. *Jewish Life and Thought among Greeks and Romans: Primary Readings.* Minneapolis: Fortress Press, 1996.

Justin. *Dialogue with Trypho.* In *The Ante-Nicene Fathers,* edited by Alexander Roberts and James Donaldson, 1.94–270. 10 vols. 1885–87; reprint; Peabody, Mass.: Hendrickson, 1994.

Malherbe, Abraham J. *Ancient Epistolary Theorists.* Sources for Biblical Studies 19. Atlanta: Scholars Press, 1988.

———. *Moral Exhortation: A Greco-Roman Sourcebook.* LEC 4. Philadelphia: Westminster, 1986.

Nadeau, Ray. "Hermogenes' *On Stases:* A Translation with an Introduction and Notes." *Speech Monographs* 31 (1964):361–424.

Neusner, Jacob. *The Mishnah: A New Translation.* New Haven: Yale Univ. Press, 1988.

Schneemelcher, Wilhelm, ed. *New Testament Apocrypha.* Rev. ed. Translated by R. McL. Wilson. 2 vols. Louisville: Westminster John Knox, 1990–91.

Trigg, Joseph W. "Augustine/Jerome, Correspondence." In *Biblical Interpretation,* 250–95. Message of the Fathers of the Church 9. Wilmington, Del.: Michael Glazier, 1988.

Vermes, Geza. *The Complete Dead Sea Scrolls in English.* 4th ed. New York: Penguin, 1997.

White, John L. *Light from Ancient Letters.* FF. Minneapolis: Fortress Press, 1986.

Whittaker, Molly. *Jews and Christians: Graeco-Roman Views.* Cambridge: Cambridge Univ. Press, 1984.

Williams, Margaret H., ed. *The Jews among the Greeks and Romans: A Diaspora Sourcebook.* Baltimore: Johns Hopkins Univ. Press, 1998.

Secondary Sources

Anderson, R. Dean, Jr. *Ancient Rhetorical Theory and Paul.* Contributions to Biblical Exegesis and Theology 18. Kampen: Pharos, 1996.

Aune, David E. *The New Testament in Its Literary Environment.* LEC 8. Philadelphia: Westminster, 1987.

———. "Review of Hans Dieter Betz's *Galatians.*" *Recherches de science religieuse* 7 (1981):323–28.

Axtell, Harold L. *The Deification of Abstract Ideas in Roman Literature and Inscriptions.* New Rochelle, N.Y.: Caratzas, 1987.

Baasland, Ernst. "Persecution: A Neglected Feature in the Letter to the Galatians." *ST* 38 (1984):135–50.

Bahr, Gordon J. "The Subscriptions in the Pauline Letters." *JBL* 87 (1968):27–41.

Banks, Marcus. *Ethnicity: Anthropological Constructions.* London: Routledge, 1996.

Barclay, John M. G. *Jews in the Mediterranean Diaspora: From Alexander to Trajan (323 B.C.E.–117 C.E.).* Edinburgh: T. & T. Clark, 1996.

———. "Mirror-Reading a Polemical Letter: Galatians as a Test Case." In *The Pauline Writings: A Sheffield Reader*, edited by Stanley E. Porter and Craig A. Evans, 247–67. Sheffield: Sheffield Academic Press, 1995.

———. *Obeying the Truth: Paul's Ethics in Galatians.* Minneapolis: Fortress Press, 1988.

Barth, Fredrik. "Introduction." In *Ethnic Groups and Boundaries: The Social Organization of Culture Difference*, edited by F. Barth, 9–38. Boston: Little, Brown, 1969.

Bassler, J. M., ed. *Pauline Theology.* Vol. 1: *Thessalonians, Philippians, Galatians, Philemon.* Minneapolis: Fortress Press, 1991.

Bauer, Walter. *A Greek-English Lexicon of the New Testament and Other Early Christian Literature.* 2d ed. Rev. by F. Wilbur Gingrich and Frederick W. Danker. Chicago: Univ. of Chicago Press, 1979.

Baur, Ferdinand Christian. *Paul the Apostle of Jesus Christ: His Life and Work, His Epistles, and His Doctrine.* Translated by A. Menzies from 2d ed. Edited by Eduard Zeller. 2 vols. 1845; London: Williams & Norgate, 1873–75.

Beard, Mary, John North, and Simon Price. *Religions of Rome.* Vol. 1: *A History;* vol. 2: *A Sourcebook.* Cambridge: Cambridge Univ. Press, 1998.

Becker, U. "Gospel, Evangelize, Evangelist." In *NIDNTT*, edited by Colin Brown, 2.107–15. Grand Rapids: Zondervan, 1977.

Beker, J. Christiaan. *Paul the Apostle: The Triumph of God in Life and Thought.* Philadelphia: Fortress Press, 1980.

Bell, Catherine. *Ritual Theory, Ritual Practice.* New York: Oxford Univ. Press, 1992.

Berchman, Robert M. "Galatians (1:1-5): Paul and Greco-Roman Rhetoric." In *Judaic and Christian Interpretation of Texts: Context and Contexts,* edited by J. Neusner and E. S. Frerichs, 1–15. New Perspectives on Ancient Judaism 3. Lanham, Md.: Univ. Press of America, 1987.

Berger, Peter L., and Thomas Luckmann. *The Social Construction of Reality: A Treatise in the Sociology of Knowledge.* New York: Doubleday, 1966.

Bertram, Georg. "Μεταστρέφω." In Kittel and Friedrich, eds. *TDNT* 7.729.

Betz, Hans Dieter. *Galatians: A Commentary on Paul's Letter to the Churches in Galatia.* Hermeneia. Philadelphia: Fortress Press, 1977.

———. "The Literary Composition and Function of Paul's Letter to the Galatians." *NTS* 21 (1975):353–79.

Betz, Otto. "Jesus' Gospel of the Kingdom." In *The Gospel and the Gospels,* edited by P. Stuhlmacher, 53–74. Grand Rapids: Eerdmans, 1991.

Bitzer, Lloyd F. "Functional Communication: A Situational Perspective." In *Rhetoric in Transition: Studies in the Nature and Uses of Rhetoric,* edited by Eugene E. White, 21–38. University Park: Pennsylvania State Univ. Press, 1980.

———. "The Rhetorical Situation." *Philosophy and Rhetoric. Supplementary Issue,* 1–14. 1968; University Park: Pennsylvania State Univ. Press, 1992.

Bligh, John. *Galatians in Greek: A Structural Analysis of St. Paul's Epistle to the Galatians with Notes on the Greek.* Detroit: Univ. of Detroit Press, 1966.

Boers, Hendrikus. *The Justification of the Gentiles: Paul's Letters to the Galatians and Romans.* Peabody, Mass.: Hendrickson, 1994.

Boissevain, Jeremy. *Friends of Friends: Networks, Manipulators, and Coalitions.* Oxford: Blackwell, 1974.

Bolchazy, Ladislaus J. *Hospitality in Antiquity: Livy's Concept of Its Humanizing Force.* Chicago: Ares, 1995.

Booth, Wayne C. *The Rhetoric of Irony.* Chicago: Univ. of Chicago Press, 1974.

Borgen, Peder. "Paul Preaches Circumcision and Pleases Men." In *Paul and Paulinism: Essays in Honour of C. K. Barrett,* edited by M. D. Hooker and S. G. Wilson, 37–46. London: SPCK, 1982.

———. "'Yes,' 'No,' 'How Far?': The Participation of Jews and Christians in Pagan Cults." In *Paul in His Hellenistic Context,* edited by Troels Engberg-Pedersen, 30–59. Minneapolis: Fortress Press, 1995.

Botha, P. J. J. "Greco-Roman Literacy as Setting for New Testament Writings." *Neot* 26 (1992):195–215.

———. "Letter Writing and Oral Communication in Antiquity: Suggested Implications for the Interpretation of Paul's Letter to the Galatians." *Scriptura* 42 (1992):17–34.

———. "The Verbal Art of the Pauline Letters: Rhetoric, Performance, and Presence." In *Rhetoric and the New Testament,* edited by Porter and Olbricht,409–28.

Bourdieu, Pierre. *Language and Symbolic Power.* Translated by G. Raymond and M. Adamson. Cambridge: Harvard Univ. Press, 1991.

Bowersock, G. W. "The Imperial Cult: Perceptions and Persistence." In *Jewish and Christian Self-Definition.* Vol. 3: *Self-Definition in the Greco-Roman World,* edited by B. F. Meyer and E. P. Sanders, 171–82. Philadelphia: Fortress Press, 1983.

Boyarin, Daniel. *A Radical Jew: Paul and the Politics of Identity.* Berkeley: Univ. of California Press, 1994.

Braithwaite, John. *Crime, Shame, and Reintegration.* Cambridge: Cambridge Univ. Press, 1989.

Brent, Allen. *The Imperial Cult and the Development of Church Order: Concepts and Images of Authority in Paganism and Early Christianity before the Age of Cyprian.* Supplements to Vigiliae Christianae 45. Leiden: Brill, 1999.

Breytenbach, Cilliers. *Paulus und Barnabas in der Provinz Galatien: Studien zu Apostelgeschichte 13f.; 16,6; 18,23 und den Adressaten des Galaterbriefes.* AGAJU 38. Leiden: Brill, 1996.

Brichto, Herbert Chanan. *The Problem of "Curse" in the Hebrew Bible.* SBLMS 13. Philadelphia: Society of Biblical Literature, 1968.

Brinsmead, Bernard Hungerford. *Galatians—Dialogical Response to Opponents.* SBLDS 65. Atlanta: Scholars Press, 1982.

Bruce, F. F. *The Epistle to the Galatians: A Commentary on the Greek Text.* New International Greek Testament Commentary. Grand Rapids: Eerdmans, 1982.

———. "Galatian Problems: 3. The 'Other' Gospel." *BJRL* 53 (1971):253–71.

Burton, Ernest De Witt. *A Critical and Exegetical Commentary on the Epistle to the Galatians.* International Critical Commentary. Edinburgh: T. & T. Clark, 1921.

Calvin, John. *Commentaries on the Epistles of Paul to the Galatians and Ephesians.* Translated by W. Pringle. Grand Rapids: Eerdmans, 1955.

Cameron, Peter S. "An Exercise in Translation: Galatians 2.11-14." *Bible Translator* 40: 135–45 (1989).

Camery-Hoggatt, Jerry. *Irony in Mark's Gospel: Text and Subtext.* Cambridge: Cambridge Univ. Press, 1992.

Campbell, J. Y. "The Origin and Meaning of the Christian Use of the Word *ΕΚΚΛΗΣΙΑ*." *JTS* 49 (1948):130–42.

Campbell, William S. *Paul's Gospel in an Intercultural Context: Jew and Gentile in the Letter to the Romans.* Frankfurt: Lang, 1992.

Classen, C. J. "St. Paul's Epistles and Ancient Greek and Roman Rhetoric." In *Rhetoric and the New Testament,* edited by Porter and Olbricht, 265–91.

Cohen, Anthony P. *Self-Consciousness: An Alternate Anthropology of Identity.* London: Routledge, 1994.

———. *The Symbolic Construction of Community.* London: Routledge, 1985.

Cohen, Shaye J. D. *The Beginnings of Jewishness: Boundaries, Varieties, Uncertainties.* Berkeley: Univ. of California Press, 1999.

———. "*Ioudaios:* 'Judaean' and 'Jew' in Susanna, First Maccabees, and Second Maccabees." In *Geschichte—Tradition—Reflection: Festschrift für Martin Hengel zum 70. Geburtstag.* Vol. 1: *Judentum,* edited by H. Cancik and others, 211–20. Tübingen: Mohr/Siebeck, 1996.

Cohen, S. J. D., and E. S. Frerichs, eds. *Diasporas in Antiquity.* BJS 288. Atlanta: Scholars Press, 1993.

Collins, John J. *The Scepter and the Star: The Messiahs of the Dead Sea Scrolls and Other Ancient Literature.* Anchor Bible Reference Library. New York: Doubleday, 1995.

Conrad, Carl. "*HOI ΠERITEMNOMENOI* in Gal. 6:13." Posted on B-Greek mailing list on 24 January 2000.

Cooper, Stephen A. "*Narratio* and *Exhortatio* in Galatians According to Marius Victorinus Rhetor." *ZNW* 91 (2000):107–35.

Cornelius, E. M. "The Relevance of Ancient Rhetoric to Rhetorical Criticism." *Neot* 28 (1994):457–67.

Coser, Lewis A. *The Functions of Social Conflict.* New York: The Free Press, 1956.

Cosgrove, Charles H. *The Cross and the Spirit: A Study in the Argument and Theology of Galatians.* Macon, Ga.: Mercer Univ. Press, 1988.

Cotter, Wendy. "The Collegia and Roman Law: State Restrictions on Voluntary Associations, 64 B.C.E.–200 C.E." In *Voluntary Associations in the Graeco-Roman World,* edited by Kloppenborg and Wilson, 74–89.

Cronjé, J. Van W. "Defamiliarization in the Letter to the Galatians." In *A South African Perspective on the New Testament,* edited by Petzer and Hartin, 214–27.

Dahl, Nils Alstrup. "Paul's Letter to the Galatians: Epistolary Genre, Content, and Structure." Paper presented at the SBL Paul Seminar, Chicago, 1973.

Dane, Joseph A. *The Critical Mythology of Irony.* Athens: Univ. of Georgia Press, 1991.

Davies, W. D. *Jewish and Pauline Studies.* Philadelphia: Fortress Press, 1984.

de Ste. Croix, G. E. M. *The Class Struggle in the Ancient Greek World: From the Archaic Age to the Arab Conquests.* Ithaca, N.Y.: Cornell Univ. Press, 1981.

———. "Why Were the Early Christians Persecuted? A Rejoinder." *Past & Present* 27 (1964):28–33.

Deissmann, Adolf. *Light from the Ancient East: The New Testament Illustrated by Recently Discovered Texts of the Graeco-Roman World.* Translated by L. R. M. Strachan. 1923; Grand Rapids: Baker, 1965.

Deist, Ferdinand. "Boundaries and Humour: A Case Study from the Ancient Near East." *Scriptura* 63 (1997):415–24.

Dix, Gregory. *Jew and Greek: A Study in the Primitive Church.* London: Dacre, 1953.

Dodd, Brian J. *Paul's Paradigmatic "I": Personal Example as Literary Strategy.* JSNTSup 177. Sheffield: Sheffield Academic, 1999.

Dodds, E. R. *The Greeks and the Irrational.* Berkeley: Univ. of California Press, 1951.

Donaldson, Terence L. "'The Gospel That I Proclaim among the Gentiles' (Gal. 2.2): Universalistic or Israel-Centred?" In *Gospel in Paul,* edited by Jervis and Richardson, 166–93.

———. *Paul and the Gentiles: Remapping the Apostle's Convictional World.* Minneapolis: Fortress Press, 1997.

———. "Preaching Circumcision: Gal 5:11 and the Origin of Paul's Gentile Mission." Paper presented at the Canadian SBL meeting, 1988.

———. "Rural Bandits, City Mobs, and the Zealots." *Journal for the Study of Judaism* 21 (1990):19–40.

Doty, William G. *Letters in Primitive Christianity.* GBS. Philadelphia: Fortress Press, 1973.

Driver, Tom F. *The Magic of Ritual: Our Need for Liberating Rites that Transform Our Lives and Our Communities.* San Francisco: HarperSanFrancisco, 1991.

Du Toit, A. B. "Alienation and Re-Identification as Pragmatic Strategies in Galatians." *Neot* 26 (1992): 279–95.

———. "Vilification as a Pragmatic Device in Early Christian Epistolography." *Bib* 75 (1994): 403–12.

Duff, A. M. *Freedmen in the Early Roman Empire.* Cambridge: Heffer, 1958.

Duke, Paul D. *Irony in the Fourth Gospel.* Atlanta: John Knox, 1985.

Dundes, Alan, ed. *The Evil Eye: A Folklore Casebook.* New York: Garland, 1981.

Dunn, James D. G. *The Epistle to the Galatians.* Black's New Testament Commentaries. Peabody, Mass.: Hendrickson, 1993.

———. "In Search of Common Ground." In *Paul and the Mosaic Law,* edited by J. D. G. Dunn, 309–34. Tübingen: Mohr/Siebeck, 1996.

———. *Jesus, Paul, and the Law: Studies in Mark and Galatians.* Louisville: Westminster John Knox, 1990.

———. *The Partings of the Ways between Christianity and Judaism and Their Significance for the Character of Christianity.* Philadelphia: Trinity Press International, 1991.

———. "The Theology of Galatians: The Issue of Covenantal Nomism." In *Pauline Theology,* edited by Bassler, 125–46.

———. *The Theology of Paul the Apostle.* Grand Rapids: Eerdmans, 1997.

———. *The Theology of Paul's Letter to the Galatians.* New Testament Theology. Cambridge: Cambridge Univ. Press, 1993.

Elliott, James K. "The Use of ἕτερος in the New Testament." *ZNW* 60 (1969):140–41.

Elliott, John H. "Paul, Galatians, and the Evil Eye." *Currents in Theology and Mission* 17 (1990):262–73.

Elliott, Neil. *Liberating Paul: The Justice of God and the Politics of the Apostle.* Maryknoll, N.Y.: Orbis, 1994.

———. "Paul and the Politics of Empire: Problems and Prospects." In *Paul and Politics: Ekklesia, Israel, Imperium, Interpretation,* edited by Richard A. Horsley, 17–39. Harrisburg, Pa.: Trinity Press International, 2000.

———. "Review of Mark Nanos, *The Mystery of Romans,*" *CBQ* 59 (1997): 587–89.

Elliott, Robert C. *The Power of Satire: Magic, Ritual, Art.* Princeton: Princeton Univ. Press, 1960.

Elliott, Susan M. "Choose Your Mother, Choose Your Master: Galatians 4:21—5:1 in the Shadow of the Anatolian Mother of the Gods." *JBL* 118 (1999):661–83.

———. "The Rhetorical Strategy of Paul's Letter to the Galatians in Its Anatolian Cultic Context: Circumcision and the Castration of the Galli of the Mother of the Gods." 3 vols. Ph.D. diss., Loyola University, Chicago, 1997.

Ellis, E. Earle. "Paul and His Opponents: Trends in Research." In *Christianity, Judaism, and Other Greco-Roman Cults: Studies for Morton Smith at Sixty*. Part 1: *New Testament*, edited by Jacob Neusner. 264–98. Studies in Judaism in Late Antiquity 12. Leiden: Brill, 1975.

Elworthy, Frederick Thomas. *The Evil Eye: An Account of the Ancient and Widespread Superstition*. London: Murray, 1895.

Enslin, Morton Scott. *Christian Beginnings*. New York: Harper & Brothers, 1938.

Esler, Philip F. *The First Christians in Their Social Worlds: Social-Scientific Approaches to New Testament Interpretation*. London: Routledge, 1994.

———. *Galatians*. New Testament Readings. London: Routledge, 1998.

———. "Making and Breaking an Agreement Mediterranean Style: A New Reading of Galatians 2:1–14." *BibInt* 3 (1995):285–314.

Etzioni, Amitai. "Social Control: Organizational Aspects." In *International Encyclopedia of the Social Sciences*, edited by D. Sills, 14:396–402. New York: Macmillan, 1968.

Fairweather, Janet. "The Epistle to the Galatians and Classical Rhetoric: Parts 1 & 2." *TynBul* 45 (1994):1–38.

———. "The Epistle to the Galatians and Classical Rhetoric: Part 3." *TynBul* 45 (1994):213–43.

Feldman, Louis H. *Jew and Gentile in the Ancient World: Attitudes and Interactions from Alexander to Justinian*. Princeton: Princeton Univ. Press, 1993.

Finn, Thomas M. *From Death to Rebirth: Ritual and Conversion in Antiquity*. New York: Paulist, 1997.

Fish, Stanley. "Short People Got No Reason to Live: Reading Irony." In *Doing What Comes Naturally: Change, Rhetoric, and the Practice of Theory in Literary and Legal Studies*, 180–96. Post-Contemporary Interventions. Durham, N.C.: Duke Univ. Press, 1989.

Fishwick, Duncan. *The Imperial Cult in the Latin West: Studies in the Ruler Cult of the Western Provinces of the Roman Empire*. EPRO 108. Leiden: Brill, 1992.

Fitzgerald, John T. "The Catalogue in Ancient Greek Literature." In *The Rhetorical Analysis of Scripture*, edited by Porter and Olbricht, 275–93.

Fletcher, Douglas K. "The Singular Argument of Paul's Letter to the Galatians." Ph.D. diss., Princeton University, 1982.

Foster, George M. "The Anatomy of Envy: A Study in Symbolic Behavior." *Current Anthropology* 13 (1972):165–202.

———. "Peasant Society and the Image of Limited Good." *American Anthropologist* 67 (1965):293–315.

Fredriksen, Paula. *From Jesus to Christ: The Origins of the New Testament Images of Jesus*. New Haven: Yale Univ. Press, 1988.

———. "Judaism, the Circumcision of Gentiles, and Apocalyptic Hope: Another Look at Galatians 1 and 2." *JTS* 42 (1991):532–64.

Friedrich, Gerhard. "Εὐαγγελίζομαι." In Kittel and Friedrich, eds. *TDNT* 2.707–37.

Fuchs, Ernst. "κατασκοπέω," In Kittel and Friedrich, eds. *TDNT* 7.417.

Fung, Ronald Y. K. *The Epistle to the Galatians*. NICNT. Grand Rapids: Eerdmans, 1953.

Garnsey, Peter D. A. "Descendants of Freedmen in Local Politics: Some Criteria." In *The Ancient Historian and His Materials: Essays in Honour of C. E. Stevens on His Seventieth Birthday*, edited by B. Levick, 167–80. Farnborough, Hants.: Gregg, 1975.

Garnsey, Peter, and Richard Saller. *The Roman Empire: Economy, Society, and Culture*. Berkeley: Univ. of California Press, 1987.

Garrison, Vivian, and Conrad M. Arensberg. "The Evil Eye: Envy or Risk of Seizure? Paranoia or Patronal Dependency." In *The Evil Eye*, edited by C. Maloney, 287–328. New York: Columbia Univ. Press, 1976.

Gaston, Lloyd. "Judaism of the Uncircumcised in Ignatius and Related Writers." In *Anti-Judaism in Early Christianity*. Vol. 2: *Separation and Polemic*, edited by S. G. Wilson, 33–44. Waterloo, Ontario: Wilfrid Laurier Univ. Press, 1986.

———. *Paul and the Torah*. Vancouver: Univ. of British Columbia Press, 1987.

Goldstein, Jonathan. "Jewish Acceptance and Rejection of Hellenism." In *Jewish and Christian Self-Definition*. Vol. 2: *Aspects of Judaism in the Graeco-Roman World*, edited by E. P. Sanders et al., 64–87. Philadelphia: Fortress Press, 1981.

Good, Edwin M. *Irony in the Old Testament*. London: SPCK, 1965; reprinted Sheffield: Almond, 1981.

Goodman, Martin. "Jews, Greeks, and Romans." In *Jews in a Graeco-Roman World*, edited by M. Goodman, 3–14. Oxford: Clarendon, 1998.

———. *Mission and Conversion: Proselytizing in the Religious History of the Roman Empire*. Oxford: Clarendon, 1994.

———. *The Roman World 44 B.C.–A.D. 180*. London: Routledge, 1997.

———. *The Ruling Class of Judaea: The Origins of the Jewish Revolt against Rome A.D. 66–70*. Cambridge: Cambridge Univ. Press, 1987.

———. *Who Was a Jew?* Oxford: The Yarnton Trust for the Oxford Centre for Postgraduate Hebrew Studies, 1989.

Gordon, Mary L. "The Freedman's Son in Municipal Life." *JRS* 21 (1931):65–77.

Gordon, T. David. "The Problem at Galatia." *Int* 41 (1987):32–43.

Goulder, Michael. *St. Paul versus St. Peter: A Tale of Two Missions*. Louisville: Westminster John Knox, 1995.

Gouldner, Alvin W. *Enter Plato: Classical Greece and the Origins of Social Theory*. New York: Basic, 1965.

Grenholm, Cristina, and Daniel Patte, eds. "Overture: Receptions, Critical Interpretations, and Scriptural Criticism." In *Reading Israel in Romans: Legitimacy and Plausibility of Divergent Interpretations*, 1–54. Harrisburg, Pa.: Trinity Press International, 2000.

Gunther, John. *St. Paul's Opponents and Their Background: A Study of Apocalyptic and Jewish Sectarian Teachings*. Supplement to Novum Testamentum 35. Leiden: E. J. Brill, 1973.

Hall, Jonathan M. *Ethnic Identity in Greek Antiquity*. Cambridge: Cambridge Univ. Press, 1997.

Hall, Robert G. "The Rhetorical Outline for Galatians: A Reconsideration." *JBL* 106 (1987):277–88.

Hamilton, Richard F. *The Social Misconstruction of Reality: Validity and Verification in the Scholarly Community*. New Haven: Yale Univ. Press, 1996.

Hansen, G. Walter. *Abraham in Galatians: Epistolary and Rhetorical Contexts*. JSNTSup 29. Sheffield: Sheffield Academic Press, 1989.

———. *Galatians*. Downers Grove, Ill.: InterVarsity Press, 1994.

———. "A Paradigm of the Apocalypse: The Gospel in the Light of Epistolary Analysis." In *Gospel in Paul*, edited by Jervis and Richardson, 194–209.

Harnack, Adolf. *The Constitution and Law of the Church in the First Two Centuries.* Translated by F. L. Pogson. Edited by H. D. A. Major. New York: Putnam, 1910.

Harvey, A. E. "The Opposition to Paul." In *Studia Evangelica.* Vol. 4, part 1: *The New Testament Scriptures,* edited by F. L. Cross, 319–32. Berlin: Akademie, 1968.

Hatina, Thomas R. "The Perfect Tense-Form in Recent Debate: Galatians as a Case Study." *Filologia Neotestamentica* 8 (15) (1995):3–22.

Hawkins, John G. "The Opponents of Paul in Galatia." Ph.D. diss., Yale University, 1971.

Hays, Richard B. "Crucified with Christ: A Synthesis of the Theology of 1 and 2 Thessalonians, Philemon, Philippians, and Galatians." In *Pauline Theology,* edited by Bassler, 227–46.

———. *The Faith of Jesus Christ: An Investigation of the Narrative Substructure of Galatians 3:1—4:11.* SBLDS 56. Chico, Calif.: Scholars Press, 1983.

Hengel, Martin. *Judaism and Hellenism: Studies in Their Encounter in Palestine during the Early Hellenistic Period.* 2 vols. Translated by J. Bowden. Philadelphia: Fortress Press, 1974.

Herzog, William R. II. *Parables as Subversive Speech: Jesus as Pedagogue of the Oppressed.* Louisville: Westminster John Knox, 1994.

Hester, James D. "Placing the Blame: The Presence of Epideictic in Galatians 1 and 2." In *Persuasive Artistry: Studies in New Testament Rhetoric in Honor of George A. Kennedy,* edited by D. F. Watson, 281–307. JSNTSup 50. Sheffield: Sheffield Academic Press, 1991.

———. "Rhetoric and the Composition of the Letters of Paul." Paper presented at the Claremont Conference on Alexander and Hellenism, 1997.

———. "The Rhetorical Structure of Galatians 1:11—2:14." *JBL* 103 (1984):223–33.

———. "Speaker, Audience and Situations: A Modified Interactional Model." *Neot* 32 (1998):251–71.

———. "The Use and Influence of Rhetoric in Galatians 2:1–14." *Theologische Zeitschrift* 42 (1986):386–408.

Hirsch, Emanuel. "Zwei Fragen zu Galater 6." *ZNW* 29 (1930):192–97.

Hoffman, Lawrence A. *Covenant of Blood: Circumcision and Gender in Rabbinic Judaism.* Chicago: Univ. of Chicago Press, 1996.

Hogg, Michael A., and Dominic Abrams. *Social Identifications: A Social Psychology of Intergroup Relations and Group Processes.* London: Routledge, 1988.

Hogg, Michael A., and Graham M. Vaughan. *Social Psychology.* 2d ed. London: Prentice-Hall Europe, 1995.

Holland, Glenn. "Paul's Use of Irony as a Rhetorical Technique." In *The Rhetorical Analysis of Scripture,* edited by Porter and Olbricht, 234–48.

Holmberg, Bengt. *Paul and Power: The Structure of Authority in the Primitive Churches Reflected in the Pauline Epistles.* Philadelphia: Fortress Press, 1978.

Holmstrand, Jonas. *Markers and Meaning in Paul: An Analysis of 1 Thessalonians, Philippians, and Galatians.* ConBNT 28. Stockholm: Almqvist & Wiksell, 1997.

Horbury, William. "The Temple Tax." In *Jesus and the Politics of His Day,* edited by Ernst Bammel and C. F. D. Moule, 265–86. Cambridge: Cambridge Univ. Press, 1984.

Horsley, Richard A. *Jesus and the Spiral of Violence: Popular Jewish Resistance in Roman Palestine.* 1987; Minneapolis: Fortress Press, 1993.

———, ed. *Paul and Empire: Religion and Power in Roman Imperial Society.* Harrisburg, Pa.: Trinity Press International, 1997.

Horsley, Richard A., and John S. Hanson. *Bandits, Prophets, and Messiahs: Popular Movements in the Time of Jesus.* San Francisco: Harper & Row, 1987; reprinted Harrisburg, Penn.: Trinity Press International, 1999.

Howard, George. *Paul: Crisis in Galatia: A Study in Early Christian Theology.* 2d ed. SNTSMS 35. Cambridge: Cambridge Univ. Press, 1990.

Hughes, Frank W. *Early Christian Rhetoric and 2 Thessalonians.* JSNTSup 30. Sheffield: JSOT Press, 1989.

———. "The Gospel and Its Rhetoric in Galatians." In *Gospel in Paul,* edited by Jervis and Richardson, 210–21.

Hutcheon, Linda. *Irony's Edge: The Theory and Politics of Irony.* London: Routledge, 1994.

Iser, Wolfgang. *The Act of Reading: A Theory of Aesthetic Response.* Baltimore: Johns Hopkins Univ. Press, 1978.

Jegher-Bucher, Verena. *Der Galaterbrief auf dem Hintergrund antiker Epistolographie und Rhetorik: Ein anderes Paulusbild.* Abhandlungen zur Theologie des Alten und Neuen Testaments 78. Zurich: Theologischer Verlag, 1991.

Jenkins, Richard. *Social Identity.* Key Ideas. London: Routledge, 1996.

Jervell, Jacob. *Luke and the People of God: A New Look at Luke-Acts.* Minneapolis: Augsburg, 1972.

———. "The Mighty Minority." *ST* 34 (1980):13–38.

Jervis, L. Ann, and Peter Richardson, eds. *Gospel in Paul: Studies on Corinthians, Galatians and Romans for Richard N. Longenecker.* JSNTSup 108. Sheffield: Sheffield Academic Press, 1994.

Jewett, Robert. "The Agitators and the Galatian Congregation." *NTS* 17 (1970–71):198–212.

———. *A Chronology of Paul's Life.* Philadelphia: Fortress Press, 1979.

Jones, Siân, and Sarah Pearce, eds. *Jewish Local Patriotism and Self-Identification in the Graeco-Roman Period.* JSPSup 31. Sheffield: Sheffield Academic Press, 1998.

Jónsson, Jakob. *Humour and Irony in the New Testament: Illuminated by Parallels in Talmud and Midrash.* Reykjavík: Bókaútgáfa Menningarsjóds, 1965.

Judge, Edwin A. "The Decrees of Caesar at Thessalonica." *RTR* 30 (1971):1–7.

———. *Rank and Status in the World of the Caesars and St Paul.* University of Canterbury Publications 29. Christchurch, New Zealand: Univ. of Canterbury Press, 1982.

Juel, Donald H. *A Master of Surprise: Mark Interpreted.* Minneapolis: Fortress Press, 1994.

Kasher, Aryeh. "The Civic Status of the Jews in Prolemaic [*sic*] Egypt." In *Ethnicity in Hellenistic Egypt*, edited by P. Bilde et al., 100–121. SHC 3. Aarhus, Denmark: Aarhus Univ. Press, 1992.

Kaufman, Gershen. *Shame: The Power of Caring.* 3d ed. Rochester, Vt: Schenkman, 1992.

Kennedy, George A. *Classical Rhetoric and Its Christian and Secular Tradition.* Chapel Hill: Univ. of North Carolina Press, 1980.

———. *A New History of Classical Rhetoric.* Princeton: Princeton Univ. Press, 1994.

———. *New Testament Interpretation through Rhetorical Criticism.* Chapel Hill: Univ. of North Carolina Press, 1984.

Kern, Philip H. *Rhetoric and Galatians: Assessing an Approach to Paul's Epistle.* SNTSMS 101. Cambridge: Cambridge Univ. Press, 1998.

Kertzer, David I. *Ritual, Politics, and Power.* New Haven: Yale Univ. Press, 1988.

Kierkegaard, Søren. *The Concept of Irony with Constant Reference to Socrates.* Translated by L. M. Capel. New York: Harper & Row, 1965.

Kittel, Gerhard, and Gerhard Friedrich, eds. *Theological Dictionary of the New Testament.* Translated by G. W. Bromiley. 10 vols. Grand Rapids: Eerdmans, 1964–76.

Kloppenborg, John S. "Edwin Hatch, Churches and Collegia." In *Origins and Method*, edited by Bradley H. McLean, 212–38.

Kloppenborg, John S., and Stephen G. Wilson, eds. *Voluntary Associations in the Graeco-Roman World*. London: Routledge, 1996.

Knox, Norman D. "Irony." In *Dictionary of the History of Ideas*, edited by P. P. Wiener, 2.626–34. New York: Scribner, 1973.

———. *The Word Irony and Its Context, 1500–1755*. Durham, N.C.: Duke Univ. Press, 1961.

Koester, Helmut. "From the Kerygma-Gospel to Written Gospels." *NTS* 35 (1989):361–81.

Koptak, Paul E. "Rhetorical Identification in Paul's Autobiographical Narrative: Galatians 1.13—2.14." *JSNT* 40 (1990):97–115.

Kosmala, Hans. *Hebräer—Essener—Christen*. Studia Post-Biblica 1. Leiden: Brill, 1959.

Kraabel, A. Thomas. "The Roman Diaspora: Six Questionable Assumptions." In *Diaspora Jews and Judaism*, edited by Overman and MacLennan, 1–20.

Kraftchick, Steven John. "Ethos and Pathos Appeals in Galatians Five and Six: A Rhetorical Analysis." Ph.D. diss., Emory University, 1985.

———. "Why Do the Rhetoricians Rage?" In *Text and Logos: The Humanistic Interpretation of the New Testament*, edited by T. W. Jennings Jr., 55–79. Scholars Press Homage Series. Atlanta: Scholars Press, 1990.

Lake, Kirsopp. "Galatians II.3–5." *Expositor* 1 (1906):236–45.

Lambert, John C. "'Another Gospel That Is Not Another': Galatians i. 6, 7." *ExpT* 12 (1900–1901):90–93.

Lanci, John R. "Behind the Boasting: The Complex World of Freedpersons at Corinth." Paper presented at the SBL annual meeting, Chicago, 1994.

Lategan, Bernard C. "The Argumentative Situation of Galatians." *Neot* 26 (1992):257–77.

———. "Levels of Reader Instructions in the Text of Galatians." *Semeia* 48 (1989):171–84.

Leach, Edmund R. "Ritual." In *International Encyclopedia of the Social Sciences*, edited by D. L. Sills, 13.520–26. New York: Macmillan, 1968.

Leary, Mark R., and Robin M. Kowalski. *Social Anxiety*. Emotions and Social Behavior. New York: Guilford, 1995.

Lemmer, Richard. "Why Should the Possibility of Rabbinic Rhetorical Elements in Pauline Writings (e.g., Galatians) Be Reconsidered?" In *Rhetoric, Scripture, and Theology: Essays from the 1994 Pretoria Conference*, edited by S. E. Porter and T. H. Olbricht, 161–79. JSNTSup 131. Sheffield: Sheffield Academic Press, 1996.

Levine, Lee I. *The Ancient Synagogue: The First Thousand Years*. New Haven: Yale Univ. Press, 2000.

Lewis, Naphtali, and Meyer Reinhold, eds. *Roman Civilization: Selected Readings*. 3d ed. 2 vols. New York: Columbia Univ. Press, 1990.

Lieu, Judith M., and others, eds. *The Jews among Pagans and Christians: In the Roman Empire*. London: Routledge, 1992.

Lightfoot, J. B. *St. Paul's Epistle to the Galatians*. London: Macmillan, 1865; reprinted Lynn, Mass.: Hendrickson, 1981.

Lohse, Eduard. "εὐπροσωπέω," In Kittel and Friedrich, eds. *TDNT* 6.779.

Longenecker, Bruce W. *The Triumph of Abraham's God: The Transformation of Identity in Galatians*. Nashville: Abingdon, 1998.

———. "'Until Christ Is Formed in You'; Suprahuman Forces and Moral Character in Galatians." *CBQ* 61 (1999):92–108.

Longenecker, Richard N. *Galatians*. Word Biblical Commentary 41. Dallas: Word, 1990.

Loubser, J. A. "Orality and Literacy in the Pauline Epistles: Some New Hermeneutical Implications." *Neot* 29 (1995):61–74.

Louw, Johannes P. *Semantics of New Testament Greek*. Atlanta: Scholars Press. 1982.

Louw, Johannes P., and Eugene A. Nida, eds. *Greek-English Lexicon of the New Testament Based on Semantic Domains*. 2d ed. 2 vols. New York: United Bible Societies, 1988–89.

Lüdemann, Gerd. *Opposition to Paul in Jewish Christianity*. Translated by M. E. Boring. Minneapolis: Fortress Press, 1989.

Lüderitz, Gert. "What is the Politeuma?" In *Studies in Early Jewish Epigraphy*, edited by Jan Willem van Henten and Pieter Willem van der Horst, 183–225. AGAJU 21. Leiden et al: Brill, 1994.

Lull, David John. *The Spirit in Galatia: Paul's Interpretation of* 'PNEUMA' *as Divine Power*. SBLDS 49. Atlanta: Scholars Press, 1980.

Lütgert, Wilhelm. *Gesetz und Geist: Eine Untersuchung zur Vorgeschichte des Galaterbriefes*. Beiträge zur Förderung christlicher Theologie 1/22/6. Gütersloh: Bertelsmann, 1919.

Luther, Martin. *A Commentary on Saint Paul's Epistle to the Galatians*. Grand Rapids: Baker Book House, 1979.

Lyons, George. *Pauline Autobiography: Toward a New Understanding*. SBLDS 73. Atlanta: Scholars Press, 1985.

Mack, Burton L. *Rhetoric and the New Testament*. GBS. Minneapolis: Fortress Press, 1990.

MacMullen, Ramsay. *Paganism in the Roman Empire.* New Haven: Yale Univ. Press, 1983.

Malina, Bruce J. *Christian Origins and Cultural Anthropology: Practical Models for Biblical Interpretation.* Atlanta: John Knox, 1986.

———. *The New Testament World: Insights from Cultural Anthropology.* Rev. ed. Louisville: Westminster John Knox Press, 1993.

———. *The Social World of Jesus and the Gospels.* London: Routledge, 1996.

Marcus, Joel. "The Circumcision and the Uncircumcision in Rome." *NTS* 35 (1989):67–81.

Martin, Troy. "Apostasy to Paganism: The Rhetorical Stasis of the Galatian Controversy." *JBL* 114 (1995):437–61.

———. "Pagan and Judeo-Christian Time-Keeping Schemes in Gal. 4:10 and Col. 2:16." *NTS* 42 (1996):120–32.

Martyn, J. Louis. *Galatians.* Anchor Bible 33A. New York: Doubleday, 1997.

———. "A Law-Observant Mission to Gentiles: The Background of Galatians." *SJT* 38 (1985):307–24.

———. *Theological Issues in the Letters of Paul.* Studies of the New Testament and Its World. Nashville: Abingdon, 1997.

Marxsen, Willi. *Introduction to the New Testament: An Approach to Its Problems.* Translated by G. Buswell. Philadelphia: Fortress Press; Oxford: Blackwell, 1968.

Matera, Frank J. *Galatians.* Sacra pagina 9. Collegeville, Minn.: Liturgical, 1992.

Maurer, Christian. "Μετατίθημι, Μετάθεσις." In Kittel and Friedrich, eds. *TDNT* 8.161–62.

McCready, Wayne O. "*Ekklēsia* and Voluntary Associations." In *Voluntary Associations in the Graeco-Roman World,* edited by Kloppenborg and Wilson, 59–73.

McLean, B. H., ed. *Origins and Method: Towards a New Understanding of Judaism and Christianity: Essays in Honour of John C. Hurd.* JSNTSup 86. Sheffield: Sheffield Academic Press, 1993.

Meeks, Wayne A. *The First Urban Christians: The Social World of the Apostle Paul.* New Haven: Yale Univ. Press, 1983.

———. "Review of Hans Dieter Betz's *Galatians.*" *JBL* 100 (1981):304–7.

Milgram, Stanley. *Obedience to Authority: An Experimental View.* New York: Harper & Row, 1974.

Mitchell, Lynette G. *Greeks Bearing Gifts: The Public Use of Private Relationships in the Greek World, 435–323 B.C.* Cambridge: Cambridge Univ. Press, 1997.

Mitchell, Margaret M. *Paul and the Rhetoric of Reconciliation: An Exegetical Investigation of the Language and Composition of I Corinthians.* Louisville: Westminster John Knox, 1992.

Mitchell, Stephen. *Anatolia: Land, Men, and Gods in Asia Minor.* Vol. 1, *The Celts in Anatolia and the Impact of Roman Rule.* Vol. 2: *The Rise of the Church.* Oxford: Clarendon, 1993.

Mitternacht, Dieter. *Forum für Sprachlose: Eine kommunikationspsychologiche und epistolär-rhetorische Untersuchung des Galaterbriefs.* ConBNT 30. Stockholm: Almqvist & Wiksell, 1999.

Morland, Kjell Arne. *The Rhetoric of Curse in Galatians: Paul Confronts Another Gospel.* Emory Studies in Early Christianity 5. Atlanta: Scholars Press, 1995.

Muddiman, John. "The Anatomy of Galatians." In *Crossing the Boundaries: Essays in Biblical Interpretation in Honour of Michael Goulder*, edited by S. E. Porter et al., 257–70. BibIntSer 8. Leiden: Brill, 1994.

Muecke, D. C. *The Compass of Irony.* London: Methuen, 1969.

———. *Irony.* London: Methuen, 1970.

Mullins, Terence Y. "Formulas in New Testament Epistles." *JBL* 91 (1972):380–90.

Munck, Johannes. *Paul and the Salvation of Mankind.* Translated by Frank Clarke. Richmond: John Knox, 1959.

Murdock, George Peter. *Theories of Illness: A World Survey.* Pittsburgh: Univ. of Pittsburgh Press, 1980.

Mussner, Franz. *Der Galaterbrief.* HTKNT 9. Freiburg et al: Herder, 1977.

Nanos, Mark D. "*AΛΛON & HETERON* Luke 7:19,20 (Gal.1:6–7)." Posted on B-Greek mailing list on 1 April 1999. http://franklin.oit.unc.edu/cgi-bin/lyris.pl?sub=84634$id=153357418.

Nanos, Mark D., ed. *The Galatians Debate.* Peabody, Mass.: Hendrickson, forthcoming.

———. "The Inter- and Intra-Jewish Political Contexts of Paul and the Galatians." In *Paul and Politics: Ekklesia, Israel, Imperium, Interpretation*, edited by R. A. Horsley, 146–59. Harrisburg, Pa.: Trinity Press International, 2000.

———. "Intruding 'Spies' and 'Pseudo' Brethren: The Intra-Jewish Context of 'Those of Repute' in Jerusalem (Gal. 2:1–10)." Paper presented at the International Research Consultation: "Ideology, Power, and Interpretation," Birmingham, England, 1997.

———. *The Mystery of Romans: The Jewish Context of Paul's Letter.* Minneapolis: Fortress Press, 1996.

———. "'O Foolish Galatians, Who Has Cast the Evil Eye [of Envy] upon You?' (Gal 3:1a-b): The Belief System and Interpretive Implications of Paul's Accusation." Paper presented at the SBL annual meeting, Boston, 1999.

Nemeth, Charlan Jeanne. "Intergroup Relations between Majority and Minority." In *Psychology of Intergroup Relations,* edited by S. Worchel and W. G. Austin, 229–43. 2d ed. Nelson-Hall Series in Psychology. Chicago: Nelson-Hall, 1986.

Neusner, Jacob, and E. S. Frerichs, eds.. *"To See Ourselves as Others See Us": Christians, Jews, "Others" in Late Antiquity.* Scholars Press Studies in the Humanities. Chico, Calif.: Scholars Press, 1985.

Neyrey, Jerome H. *Paul, in Other Words: A Cultural Reading of His Letters.* Louisville: Westminster John Knox Press, 1990.

Nolland, John. "Uncircumcised Proselytes?" *JSNT* 12 (1981): 173–94.

North, John. "The Development of Religious Pluralism." In *The Jews among Pagans and Christians,* edited by Lieu and others, 174–93.

Novak, David. *The Image of the Non-Jew in Judaism: An Historical and Constructive Study of the Noahide Laws.* Toronto Studies in Theology 14. New York: Mellen, 1983.

Oepke, Albrecht. *Der Brief des Paulus an die Galater.* 3d ed. THKNT 9. 1937; Berlin: Evangelische Verlag, 1973.

O'Neill, J. C. *The Recovery of Paul's Letter to the Galatians.* London: SPCK, 1972.

Overman, J. Andrew, and Robert S. MacLennan, eds. *Diaspora Jews and Judaism: Essays in Honor of, and in Dialogue with, A. Thomas Kraabel.* South Florida Studies in the History of Judaism 41. Atlanta: Scholars Press, 1992.

Parunak, H. Van Dyke. "Dimensions of Discourse Structure: A Multidimensional Analysis of the Components and Transitions of Paul's Epistle to the Galatians." In *Linguistics and New Testament Interpretation: Essays on Discourse Analysis,* edited by D. A. Black, 207–39. Nashville: Broadman, 1992.

Pearce, Sarah. "Belonging and Not Belonging: Local Perspectives in Philo of Alexandria." In *Jewish Local Patriotism,* edited by Jones and Pearce, 79–105.

Pelser, G. M. M., A. B.du Toit, M. A. Kruger, H. R. Lemmer, and J. H. Roberts, "Discourse Analysis of Galatians." *Addendum to Neotestamentica* 26 (2) (1992):1-41.

Perelman, Ch., and L. Olbrechts-Tyteca. *The New Rhetoric: A Treatise on Argumentation.* Translated by J. Wilkinson and P. Weaver. Notre Dame: Univ. of Notre Dame Press, 1969.

Peristiany, J. G., ed. *Honour and Shame: The Values of Mediterranean Society.* Chicago: Univ. of Chicago Press, 1966.

Petzer, J. H., and P. J. Hartin, eds. *A South African Perspective on the New Testament.* New Testament Tools and Studies 15. Leiden: Brill, 1986.

Pitt-Rivers, Julian. "Honor." In *International Encyclopedia of the Social Sciences,* edited by D. Sills, 6:503–11. New York: Macmillan, 1968.

———. "Honour and Social Status." In *Honour and Shame,* edited by Peristiany, 19–77.

Pitts, Jesse R. "Social Control: The Concept." In *International Encyclopedia of the Social Sciences,* edited by D. Sills, 14:381–96. New York: Macmillan, 1968.

Plank, Karl A. *Paul and the Irony of Affliction.* Semeia Studies. Atlanta: Scholars Press, 1987.

Porter, Stanley E. "Ancient Rhetorical Analysis and Discourse Analysis of the Pauline Corpus." In *The Rhetorical Analysis of Scripture,* edited by Porter and Olbricht, 249–74.

———. *Idioms of the Greek New Testament.* 2d ed. Biblical Languages, Greek 2. Sheffield: Sheffield Academic Press, 1994.

———. "Paul of Tarsus and His Letters." In *Handbook of Classical Rhetoric,* edited by Porter, 533–85.

———. "The Theoretical Justification for Application of Rhetorical Categories to Pauline Epistolary Literature." In *Rhetoric and the New Testament,* edited by Porter and Olbricht, 100–122.

———, ed. *Handbook of Classical Rhetoric in the Hellenistic Period 330 B.C.–A.D. 400.* Leiden: Brill, 1997.

Porter, Stanley E., and T. H. Olbricht, eds. *Rhetoric and the New Testament: Essays from the 1992 Heidelberg Conference.* JSNTSup 90. Sheffield: Sheffield Academic Press, 1993.

———, eds. *The Rhetorical Analysis of Scripture: Essays from the 1995 London Conference.* JSNTSup 146. Sheffield: Sheffield Academic Press, 1997.

Porton, Gary G. *The Stranger within Your Gates: Converts and Conversion in Rabbinic Literature.* Chicago: Univ. of Chicago Press, 1994.

Price, S. R. F. *Rituals and Power: The Roman Imperial Cult in Asia Minor.* Cambridge: Cambridge Univ. Press, 1984.

Rabinowitz, Peter J. *Before Reading: Narrative Conventions and the Politics of Interpretation.* Columbus: Ohio State Univ. Press, 1998.

Rajak, Tessa. "The Synagogue within the Greco-Roman City." In *Jews, Christians, and Polytheists in the Ancient Synagogue: Cultural Interaction during the Greco-Roman Period*, edited by S. Fine, 161–73. London: Routledge, 1999.

———. "Was There a Roman Charter for the Jews?" *JRS* 74 (1984):107–23.

Rambo, Lewis R. *Understanding Religious Conversion.* New Haven: Yale Univ. Press, 1993.

Ramsay, William M. *Historical Commentary on Galatians.* Edited by Mark Wilson. London: Hodder and Stoughton, 1900; reprinted Grand Rapids: Kregel, 1997.

Reed, Jeffrey T. "The Epistle." In *Handbook of Classical Rhetoric*, edited Porter, 171–93.

———. "Using Ancient Rhetorical Categories to Interpret Paul's Letters: A Question of Genre." In *Rhetoric and the New Testament*, edited by Porter and Olbricht, 292–324.

Reumann, John. "St. Paul's Use of Irony." *Lutheran Quarterly* 5 (1955):140–45.

Richards, E. Randolph. *The Secretary in the Letters of Paul.* WUNT 2/42. Tübingen: Mohr/Siebeck, 1991.

Richardson, Peter. *Israel in the Apostolic Church.* Cambridge: Cambridge Univ. Press, 1969.

Richardson, Peter, and Valerie Heuchan. "Jewish Voluntary Associations in Egypt and the Roles of Women." In *Diaspora Jews and Judaism*, edited by Overman and MacLennan, 226–51.

Roberts, J. H. "*ΘΑΥΜΑΖΩ:* An Expression of Perplexity in Some Examples from Papyri Letters." *Neot* 25 (1991):109–21.

———. "Paul's Expression of Perplexity in Galatians 1:6: The Force of Emotive Argumentation." *Neot* 26 (1992):329–37.

———. "Transitional Techniques to the Letter Body in the *Corpus Paulinum.*" In *A South African Perspective on the New Testament*, edited by Petzer and Hartin, 187–201.

Robinson, D. W. B. "The Distinction between Jewish and Gentile Believers in Galatians." *Australian Biblical Review* 13 (1965):29–48.

Ropes, James Hardy. *The Singular Problem of the Epistle to the Galatians.* HTS 14. Cambridge: Harvard Univ. Press, 1929.

Rosenbaum, H. Jon, and Peter C. Sederberg. "Vigilantism: An Analysis of Establishment Violence." In *Vigilante Politics*, edited by H. J. Rosenbaum and P. C. Sederberg, 3–29. Philadelphia: Univ. of Pennsylvania Press, 1976.

Russell, Walter B., III. "Rhetorical Analysis of the Book of Galatians, Parts 1 and 2." *BibSac* 150 (1993):341–58, 416–39.

Saldarini, Anthony J. "Boundaries and Polemics in the Gospel of Matthew." *BibInt* 3 (1995):239–65.

Sanders, E. P. "Common Judaism and the Synagogue in the First Century." In *Jews, Christians, and Polytheists in the Ancient Synagogue: Cultural Interaction During the Greco-Roman Period*, edited by Steven Fine, 1–17. London: Routledge, 1999.

———. *Paul and Palestinian Judaism: A Comparison of Patterns of Religion*. Philadelphia: Fortress Press, 1977.

———. *Paul, the Law, and the Jewish People*. Philadelphia: Fortress Press, 1983.

Schäfer, Peter. *Judeophobia: Attitudes toward the Jews in the Ancient World*. Cambridge: Harvard Univ. Press, 1997.

Schlier, Heinrich. *Der Brief an die Galater*. KEK 7. 1962; Göttingen: Vandenhoeck & Ruprecht, 1971.

Schmidt, K. L. "ἐκκλησία." In Kittel and Friedrich, eds. *TDNT* 3.501–36.

Schmithals, Walther. *Paul and James*. Translated by D. M. Barton. Studies in Biblical Theology 1/46. Naperville, Ill.: Allenson, 1965.

———. *Paul and the Gnostics*. Translated by J. E. Steely. Nashville: Abingdon, 1972.

Schoeck, Helmut. *Envy: A Theory of Social Behavior*. Indianapolis: Liberty, 1970.

Schoeps, Hans Joachim. *Paul: The Theology of the Apostle in the Light of Jewish Religious History*. Translated by H. Knight. Philadelphia: Westminster, 1961.

Schultz, Joseph P., and Lois Spatz. *Sinai and Olympus: A Comparative Study*. Lanham, Md.: Univ. Press of America, 1995.

Schürer, Emil. *The History of the Jewish People in the Age of Jesus Christ (175 B.C.–A.D. 135)*. 4 vols. Revised and edited by G. Vermes, F. Millar, and M. Goodman. Edinburgh: T. & T. Clark, 1973–87.

Schütz, John Howard. *Paul and the Anatomy of Apostolic Authority*. SNTSMS 26. Cambridge: Cambridge Univ. Press, 1975.

Scott, James M. *Adoption as Sons of God: An Exegetical Investigation into the Background of ΥΙΟΘΕΣΙΑ in the Pauline Corpus*. WUNT 2/48. Tübingen: Mohr/Siebeck, 1992.

———. *Paul and the Nations: The Old Testament and Jewish Background of Paul's Mission to the Nations with Special Reference to the Destination of Galatians*. WUNT 84. Tübingen: Mohr/Siebeck, 1995.

Segal, Alan F. "Conversion and Universalism: Opposites that Attract." In *Origins and Method*, edited by McLean, 162–89.

———. *Paul the Convert: The Apostolate and Apostasy of Saul the Pharisee*. New Haven: Yale Univ. Press, 1990.

Seland, Torrey. *Establishment Violence in Philo and Luke: A Study of Non-Conformity to the Torah and Jewish Vigilante Reactions*. Leiden: Brill, 1995.

Sieffert, Friedrich. *Der Brief an die Galater.* KEK 7. 9th ed. Göttingen: Vandenhoeck & Ruprecht, 1899.

Silva, Moisés. "Eschatological Structures in Galatians." In *To Tell the Mystery: Essays on New Testament Eschatology in Honor of Robert H. Gundry*, edited by Thomas E. Schmidt and Moisés Silva, 140–62. JSNTSup 100. Sheffield: Sheffield Academic Press, 1994.

———. *Explorations in Exegetical Method: Galatians as a Test Case*. Grand Rapids: Baker, 1996.

———. "Text and Language in the Pauline Corpus: with Special Reference to the Use of Conjunctions in Galatians." *Neot* 24 (1990):273-81.

Smallwood, E. Mary. *The Jews under Roman Rule: From Pompey to Diocletian*. Rev. ed. Studies in Judaism in Late Antiquity 20. Leiden: Brill, 1981.

Smit, Joop. "The Letter of Paul to the Galatians: A Deliberative Speech." *NTS* 35 (1989):1–26.

Smith, Christopher C. "Εκκλείσαι in Galatians 4:17: The Motif of the Excluded Lover as a Metaphor of Manipulation." *CBQ* 58 (1996):480–99.

Smith, Craig R., and Scott Lybarger. "Bitzer's Model Reconstructed." *Communication Quarterly* 44 (1996):197–213.

Smith, Jonathan Z. "Fences and Neighbors: Some Contours of Early Judaism." In *Approaches to Ancient Judaism*, edited by W. S. Green, 2:1–25. BJS 9. Chico, Calif.: Scholars Press, 1980.

Snow, David A., and Richard Machalek. "The Convert as a Social Type." In *Jossey-Bass Social and Behavioral Science Series*, edited by Randall Collins, 259–89. San Francisco: Jossey-Bass, 1983.

Spallek, Andrew J. "The Origin and Meaning of Εὐαγγέλιον in the Pauline Corpus." *CTQ* 57 (3) (1993):177–90.

Spencer, Aida Besançon. "The Wise Fool (and the Foolish Wise): A Study of Irony in Paul." *NovT* 23 (1981):349–60.

Spicq, Ceslas. *Theological Lexicon of the New Testament.* 3 vols. Translated and edited by J. D. Ernest. Peabody, Mass.: Hendrickson, 1994.

Stählin, Gustav. "ἀποκόπτω," In Kittel and Friedrich, eds. *TDNT* 3.855.

———. "ξένος," In Kittel and Friedrich, eds. *TDNT* 5.1–19.

Stamps, Dennis L. "Rethinking the Rhetorical Situation: The Entextualization of the Situation in New Testament Epistles." In *Rhetoric and the New Testament,* edited by Porter and Olbricht, 193–210.

Stanley, Christopher D. "'Neither Jew Nor Greek': Ethnic Conflict in Graeco-Roman Society." *JSNT* 64 (1996):101–24.

Staples, Clifford L., and Armand L. Mauss. "Conversion or Commitment? A Reassessment of the Snow and Machalek Approach to the Study of Conversion." *Journal for the Scientific Study of Religion* 26 (1967):133–47.

Stark, Rodney. *The Rise of Christianity: A Sociologist Reconsiders History.* Princeton: Princeton Univ. Press, 1996.

Stirewalt, M. Luther, Jr. *Studies in Ancient Greek Epistolography.* Resources for Biblical Study 27. Atlanta: Scholars Press, 1993.

Stowers, Stanley K. *Letter Writing in Greco-Roman Antiquity.* LEC 5. Philadelphia: Westminster, 1986.

———. *A Rereading of Romans: Justice, Jews, and Gentiles.* New Haven: Yale Univ. Press, 1994.

———. "Social Typification and the Classification of Ancient Letters." In *The Social World of Formative Christianity and Judaism: Essays in Tribute to Howard Clark Kee,* edited by Jacob Neusner et al., 78–90. Philadelphia: Fortress Press, 1988.

Stuhlmacher, Peter. "The Pauline Gospel." In *The Gospel and the Gospels,* edited by Stuhlmacher, 149–72.

———. *Das paulinische Evangelium.* Vol. 1, *Vorgeschichte.* FRLANT 95. Göttingen: Vandenhoeck & Ruprecht, 1968.

———. "The Theme: The Gospel and the Gospels." In *The Gospel and the Gospels,* edited by Peter Stuhlmacher, 1–25.

———, ed. *The Gospel and the Gospels.* Grand Rapids: Eerdmans, 1991.

Sumney, Jerry L. *'Servants of Satan', 'False Brothers' and Other Opponents of Paul.* JSNTSup 188. Sheffield: Sheffield Academic Press, 1999.

Swanson, Reuben J., ed. *New Testament Greek Manuscripts: Variant Readings Arranged in Horizontal Lines against Codex Vaticanus: Galatians.* Wheaton, Ill.: Tyndale, 1999.

Swartz, Marc J., Victor W. Turner, and Arthur Tuden, eds. *Political Anthropology.* Chicago: Aldine, 1966.

Tajfel, Henri. *Differentiation between Social Groups: Studies in the Social Psychology of Intergroup Relations.* London: Academic, 1978.

———. "Social Stereotypes and Social Groups." In *Intergroup Behaviour*, edited by J. C. Turner and H. Giles, 144–67. Oxford: Blackwell, 1981.

Tarazi, Paul N. *Galatians: A Commentary.* Orthodox Biblical Studies. Crestwood, N.Y.: St. Vladimir's Seminary Press, 1994.

Taylor, Nicholas. *Paul, Antioch, and Jerusalem: A Study in Relationships and Authority in Earliest Christianity.* JSNTSup 66. Sheffield: Sheffield Academic Press, 1992.

Tcherikover, Victor. *Hellenistic Civilization and the Jews.* Translated by S. Applebaum. Philadelphia: Jewish Publication Society of America, 1961.

Thurén, Lauri. *Derhetorizing Paul: A Dynamic Perspective on Pauline Theology and the Law.* WUNT 124. Tübingen: Mohr/Siebeck, 2000.

Thyen, Hartwig. *Der Stil der jüdisch-hellenistischen Homilie.* FRLANT 47. Göttingen: Vandenhoeck & Ruprecht, 1955.

Tibbetts, A. M. *The Strategies of Rhetoric.* Assisted by Frank Moake. Glenview, Ill.: Scott, Foresman, 1969.

Tomson, Peter J. *Paul and the Jewish Law: Halakha in the Letters of the Apostle to the Gentiles.* CRINT. Section Three: Jewish Traditions in Early Christian Literature. Vol. 1. Minneapolis: Fortress Press, 1990.

Trebilco, Paul R. *Jewish Communities in Asia Minor.* SNTSMS 69. Cambridge: Cambridge Univ. Press, 1991.

Turner, Victor. *The Forest of Symbols: Aspects of Ndembu Ritual.* Ithaca, N.Y.: Cornell Univ. Press, 1967.

———. *The Ritual Process: Structure and Anti-Structure.* Ithaca, N.Y.: Cornell Univ. Press, 1969.

Tyson, Joseph B. "Paul's Opponents in Galatia." *NovT* 10 (1968):241–54.

van Gennep, Arnold. *The Rites of Passage.* Translated by M. B. Vizedom and G. L. Caffee. 1908; Chicago: Univ. of Chicago Press, 1960.

Verseput, D. J. "Paul's Gentile Mission and the Jewish Christian Community: A Study of the Narrative in Galatians 1 and 2." *NTS* 39 (1993):36–58.

Violi, Patrizia. "Letters." In *Discourse and Literature*, edited by T. A. van Dijk, 149–67. Amsterdam: Benjamins, 1985.

Voelz, James W. *Fundamental Greek Grammar.* 2d ed. St. Louis: Concordia Publishing House, 1993.

Vorster, J. N. "Dissociation in the Letter to the Galatians." *Neot* 26 (1992):297–310.

———. "Why Opt for a Rhetorical Approach?" *Neot* 29 (1995):393–418.

Vos, Johan S. "Paul's Argumentation in Galatians 1–2." *HTR* 87 (1994):1–16.

Vouga, François. "Der Galaterbrief: kein Brief an die Galater? Essay über den literarischen Charakter des letzten grossen Paulusbriefes." In *Schrift und Tradition: Festschrift für Josef Ernst zum 70. Geburtstag,* edited by K. Backhaus and F. G. Untergassmair, 243–58. Paderborn: Schöningh, 1996.

Walcot, Peter. *Envy and the Greeks: A Study of Human Behaviour.* Warminster, England: Aris & Phillips, 1978.

Walker-Ramisch, Sandra. "Graeco-Roman Voluntary Associations and the Damascus Document: A Sociological Analysis." In *Voluntary Associations in the Graeco-Roman World,* edited Kloppenborg and Wilson, 128–45.

Walter, Nikolaus. "Paulus und die Gegner des Christusevangeliums in Galatien." In *L'Apôtre Paul: Personnalité, Style et Conception du Ministére,* edited by A. Vanhoye, 351–56. Leuven: Leuven Univ. Press, 1986.

Ward, Roy Bowen. "The Opponents of Paul." *Restoration Quarterly* 10 (4) (1967):185–95.

Watson, Duane F. "Rhetorical Criticism of the Pauline Epistles Since 1975." *Current Research: Biblical Studies* 3 (1995):219–48.

Watson, Francis. *Paul, Judaism and the Gentiles: A Sociological Approach.* SNTSMS 56. 1986; Cambridge: Cambridge Univ. Press, 1989.

Weaver, P. R. C. "Social Mobility in the Early Roman Empire: The Evidence of the Imperial Freedmen and Slaves." In *Studies in Ancient Society,* edited by M. I. Finley, 121–40. London: Routledge and Kegan Paul, 1974.

Weima, Jeffrey A. D. *Neglected Endings: The Significance of the Pauline Letter Closings.* JSNTSup 101. Sheffield: Sheffield Academic Press, 1994.

———. "What Does Aristotle Have to Do with Paul?: An Evaluation of Rhetorical Criticism." *Calvin Theological Journal* 32 (1997):458–68.

White, John L. "Apostolic Mission and Apostolic Message: Congruence in Paul's Epistolary Rhetoric, Structure, and Imagery." In *Origins and Method,* edited by McLean, 145–61.

———. *The Form and Function of the Body of the Greek Letter: A Study of the Letter-Body in the Non-Literary Papyri and in Paul the Apostle.* SBLDS 2. Missoula, Mont.: Society of Biblical Literature, 1972.

———. "Introductory Formulae in the Body of the Pauline Letter." *JBL* 90 (1971):91–97.

———. "New Testament Epistolary Literature in the Framework of Ancient Epistolography." In *Aufstieg und Niedergang der römischen Welt: Geschichte und Kultur Roms im Spiegel der neueren Forschung,* edited by H. Temporini and W. Haase, II.25/2:1730–56. Berlin: de Gruyter, 1984.

———. "Saint Paul and the Apostolic Letter Tradition." *CBQ* 45 (1983):433–44.

White, L. Michael. *The Social Origins of Christian Architecture: Building God's House in the Roman World: Architectural Adaptation among Pagans, Jews and Christians.* 2 vols. HTS 42. Valley Forge, Pa.: Trinity Press International, 1990.

Williams, Sam K. "Promise in Galatians: A Reading of Paul's Reading of Scripture." *JBL* 107 (1988):709–20.

———. *Galatians.* Abingdon New Testament Commentaries. Nashville: Abingdon Press, 1997.

Wilson, Brian R. *Magic and the Millennium: A Sociological Study of Religious Movements of Protest Among Tribal and Third-World Peoples.* New York: Harper & Row, 1973.

Wilson, R. McL. "Gnostics in Galatia?" In *Studia Evangelica.* Vol. 4, part 1: *The New Testament Scriptures,* edited by F. L. Cross, 358–67. Berlin: Akademie, 1968.

Winbery, Carlton. "Gal. 1:6." Posted on B-Greek mailing list on 9 December 1999.

Winger, Michael. "Tradition, Revelation, and Gospel: A Study of Galatians." *JSNT* 53 (1994):65–86.

Winter, Bruce W. "Acts and Roman Religion: The Imperial Cult." *In The Book of Acts in Its Graeco-Roman Setting,* 2, edited by Gill and Gempf, 93–103. The Book of Acts in Its First Century Setting, Grand Rapids: Eerdmans, 1994.

———. "The Problem with 'Church' for the Early Church." In *In the Fullness of Time: Biblical Studies in Honour of Archbishop Donald Robinson,* edited by D. Peterson and J. Pryor, 203–17. Homebush West, NSW, Australia: Lancer, 1992.

———. *Seek the Welfare of the City: Christians as Benefactors and Citizens.* Grand Rapids: Eerdmans, 1994.

Witherington, Ben, III. *Grace in Galatia: A Commentary on St Paul's Letter to the Galatians.* Grand Rapids: Eerdmans, 1998.

Worcester, David. *The Art of Satire.* 1940; reprinted New York: Norton, 1969.

Wright, N. T. "Gospel and Theology in Galatians." In *Gospel in Paul*, edited by Jervis and Richardson, 222–39.

Wuellner, Wilhelm. "Where Is Rhetorical Criticism Taking Us?" *CBQ* 49 (1987):448–63.

Zaidman, Louise Bruit, and Pauline Schmitt Pantel. *Religion in the Ancient Greek City*. Translated by P. Cartledge. Cambridge: Cambridge Univ. Press, 1989.

INDEX OF ANCIENT SOURCES

Dead Sea Scrolls (Qumran)

Philo

Josephus

Early Christian Writings

Papyri

INDEX OF SELECTED SUBJECTS

INDEX OF MODERN AUTHORS